East-Central Europe Under the Communists

HUNGARY

EAST-CENTRAL EUROPE

UNDER THE COMMUNISTS

ROBERT F. BYRNES, *General Editor*

Albania

Stavro Skendi, Assistant Professor of Albanian and South Slavic, Columbia University, and Research Supervisor, Mid-European Studies Center, editor

Bulgaria

L. A. D. Dellin, Lecturer, Columbia University, and Research Supervisor, Mid-European Studies Center, editor

Czechoslovakia

Vratislav Busek, former Professor of Canon Law at Charles University in Prague, and Nicolas Spulber, Associate Professor of Economics, Indiana University, editors

Hungary

Ernst C. Helmreich, Professor of History, Bowdoin College, editor

Poland

Oscar Halecki, Professor of History, Fordham University, editor

Romania

Stephen Fisher-Galati, Assistant Professor of History, Wayne University, editor

Yugoslavia

With an Introduction by Robert F. Byrnes, Professor of History, Indiana University

HUNGARY

ERNST C. HELMREICH, *Editor*

Published for the
MID-EUROPEAN STUDIES CENTER of the
FREE EUROPE COMMITTEE, INC., by

FREDERICK A. PRAEGER — New York

Books that Matter

Copyright © *1957 by the Free Europe Committee, Inc.*

First published in the United States of America in 1956 by
Frederick A. Praeger, Inc., *Publishers, 15 West 47th Street*
New York 36 N. Y.

This is Volume Number 49
of Praeger Publications in Russian History and World Communism

Library of Congress Catalog Card Number 57-9335
Printed in the United States of America

FOREWORD

The Mid-European Studies Center, a unit of the Free Europe Committee, Inc. (formerly the National Committee for a Free Europe), was founded in the summer of 1950 principally to help maintain the intellectual traditions and cultural heritage of the peoples of Central and Eastern Europe now under Communist control, to assist exiles of scholarly competence to continue their work against Communist tyranny, and to increase the fund of information available on this area, which is a *terra incognita* for even most educated Americans. The Center has completed and published a large number of studies, and has probably been the principal research institute in the world concentrating on East-Central Europe.

This volume, *Hungary Under the Communists*, is one of a series of seven. The series was conceived in the spring of 1954 by Mr.Stetson S. Holmes, then Director of the Mid-European Studies Center, by Mr. Jacob B. Hoptner, then Director of Research of the Mid-European Studies Center, and by Dr. Stephen Fischer-Galati, then a staff member. It was organized as a joint project of refugee scholars and of American specialists, and it was hoped that the volumes would not only increase the fund of information, but would also help define the boundaries of our knowledge and the areas in which research and analysis were most needed. The books are designed to provide thorough, accurate, and well-organized information on Albania, Bulgaria, Czechoslovakia, Hungary, Poland, Romania, and Yugoslavia since they have been under Communist rule. Eastern Germany and the Baltic states, Lithuania, Latvia, and Estonia, all important parts of the Soviet empire in East-Central Europe, were omitted because the Center lacked both the personnel and materials for volumes on these states.

The series is a massive project, which the Mid-European Studies Center is particularly well qualified to prepare and to publish. As the research division of the Free Europe Committee, it possesses a small but highly qualified staff of experts on this area. Some of these specialists lived for years in East-Central Europe, were educated there, and held important positions in cultural, political, and government life; others have American academic training. In addition, the Center has developed close relations with specialists on this area teaching in American colleges and universities or working in research institutions. Finally, the Free Europe Committee, of which the Center is a part, has the largest collection of materials available in the non-Communist world, particularly on developments within the last six years.

However, this material is often fragmentary. Moreover, Communist data must be examined with great care, because all Communist material has a political purpose. In addition, little analysis has been made anywhere in the world of recent developments in East-Central Europe, so that there are few secondary studies available. In a sense, each chapter of each volume—in other words, the 150 chapters in the series—represents pioneer research, with all the faults and weaknesses from which such research suffers. This explains why each volume contains quantities of useful information, but lacks generally the kind of analysis one would find in studies of areas where American research has had a longer and richer tradition.

Dr. Fischer-Galati at the beginning was entrusted with the administration and direction of the series. He prepared the outline for the seven volumes, selected the original contributors, reviewed many of the preliminary drafts, and managed the enterprise generally until he accepted appointment as assistant professor of history at Wayne University in the summer of 1955. At that time, I assumed the editorship, with Dr. Alexander Rudzinski and Dr. Bernard Ziffer as close associates, and all the resources of the Center were mobilized to complete the series by the summer of 1956.

When the editorial process was begun by the Center's staff and by the editors of the individual volumes, we discovered that some chapters were excellent, but that others failed to meet the standards set for the work as a whole, because of the wide variety of training, experience, and political points of view of the authors. It also became clear that many important and interesting issues and problems had not been included in the initial outline. Consequently, within a limited budget and period of time, some additional chapters were added, and substantial editing, revising, and, in some cases, complete rewriting were undertaken. This task was assumed and completed with skill and diligence by the staff of the Mid-European Studies Center.

The difficulties were all grievously compounded when, as the various volumes were nearing completion, the flow of information from the Soviet Union and from the countries under Communist control suddenly increased sharply. In some cases, the new data constituted the first solid information on important aspects of the economies of these countries; in other cases, the new information supplemented or replaced estimates derived from many scraps of information. All this information had to be carefully analyzed and incorporated. Just as this task was being completed, the Twentieth Congress of the Soviet Communist Party, the extraordinary attacks on Stalin and Stalinism which accompanied and followed it throughout East-Central Europe and subsequent policy shifts brought considerable revisions and additions to many sections of the books.

This volume reflects the state of American scholarship, and of Western scholarship generally, on developments within Communist Hungary. Its authors and editors have sought to ensure that it be an accurate and objective description and analysis of what has happened in Hungary under Communist rule. The manuscript was delivered to the publisher in August 1956, so that it reflects data available at that time.

The editor of this volume, Dr. Ernst C. Helmreich, is Professor of History and Government and Chairman of the History Department at Bowdoin College. Born and educated in Illinois, he received his Ph. D. from Harvard University in 1932 and has taught at Purdue University, Radcliffe College, and the Fletcher School of Law and Diplomacy. He is the author of *Diplomacy of the Balkan Wars, 1912-1913* (Cambridge, 1938). He was associated with Professor Joseph S. Roucek and others in publishing *Central-Eastern Europe* (New York, 1948), and was co-author with Professor Cyril E. Black of *Twentieth Century Europe: A History* (New York, 1950). He has also contributed a number of articles to European and American scholarly journals.

ROBERT F. BYRNES

PREFACE

This volume on Hungary, as part of a series of volumes on the East-Central European countries sponsored by the Mid-European Studies Center, has necessarily been influenced by the general organization and scope of this series. Originally designed to have parallel chapters to those of other volumes, circumstances and general editorial policy caused some alterations in the plan. There were also certain limitations as to length. Some topics on which chapters appear in other volumes have here been reduced to sections in related chapters. Accordingly, while some readers may not find all the information they desire on a particular subject, the volume should prove useful to many for it contains a wealth of material.

Special mention should be made of the work of Dr. Stephen Fischer-Galati, who was largely responsible for the preliminary planning of the volume and the selection of authors. Dr. Robert F. Byrnes, former Director of the Mid-European Studies Center, not only supervised the whole series, but gave generously of his knowledge and skill in the preparation of this volume. More than any one individual, Dr. Fred S. Pisky of the Mid-European Studies Center deserves appreciation and gratitude for his over-all efforts in making the publication of this volume on Hungary possible. Appreciation is also due those authors who, for various reasons, must remain anonymous, and to Peter Julian, the pseudonym of a distinguished Hungarian novelist whose family still lives in Hungary.

The project also benefited from the help of several other scholars who have read chapters in their special fields. Outside of his own chapter, which is only meant to provide a brief historical setting for the volume, the editor's contribution has been largely limited to suggestions and routine editorial tasks.

After the volume was in galleys, the Hungarian revolution erupted. The escapees brought a flow of invaluable Hungarian data to the West, and the Kadar regime released much new statistical information. It was thought best to add a short factual chapter on this, one of the most heroic episodes in Hungarian history, rather than have the individual authors rewrite their chapters.

ERNST C. HELMREICH

CONTENTS

MAPS

NOTE

GUIDE TO PRONUNCIATION

Pronunciation of Hungarian is based on fixed rules to which there is no exception.

The accent in all Hungarian words (or in the case of compounds, in all self-contained components) is on the first syllable. There is no exception to this rule even in the case of imported words.

Hungarian letters are pronounced as follows:[1]

Letter	Pronounced as	Letter	Pronounced as
a	*o* in "hot"	ny	*n* in "tenure"
á	*a* in "father"	o	*o* in "form"
b	in English	ó	*o* in "note"
c	*ts* in "lets"	ö	*i* in "girl" (German *ö*)
cs	*ch* in "church"	ő	*i* in "sir"
d	in English	p	in English
e	*e* in "bet"	q	in English
é	*a* in "date"	r	in English (always audible)
f	in English	s	*sh* in "show"
g	*g* in "give"	sz	*s* in "us"
gy	*d* in "verdure"	t	in English
h	*h* in "hot"	ty	*t* in "tune"
i	*i* in "winter"	u	*oo* in "book"
í	*ee* in "feet"	ú	*oo* in "moon"
j	*y* in "yet"	ü	*u* in French "*rue*"
k	in English	ű	above but longer
l	in English	v	in English
ly	*ll* in "allure"	w	*v* in "verve"
lj	*ll* in "allure"	x	in English
m	in English	y	*y* in "grassy"
n	in English	z	*z* in "zone"
		zs	*s* in "pleasure"

[1] Although no accents are used in this volume, the pronunciation of accented letters is included here.

The Hungarian language lacks the English *th* sound.

Doubled consonants (*kk, mm, tt,* etc.) indicate that the consonant is emphasized, for example, *kk* in "blackcat."

Each vowel is pronounced separately, even though two vowels are together, for example, *"bead"* (hand in, file), which is composed of *"be"* and *"ad."* Vowels are only doubled in compound words, such as *"összeesik"* (collapse), which is composed of *"össze"* and *"esik,"* and both *e*'s are pronounced.

Equivalent Values

The American equivalents of continental measures used in this volume are as follows:

1 kilometer (km.) $= 0.62$ mile
1 square kilometer (km²) $= 0.386$ square mile
1 hectare (ha.) $= 2.47$ acres
1 cadastral yoke (*hold*) $= 1.42$ acres
1 kilogram (kg.) $= 2.20$ lbs. avoirdupois
1 quintal $= 220.46$ lbs. avoirdupois
1 hectoliter $= 2.84$ U.S. bushels

References to "tons" indicate metric tons (1 metric ton $= 1.1023$ short tons). As quintal is a measure of weight and bushel of capacity, it is difficult in the measurements of crop yields to convert quintals into bushels, each bushel varying with the crop.

The following symbols have been used in the tables:

Dots (...) indicate that data are not available.
A dash (—) indicates that the amount is nil or negligible.

I. Introduction

1. HUNGARY IN HISTORY

The conflict between East and West for the control of Europe has world-wide implications today. This stems partly from a conflict of ideologies and partly from the simple fact that speed and ease of communication have narrowed the circumference of the globe. Yet the conflict itself is not a new phenomenon, and Hungary has always been involved to some extent.

When the first Magyars, originally resident east of the Urals, crossed the Carpathians in the winter of 895-96, they established an eastern outpost in the Danubian Basin. Their initial conquests ended the extensive Moravian kingdom and permanently separated the Western and Northern Slavs (Poles, Slovaks, and Czechs) from the Southern Slavs (Slovenes, Croatians, and Serbians). These early Magyars were a collection of tribes, and they raided deep into Western Europe, into Italy, and to the southeast to the walls of Constantinople. In 955, they suffered a catastrophic defeat at Lechfeld, near Augsburg, at the hands of Emperor Otto I, who reorganized the Ost Mark (Austria) as a barrier against further Magyar inroads into Western Europe. The defeat apparently had a sobering effect, for the Magyars settled down permanently in the lands where they have ever since remained.

A chieftain, hardly to be called king, by the name of Arpad is credited with having led the Magyars into Europe. Although he gave his name to the first great Hungarian dynasty, which ruled until 1301, his immediate successors by no means exercised royal rights. It was Duke Geza (972-97) who organized the princely power and began to weld the tribes into a kingdom. At this time, the Byzantine Empire had taken a new lease on life and was threatening to extend its power again beyond the Danube. Geza, who realized he could no longer live in pagan isolation, decided to accept Roman Christianity at the hands of German missionaries to avoid subjugation to the Church at Constantinople. Nevertheless, he was fearful of coming under German domination, an attitude which has characterized Hungarian history through the ages.

2

Geza's son, Stephen I (997-1038), was the real founder of the Hungarian Kingdom. He established direct contacts with Pope Sylvester II, who favored him with special temporal and spiritual privileges. The Pope sent him a special crown (1001) and granted him the title of Apostle, supposedly in recognition of his conversion of many souls to Christianity and his sturdy opposition to the Eastern Orthodox Church. From being an outpost of the East, Hungary more and more became an outpost of the West against the East. The Pope gave to Stephen and his successors the right to found episcopal sees, and Hungary was made independent of German episcopal control. The Hungarian king appointed bishops, abbots, and other high ecclesiastical dignitaries, simply informing the Pope of his choice. The bitter conflict over lay investiture which developed between the Pope and the Holy Roman Emperor and other West European rulers was unknown in Hungary. The king acted as patron of the Church and endowed it with vast lands and wealth. Under Stephen I, Benedictines entered Hungary. Every monastery not only became a center of religion, but a center of Western civilization. The monks cleared the lands, introduced Western methods of agriculture, and became the first teachers. Very early a Latin alphabet was invented for the Magyar language, and thus another link with the West was forged.

The tie between the Hungarian king and the Papacy proved beneficial to both parties. Although the kings acted as patrons of the Church, they were always careful to maintain their special privileges. Especially through the power of appointment, they kept a guiding hand on the hierarchy, which was recruited from the leading families of the realm. The Church in turn became a strong supporter of the crown, helped to administer the realm, and took charge of education and other social services. The close relation between Church and state, begun under Stephen I, survived the Reformation and even the overthrow of the Hapsburgs in 1918. The attempts of the present regime to cut these century-old ties is indeed not only a religious revolution, but a major civil revolution as well.

Stephen I was canonized in 1083, and this added a special aura to his reign. Not only were his successors known as Apostolic Kings of Hungary, but the Holy Crown of St. Stephen became a symbol of the Hungarian nation. It was not the lands inhabited by Magyars that constituted Hungary, but rather the lands constituting the Realm of St. Stephen. This concept is of extreme importance in Hungarian history. After 1526, Hungary was connected with Austria by common sovereigns, but the concept of the unity of the crown lands was a major political factor in preventing a successful reorganization of the multi-national Hapsburg domain. After World War I, when the historic kingdom was torn apart, reuniting the lands of the Crown of St. Stephen became a rallying cry for Hungarian revisionists.

Stephen I also brought about internal reforms which shaped Hungarian history. He abolished the old tribal organization and the system of communal ownership of land. Although he made some grants of land on condition of military service, he did not organize his kingdom on a feudal basis. Instead, he divided the realm into counties administered by counts, after the fashion of Charlemagne's Empire. Two-thirds of the revenue from each county went to the royal treasury, and one third to the count for administrative purposes. These counties not only became important units of administration, but also the foundations of local autonomy and self-government. The free men (nobility) met in county assemblies, and eventually the counties sent deputies to parliament. The counties continued to play an important role down to very recent times, and the history of the development of Hungarian government is rooted in the county organization.

The Hungarian concept of the lands of St. Stephen was clear, but the state was not compact and its boundaries were rather indeterminate. The territory which we know today as Slovakia had been conquered by the Magyars in their first invasions. Stephen had established claim to Transylvania, which was henceforth ruled as a Hungarian province. Considerable change took place under Stephen's immediate successors, who expanded the kingdom to the south and west. In the eleventh century, a Slavonian banat was organized, and the representatives of Croatia, which then extended as far as Montenegro, crowned Kalman King of Dalmatia and Croatia. Dalmatia broke away, and although several times reconquered eventually was lost by the Hungarian crown. Croatia, however, retained its connection with Hungary as an associated state to the Crown of St. Stephen until October 1918. It had its own laws and at times was so separate that ownership of land within Croatia was forbidden to Magyars.

Three developments of the thirteenth century deeply influenced Hungarian history. One was the granting of the Golden Bull of 1222 to the gentry by the king. This was a charter of liberties not unlike the Magna Charta of 1215 in England. Like the latter, the Golden Bull has been variously interpreted. It was no doubt primarily a guarantee of feudal privileges, which at times were used to curb the power of the king. The Golden Bull was confirmed by later sovereigns and was incorporated into Werboczy's *Tripartitum Opus Juris Hungarici,* a compilation of laws in 1514. Hungary did not develop a written constitution, and the Golden Bull has always been considered one of the cornerstones of Hungarian government. (See page 74.)

At this time, of course, there was no thought of Magyarization of the various groups who lived within the kingdom. Many tribes, such as the Cumans, Jazyes, and Petchenecs, all of a common Turki background, were easily absorbed. The kings welcomed immigrants and brought in large groups of Germans, who worked the gold mines of the Zips and who also settled in the border province of Transylvania. It was normal procedure to grant such foreign groups special privileges, and the thirteenth century brought a grant of extensive privileges to the Saxons of Transylvania (1224), who established an island of German culture and maintained their special position until the dislocations of World War II. They developed seven important municipal centers and are often referred to as the Siebenbürgen Saxons. At the time of the Reformation, they became Lutheran and along with some Slovak groups were the chief representatives of that faith in Hungary. The special status of the Transylvanian Saxons always complicated the history of Transylvania. On the other hand, the Saxons were an important avenue for the extension of Western influences to this part of Europe.

The thirteenth century also saw the great Mongol invasion of 1241, which left the country devastated. Fortunately, the Mongols did not remain long. To guard against further depredations, the nobility were allowed to build castles, and these not only became bases for feudal conflicts among themselves, but also centers for opposition to the king. King Bela IV and his successors were generally weak and, to add to the confusion, the Arpad dynasty came to an end in 1301. After a period of civil war, the nobles elected Charles I of Anjou (1310-42) as their sovereign. He had a remote hereditary claim to the throne but, more important, he had the strong support of the Pope. He proved to be an able ruler and paved the way for the reign of Louis the Great (1342-82), under whom Hungary was at the peak of its power.

Louis confirmed the Golden Bull in 1351, but abrogated a clause under which the nobles had the right to alienate their lands. This was done in the interest of preserving the large feudal estates as part of the feudal military system. The law remained in effect until 1848 and, along with the Hapsburg donations, played a considerable role in building up the large estates characteristic of Hungary. The owners of these holdings came to be known as magnates, a group distinct from the lesser nobility or gentry. Louis was an able administrator, encouraged trade, granted many municipal charters, and founded the Uni-

versity of Pecs. However, he was not so successful in opposing the
Ottoman Turks, who began their march northward in the Balkan
Peninsula during his reign. He attempted to surround Hungary on the
south with a circle of tributary princes (Bosnia, Serbia, Bulgaria,
Wallachia, and Moldavia), but these princes were never loyal because
of his antagonism to the Orthodox Church. Louis was also elected King
of Poland, and he ruled over a vast empire which extended from the
middle Vistula to the Adriatic and deep into the Balkans. The union
of the Hungarian and Polish crowns was repeated again in the late
Middle Ages, and at times there was also a union with the Bohemian
crown. This large East-Central state never developed into a united
political entity, but it is an interesting precursor of some modern plans
for a large East-Central European Federation.

Hungary's location made it a natural leader in the attempt to block
the spread of the Turks and of the Mohammedan religion to Western
Europe. The Pope encouraged the Hungarian kings to make a number
of crusades. Sigismund I, who ruled Hungary from 1387 to 1437, and
who was also elected Holy Roman Emperor and King of Bohemia, for
a time held off the Turks. His activity in the Council of Constance in
ending the schism in the Church, as well as his attempt to suppress the
Hussite heresy, were at least in part designed to unite Western Chris-
tendom in a common front against the new Eastern menace. Time
and time again the Hungarians fought the battles of the West. In the
next reign, John Hunyadi, ruler of Transylvania, won fame for his
victories over the Turks. However, a disastrous defeat at Varna (1444)
marked the end of Hungarian campaigns deep to the south. Another
crusade was launched in 1456. Hunyadi died shortly after the Turks
were turned back from their seige of Belgrade.

Two years later, Hunyadi's son, Mathias Corvinus (1458-90), was
elected King of Hungary. He gave the country a brief period of prosperity and glory. In keeping with the practices of the time, he did
away with feudal levies and organized a strong, efficient mercenary
army. He stressed the light cavalry and is credited with being the
originator of the famous Hungarian hussars. He consolidated his realm
and curbed the lawlessness of the nobility. A patron of Renaissance
learning, he did much to advance the intellectual life of his kingdom.
He founded a university at Pressburg and revived the universities at
Pecs and Buda. He was able to keep the Turks at bay and advanced to
the west, winning control over parts of Austria and Bohemia.

The nobility chafed under Mathias' firm rule and at his death elected
as their king Ladislas II, who was also King of Bohemia. In him,
the nobility had a man they could control, and many of the re-

forms of the previous reign were nullified. The high prelates of the
Church were typical "Renaissance men," more interested in worldly
pleasures than in religious piety. A serious peasant uprising which
occurred in 1514 was suppressed with great severity and virtual en-
slavement of the peasantry. It was a Hungary weakened by the riotous
living of the governing classes which was called upon to meet the
aggressive and revitalized Turkey of Suleiman the Magnificent. On
August 29, 1526, at Mohacs, Louis Jagiello, King of Hungary and
Bohemia, and his army perished. His death paved the way for the
Hapsburg claims to both the Hungarian and Bohemian thrones. The
Sultan swept on to Buda, from which he returned to Constantinople,
taking tremendous booty and some 105,000 captives.

In Hungary, a dispute over the succession arose. John Zapolya, the
powerful Prince of Transylvania, called a Diet and was elected king.
Another assembly, which met in western Hungary, elected Ferdinand
of Hapsburg. The latter not only had a hereditary claim to the throne,
but also because of his wealth and position held out prospects of material support against the Turks. He was also elected King of Bohemia,
and henceforth the crowns of Hungary, Bohemia, and Austria were to
be in the possession of a Hapsburg. With the death of Emperor Charles
V (1519-56), Ferdinand was also elected Emperor of the Holy Roman
Empire. His successors always held this title. Although Hungary never
was part of the Empire, by these dynastic connections it became closely
involved in imperial policies. More and more Hungary was drawn into
the orbit of Western European affairs.

With two claimants to the throne, Hungary was rent by civil war.
Ferdinand proved the stronger and drove Zapolya back to the mountains of Transylvania. Suleiman took the part of Zapolya and restored
him to the Hungarian throne at Buda in 1529. Pressing up the Danube,
the Sultan unsuccessfully laid seige to Vienna. His retreat led to renewed civil war, which was finally ended by partition of Hungary
between the two rulers, with the understanding that at Zapolya's death
Ferdinand or his heirs should rule all Hungary. Despite this agreement,
the nobility on Zapolya's death in 1541 elected his infant son, John
Sigismund, king. Again civil war engulfed the country, as Ferdinand
attempted to make good his claim and the Sultan, determined that no
Hapsburg should rule in Buda, intervened against him. Eventually, the
Sultan's involvements in Persia led to a truce with Ferdinand. In
return for a handsome annual tribute, Ferdinand was to rule over
forty-five western counties, including Croatia and Slavonia. The central
portion of the Hungarian kingdom the Sultan kept for himself, annex-
ing it to the Turkish Empire. Transylvania and sixteen adjacent coun-

ties were granted to John Sigismund, who ruled as Prince under the suzerainty of the Sultan. Thus, the lands of the Crown of St. Stephen were divided into three parts.

The Turkish invasion and the civil war devastated the country and brought great material hardship. These were also the years of the Reformation, and Protestant doctrines swept Hungary. The Turkish rulers had no intention of forcing Mohammedanism on their conquered peoples. On the other hand, they disliked the Papacy, which had constantly preached crusades and instigated kings to fight against them. To the Turkish rulers, Protestantism was less objectionable than Catholicism, and they permitted it to spread. It was, however, the Reformed doctrines of Calvinism that appealed to the Magyars. In those days, Lutheranism was associated with German influence. By accepting Calvinism, many Magyars expressed both anti-Catholic and anti-German sentiments. Religious liberalism was also manifested in the toleration of Unitarianism in Transylvania. Here as early as 1571, Roman Catholicism, Lutheranism, Calvinism, and Unitarianism received official recognition and toleration.

The Hapsburg rulers were occupied for about a century with the religious conflicts of the Reformation and Counter Reformation (about 1550-1650). A second unsuccessful Turkish siege of Vienna in 1683 prefaced a renewed attack on the Turks, in which Russia, Poland, and Austria with its allies participated. Gradually, the Turks were pushed back. By 1718 Hapsburg arms (Peace of Passarowitz) had freed the Kingdom of Hungary from Turkish rule. The advancing Hapsburg forces and the Jesuits who followed in their train did much to restore the Catholic Church to its old privileged position. Only Transylvania and northeastern Hungary, which lay outside the paths of the Hapsburg armies, remained important centers of Protestantism.

To populate and defend the territories freed from the Turks, the government resorted to an active policy of colonization, and immigrants and settlers came from all over Europe. Germans and Slovaks were settled in the southern regions. Many Serbs sought refuge from Turkish rule and were welcomed as settlers in the newly acquired Banat of Temesvar. Military frontier regions were established, and the people who manned the fortifications were given special privileges. At the time, this policy strengthened the state, but later, when the spirit of nationalism had developed into a strong historical force, the conglomeration of settlements was to present grave problems.

The reconquest of Hungary also revived old issues. The recurring problem of preserving Hungarian independence and combating German influence presented itself in new forms. Even before Passarowitz, there were evidences of Magyar resistance to the Hapsburgs. Francis Rakoczi headed a large armed movement of protest against domination from Vienna. In order to obtain international recognition, the Hungarian Diet proclaimed the dethronement of the House of Hapsburg and elected Rakoczi "Ruling Prince." Louis XIV of France provided some support during the War of the Spanish Succession. Rakoczi's troops occupied most of Hungary. However, when the Hapsburg army was released from the west, the long insurrection (1703-11) was suppressed. A truce was arranged in 1711 which granted full religious liberty and recognized the inviolability of the ancient rights and privileges of the Magyars. The sovereigns were now considered primarily German, and royal policy was viewed with skeptical eyes. Through his power of appointment, the sovereign could name officials, particularly Church officers, who were at times considered too prone to "foreign" influence. Hapsburg, German, Catholic, all too often were lumped together as not sufficiently Magyar. This accounts for the fact that the Magyar Protestants, although a minority, have been prominent in the struggle for the maintenance of Hungarian rights and privileges. The magnates, who were generally Catholic, gravitated to Vienna, and the Hapsburgs in return showered them with favors.

Maria Theresa (1740-80) particularly had the favor of the magnates, but she also received a surprising amount of support from the gentry, the constant defenders of Hungarian rights. Her father had persuaded the Hungarian Diet in 1723 to accept the Pragmatic Sanction, which provided that the lands belonging to the Hapsburg crown were indivisible and that in default of male heirs, a female might inherit the throne. This became the first constitutional tie binding Hungary to Austria. Henceforth, the Hungarian crown was not to be elective, but was indissolubly connected with the crown of Austria. In return for this promise of loyalty, the Hapsburg rulers agreed to preserve intact the Hungarian constitution with all its rights, laws, privileges, and customs.

While Maria Theresa did much to bring together her multiple holdings, it was Joseph II (1780-90), as the exponent of enlightenment, who made the most drastic effort to create uniformity in the administration of the Hapsburg lands. In Hungary, he encountered the determined opposition of the county gentry, in whose hands lay the administration of law and justice. Opposing the intercession of a German bureaucracy, the Hungarians were able to maintain historic Hungarian customs, and Hungary retained its separateness. This continued even after the Hapsburgs proclaimed themselves emperors of an Austrian Empire and the Holy Roman Empire was dissolved (1806). To the Hungarians, the emperor remained simply King of Hungary.

In the 1840's, the rising revolutionary spirit that was sweeping Europe reached Austria as well as Hungary. The leaders of the Hungarian "reform period," Istvan Szechenyi, Lajos Kossuth, and Miklos Wesselenyi, pressed Emperor Ferdinand I for substantially greater political concessions. (See pages 104 ff.) In 1848, the political tension erupted in the Hungarian Revolution, which was suppressed only with the aid of Russia. The Hapsburgs placed Hungary under martial law, and a stern period of confiscation and reprisal was inaugurated. Thirteen leading generals were either shot or hanged at Arad, and the memory of these "martyrs" has since remained a stimulus to Hungarian patriotic fervor.

The new emperor, Francis Joseph, attempted to rule Hungary from Vienna under a policy of centralization, known from its orginator as the Bach system. Bach staffed his adminstration with German, Czech, and Polish officials, who did not know the language of the people, and German became the official language. Bach also detached Croatia, Transylvania, and southern Hungary from the kingdom, making them into separate provinces. The Magyars refused to accept the system, although Bach introduced some needed reforms and raised the material prosperity of the country. Modern roads and railroads were built. At long last, the Hapsburg lands were united under one tariff system.

The war with Italy and France in 1859 convinced the government in Vienna that concessions were necessary. Makeshift constitutional reforms were undertaken by the October Diploma of 1860 and the February Patent of 1861. Although these projects received some support in Hungary, the Diet refused to accept them and petitioned for the restoration of the territorial integrity of the kingdom and the restitution of the fundamental laws. The Hapsburgs were never rulers to act in haste. Not until after the defeat by Prussia in 1866, with dire consequences for Austrian power in Germany and Italy, did they bring themselves to make concessions to the Hungarians.

The Compromise *(Ausgleich)* of 1867 established the Dual Monarchy of Austria-Hungary. Under the Compromise, the territorial integrity of Hungary was restored, with Croatia retaining its autonomy, but with Transylvania becoming an integral part of Hungary. The Compromise represented recognition of Hungary's constitutional status by the Hapsburgs after a struggle of three centuries. There were henceforth two entirely separate states: the Empire of Austria with its Parliament and the Kingdom of Hungary with its Parliament.

In one, Francis Joseph was to rule as emperor, in the other as king. There were three common ministers, those for foreign affairs, war, and finance. Moreover, for important measures, these ministers had to obtain the consent of the prime ministers of each state. Both Parliaments elected special committees called Delegations which enacted legislation to carry out joint affairs. If the two houses of Delegations failed to agree, they then held a joint session and without debate voted. A common army was provided, and after its quota was filled recruits were assigned to serve in the state militias. Customs rates and the quota each state was to pay to the common financial budget were to be settled by treaty every ten years.

Under the Compromise, Hungary and Austria each went its own way in internal affairs. Hungary's government to a great extent remained based on its county organization. Suffrage remained limited, with open ballot, and the nobility continued to wield great influence. The Catholic Church retained its privileged position and played an important role in political, cultural, and social life. The lesser national groups, Romanians, Ruthenians, Slovaks, Croatians, Serbians, and Germans did not share equally in political privileges, and the Hungarian government pressed a policy of Magyarization, especially after the 1880's. Official, as well as public, opinion was unalterably opposed to any arrangement of territories which would have converted the Dual Monarchy into a triple monarchy, with a third South-Slav state under Hapsburg rule. Neither this project nor any other touching the unity of the lands of the Crown of St. Stephen stood the slightest chance of receiving Hungarian approval.

Although Austrian and Hungarian troops fought valiantly side by side during World War I, the two states were not brought closer together. In Austria, Parliament was adjourned during most of the war, and authority was exercised by a military dictatorship. In Hungary, Parliament remained in session. While it was not an active or aggressive body, for it was completely dominated by Premier Count Tisza until May 1917, it was important in supporting independent Hungarian action. Military absolutism did not control Hungary, as it did Austria. The two countries supposedly formed one economic unit, but as food shortages became acute, the Hungarian government placed an embargo on the export of grain to Austria, permitting intermittent shipments in return for certain Austrian manufactured goods. With the disintegration of the Dual Monarchy at the end of the war, Hungary declared the Compromise of 1867 annulled. The only remaining tie with Austria was the personal union with King Charles. On November 13, 1918, King Charles, having already withdrawn from Austrian affairs, surrendered his powers as King of Hungary. He did not abdicate, a technicality which held open his claims to the throne if either Austria or Hungary chose to continue monarchial government.

The new government of Hungary, headed by Mihaly Karolyi, a liberal aristocrat, concluded a separate armistice with the Allies and proceeded to operate as a sovereign state. However, the Allies refused to permit Hungary to abandon the obligations of the old Dual Monarchy and treated her as a defeated state. Romania laid claim to the Hungarian territory promised her in 1916, before she entered the war. The Allies ordered the Hungarians to turn over historic Transylvania to Romanian occupation troops. In addition, certain Czech demands were incorporated in the Allied note presented to Karolyi who, despairing of reaching a tolerable settlement, resigned. This provided a favorable moment for Bela Kun, a returned revolutionary from Russia, who proceeded to establish a Soviet Republic. Since the Allies would not negotiate with a Communist regime, the conclusion of a peace treaty was postponed. In order to bolster his regime by the defense of Hungarian soil, Bela Kun first attacked Czechoslovak troops and occupied a considerable part of Slovakia. This military operation was stopped by an order from Paris. Kun then moved his troops against the Romanian forces, which sought to extend their occupation zone. The Romanian armies rolled westward toward Budapest. These events, as well as rising popular resistance, compelled Bela Kun to flee to Vienna on August 1, 1919. Meanwhile, a rightist movement had been gaining strength, and Admiral Miklos Horthy, commander in chief of the forces, took over the government as regent and head of state. On March 23, 1920, Hungary was declared a kingdom with the throne vacant. A conservative reaction set in which prevented radical changes in internal affairs. (See also pages 109 ff.)

This government was forced to sign the Treaty of Trianon on June 4, 1920. The peace treaty was modeled on those which had previously been concluded with Germany, Austria, and Bulgaria. It included the League of Nations Covenant and the International Labor Statute. Hungary along with her allies had to acknowledge responsibility for the war and to share a heavy reparations payment. Her army was restricted to 35,000 men. Although few minority groups were left within its boundaries, Hungary had to accept provisions placing them under the supervision and protection of the League. The most drastic provisions of the treaty were the territorial settlements, because the lands of the Crown of St. Stephen were distributed without negotiation and without plebiscite.

Of the Old Kingdom only 28.6 per cent made up the new Hungary; 31.5 per cent went to Romania (primarily Transylvania and two-thirds of the Banat); 19.6 per cent went to Yugoslavia (primarily Croatia-Slavonia and one-third of the Banat); 18.9 per cent to Czechoslovakia (primarily Slovakia, sub-Carpathian Ruthenia, and the city of Pressburg); 1.2 per cent to Austria (Burgenland); .2 per cent to Poland (part of Orava and Spis); and less than .004 per cent to Italy, an area of five square miles of the city of Fiume. Hungary lost 71.4 per cent of its territory which contained about 60 per cent of its former population.[1]

The treaty naturally aroused great opposition in Hungary. The refusal to grant plebiscites was particularly resented. When a plebiscite was later arranged for a part of Burgenland, the people of Sopron (Odenburg) voted to remain with Hungary. Also, the boundaries as drawn left large compact groups of Magyars living in territories adjacent to Hungary within the jurisdiction of other states (see Map 1, page 15). These new frontiers often seemed an unnecessarily violent violation of the principle of self-determination. The Allies, however, wanted Czechoslovakia and Romania to have a common frontier, and they did not look favorably on Hungary as a neighbor of Poland. There was also the problem of railroads, which could not be allowed to meander back and forth across frontiers. The territorial settlement was never accepted by the Hungarian people, and *Nem, Nem, Soha* became the watchword. "No, No, Never" would the boundaries of the Treaty of Trianon be accepted; the lands of the Crown of St. Stephen must again be reunited.

For the first ten years, the new kingless Hungarian kingdom was under the guidance of Count Istvan Bethlen, a true representative of the old aristocracy which had dominated Hungary for many years. He ended the policy of land distribution and on the whole rebuilt the social institutions and practices of prewar Hungary. Public voting was reintroduced in the rural districts, and the government was always able to swing the elections. A loyal bureaucracy was recruited, and Hungary was a well-managed state. However, the economy suffered, and the great depression proved too much for Bethlen. Count Gyula Karolyi briefly acted as Prime Minister, followed by General Gyula Gombos (1932-35). The latter had distinct dictatorial leanings, but was not sufficiently skillful or dynamic to overthrow the established

---

[1] C. E. Black and E. C. Helmreich, *Twentieth Century Europe; A History* (New York, 1950), pp. 150-51; based on Sophia Saucerman, *International Transfers of Territory in Europe* (Washington, 1937), p. 53.

system of government. The anti-Semitic tone to his regime increased under that of his successor, Kalman Daranyi (1936-38). Gombos was responsible for a law which inaugurated a *numerus clausus* of 20 per cent (reduced later to 6 per cent) for Jewish employment in business and the professions. In this period, various small fascist parties came into prominence. Among these, the best-known was the Arrow Cross group, which did not have sufficient power to seize the government, but was influential. Prime Minister Bela Imredy, who succeeded Daranyi, was a conservative, yet he introduced a measure calling for gradual redistribution of land. He also tightened anti-Semitic legislation, only to have his opponents discover that his grandfather had been a Jew. Although legally not disqualified, Imredy found it necessary to resign. His successor was Count Paul Telecki (1939-41), a distinguished geographer and friend of Count Bethlen, who dissolved some of the fascist parties, but did not basically change state policy.

In the interwar years, the key to Hungary's foreign policy was the desire to regain the lost territories. To block this, Czechoslovakia, Yugoslavia, and Romania negotiated a series of bilateral agreements. France extended its blessings to these agreements, and the Little Entente, as the group came to be called, was an important link in the French security system. While Czechoslovakia, Yugoslavia, and enlarged Romania owed their existence to the peace treaties, Hungary's interests clearly lay in revision of the Paris peace settlements. Ties were first established with Italy, the so-called Rome protocols (valid from 1934 to 1936), which provided for cooperation among Austria, Hungary, and Italy. Italo-German *rapprochement* eventually led to agreements with Nazi Germany. Hungary achieved considerable territorial revisions with the support of the Axis Powers.

After the Munich agreement in 1938, Ciano and Ribbentrop arbitrated a major frontier readjustment between Hungary and Czechoslovakia, called the First Vienna Award. Hitler's seizure of Prague led to Hungarian occupation of Ruthenia (Carpatho-Ukraine) on March 15, 1939. After the fall of France, Soviet seizure of Bessarabia and part of Bukovina from Romania led to further territorial adjustments. On August 30, 1940, under the Second Vienna Award, Northern Transylvania was given to Hungary by Ciano and Ribbentrop. The following November, Hungary along with Romania and Slovakia, adhered to the Tripartite Pact (Germany, Italy, and Japan). Hungary was more and more drawn into the wake of the Axis, and when Hitler attacked Yugoslavia in April 1941, Hungarian troops occupied Vojvodina, formerly called Bacska, the triangle of Baranya, and two small territories along the Mura River. Premier Teleki was opposed to this

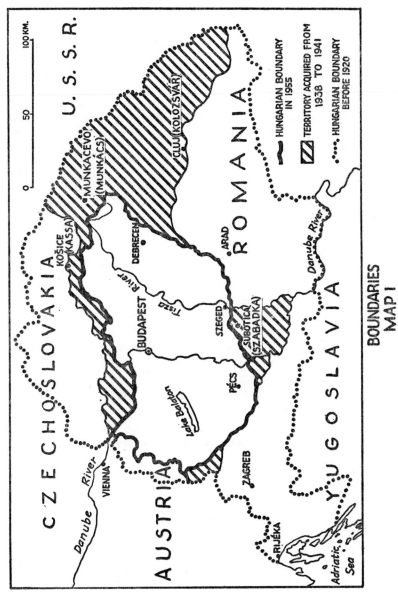

BOUNDARIES
MAP I

HUNGARIAN BOUNDARY
IN 1955

TERRITORY ACQUIRED FROM
1938 TO 1941

HUNGARIAN BOUNDARY
BEFORE 1920

policy sanctioned by the Cabinet and committed suicide. Subsequently, Hungary sent a limited number of troops to the Russian front, but maintained a surprising amount of freedom from German domination. Budapest was not blacked out, and did not suffer from Allied air raids. In fact, Allied airplanes, unmolested in their flights over Hungary, used Hungarian air space as a rendezvous for attacks on Vienna and on Romania. The government under Miklos Kallay was also able to resist the demands of Germany and of Hungarian extremists to enforce a ruthless program of racial discrimination. When it was clear that, in addition to the policy of lukewarm cooperation, Hungarian leaders were in contact with the Allies, Hitler on March 19, 1944 seized control of the country and installed a puppet government. For a time, Admiral Horthy remained regent, but on October 15, 1944, the Nazis put Ferenc Szalasi in his place. (See page 111.)

As Soviet forces entered the country, a provisional government was established in Debrecen, a town in northeastern Hungary. This government signed an armistice in Moscow on January 20, 1945. Meanwhile, fighting continued and brought great destruction to Budapest before the German forces cleared the city. Even before the war in Europe was officially ended, Stalin on March 12, 1945 turned Northern Transylvania back to Romania. The Russians dominated the inter-Allied occupation regime which was established in Budapest. By the Peace Treaty of February 1947, Hungary not only was confined to the Trianon frontiers, but was forced to cede a small bridgehead opposite Bratislava to Czechoslovakia. The lands of the Crown of St. Stephen were smaller than ever.

Under the peace treaty, Russian troops continued to occupy Hungary and Soviet authorities supervised and molded the new Hungary. Just how this was done and how Hungary has been changed in this effort to make her a western outpost of the Soviet bloc will be described in the following chapters.

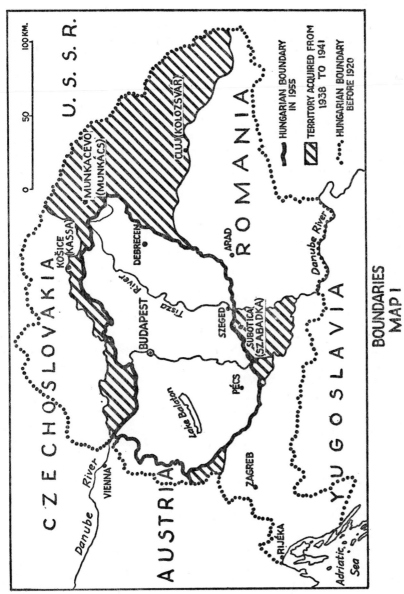

BOUNDARIES
MAP I

policy sanctioned by the Cabinet and committed suicide. Subsequently, Hungary sent a limited number of troops to the Russian front, but maintained a surprising amount of freedom from German domination. Budapest was not blacked out, and did not suffer from Allied air raids. In fact, Allied airplanes, unmolested in their flights over Hungary, used Hungarian air space as a rendezvous for attacks on Vienna and on Romania. The government under Miklos Kallay was also able to resist the demands of Germany and of Hungarian extremists to enforce a ruthless program of racial discrimination. When it was clear that, in addition to the policy of lukewarm cooperation, Hungarian leaders were in contact with the Allies, Hitler on March 19, 1944 seized control of the country and installed a puppet government. For a time, Admiral Horthy remained regent, but on October 15, 1944, the Nazis put Ferenc Szalasi in his place. (See page 111.)

As Soviet forces entered the country, a provisional government was established in Debrecen, a town in northeastern Hungary. This government signed an armistice in Moscow on January 20, 1945. Meanwhile, fighting continued and brought great destruction to Budapest before the German forces cleared the city. Even before the war in Europe was officially ended, Stalin on March 12, 1945 turned Northern Transylvania back to Romania. The Russians dominated the inter-Allied occupation regime which was established in Budapest. By the Peace Treaty of February 1947, Hungary not only was confined to the Trianon frontiers, but was forced to cede a small bridgehead opposite Bratislava to Czechoslovakia. The lands of the Crown of St. Stephen were smaller than ever.

Under the peace treaty, Russian troops continued to occupy Hungary and Soviet authorities supervised and molded the new Hungary. Just how this was done and how Hungary has been changed in this effort to make her a western outpost of the Soviet bloc will be described in the following chapters.

2. HUNGARY IN INTERNATIONAL AFFAIRS
SINCE 1945

The period between the world wars was an unprecedented experience for Hungary. She had become one of the small "succession" states which replaced the Hapsburg Empire. For the first time in modern history, no great power existed in the Danubian region, and the new era found Hungary in a most precarious predicament. The Treaty of Trianon attached more than three million Hungarians to neighboring states.[1] Moreover, it generated a whole series of economic difficulties. Most of the factories and industrial areas remaining in Hungary were deprived of their markets and were cut off from their sources of raw materials within its newly created neighbors. These and numerous related issues generated a strong desire in Hungary for revision of the *status quo*, the maintenance of which was the chief aim of her neighbors. Revisionism persisted throughout the interwar period and made impossible a sensible compromise and cooperation between Hungary and her Danubian and Balkan neighbors. Revisionism and anti-Bolshevism became the leitmotiv of Hungarian foreign policy. In the 1930's, a pro-Axis orientation was almost inevitable.

On the eve of the second World War Hungary, however, followed a cautious policy. Her desire for a *rapprochement* with the Little Entente became manifest through the Bled Agreement of August 23, 1938. The turn of European events nonetheless defeated this conciliatory course, and the Munich Conference made it clear that the Western democracies intended to remain aloof from Central European affairs. The subsequent Hitler-Stalin deal of August 1939 caught the whole Danubian area between the upper and nether millstones.

With the outbreak of hostilities, Prime Minister Paul Teleki sought to maintain a nonbelligerent status and some measure of independence

Note: We wish to thank Stephen D. Kertesz and the University of Notre Dame Press for granting permission to reprint this shortened version of the chapter "Hungary" from the publication, Stephen Kertesz (editor), *The Fate of East Central Europe: Hopes and Failures of American Foreign Policy* (Notre Dame, 1956).
[1] Harold Temperley, "How the Hungarian Frontiers Were Drawn," *Foreign Affairs,* VI (1928), 432-447.

for Hungary, despite initial territorial readjustments obtained with
the help of the Axis powers. Teleki rejected German demands to use
a Hungarian railroad line to attack the Polish Army from the rear.
But such an energetic manifestation of Hungary's independence could
not last for long. Geography, revisionism, and the weakness of the
Western democracies soon influenced Hungarian foreign policy;
Teleki committed suicide when German troops crossed Hungary's
boundaries to attack Yugoslavia and the Hungarian Government decided to cooperate with Germany. In Winston Churchill's words, Teleki's suicide was "a sacrifice to absolve himself and his people from
guilt in the German attack upon Yugoslavia. It clears his name before
history. It could not stop the march of the German armies nor the
consequences." [2]

Although Hungary's limited participation in Hitler's war against the
Soviet Union eventually caused a state of war with the English-speaking
powers, Hungarian contingents did not fight against American or
British troups. After the calamitous defeat suffered by the Hungarian
Army at Voronezh in January 1943, military help for Germany in
Russia was reduced to a badly equipped token force. Soon afterwards,
emissaries of the Hungarian Government contacted British and American representatives to secure the earliest possible armistice. But, despite some preliminary agreements, this policy could not succeed,
because it was based on the assumption that Europe would be invaded
from the southeast. Limited cooperation between Hungary and the
English-speaking powers nevertheless resulted, and the Western powers
did not bomb Hungarian territory until Germany occupied the country
in a surprise move on March 19, 1944. Three days before the German
occupation, a United States military mission was parachuted to Hungarian soil. The members of this mission soon became German war
prisoners, and American army personnel trained for occupation duty
in Hungary never were used.

At the end of hostilities, geography proved decisive in the misfortune
of Hungary, which was situated in the inner circle of the German
power sphere. Regent Nicolas Horthy's ill-prepared endeavor to conclude an armistice failed. His armistice proclamation, read over the
Budapest radio on October 15, 1944, had little effect. Most of the
ranking government officials left the country with the retreating German troops and the remainder of the Hungarian Army. When news

---

[2] Winston S. Churchill, *The Grand Alliance*, Vol. III of *The Second World War*
(Boston, 1950), p. 168. For Hungary's wartime policy, see Stephen D. Kertesz,
Diplomacy in a Whirlpool: Hungary Between Nazi Germany and Soviet Russia (Notre
Dame, 1953) and Nicholas Kallay, *Hungarian Premier* (New York, 1954).

spread about the behavior of the invading Red Army, even lesser officials fled. The country was first ravaged by the Germans, then systematically looted by the Russians. Because of all these circumstances, in no other Axis satellite state were the physical destruction and the vacuum of political power and administrative authority so extensive as in Hungary.

WESTERN AND SOVIET POLICIES AT THE CLOSE OF HOSTILITIES

While Budapest and Western Hungary were still in German hands, a provisional National Assembly was organized in Debrecen, the chief town in northeastern Hungary. In the "liberated" areas, representatives to the Assembly were elected by acclamation. The Assembly then elected a provisional National Government, and authorized it to conclude an armistice with the Allied Powers.

In point of time, Hungary was the last of the Axis satellites to conclude an armistice agreement with the three major Allies (January 20, 1945). The agreement contained obligations of a military, political, economic, and financial nature, and reduced Hungarian sovereignty to a minimum. It established an Allied Control Commission (ACC) under Russian chairmanship. The Chairman was Marshal Klementy Voroshilov. Hungarian authorities were to carry out orders and instructions issued by the Soviet High Command or the ACC. In practice Voroshilov or his deputy acted in the name of both. The ACC had American and British sections along with the Russian section but for all practical purposes was run exclusively by the Russians, who were in effective occupation of the country. Through this instrument, the Russians freely intervened in Hungary's domestic and foreign affairs. In the entire armistice period, the Soviet technique in Hungary was to act in the name of the three major allies while keeping Britain and the United States from effective action.

During negotiation of the armistice agreement, the Russians were unwilling to accept American proposals aiming at equal participation of the three Allied governments in the work of the ACC. Later, in Budapest, the American section prepared an elaborate plan for the operation of the ACC. An important feature of the plan was establishment of a Secretariat, which would have the function, *inter alia*, of receiving and translating all incoming and outgoing communications, and furnishing copies to each section of the ACC. Voroshilov buried the proposal with the comment that the armistice agreement said nothing about a Secretariat.

As appears from the armistice agreement, the ACC was under the general direction of the Soviet High Command during the hostilities against Germany.[3] The fact that the Soviet chairmanship was restricted to this period implied a promise for larger Western participation between the termination of hostilities and the conclusion of peace. Consequently, at Potsdam in July 1945 the three Allied governments

> took note that the Soviet Representatives on the Allied Control Commission in Romania, Bulgaria, and Hungary have communicated to their United Kingdom and United States colleagues proposals for improving the work of the Control Commissions, now that hostilities in Europe have ceased.
>
> The three Governments agreed that the revision of the procedures of the Allied Control Commissions in these countries would now be undertaken, taking into account the interests and responsibilities of the three Governments which together presented the terms of armistice to the respective countries, and accepting as a basis, in respect of all these countries, the Soviet Government's proposals for Hungary as annexed thereto.[4]

When President Truman returned from Potsdam, he reaffirmed in a radio address to the American people the joint responsibility of the three major powers to establish in the liberated nations of Europe governments broadly representative of the democratic elements of the population. With particular reference to Romania, Bulgaria, and Hungary, he stated that these nations

> are not to be spheres of influence of any one power. They are now governed by Allied control commissions composed of representatives of the three governments which met at Yalta and Berlin. These con-

[3] This was provided for in paragraph 2 of Article 18 in the Bulgarian and Hungarian armistice agreements. The corresponding article of the earlier Romanian armistice agreement revealed Soviet intentions more clearly, for it simply stated that an Allied Control Commission "will undertake until the conclusion of peace the regulation of and control over the execution of the present terms under the general direction and orders of the Allied (Soviet) High Command, acting on behalf of the Allied Powers." As a result of American diplomatic efforts paragraph 2 was added to Article 18 in the Bulgarian and Hungarian armistice agreements, which established Soviet chairmanship for the period of hostility against Germany.

[4] There then followed a citation to "Annex I," the rather vague text of a letter sent by the Soviet Government on July 12, 1945, to the representatives of the American and British Governments on the ACC in Hungary. The Soviet Government promised in this letter that the President of the ACC would call conferences with the British and American representatives once every ten days, or more frequently in case of need. American and British representatives were promised free movement. Moreover, it was provided that directives of the ACC on "questions of principle" would be issued to the Hungarian authorities by the ACC after agreement on these directives with the British and American representatives. These and other pledges concerning the new order of work for the ACC were not kept.

trol commissions, it is true, have not been functioning completely to our satisfaction, but improved procedures were agreed upon at Berlin. Until these states are re-established as members of the international family, they are the joint concern of all of us.[5]

The revised statutes of the ACC accordingly set forth that the American and British representatives of the ACC should have the right "to receive copies of all communications, reports and other documents which may interest the Government of the United States and the United Kingdom."[6] In practice, no change took place. The famous 50-50 settlement, agreed upon by Churchill and Stalin concerning Russian and Western influence in Hungary,[7] was never applied. Control Commissions in the Danubian states remained under Russian domination throughout their existence. These commissions brought pressure on the local governments and, in close cooperation with the local Communist parties, engineered the political transformations of these countries.

Contacts between Russians and the Americans and British in Hungary were, of course, only a small segment of their larger relationships. The heads of the American, British, and Soviet diplomatic missions were political advisers to the ACC and were not accredited to the Hungarian Government. An American representative with the personal rank of minister, H. F. Arthur Schoenfeld, arrived in Budapest in May 1945. He functioned as the United States representative in Hungary for the general protection of American interests in addition to and separate from the ACC. Schoenfeld told Foreign Minister Janos Gyongyosi at their first meeting that the American Government intended to help the reconstruction and rehabilitation of Hungary. Moreover, he made it clear that the American authorities did not intend to seize as war booty the property removed forcibly by the Nazis from Hungary to the American zone of Germany, but intended to restore all identifiable displaced property. As for war guilt, he declared that the United States advocated punishment of war criminals but opposed application to any particular nation of the principle of collective responsibility. An American note expressed willingness to receive an unofficial Hungarian representative in Washington even before the renewal of official diplo-

---

[5] *New York Times*, August 10, 1945.
[6] Art. 6. c. *The Department of State Bulletin*, XVI (1947), 1161. (Hereafter referred to as *Bulletin*.)
[7] Winston S. Churchill, *Triumph and Tragedy*, Vol. VI of *The Second World War* (Boston, 1953), p. 227; Stephen G. Kydis, "The Secret Anglo-Soviet Agreement on the Balkans of October 9, 1944," *Journal of Central European Affairs*, XV (1955), 248-271.

matic relations. This offer was reiterated, but because of Soviet opposition the Hungarian Government could not accept.

The British political representative, Alvary D. F. Gascoigne, repeatedly pointed out to the Foreign Minister the shortcomings of Hungarian democratic practices—for example, the lack of freedom of speech or guarantees of personal liberties. Gascoigne particularly objected to the abuses committed by the political police. Ernest Bevin, in his first speech in the House of Commons as Foreign Secretary on August 20, 1945, had aptly characterized the shortcomings of the new regimes established in the Danubian states. In speaking of the situation in Bulgaria, Romania and Hungary, Bevin observed:

> The Governments which have been set up do not, in our view, represent the majority of the people, and the impression we get from recent developments is that one kind of totalitarianism is being replaced by another. This is not what we understand by that very much overworked word democracy, which appears to need definition, and the forms of government which have been set up as a result do not impress us as being sufficiently representative to meet the requirements of diplomatic relations.

Although American and British goodwill towards Hungary was displayed mainly in the form of advice and friendly gestures, there also were the humanitarian gifts badly needed in the impoverished country. One of the first American moves was a considerable gift of medicine to the Hungarian Red Cross. Later, the United States granted credits totaling $30,000,000 for the purchase of surplus property. Moreover, UNRRA relief supplies valued at over four million dollars were sent to Hungary.

At the first meeting of the Council of Foreign Ministers, which opened in London on September 11, 1945, Secretary Byrnes declared that the United States would not sign treaties with the existing unrepresentative governments of Romania and Bulgaria, but was ready to recognize the government of Hungary on receipt of a pledge of free elections. This move clearly aimed at strengthening non-Communist elements in the Hungarian coalition. Molotov countered by immediate and unconditional recognition of the Hungarian Government. Thus, the American and Russian missions were changed to legations, and the American and Russian diplomatic representatives to the ACC presented their credentials to the Hungarian Government as plenipotentiary ministers. Great Britain manifested a more reserved attitude. She was not willing to re-establish regular diplomatic relations with Hungary, a country still technically at war with the Allied Powers, and appointed Gascoigne as British political representative to Hungary.

But renewal of diplomatic relations did not strengthen the position of the British and American representatives in the ACC. In the course of the execution of the Armistice Agreement, the Russians committed many abuses, notably in enforcing their interpretation of "democracy" and "fascism." They had a wide choice of means in exerting pressure on Hungarian authorities. Personal liberty as well as the daily bread of the population, in fact, all the necessities of life, depended entirely upon them. Devastated Hungary had to feed an occupying force of several hundred thousand men. Civilians by the thousands, including women, were deported to the Soviet Union as prisoners of war. There was no authority capable of giving protection against the Russians. The mass deportation of civilians and selected politicians was but one of the means to frighten the population into conformity with Soviet wishes. Such actions made the Russians and the Communists unpopular, but at the same time created a feeling of helplessness. The effect was cumulative, since this feeling of fear and insecurity prepared the way for subsequent Soviet political actions.

HUNGARIAN FOREIGN AFFAIRS AND AMERICAN DIPLOMACY

The foreign affairs of postwar Hungary may be divided into two periods. In the first, non-Communist political leaders tried to build up friendly relations with the Soviet Union, but at the same time considered Hungary to be an independent member of the free community of nations and in close relations with the Western democracies. Probably the last manifestation of this attitude was the decision of the Dinnyes Government in July 1947 to accept an invitation to the Paris Conference on United States aid to Europe. But a Soviet veto prevented Hungary's participation.[8] Shortly thereafter, Hungary became a mem-

[8] On July 7, 1947, the Hungarian Telegraph Agency reported that great interest was being taken by the government in the Marshall offer and in the proposal for a European economic program. The communiqué added cautiously that Hungary "would have great difficulties in taking an attitude different from other southeast European ex-enemy states." Furthermore, it was reported that the Prime Minister had decided to ask the ACC for permission for his government to accept the invitation to the Paris Conference on United States aid to Europe. The Hungarian note handed to the British Political Mission in Budapest on July 10 obviously reflected the answer the Hungarian Government received for its inquiry. This note emphasized that Hungary "cannot take part at a conference on the object of which the Great Powers concerned could not come to an understanding." According to the text of the communiqué issued on the same day, the Hungarian Government could not send delegates to Paris because of the disagreement existing among the Great

ber of the Soviet alliance system, and Hungarian foreign policy was integrated into the foreign political machinery of the Soviet Union. Ever since, she has been faithfully echoing Moscow's propaganda slogans, and her foreign policy is as independent as that of the Ukraine and Byelorussia. As has been described above, Soviet interferences in Hungary's foreign and domestic relations took place from the outset of the occupation, when the ACC proved a convenient channel for this usurpation of power. When the Hungarian Government, in its peace preparatory notes addressed to the three major powers, advocated close political, economic and cultural collaboration among the Danubian states,[9] international control of the Danube,[10] the internationalization of all rivers and canals in the Danube Valley, and close collaboration of the Danubian countries to improve the Danube water system, the Russian and Hungarian Communist leaders objected on the grounds that these propositions were premature. The Danubian countries, they claimed, were still reactionary. As soon as these countries became truly democratic, cooperation would come into being.

The strong American stand at Potsdam for free elections,[11] and the

Powers. The reference to the "disagreement" meant the Russian veto. Prior to this veto, the Smallholder and Socialist parties decided that Hungary should send representatives to Paris, and even the head of the Hungarian delegation was tentatively designated.

Almost all East Central European states desired to participate in the Paris Conference on United States aid to Europe. The local Communist parties could not have resisted this popular trend without a peremptory Russian veto.

[9] See the notes of August 14 and November 12, 1945 and May 8, 1946, addressed to the United States, British and Soviet Governments. *La Hongrie et la Conférence de Paris* (Budapest, 1947), pp. 7-14, 21-36, 56-62.

[10] Cavendish W. Cannon, head of the American delegation at the Danubian Conference in Belgrade on August 13, 1948, declared:

"It is interesting to note that the postwar government of Hungary, on November 12, 1945, addressed a note to the United States, British and Soviet Governments giving its views on the Danube question. It called attention to the great importance to Hungary of a regime which guarantees full freedom of navigation. It suggested that the prewar system of international navigation be reconstituted with provisions for changes required by new conditions. The Hungarian Government did not envisage elimination of non-riparian representation, for it suggested consolidation into one Commission of the European Commission of the Danube and the International Commission of the Danube. Both Commissions, as the Conference is aware, had non-riparian representation. There have been changes since 1946 but we believe the long-term economic interests of Hungary remain the same." *Bulletin*, XIX (1948), 283.

The Hungarian representative, Foreign Minister of the by then completely Communist-dominated Hungarian Government, did not reply other than by his one hundred per cent support of the Soviet position, which in fact denied that freedom of navigation for which the Hungarian Government had dared to raise its voice three years before.

[11] The Russians did not make a secret of their intentions in connection with the Yalta pledges and the fate of the East-Central European countries. "A freely elected government in any of these countries would be anti-Soviet, and that we cannot allow," declared Marshal Stalin at Potsdam, according to a member of the American delegation. Philip E. Moseley, *Face to Face with Russia*, Foreign Policy Association, Headline Series, no. 70, 1948, 23.

fact that the final agreement reached there looked forward to an early conclusion of a peace treaty and Hungary's admission into the United Nations, favorably impressed the Hungarian public. Western representatives in Budapest strengthened the determination of non-Communist political leaders by stating that their governments would not regard elections based on a single electoral list as free elections corresponding to the Yalta Declaration. Despite such encouraging factors the Potsdam Agreement, in several respects further deteriorated Hungary's position. It did not change Soviet preponderance in the ACC; moreover, the undefined category of "German external assets" in Hungary, granted to Russia as reparations, opened new possibilities for Russian abuses.

Furthermore, the Potsdam agreement wrongly assimilated the problem of the Germans in Hungary to the German problems in Poland and Czechoslovakia, and declared that transfer to Germany of the German population in these three countries "will have to be undertaken." Subsequently, the Allied Control Council for Germany, on November 20, 1945, put the number of the Germans to be moved from Hungary at 500,000,[12] a higher figure than the actual number of Germans in the country.

The Russians and Hungarian Communists interpreted the Potsdam text and the decisions of the Council as orders addressed to the Hungarian Government by the victorious allies, and although the Hungarian Government repeatedly protested against application of the principle of collective responsibility and asked for explanations from the British and United States governments, under Soviet and Communist pressure it issued a severe decree concerning the transfer of Germans. The American reply, which supported the original Hungarian position and expressed the opinion that the decision of the Allied Council did not oblige the Hungarian Government to expel all the Germans, arrived only after promulgation of the decree. An interplay of actions and circumstances hindered an all-out transfer of Germans from Hungary. In 1945, the Smallholder Party and the Hungarian Foreign Ministry delayed preparations; in the following year, United States policy began to change, and by the end of 1946 the United States Zone of Germany ceased to accept expellees. Altogether, the number of German expellees from Hungary was somewhat over 200,000, three-fourths of them being transferred to the American zone, and the rest to Eastern Germany.[13]

[12] *Bulletin,* XIII (1945), 937.
[13] For the details of this complicated affair, see Stephen Kertesz, "The Expulsion of the Germans from Hungary; A Study in Postwar Diplomacy," *Review of Politics,* XV (1953), 179-208.

Moscow's support of German expulsion actually was only part of the Soviet policy of *divide et impera* which fostered hostile feelings among neighboring nations. Other examples of this policy are evident in Hungaro-Czechoslovak and Hungaro-Romanian relations. At the close of hostilities, the Prague Government announced that Czechoslovakia was going to be transformed into a national state. In harmony with this policy, the Czechoslovak actions aiming at expulsion of all Hungarians from the Republic, as an introductory measure to carry out an exchange of population between the two countries, were energetically supported by the Soviet Union.[14] In addition to direct pressure, Marshal Voroshilov and Soviet diplomats repeatedly alluded to the fact that Hungary might get some territorial compensation from another ex-Nazi satellite, Romania, if she behaved well and accepted the Czechoslovak proposals. Nor were Hungarian ambitions for a boundary revision in Transylvania discouraged by Stalin, when such claims were expressed to him by members of the Hungarian Government in April 1946. Molotov himself explained on this occasion that the Romanian armistice treaty gave an opportunity to the Hungarians to raise the issue.[15] This benevolent attitude notwithstanding, Molotov previously and subsequently opposed in the Council of Foreign Ministers an American proposal for modifying the Transylvanian boundary line in favor of Hungary.

To counteract Czechoslovak actions, the Hungarian Government between April 1945 and July 1946 addressed a total of 184 notes to the ACC protesting specific cases of persecution in Czechoslovakia.[16] Because the Russian-dominated ACC could not react at all, the Hungarian Government simultaneously sent separate notes and memoranda to the three major powers. While the Soviet Union openly encouraged Czechoslovakia, the English-speaking powers remained unresponsive to Hungarian suggestions and refused to entertain requests for establishment of a Commission of Inquiry and proposals for great power intervention in the Hungarian-Czechoslovak conflict. Although the United States opposed collective punishment of ethnic groups, she

---

[14] During the war, Benes obtained Moscow's promise for support of the expulsion of the "guilty minority population" from Czechoslovakia. Eduard Taborsky, "Benes and Stalin—Moscow 1943 and 1945," *Journal of Central European Affairs*, XIII (1953), 168.

[15] Ferenc Nagy, *The Struggle Behind the Iron Curtain* (New York, 1948), pp. 209-210. It should be noted that during the second World War German diplomacy exploited Hungarian and Romanian territorial claims concerning Transylvania.

[16] For the list of these notes, see *Hungary and the Conference of Paris*, II (Budapest, 1947), pp. 155-163. For the anti-Hungarian discriminatory laws and decrees, see *ibid.*, IV., pp. 176-186.

approved population transfers when those took place in accordance with international agreements and "in an orderly way." [17]

Eventually, continued persecution of Hungarians in Slovakia, together with Russian pressure and the negative Western attitude, compelled the Hungarian Government to conclude a population exchange agreement with Czechoslovakia in February 1946.[18] This treaty, containing a series of unilateral benefits for Czechoslovakia, was the price for a Czechoslovak pledge that the bulk of the Hungarians in Czechoslovakia could remain until the decision of the Peace Conference. In the course of the population exchange, 60,000 Slovaks left Hungary and the number of Hungarians who were exchanged or forced to leave Slovakia was about 93,000. These events greatly deteriorated the relations between the two countries, and the large-scale deportation of Hungarians to the Sudetenland caused further resentment in Hungary.[19] Thus, cooperation between two Western-minded states was prevented before the Communist seizure of power.

Before the peace settlement, a Government Delegation under the leadership of Prime Minister Ferenc Nagy visited Moscow, Washington, and London in April and May 1946 and asked the three major powers for support. This open appeal to the West by a country occupied by the Red Army clearly showed that the postwar regime of Hungary wanted to maintain close relations with the Western powers. Hungary's position improved in the West, but friendly feeling for her and some economic help could not change the realities of power politics along the Danube. Nor did the process of peacemaking have the expected favorable impact on the fate of Hungary.

In the Council of Foreign Ministers and at the Paris Conference (July-October, 1946), Hungarian proposals for reorganization of Danubian Europe on a cooperative basis and for settling other fundamental issues of the Danubian states were not even considered. The United States delegation did submit to the Conference a proposal to reduce the total amount of reparations to be paid by Hungary from 300 million to 200 million dollars but the Conference did not accept this proposal.[20]

[17] These exchanges of notes were published in *Hungary and the Conference of Paris*, II, pp. 1-29, 50-55, 90-91.

[18] For the agreement and preceding negotiations see *ibid.*, pp. 30-49, 56-90.

[19] *The Deportation of the Hungarians of Slovakia*, published by Hungarian Society for Foreign Affairs (Budapest, 1947).

[20] *Paris Peace Conference 1946*. Selected Documents. U.S. Government Printing Office (Washington), 1123, 1153, 1194-1195. For the full text of the declaration of the American Delegate, Willard L. Thorp, see *Bulletin*, XV (1946), 746-748. For Hungary's preparations for, and position at, the Peace Conference, see Kertesz, *op. cit.*, pp. 163-187.

The greatest direct threat to Hungary at the Peace Conference was a Czechoslovak proposal openly sponsored by the Soviet Union to insert in the peace treaty a provision authorizing expulsion of 200,000 Hungarians from Czechoslovakia. Determined Hungarian opposition to this proposal would have been futile without the support of the United States and other Western delegations. The Czechoslovak proposal was defeated, and Article 5 of the peace treaty instructed Hungary to enter into negotiations with Czechoslovakia for the solution of the problem of the Hungarians in Czechoslovakia. The conflict was easily solved by repeal of the anti-Hungarian discriminatory measures as soon as the Communists seized power in both Hungary and Czechoslovakia.

The Paris Conference obliterated Hungarian endeavors for a territorial revision in Transylvania. Czechoslovakia obtained three Hungarian villages on the right bank of the Danube opposite Bratislava. Otherwise the Trianon frontiers were re-established. Generally speaking, the peace settlement did little more than recast the harsh terms of the armistice agreement in a peace treaty which authorized the Soviet Union to keep armed forces in Hungary for the maintenance of the lines of communication with the Red Army in Austria.

President Truman, upon ratification of the peace treaties, expressed regret that the Yalta commitments remained unfulfilled in Hungary, Romania and Bulgaria.[21] On March 17, 1948 in an address before a joint session of Congress he stated that

> The agreements we [the Allied victors in the second World War] did obtain, imperfect though they were, could have furnished the basis for a just peace—if they had been kept. But they were not kept. They have been persistently ignored and violated by one nation.[22]

[21] In the statement released to the press by the White House on June 14, 1947, the President declared:
"At the time of ratification of the treaties establishing peace with Hungary, Romania, and Bulgaria, I feel I must publicly express regret that the governments of those countries not only have disregarded the will of the majority of the people but have resorted to measures of oppression against them. Ever since the liberation of these countries from the Nazi yoke and the commitments undertaken by the three Allies at Yalta, I had hoped that governments truly representative of the people would be established there. Such governments do not exist today in those three countries.
"It is, however, in the interests of the Hungarian, Romanian, and Bulgarian peoples to terminate the state of war which has existed between their governments and the United States for over five years. The establishment of peace will mean that all occupation forces (not including Soviet units needed to maintain lines of communication to the Soviet Zone of occupation in Austria) will be withdrawn from these countries and armistice Control Commissions terminated." *Bulletin*, XVI (1947), 1214.
[22] *New York Times*, March 18, 1948.

Although American diplomacy in Hungary itself has always been friendly and helpful, in the period following the close of hostilities it has reflected Western aloofness from political realities. Secretary Byrnes' actions as late as December 1945, in Moscow, stemmed from the hope "that the Soviet Union and the United States had a common purpose."[23] When Hungarian politicians, in view of flagrant Russian interferences and encroachments, asked for the support of the other signatories of the Yalta agreement, they received baffling answers. As the American Minister to Hungary put it, the representatives of the Western Allies

> were frequently sounded out as to how much help they would pro-
> vide to the non-Communist political groups. When our invariable
> reply was that American diplomatic practice excluded the possibility
> of such interference in the internal political affairs of foreign coun-
> tries, there was bewilderment at what seemed so unrealistic an atti-
> tude compared with that of the Russians.[24]

The same American policy was expressed even more directly in the following passage of a letter addressed by Minister Schoenfeld to Joseph Cardinal Mindszenty, December 27, 1946:

> It is noted that your letters of December 12 and December 16,
> touching on internal political problems of Hungary, requested the
> assistance of the United States Government in altering certain con-
> ditions which Your Eminence deplores. In this connection you are
> of course aware of my Government's long standing policy of non-
> interference in the internal affairs of other nations. This policy has
> proven over a long period of time and through many trying situa-
> tions the best guarantee of spontaneous, vigorous and genuine
> democratic development. It will be clear to Your Eminence that it
> necessarily precludes action by this Legation which could possibly
> be construed as interference in Hungarian domestic affairs or which
> lies outside the normal functions of diplomatic missions.[25]

Although this reserved American attitude corresponded to the traditional precepts of diplomacy, it seemed strange to the Hungarians, in view of the tripartite Yalta agreement and Russian interventions

---

[23] James F. Byrnes, *Speaking Frankly* (New York, 1947), p. 255.

[24] F. A. Schoenfeld, "Soviet Imperialism in Hungary," *Foreign Affairs*, XXVI (1948), 558.

[25] A photograph of this letter was published in the Yellow Book of the Hungarian Government: *Documents on the Mindszenty Case* (Budapest, 1949), p. 54. There are probably many forgeries in this volume, but this particular letter was not disavowed.

in domestic affairs of Hungary. In reality, American diplomatic caution may have been only the refuge of impotence. Decisive factors in Hungary were the Red Army, Soviet leadership in the ACC, and the key power positions seized by the Hungarian Communist Party, which operated as a disguised branch of Soviet administration. These conditions hardly could have been changed or influenced on a purely diplomatic level without the threat or application of forceful measures.

The first Western protest to the Hungarian Government took place against the expropriation of the landed properties of British and American citizens. Although such seizures violated article 13 of the armistice agreement, the protests of the "imperialistic capitalist" powers opened up propaganda possibilities to the Communists. When Soviet bad faith became altogether too conspicuous, American policy slowly underwent a change,[26] and as time went on American protests increased in number, became stronger in tone, and embraced a variety of political and economic problems. In Hungary, the first really energetic political action took place almost simultaneously with enunciation of the Truman doctrine: the United States proposed concerted action to investigate political conditions and the alleged political plot by the Smallholder Party in Hungary. The acting Chairman of the ACC promptly refused, because the investigation "would appear to be an open intervention into the internal affairs of the Hungarian Republic." On the other hand, he considered American concern with regard to the arrest of the Secretary General of the Smallholders "as an attempt to infringe on the legal rights of the Soviet occupation authorities to defend their armed forces located on Hungarian territory."[27]

The conclusion of the peace treaty did not bring a change for the better in Hungary. The Hungarian Government simply disregarded the provisions of the treaty concerning human rights and fundamental freedoms, rejected English and American protests, and refused to participate in the creation of a commission provided for by the Peace Treaty for the solution of disputes. Although the peace treaty limited the Hungarian Army to 70,000 men, Hungary at the present writing has over 300,000 men in various military establishments. The army has been practically integrated into the Red Army, through its high command, armaments and general organization. The establishment of a unified military command for the Soviet Union and the captive

---

[26] Secretary Byrnes stated that the firmer attitude toward the Soviet Union began in February 1946. Byrnes, op. cit., p. 255. Russia's refusal to evacuate Northern Iran and Stalin's speech on February 14, 1946, in which he advocated further development of heavy industry and armaments, opened the eyes of the American policy-makers.
[27] Bulletin, XVI (1947), 584.

countries by the Warsaw treaty on May 14, 1955 was only the formal recognition of conditions which have existed in Hungary since 1948. Hungary not only became part of the Soviet alliance and economic system in Europe, but she ostentatiously developed friendship and intercourse with such Asiatic Communist countries as China, North Korea and North Vietnam.

Diplomatic relations between the United States and Hungary since 1947 have consisted of a sorry chain of incidents, characterized by arrest and imprisonment of American citizens, seizure and confiscation of American property, charges and measures against American diplomatic representatives including restriction of their movement and their practical isolation, closure of the United States information center in Budapest, jailing and sentencing of four downed American fliers and refusal to submit the case to the International Court of Justice, and denial to American representatives of access to arrested American citizens, such as Paul Ruedmann and Robert A. Vogeler.[28] The long list of American diplomats declared *persona non grata* in Hungary included Selden Chapin, Minister to Hungary in 1947-49. Briefly, Hungary, like the other Soviet satellites, has disregarded accepted diplomatic standards. Protection of American citizens and interests has become increasingly difficult. The arrest of Hungarian employees of the United States Legation and correspondents for the Associated Press and the other American news agencies has been a frequent occurrence. The United States repeatedly retaliated, as in the invalidation of American passports for travel to Hungary, closure of Hungarian consulates in New York and Cleveland, and travel restrictions on Hungarian Legation personnel in Washington.

Since Stalin's death some improvements have taken place in formal contacts between the United States and Hungary. For example, travel restrictions on diplomatic representatives have been liberalized. Such changes, however, are but a small segment in the large picture of Soviet-American relations. Their substantial elements and the totality of Hungaro-American relations depend on further developments in great-power politics.

[28] The *Bulletin* published the notes and other official documents concerning these cases. Cf. *Report on the MAORT Sabotage*, Hungarian Ministry of Home Affairs (Budapest, 1948): Paul Ruedemann, "I Learned About Communism the Hard Way," *Saturday Evening Post*, May 28, 1949; *Standard Oil Company and Oil Production in Hungary by MAORT*, European Gas and Electric Company (1948); *R. Vogeler, E. Sanders and Their Accomplices Before the Criminal Court*, Hungarian State Publishing House (Budapest, 1950); Robert A. Vogeler, *I Was Stalin's Prisoner* (New York, 1952); *Documents on the Hostile Activity of the United States Government Against the Hungarian People's Republic*, Hungarian State Publishing House (Budapest, 1951).

II. Geography and Demography

3. THE LAND

The 93,000 square kilometer (35,907 square mile) territory of Hungary lies largely in the largest sea-bottom basin of Central Europe, the Middle Danube depression, also called the Hungarian Carpathian, or Pannonian, Basin. Hungary occupies a compact area, approximately 122 miles wide and 280 miles long. It falls between 45°48' and 48°31' north latitude and between 16°01' and 22°58' east longitude. Hungary has only two stretches of natural frontier, the Danube and Ipoly rivers along the western half of the northern border, and the Drava and Mura rivers in the southwest. The total length of the present boundaries is approximately 1,400 miles, of which 228 miles border on Austria in the west, 446 miles on Czechoslovakia in the north, 66 miles on the Soviet Union in the northeast, 268 miles on Romania in the east, and 397 miles on Yugoslavia in the south.

Prior to 1920, the Hungarian Kingdom was bounded by the main ranges of the Carpathian Mountains on the north and northeast and by the Transylvania Alps to the east and southeast. The mountain ranges turned west and reached the Danube line. On the west, the boundary extended to the foothills of the Austrian Alps. Within this area, the river system showed a hydrographical unity. The rivers coming from the mountainous area flowed into the two main rivers, the Danube and the Tisza. Thus, Hungary historically formed something of a geographical unit. However, the boundaries established by the Treaty of Trianon bear little relation to the geography of the area.

One of the decisive geographical facts that has affected the history and economy, as well as the general outlook of Hungary, is her land-locked, continental position. Only six other European countries are without direct outlet to the sea. Another geopolitical factor is the strategic location of the Hungarian Plain, through which the major roads lead east and south. Since prehistoric times, foreign conquerors coming from the east, south, or west have had to force their way through the Hungarian Basin, which has witnessed many decisive battles in the course of the past thousand years.

PRINCIPAL GEOGRAPHICAL REGIONS

In contrast to her neighbors, which are covered by the rugged high ranges of the Carpathian and Alpine systems, Hungary is a flat country. It is the bottom of the Carpathian Basin, a depression once occupied by the Tertiary Pannonian Sea, which left flat sediments. The almost perfectly flat plain covers almost two-thirds of the central and eastern parts of Hungary. To the west and north, some ridges and hills represent the outcropping of Miocene small volcanic limestone thrusts.

On the basis of the present geological setting, relief, and climate, Hungary may be divided into three major geographical regions: Transdanubia, the Great Plain, and the Northern Upland.

Transdanubia

Transdanubia comprises 14,170 square miles, or about 39.5 per cent, of Hungarian territory. It forms a rough square bounded on the north and east by the Danube, on the west by the last outliers of the Alps, and on the south by the Mura and Drava rivers. The landscape of Transdanubia is characterized by a diversity of land forms. Hills alternate with valleys, and undulating plains are surrounded by blocks of unfolded mountains. The main structural elements of the relief consist of the folded ranges of the Western Mountains, the unfolded blocks of the Transdanubian Middle Mountains, and finally of the Little Plain in the northwestern corner of the region.

The mountains originated in various geological eras. Along the western border lies the youngest formation, the easternmost outliers of the Alpine system, called the Western Mountains. It was folded in the Upper Mesozoic and in the Tertiary eras. Its highest peak, Irottko, reaches 2,650 feet.

Southeast of the Little Plain, blocks of unfolded rocks form the Transdanubian Middle Mountains. In its southern corner emerge the isolated and geologically complex mass of the Mesozoic Mecsek and Villany mountains. Their highest peak, Zengo, is 2,894 feet above sea level. They form an island of older rocks rising from beneath the surrounding young alluvial deposits. The limestone and sandstone of the mountains contain some bituminous coal in the Mecsek and bauxite in the Villany.

Lakes Balaton and Velence are situated northward, along a fault line running southwest and northeast. Along the northern side of this fault line runs a forested mountain group built mainly by Mesozoic strata. Tectonic movements cut the group into several well-defined blocks, beginning with the Bakony (peak at Mount Koroshegy, 2,339 feet) in the southwestern end of the group, continuing with Vertes (Kortvelyes peak, 1,560 feet), Gerecse (about 1,800 feet), and Pilis Mountains (highest elevation, 2,484 feet), and ending with the Duna-zug Mountain at the sharp southerly turn of the Danube River near the old town of Esztergom.

The most impressive ridge of Transdanubia is formed by the Bakony Mountains overlooking Lake Balaton. Some granite and limestone outcroppings in the ridge and a few basaltic hillocks attest to the volcanism caused by tectonic strains.

In the northwestern corner of Transdanubia, there is a small moun-tain-ringed replica of the Great Plain, called the Little Plain. Including its extension across the Danube into Czechoslovakia, it covers approxi-mately 3,600 square miles, and its general features resemble the basins of Austria and Moravia, with great expanses of loess, sand, and gravel deposited in the Quarternary era by the Danube and Raba rivers. In the northwestern corner of the Little Plain, is Lake Ferto, surrounded by swamps and marshlands; it is Hungary's second largest lake. The Raba River coming from the Styrian Alps cuts through the plain and joins the Danube at the industrial town of Gyor.

The Great Plain

The Great Plain, occupying five-ninths of the country, approximately 20,000 square miles, constitutes the most characteristic region of Hun-gary. This open, flat expanse lies east of the Danube and south of the hills of the Northern Upland, in the central and eastern parts of the country. It reaches over the Tisza River and extends along the Hungar-ian borders into Ruthenia (Carpatho-Ukraine), Romania, and Yugo-slavia. The total area amounts to roughly 36,000 square miles, of which approximately 20,000 square miles are within Hungary. It has an elevation of 300-350 feet above sea level, and is the lowest point in the Danube Basin. Its most fertile sections, the Banat and the Bacska, which have belonged to Romania and Yugoslavia since the Trianon Treaty, are of the so-called black earth category. Only a small border zone along the Hungarian-Yugoslav frontier has the same quality of soil. The so-called chestnut-brown soil ranks second to it and is the dominating type of the fertile Great Plain.

The basic structure of the relief was formed during the Tertiary era, when the area was occupied by the Pannonian Sea. Later, it was covered by Quaternary loess and, more recently, by alluvial deposits. Between the Danube and Tisza rivers the monotonous flatness of the region is interrupted by ridges of sand dunes.

The erratic climate has turned large parts of this region into a grassland, almost like the prairies of North America. Formerly, these grasslands, called *puszta,* were used for extensive livestock grazing. However, systematic draining of the once swampy area of the eastern part of the Plain, as well as the introduction of intensive agriculture, have almost completely eliminated the *puszta* character of the section between the Danube and Tisza rivers, often referred to as the "Inter-river Plain." Since the middle of the nineteenth century, the sand dunes have been anchored by vegetation. Viticulture, fruit gardening, and planted acacia woods have also anchored the layer of loess and sand, enabling the *puszta* to support a dense population.

The only sub-area that has long preserved its *puszta* character is the Hortobagy, located in the Trans-Tisza region, west of the city of Debrecen. Here there are still extensive tracts of wild grassland. However, this area also is in the process of change. Irrigation projects have been initiated in the southern region of the Hortobagy, which is now designed for rice production.

The Danube, the Tisza, and its tributaries, the Sajo, Szamos, Koros, Berettyo, and Maros rivers, are the main water resources of the region.

Northern Upland

The Northern Upland, the third main geographical region, parallels in a way the political boundaries on the north. It extends from the gorge of the Danube near the city of Esztergom to the northeastern corner of the country. According to Professor Geza Teleki, the entire region structurally belongs to the inner volcanic zone of the Carpathians, with the exception of the Bukk Mountains, a group similar to the Bakony Mountains in Transdanubia.

The well-forested mountains are separated by the Zagyva River valley between the Cserhat and Matra and by the Tarna River valley between the Matra and the Bukk ranges. Narrow, valleylike river beds and ravines are formed by minor brooks which are affluents of these rivers. The last part of the mountain range, east-northeast of the Bukk Mountains, is the hilly Satorhegy, which extends toward Kassa (Kosice) in Slovakia.

Wedged between the Bukk Mountains and Satorhegy, the plateau-like Cserhat range has an average elevation of 1,000 feet (the major peak, Mount Nagyszal, reaches 2,139 feet). The Ban, Bodva, Sajo, and

Hernad river valleys separate these highland areas from one another. They come together around the city of Miskolc and run into the Tisza. The major peak of the Borzsony Mountains is Mount Csovanyos at 3,080 feet.

The Matra Mountains are described as a southern spur of the Carpathians. Stretching from the Zagyva valley to the Tarna valley, the highest elevation is Mount Kekes, 3,330 feet, the highest peak in Hungary. The city of Gyongyos lies at its southern foot. The Bukk Mountains, between the Eger River and Miskolc, reach 3,145 feet at Mount Istallosko.

Generally speaking, the river valleys are densely populated, while the forested mountain areas contain minerals and mining projects. Intensive viticulture is practiced in the foothills, particularly along their southern slopes, Gyongyos, Eger, and Tokaj.

THE CLIMATE

Hungary lies at the meeting point of three distinct climatic zones. On the northwest is the mild Oceanic climate of the Atlantic coast type. To the south is the Mediterranean climate, with rainy winters and hot dry summers. From the east comes the dry, cold influence of the Asiatic or Continental climate.

The Oceanic climate is dominated by a steady wind blowing from the Atlantic Ocean and carrying the warm moisture of the Gulf Stream over Western Europe. Because of the steady wind, the precipitation is evenly distributed in the main seasons of the year. Summer is cool, while winter is not severe. The difference between the average temperature of the coldest and warmest months does not exceed 40° F. The Mediterranean climate is characterized by very dry and warm summers, rainy springs and falls, and mild winters. The Continental climate dominates the wide, open plains of East-Central Europe. In winter, cold winds blowing from the Eurasian high pressure system produce the lowest temperatures in Europe. On the other hand, short, very hot summers stem from the low pressure system. Maximum precipitation occurs in June. Extreme cold and heat are the features of the Continental type.

These combined factors create a unique climate, for all the major elements of the three European climatic types are present, in varying degrees. The intensity of their influence varies from year to year. One year, the Oceanic climate dominates, causing mild winters and temperate summers with evenly distributed precipitation. Another year, under the influence of the Mediterranean climate, a dry hot summer and rainy fall occurs. Finally, the Continental climate may bring an extremely cold winter and a hot summer, with maximum precipitation in June.

Roughly speaking, however, the country may be divided into two climatic districts, according to the annual average temperature. The dividing line between the cold and mild zone runs as follows: the "cold area" lies mainly north and east of the Zalaegerszeg-Szombathely line. From Szombathely, it makes a big elbow around the city of Gyor and turns southward to include the Bakony-Vertes-Pilis area. It then comes north again, along the Danube, and makes a similar curve around Budapest, whence it runs across the Great Plain. Meeting the Tisza River at the Zagyva-Tisza junction, it proceeds east and south of Debrecen and turns toward Nagyvarad (Romania) along the foothills of the Transylvanian Mountains.

The mean annual temperature of this cold zone varies from 41° to 48° F. (10° to 11° C.); while the variation in the mild zone is about 51° to 52° F. This is, however, not true in the sense of "mildness" or "coldness," since the Great Plain has a temperature of extremities, from 104° F. (40° C.) to –29° F. (–34° C.). The average temperature in January varies between 32° F. and 28.5° F. (0° and —2° C.) and in July between 68° F. and 72° F. (20° and 22° C.). The annual total of heat observed amounts to 3,800-4,100 C. The summer total of heat is almost equal to that of the French Riviera. Even the distribution of rainfall is extreme, with an average of 90 rainy days a year.

With regard to rainfall, precipitation tends to decrease going eastward. The maximum is usually observed along the foothills of the Alps in the western border zone, around the city of Koszeg, and averages up to 800 millimeters (31.5 inches). The Northern Upland and the Bukk and Matra mountain region in the vicinity of the city of Miskolc rank next in order. In Transdanubia, in the Borzsony, Vertes, and Pilis mountain region, and in the southwestern corner of country, the annual average precipitation varies from 600 to 800 millimeters (23.5 to 31.5 inches). The Great Plain, as well as the Little Plain, have an annual average of 500 to 600 millimeters (19.5 to 23.5 inches). The driest area is roughly that bounded by the Jaszbereny-Szentes-Mezotur-Tiszafured-Jaszbereny circle. Here the annual average is somewhere between 400 and 500 millimeters (15 to 19 inches).

The average of rainy days varies between 120 and 150. Generally, the Northern Upland has a higher number than Transdanubia. The Great Plain has an average of 1,900-2,000 sunny hours per year.

Transdanubia and the Northern Upland are more cloudy and barely reach the 1,800 hour mark. The rain and snowfall are at a minimum in January and February, with the maximum in May and June, when 26 per cent of the annual total falls. The secondary maximum is in the late autumn, October, with 10 per cent of the annual total.

WATER RESOURCES

The river system of the Hungarian Basin forms a hydrographical unit, centered on the Danube. Hungarian territory once contained most of the affluent rivers of the basin. Today, only the middle or lower sections of some rivers belong to the country. Here we deal only with the Hungarian parts.

With exception of the little Poprad, which flows into the Vistula, all rivers of the basin eventually join the Danube. Most come from the mountainous rim of the basin, and therefore, their upper courses are usually rapid and precipitous. Upon reaching the Plain, the streams slow down taking on a dignified tempo. While the upper stream usually has a deep and rocky bed, the lower stream on the flat plains is usually broad and rather shallow.

Most of the rivers of Hungary freeze over during the winter, usually from about Christmas until about mid-February. Most have two flood periods; the first occurs when the ice breaks, usually late February or early March, colloquially called "white floods" or ice floods; the other flood period is known as the "green flood," which comes from mountains where snow and ice melt considerably later than on the Plain. It may come in late April, but it usually occurs in May.

Although Hungary has done a great deal of work in building up a flood-control system, controlling the green flood would also require control of the upper streams, which lie outside Hungary. Thus, the Trianon frontiers cut into half the areas of twenty-four enterprises which had managed flood control until 1920.

The Danube

The Danube enters the country below Pozsony (Bratislava, Czechoslovakia), where it is nearly 2,000 feet wide. For about 100 miles it flows through the alluvial deposits of the Little Plain. At Pozsonyligetfalu, it bifurcates and forms the isle of Csallokoz, which belongs to Czechoslovakia. The main stream bifurcates again at Somorja village to form the island of Szigetkoz. At Szob, the Danube cuts the Hungar-

ian Middle Range in two parts, forming a sharp elbow; it then bifurcates and forms the elongated island of Szentenrdre. The two branches
join near the outskirts of Budapest. Above the capital are three little
islands: Lupa Isle, Szunyogsziget (Isle of Mosquitoes), and the Isle
of the Shipyard, part of the main shipbuilding center. The Danube in
its regulated and artificially narrowed bed of 1,500 feet flows through
the capital city, separating Buda on the western bank from Pest on the
eastern bank. It forms only one small island in the capital area, Margit
(Margaret) Isle, one of the best known spas in Hungary. Maintaining
its southerly course, the Danube bifurcates again below Budapest to
form Csepel Isle. The two streams rejoin near Dunapentele, known now
as Sztalinvaros, and broadens to about 1.1 miles in width. At the city
of Kalocsa, the river is about 5,000 feet wide. It bifurcates again at
Baja, where it forms the reedy Mohacs Isle, and it leaves Hungary
below Mohacs. Its Hungarian course amounts to nearly 270 miles, all
navigable. The depth of the river bed varies form 26 to 36 feet.

Affluents of the Danube

The Danube takes up on the left the streams of the Vag (Vah),
Nyitra (Nitra), Garam (Hren), and Ipoly (Ipevl) rivers. All come
from the mountains of Slovakia and carry the water of a number of
rapid streams. They join the Danube between Pozsony (Bratislava)
and Szob.

On the right, the Lajta, a fair-sized border brook that comes from
Austria, joins the Danube at Magyarovar. The Raba (Raab) River
enters Hungary at Szentgotthard and reaches the Danube at Gyor. It
gathers many little brooks, such as the Austrian Strem, the border
brook Pinka, and the Gyongyos brook at Sarvar. It joins the Danube
with two minor streams, Repce on its left and Marcal on its right.
Beyond the Raba, except for the Bakony, there is no stream or brook
on the right bank of the Danube until the Sio Canal at Szekszard,
which connects the Danube with Lake Balaton and is reportedly navigable for river and sea-going vessels. On the southern border, the Drava
River forms a part of the boundary with Yugoslavia. It ranks next to
the Tisza as the second largest affluent of the Danube in Hungary, and
joins the Danube at Jabuka (Yugoslavia).

The Tisza River

The Tisza enters Hungary from Ruthenia at Tiszaujlak, where it is
250 feet wide, while crossing the Great Plain, it averages 500 to 650

feet in width. As it leaves the country, below Szeged, its width is approximately 1,000 feet. Its Hungarian sector is nearly 380 miles long. It is usually navigable up to Tokaj, but in an exceptionally dry summer only as far as Szolnok. With an average depth of 16 to 32 feet, it has a deep river bed and a speedy, rolling current. Since the main efforts of flood control during the last century concentrated on the Tisza, it is well regulated. Many of its bends have been eliminated, and dikes have been built at the vital spots. The old river bed in many places has been left to take up the flood waters, thus forming oxbows, lakes, and lagoons during the rest of the year.

Affluents of the Tisza

On its right bank, the Tisza receives the streams of two rapid Ruthenian brooks, the Ung (Uh) and the Latorca (Latorica). The Bodrog (Bodrok) River comes from Slovakia, enters Hungary at Satoraljaujhely, and joins the Tisza at Tokaj. The Bodrog has a wide river bed and a comparatively slow current. The Sajol (Slana) and Hernad (Hornad) rivers, both coming from the mountains, meet at Onod and join the Tisza at Polgar. Both have wooded and hilly banks, until they reach the region of Miskolc where their currents slow down. The Sajo carries smaller barges up to Miskolc. It has a few affluents coming from the Slovakian Mountains: Bodva, which enters Hungary at Bodvavendegi, the Rima (Rimava), the Murany (Muran), and the little Hungarian brook, Ban. Another small brook, Eger, comes from the Bukk Mountains and joins the Tisza below Tiszafured. The Zagyva River, which separates the Cserhat and Matra mountains, flows through a wooded, hilly area and slows before reaching the city of Hatvan. On its way to Jaszbereny, it receives the little stream of Galga on the right, and at Jaszbereny it meets its twin river the Tarna on the left. The Galga comes from the Cserhat Mountains, while the Tarna separates the Matra and Bukk mountains. The Zagyva meets the Tisza River at Szolnok.

The affluents on the left bank come from the Transylvania Mountains. The Szamos (Somes) River enters Hungary at Csenger and is one of Transylvania's main rivers. Its lazy stream in a comfortably wide bed (230-250 feet at its entrance) reaches the Tisza at Vasarosnameny. The Koros (Cris) River is sometimes called the Tripple Koros, referring to its origin in the three Koros rivers, namely the northern branch, or Sebes Koros (Swift Koros), which comes from the direction of the Transylvanian town Nagyvarad (Oradea); the middle branch, called Fekete Koros (Black Koros), which comes via Belenyes from the foothills of the Transylvanian Bihar Mountains; and the southern branch, called Feher Koros (White Koros), which batters its way down the Gyalu Mountains in the heart of Transylvania. The Sebes Koros enters Hungary at Korosharsany, the Fekete Koros enters at Kotegyan, while the Feher Koros enters at about Gyula. The Fekete and Feher Koros soon converge on their way northwest to the city of Bekes. On the other hand, the Sebes Koros on its east-west run takes up the shallow Berettyo Canal before joining its twin rivers east of the city of Gyoma. The Tripple Koros continues its slow way toward the Tisza and reaches it at the city of Csongrad. The Maros (Mures) River enters at Nagylak, coming from Transylvania as a wide but speedy affluent which reaches the Tisza just above the city of Szeged.

Lakes

Hungary has three major lakes in Transdanubia. Lake Balaton, the largest, covers an area of 160 square miles, and is 48 miles long and 3-8 miles wide, with an average level of 10 feet. Famous summer resorts are located along the shore. The other major lake is Lake Ferto, in the northwestern corner of the country, which covers an area of approximately 130 square miles, and is 22 miles long and 9 miles wide, with an average water level of 3 to 4 feet. It extends into Austria, where it is called Neusiedler See. The third lake, situated six miles east of Szekesfehervar, a major railroad center, is Lake Velence, which is 5 miles long and 1 mile wide, with an average level of 5 feet. Its reedy islands offer secure nesting places for rare water fowl, the rarest among them the gray heron. Hot underwater sulphur springs and the radium content of the lake make Lake Velence a favored spa, not only for the population of Budapest, but also for people with rheumatic and arthritic ills from all over the world.

Ports

Budapest is the largest river port and can handle ocean going vessels from the Mediterranean Sea through the Black Sea. The other major harbors can be classified according to the raw materials handled: bauxite: Gyor, Komarom, Labatlan; coal: Esztergom, Komarom, Mohacs; iron ore: Sztalinvaros (Dunapentele); oil: Csepel, Almasfuzito; cement: Labatlan, Nyergesujfalu; and lumber: Visegrad.

The Tisza ports, Tokaj, Szolnok, and Szeged, specialize mainly in grains and building materials. (See Chapter 16, "Transportation and Communications.")

Biotic Resources[1]

During the last centuries, agriculture has completely transformed Hungary's landscape. Steppes with *Stipa* grass and various types of oaks and poplars once characterized the Great Plain. However, most of the forests have disappeared, and the only large tree is the locust *(Robinia pseudocacia)*, which was imported centuries ago. Aside from the locust tree, only low scrub and brushwood remain on the steeper slopes.

Mixed forests expand around the Great Plain, especially in Transdanubia and the Northern Upland. They are composed of various species of oak, linden, and maple trees. The chestnut trees that grow in Transdanubia reflect Mediterranean climatic influence. The coniferous zone is represented in Hungary mainly in the west, along the Alps (Western Mountains). Mixed with beech, conifers also occur in the Middle Mountains and in the Northern Upland.

After World War II, only about 12 per cent of the country's area was covered with forests, although a region in this latitude should have about 20 per cent forest land to be "well balanced." In Hungary's case, only the Northern Upland surpasses this figure. Transdanubia and the Great Plain both have few forests. There are regions, such as the vicinity of Hodmezovasarhely, with only 0.2 per cent woodland, and this is soft wood, such as willow and poplar. About 32.8 per cent of the Hungarian woodland consists of various species of oak, 62.2 per cent of beech and other foliaceous trees, and about 5 per cent of coniferous forests. The coniferous forest area is composed of *Pinus sylvetris, Pinus nigra, Picea excelsa,* and trees of the Abies group.

Due to favorable climate and terrain, wildlife is abundant. The Hungarian Basin, especially the Great Plain, is one of the most important stations for bird migration between Africa and Northern Europe. Bird life is rather typically continental, with many wild ducks, herons, cranes, storks, and song birds.

[1] For mining resources, see Chapter 14, "Mining."

4. THE PEOPLE

The last census took place on January 1, 1949, but details of the census returns have not been published by the Central Bureau of Statistics. As for the figures which have appeared in print—mostly in the *Statisztikai Szemle* (Statistical Review), *Statiszitikai Tajekoztato* (Statistical Bulletin), and in *Nepegeszsegugy* (Public Health Affairs) —great care has been taken to create difficulties for Western scholars who attempt to check the statistics against corresponding figures of the period before 1945.

As interpreted by the Lenin-Stalin theoreticians, statistics are used to substantiate the political-economic course of the regime. This has often resulted in complete distortion of facts, as well as in an open contradiction of previous statements. Consequently, no method of interpolation or computation could bring satisfactory results. Sometimes a revealing sentence in a Communist leader's speech offers a clue for statistical deductions, but generally there is no possibility of checking on the accuracy of such statements.

In spite of the scarcity of accurate information, a number of international, government, and private organizations have compiled scientific projections of considerable value: the International Labour Organization of the United Nations, the United States Bureau of the Census, the Research Staff of the *Encyclopaedia Britannica,* and the Free Europe Press of the Free Europe Committee are among the most successful. Because of the nature of the task, their estimates do not agree in every respect.

DEMOGRAPHIC FACTORS

Number of Inhabitants

Hungary's population of 9,808,000 on July 1, 1955 is an estimate based on official Hungarian projections. The latest census on January 1, 1949 gave a figure of 9,204,799 inhabitants. These figures show an average annual increase of about 90,000.

The figures in Table 1 pertain to Hungary's "Paris territory," that is the political boundaries defined by the Paris Peace Treaty, effective September 15, 1947. This territory (93,011 square kilometers or

Table 1. Total Population and Population Density,[a] Selected Years 1910-1956

Year	Qualification	Population	Density per Square Mile	Net Gain or Loss Number	Net Gain or Loss Per Cent
1910	C	7,612,114	212.1	757,699	11.05
1920	C	7,986,875	222.5	374,761	4.92
1930	C	8,685,109	242.0	698,234	8.74
1941	C	9,316,074	259.5	630,965	7.27
1949	C	9,204,799	256.4	−111,275	−1.19
1950	E	9,289,000	258.8	84,200	0.90
1951	E	9,378,000	261.3	89,000	0.95
1952	E	9,459,000	263.5	81,000	0.86
1953	E	9,537,000	265.7	78,000	0.82
1954	E	9,632,000	268.3	95,000	0.99
1955	E	9,750,000	271.6	118,000	1.21
1956	P	9,870,000	275.0	120,000	1.21

Sources: Statisztikai Szemle (Statistical Review), III (March 1951), 197; Central Statistical Bureau, *Az 1949 Evi Nepszamlalas* (Population Census of 1949) (Budapest, 1952) ; *Statistische Praxis,* X (April 1955), *Karteiblatt* 1955/4; *Szabad Nep* (Free People), January 30, 1955; U.S. Bureau of the Census, *International Population Reports,* Series P-91, No. 2 (Washington, 1955).

Note: 1910-41 census figures (C) recalculated for present territory; 1910-30 census taken on December 31, each year; 1941 census on January 31, 1941; estimates (E) and projection (P) pertain to January 1 of the given year.

[a] Present territory.

35,893 square miles) is smaller than the prewar "Trianon territory" (93,073 square kilometers or 35,917 square miles), for a small bridgehead on the south bank of the Danube, opposite Bratislava, was ceded to Czechoslovakia. The ceded area (62 square kilometers or 24 square miles) covered three villages (Dunacsun, Oroszvar, Horvatjarfalu) with some 3,000 inhabitants. In proportion to the total population, this change is so small that the statistics pertaining to the Paris and Trianon territories are fairly comparable. However, Table 2 presents a tabulation of the previous census returns for the Trianon territory.

The term "Trianon territory" refers to the territory defined by the Peace Treaty of Trianon, 1920, when nearly 90,000 square miles with 12,876,000 inhabitants were ceded to neighboring states, Romania, Czechoslovakia, Yugoslavia, and Austria. On December 14, 1920 a plebiscite, based on an agreement between Austria and Hungary, returned the city of Sopron and eight small villages from Austria. Prior to Trianon, Hungary's territory covered 125,609 square miles with 20,886,000 inhabitants. The ceded areas included large settlements with a total population of over three million Hungarians. "Great Hungary," i.e. the Kingdom of Hungary as it existed within the framework of the Austro-Hungarian Monarchy up to November 1918, excluding the territory of Croatia-Slovenia (16,420 square miles), covered nearly 109,200 miles.

Table 2. Total Population and Population Density,[a] Selected Years 1910-1941

Census Year[b]	Population			Density per Square Mile	Increase	
	Total	Males	Females		Number	Per Cent
1910[c]	7,615,117	3,789,868	3,817,103	212.0	757,812	11.1
1920	7,990,202	3,875,904	4,114,298	222.4	375,084	4.9
1930	8,688,319[d]	4,250,110	4,438,209	242.0	698,117	8.7
1941	9,319,992[e]	4,562,868	4,757,124	259.5	631,673	7.3

Sources: For 1910, 1920, and 1930, Central Statistical Bureau, *Magyar Statisztikai Zsebkonyv* (Hungarian Statistical Pocketbook) (Budapest, [1947]), XIII (1946), 33-40; for 1941, Dezso Elekes, *A Mai Magyarorszag* (Hungary Today) (Budapest, 1947), p. 69.

[a] Trianon territory.

[b] December 31, except 1941, which was January 31.

[c] Recalculated to the Trianon territory in 1920, and later corrected, hence the difference of 9,146 between male-female distribution (altogether 7,615,117).

[d] The *Statistical Year-Book of the League of Nations 1933/34* (Geneva, 1934), p. 41 gives 8,328,400, which is inaccurate.

[e] If territorial gains are included, total population is 14,683,323.

The constant efforts of the Hungarian government to recover the lost areas *(terra irredenta)* resulted in temporary territorial gains:

1. On November 2, 1938, the First Vienna Award reassigned to Hungary the major Magyar-settled portions of Slovakia, an area of about 4,640 square miles with 1,057,000 population.

2. On March 15, 1939, Hungary reoccupied Ruthenia (Carpatho-Ukraine), an area of approximately 4,670 square miles with 698,000 inhabitants.

3. On August 30, 1940, the Second Vienna Award returned nearly 16,650 square miles of northern Transylvania from Romania, with a population of 2,577,000.

4. In April 1941, upon the defeat of Yugoslavia by Nazi Germany and the proclamation of Croatian independence Hungary reoccupied Vojvodina, formerly called Bacska, an area of 4,440 square miles with 1,031,000 inhabitants and two small territories along the river Mura and the triangle of Baranya.

These territorial gains extended the territory of Hungary to 66,315 square miles, with a total population of 14,683,000 until the end of World War II. All these territorial gains were surrendered anew in the Paris Peace Treaty of 1947.

The number of ethnic Hungarians in the said areas after the war, mass migration, and population exchanges, is as follows: 1,499,851 in Romania (1948), 592,400 in Czechoslovakia (1950), and 496,493 in Yugoslavia (1950). The number of Magyars by birth all over the world is approximately 13,000,000, of which 268,022 are in the United States (1950).

Population Changes and Shifts

East-Central Europe has witnessed many major shifts of population in the last fifteen years due to the expanding Nazi German empire, the mass deportations and liquidations in the German-occupied regions, the war losses, Soviet occupation, postwar agreements on population exchanges, the expulsion of Germans from the area, and finally Communist rule, which has resulted in the escape of many thousands to the West. One encounters great difficulties in drawing a "balance sheet" for any of the countries in this region. Hungary's balance sheet is particularly complicated, for there have been a number of different inward and outward movements, overlapping and counteracting one another.

One type of population shift is connected with temporary territorial gains. In 1939-41, Hungarian administration moved into the regained territories (Southern Slovakia, Ruthenia, Northern Transylvania, Vojvodina), only to be withdrawn at the end of the war. The withdrawal of the Hungarian administration resulted in a considerable migration of the civilian population toward the Trianon territory. Approximately 160,000 ethnic Hungarians fled Transylvania, 20,000 Ruthenia (Carpatho-Ukraine), and 20,000 Southern Slovakia and Vojvodina, mostly in 1944, when the front reached these areas.

War casualties form another group. Total war losses of the Hungarian Army are estimated at 200,000, of which 140,000 relate to the present territory. Civilian losses, victims of air bombardments and the siege of Budapest, were about 40,000, not including the losses of the Jewish population. As to Jewish casualties it is almost impossible to arrive at an exact figure. The 1947 Annual Report of the World Jewish Congress estimated the total number of Hungarian Jews killed during the war at 564,000. However, the majority of the victims came from regained territories and do not relate to the present territory. On the other hand, the losses sustained on the eastern front by the Army Labor Service battalions, which were manned by Jewish draftees, were recorded as military losses and included in that figure. Various estimates seem to agree on 220,000 as the approximate number of losses suffered by the Jewish population of the Trianon territory. Of this number, about 68,000 were killed in Hungary, while 152,000 met their death in German concentration camps.

Another major shift occurred at the end of the war. The Hungarian Nazi Administration withdrew to Germany, along with hundreds of thousands of civilians. Their total number, related to the present territory, was about 700,000, of which about 600,000 returned in the course of 1945 and 43,000 in 1946. This number includes about 121,000 Jews who returned from German concentration camps.

The movement of Hungarian POW's should also be entered on the balance sheet. The total number of POW's—both members of the Hungarian Army and civilians taken prisoner by the Soviet Union—was probably above 220,000, of which about 180,000 relate to the present territory. The number of those returned immediately after the war was not considerable and is tentatively estimated at 5,000. As of January 1, 1946, there were approximately 175,000 still detained by the Soviet Union. The number of POW's returned during the 1946-49 period is about 165,000. (It may be noted, however, that this number included Hungarians from Transylvania, Vojvodina, etc. who had served in the Hungarian Army.)

The Potsdam Agrement also provided for a major population shift: "The three Governments having considered the question in all its aspects, recognize that the transfer to Germany of German populations, or elements thereof, remaining in Poland, Czechoslovakia and Hungary, will have to be undertaken. . . ." The Russians demanded the transfer of about 400,000 ethnic Germans from Hungary, while the Hungarian government set the number of Germans to be expelled at 200,000 to 250,000. As of July 1947, 176,000 Germans had been transferred to Western Germany. The number of persons transferred to Eastern Germany is not known. Estimates vary as to the total number of Germans expelled from Hungary, but 200,000 had probably been expelled by the end of 1948, for the movement was considerably slowed down after July 1947.

While the expulsion of Germans meant a population shift outward from Hungary, the transfer agreement on February 27, 1946 between Czechoslovakia and Hungary resulted in an increase of the Hungarian population, by exchanging 63,000 Slovaks living in Hungary for 92,000 ethnic Hungarians from Slovakia.

The last group of population shifts covers legal as well as illegal emigration, to Israel and other countries. During 1946 and the first half of 1947, the majority of the emigrants were Hungarian Jews. The Communist *coup d'état* in June 1947, however, resulted in the flight of many thousands of anti-Communists. The total number of both categories was about 40,000 by the end of 1948. As a result of Communist police measures and border control, this movement has considerably lessened since 1949, but has not stopped completely. The total number for the period 1949-54 may be estimated at about 10,000.

The various population shifts may be tabulated in a balance sheet. Since most of the items are based on estimates, no balance sheet could claim accuracy. Table 3 gives a summary of population changes, 1939-49. The figures are computed from many sources, but the methods used and some of the results are similar to those of Gregory Frumkin in *Population Changes in Europe Since 1939*. A "residual figure"— or sum of total errors—has been allotted in order to signify that many items on the balance sheet are rounded estimates.

Table 3. Summary of Population Changes, 1939-1949

Population, January 1, 1939	9,200,000
Births, 1939-48	+1,782,000
Deaths, 1939-48	−1,299,000
Expected population, January 1, 1949	9,683,000
Military war losses	−140,000
Civilian war losses	−260,000
Emigration	−578,000
Immigration	+435,000
Residual figure (sum of total errors)	(+) 65,000
Population, January 1, 1949	9,205,000

Table 3 shows that, despite a natural increase of 500,000 during 1939-48, the total population remained unchanged. It is evident that the entire natural increase was canceled by war losses and an excess of emigration over immigration.

Population Density

Hungary is the most densely populated country in East-Central Europe: on January 1, 1955, her population density was 271.6 per square mile (or 104.8 per square kilometer), considerably above the European average of 209.6 per square mile. While the country occupies a territory somewhat smaller than the state of Indiana (36,205 square miles), her population density is 150 per cent higher than that of Indiana (108.7 per square mile).

A distinction must be made between density of population and density of settlements. In regard to the density of population, the eastern parts of Hungary—the Great Hungarian Plain and the Trans-Tisza region—are more densely inhabited than the western and northern regions, Transdanubia and the Northern Upland. Nevertheless, the Great Plain and Trans-Tisza are thinly settled. Widely scattered cities and villages with a relatively large population account for high density figures in this area.

On the other hand, Transdanubia has the highest density of settlements. With the exception of the Bakony Mountains area, Transdanubia is practically covered with villages, small communities, and towns. In this respect, Fejer County, which ranks well behind others in density of population, is the most densely settled area.

The northern region, often called the Northern Upland, is about average both as to the density of population and of settlements. Some structural changes may have occurred in Borsod-Gomor and Heves counties during the last five years, for a considerable part of the industrialization program carried out by the Five-Year Economic Plan centered around the Matra and Bukk mountains and the Sajo River valley. The density of population may have increased with the establishment of new industrial areas.

Since 1950, the "security measures" of the Hungarian government have systematically removed "unreliable" elements from the western (Austro-Hungarian) and southern (Yugoslav-Hungarian) border zones. These measures may have diminished the population density of the following counties: Gyor-Sopron, Vas, Zala, Somogy, Baranya, Bacs-Kiskun, and Csongrad.

Distribution of Population

Before 1950, Hungary consisted of twenty-five counties, traditional administrative units of various sizes. In that year, their number was reduced to nineteen by merging the smaller ones and their sizes became more or less proportionate. The counties *(megye)* are in turn subdivided into districts *(jaras)*. Table 4 lists the counties and their estimated population in 1953 (see also Map 2, page 53).

Communities, towns, and cities numbered 3,291 in 1941, and 3,288 in 1947. This number declined to 3,222 in 1950, as a result of administrative mergers. The absorption of 24 suburbs and towns to create Greater Budapest was one of the important mergers.

Table 4. Administrative Divisions, 1953

County	County Seat	Population (in thousands)
Budapest	Capital	1,728
Transdanubia		
Baranya	Pecs	384
Fejer	Szekesfehervar	352
Gyor-Sopron	Gyor	416
Komarom	Tatabanya	224
Somogy	Kaposvar	352
Tolna	Szekszard	288
Vas	Szombathely	288
Veszprem	Veszprem	352
Zala	Zalaegerszeg	256
Great Plain		
Bacs-Kiskun	Kecskemet	570
Bekes	Bekescsaba	480
Csongrad	Hodmezovasarhely	416
Hajdu-Bihar	Debrecen	512
Pest	Budapest	672[a]
Szabolcs-Szatmar	Nyiregyhaza	544
Szolnok	Szolnok	488
Northern Upland		
Borsod-Abauj-Zemplen	Miskolc	704
Heves	Eger	320
Nograd	Salgotarjan	224
Total		9,530

Source: Population figures computed by Free Europe Press based on article in *Szabad Nep*, May 5, 1953.

[a] Population of Budapest is not included.

Table 5 offers a tabulation on the distribution of population by size of community in 1941 and in 1950. According to the 1941 figures, only 9.54 per cent of the total population lived in settlements of less than 1,000 inhabitants, while 54.23 lived in small towns and communities of 1,000 to 20,000 inhabitants. Middle-sized towns claimed 18.73 per cent of the population (20,000-100,000). The rest lived in the four largest cities: Budapest (1,164,963), Szeged (136,752), Debrecen (125,933), and Miskolc (109,704).

The creation of Greater Budapest increased the total population of the capital to 1,725,000, 19 per cent of the country's inhabitants. A similar merger of the administrative center Miskolc with its industrial twin city Diosgyor promoted Miskolc to the second largest Hungarian

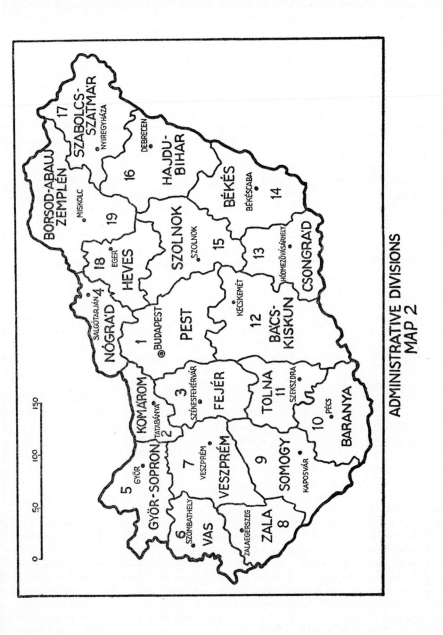

ADMINISTRATIVE DIVISIONS
MAP 2

city, with a total population of 138,000. The rapid industrialization program of the period 1949-53 has increased the population of the industrial communities (Gyor, Pecs) and has created a number of new urban communities (Sztalinvaros, Komlo, Varpalota, and Kazincbarcika). Meanwhile, the population of the large agricultural centers (Debrecen, Szeged) has remained relatively stationary.

Table 5. Distribution of Population by Size of Community,[a] 1941 and 1950

| Communities with Population of | 1941 | | | 1950 |
| | Number of Communities | Population | | Number of Communities |
		Number	Per Cent	
Less than 500	614	213,529	2.29	564
500 -1000	922	675,597	7.25	873
1001-5000	1,473	3,101,704	32.29	1,521
5001-20,000	229	2,043,710	21.94	
20,001-50,000	36	1,136,172	12.20	
50,001-100,000	9	608,820	6.53	264
100,001-1,000,000	3	372,118	3.99	
Over 1,000,000	1	1,164,963	12.51	

Sources: For 1941, *Magyar Statisztikai Zsebkonyv,* XV (1948), 41; for 1950, *Statisztikai Szemle,* III (May 1951), 451.

[a] Present territory.

The marked increase in the number of smaller communities and the population increase of the industrial settlements indicates a trend toward urbanization. The same trend is more clearly observable in Table 6 which tabulates the urban and rural population in 1941, 1949, and 1954.

Table 6. Urban-Rural Distribution of Population,[a] 1941, 1949, and 1954
(*in per cent of total population*)

Category	1941[b]	1949[c]	1954[d]
Urban including Budapest	38.2	36.5	40.0
Budapest	18.4	17.3	19.0
Rural	61.8	63.5	60.0

Source: Statistische Praxis, loc. cit.

[a] Present territory.
[b] January 31, 1941 census figures.
[c] January 1, 1949 census figures.
[d] Official mid-year (July 1) estimates.

In view of the figures on rural-urban distribution, it is interesting to note that there was an increase of 82,000 in rural population from 1941 to 1949, mainly in the 1945-49 period. This slight gain may be attributed to the relatively higher war losses of the big cities, the flight from the cities during and after the war, the higher fertility of the rural population, and the redistribution of land (land reform of 1945), which increased the need for manpower in agriculture.

On the other hand, the trend toward urbanization gained new stimulus by the rapid industrialization program of the Five-Year Plan: in four years (1949-53), the rural population decreased by some 218,000, while the urban population had an impressive 605,000 increase. This recent influx to the urban areas balanced the wartime losses, increased the number of small and middle-sized towns, and created new urban communities. Since Communist "social engineering" has always been in favor of urbanization, both in industry and agriculture, the number and proportion of urban population have not stopped growing since July 1953, under the "new course" policy.

A similar trend of urbanization and industrialization can be observed in other countries of the area. Industrial Czechoslovakia has the largest urban population (over 50 per cent), while Albania has the smallest (approximately 25 per cent) ratio.

Patterns of Settlement

In Transdanubia, where a certain continuity of settlement has existed since Roman times, unbroken even by the Turkish wars, the main centers of habitation are small or medium-sized towns serving as religious or market centers. Transdanubian towns like Szombathely or Sopron are similar to the small urban communities of other Central European countries, inhabited by people engaged in industrial, commercial, or professional occupations.

On the Great Plain, an entirely different settlement type prevails. The agricultural town of the Great Plain, a unique mixture of urban and rural elements, is almost exclusive to Hungary. Combining the functions of village and market town, its population is relatively large and mostly engaged in agriculture. The agricultural town developed in the period of the Turkish wars, when the agricultural population took refuge in large, fortified villages which developed certain urban characteristics only during the last century.

The inhabitants of these towns continued to farm, but they left their refuges only during the spring and summer to cultivate their land. For the purpose of temporary living during the crop-raising season, they built temporary dwellings called *tanya* in the centers of their farms.

This type of settlement remained even after the retreat of the Turks in the eighteenth century. Thus, the present agricultural towns in the Great Plain consist of two units. The inner settlement, a townlike community, serves as permanent winter quarters for those who are still engaged in agriculture; and an outer belt, surrounding the town in a wide circle, comprises the isolated farmsteads serving as summer residences and "workshops" for their owners. Kecskemet with 64,000 inhabitants, and Hodmezovasarhely with 50,000 inhabitants are examples of the agricultural towns of the Great Plain.

However, the agricultural towns have recently undergone profound changes. Persons engaged in industry and commerce, as well as the professions, constitute a greater number of the population. Thus, a particular settlement type results from this combination of urban and agricultural elements, which greatly contributes to raising the cultural and material level of the agricultural population of the Great Plain.

The major settlements of the Northern Upland have been developed by mining and industry. The inhabitants of the industrial towns of the Upland work in the iron and steel works or the nearby coal mines. Salgotarjan, Ozd, Rudabanya, and Diosgyor (recently merged with Miskolc) represent the industrial settlements of the Northern Upland.

Major Cities of Hungary. Budapest is the capital and the cultural and economic center of the country, with 1,725,000 inhabitants. The present city resulted from the merger of two historical towns, Buda on the hilly west bank of the Danube, and Pest on the flat-lying east bank. It grew on the Danube at the junction of the Transdanubian hills with the Great Plain, along the main crossroad of Central Europe. In 1949, Budapest incorporated its hitherto autonomous industrial suburbs.

In the fourteenth century, some centuries after the appearance of the Hungarians in the Danube Valley, Buda became the political center of the country. During the reign of Mathias (1458-90), the city became a royal residence of great splendor known throughout the Continent. A Turkish stronghold for over two centuries, Buda was depopulated by the wars; at the end of the seventeenth century, its population was probably only about a thousand persons. With the resettlement of the Great Plain, Buda and Pest became one cosmopolitan center for the peoples of Central Europe. Under the influence of Hungarian culture, it finally regained its national character.

The cultural and economic center of Hungary, Budapest is the seat of several major educational institutions and of numerous theaters and museums. The University of Budapest was established by Archbishop Peter Pazmany in 1635.

Miskolc (population, 136,000), the second largest city of Hungary, and the center of the Northern Upland, developed at the juncture of the volcanic hills of the north with the Great Plain. Heavy industry is concentrated at Miskolc, which along with Ozd, Salgotarjan, and Rudabanya form the Hungarian Ruhr. Miskolc is the seat of the only metallurgical college in Hungary.

Gyor (population, 66,000), situated at the confluence of the Raba with the Danube, is not only an important junction on the Budapest-Vienna railroad, but also a center of the machine industry. The town occupies the site of the Roman Aragona, and has always been an important center of upper Transdanubia. It is the seat of a Catholic bishopric.

Pecs (population, 87,000), the largest city of lower Transdanubia, is located equidistant from the Danube and the Drava rivers. The nearby bituminous coal mines of Mecsek have made Pecs an industrial town. It is also the seat of a university founded by King Louis II in the fourteenth century.

Other Major Cities of Transdanubia. The college of mining and forestry is located at Sopron (population, 36,000), on the Austrian border. Szombathely in a rich, vine-producing lowland and the seat of a Catholic bishopric is the center of the food industries. Szekesfehervar (population, 42,000), 25 miles southwest of Budapest, was the first capital of Hungary and is the seat of a Catholic bishopric.

Szeged (population, 88,000), the most important town in the southern half of the Great Plain, lies just below the confluence of the Maros and Tisza rivers. Because it lies along the commercial route from Transylvania to the Adriatic, it has been a trading center for centuries. It is the seat of a university and of a Catholic archbishopric.

Debrecen (population, 113,000) reigns as the center of the eastern Great Plain near the Romanian border. The headquarters of Hungarian Protestantism ever since the era of the Reformation, Debrecen has a Protestant university and seminary. Serving as market center for the agricultural population of the upper eastern Great Plain, it is an important railroad junction with six lines converging on it.

The forced industrialization of the Communist regime has recently created some new industrial towns with fast-growing populations, the most important of which is Sztalinvaros, the former Dunapentele, on the right bank of the Danube almost at equal distance from Budapest and the Yugoslav border. It was created by the first Five-Year Plan as a center of heavy industry, and its population has already reached the 30,000 mark. The blast furnaces of Sztalinvaros make steel of the iron ore of the Ukrainian Krivoj Rog, carried by river- and sea-going vessels through the Black Sea upstream on the Danube.

Sex Composition

According to the census of 1949, there were 4,423,420 male and 4,781,379 female inhabitants in Hungary. (Sex distribution in the previous census years is shown in Table 2.) The almost ideal balance of sexes was last observed in 1910, when the ratio was 995 males for every 1,000 females. World War I reduced the ratio to 952 in 1920. In 1930, the proportion rose again to 979, but declined to 959 in 1941.

World War II sharply decreased the number and percentual proportion of the male population. A tendency toward an increasing number of male births is observable in Hungary, just as in the other countries. This trend makes very slow progress, and some twenty-five to thirty years will be required to "make up for the losses," provided that no war or other major unexpected factor arises. In the course of recent years, approximately 6 per cent more boys than girls have been born. An offsetting factor is, the relatively higher death rate of the male population in infancy and in old age. Approximately 25 per cent more males than females die annually.

While no official projections have become available since 1949, when the ratio was 925 males for every 1,000 females, an unofficial estimate sets the ratio at 930 for January 1, 1955. In other words, the estimated population of Hungary, 9,750,000, consists of approximately 4,700,000 male and 5,050,000 female inhabitants.

Age Composition

Unfortunately, no official data are available for a more elaborate break-down of the age composition than those shown in Table 7. It is, however, obvious from these figures that World War II did not change the tendency of declining fertility and reproductivity. The increase in the proportion of persons over 65 years no doubt continued after 1949. By January 1, 1955, it was estimated to be nearly 9.0 per cent of the total population. Whether the proportion of young people will continue to increase will depend upon the future level of fertility. In fact, fertility would have to be substantially above the level of the recent past to assure any major increase in the number and proportion of this group. Taking into account the temporary increase in births in in recent years, the proportion of young people—under 15 years— is estimated at about 25 per cent of the total population as of January 1, 1955. The so-called working age groups follow the same pattern: the group of those between 15 and 39 years of age is expected to have decreased to about 35 per cent of the total population, while the other group, between 40 and 64 years of age, has probably increased to 31 per cent of the total population, as of January 1, 1955.

Table 7. Distribution of Population by Age Group, Selected Years 1910-1955
(*in per cent*)

Year	Under 15 Years	15-39 Years	40-60 Years	Over 65 Years
1910	34.8	38.6	21.7	4.9
1920	30.6	41.3	22.6	5.5
1930	27.5	42.6	23.6	6.3
1941	26.0	40.7	26.3	7.0
1949	24.6	37.5	30.1	7.8
1955	25.0	35.0	31.0	9.0

Sources: For 1910-41, *Magyar Statisztikai Zsebkonyv*, XIII (1946), 40; for 1949 and 1955, computed on the basis of the 1949 census.

Average Age of Total Population. The average age was 27.2 in 1910, 28.7 in 1920, 29.8 in 1930, 31.6 in 1941, and 32.4 in 1949, according to Hungarian official statistics. The preferred method of summarizing age distribution is in terms of the "median" age, rather than the arithmetic average age, given above. The median age is that age above which and below which one half of the population falls with respect to age. In other words, it is age of the "middle" man. The corresponding series of median age would give slightly lower figures (2 to 4 years) on each date, with essentially the same trend.

The trend, similar to that of most countries, shows an aging society. The same tendency has been demonstrated by the distribution of age groups. In this respect, Hungary is still "younger" than East Germany, where the median age was 35.6 years in 1946, West Germany (34.1 years in 1950), or Czechoslovakia (31.3 years in 1947), yet is "older" than, say, Poland where median age was 26.1 years in 1949.

Birth and Death Rates

Since the accuracy of vital statistics pertaining to certain periods is doubtful, birth and death rates in Table 8 were computed for five-year periods. This method eliminates some of the minor errors and empha- sizes the long-range tendencies in population movement.

Table 8 shows that Hungary's birth rate has fallen considerably. Death rates have followed a similar pattern. A tendency to balance war losses has always led to increased birth rates in early postwar years. There are indications that the Hungarian population has passed the peak of its vital revolution, and that after the present temporary re- versal, the long-range trend will resume its course. Hungary probably will reach its peak population by 1960, when the total may be as high as 10,100,000. The Hungarian official projection for January 1, 1961 is 10,026,000.

Table 8. Crude Vital Rates, 1911-13 and 1916-20—1954

(*number of births and deaths per thousand inhabitants,
excluding stillbirths and wartime military deaths*)

Year	Births	Deaths	Natural Increase
1911-13	34.3	22.9	11.4
1916-20	21.7	21.7	—
1921-25	29.4	19.9	9.5
1926-30	26.0	17.0	9.0
1931-35	20.4	15.8	4.6
1936-40	20.1	14.2	5.9
1941-45[a]	19.3	15.9	3.4
1946-50	20.4	12.5	7.9
1951	20.2	11.7	8.5
1952	19.6	11.3	8.3
1953	21.6	11.7	9.9
1954[b]	23.0	11.0	12.0

Sources: Elekes, *op. cit.,* p. 77; *Statistical Year-Book of the League of Nations 1942/44* (Geneva, 1945), p. 41; *Statisztikai Tajekoztato* (Statistical Bulletin), No. 1 (1951), 31; *ibid.,* No. 1 (1953), 36; U.N., *Demographic Yearbook 1953* (New York, 1953), pp. 138, 172; *Statistical Yearbook of the United Nations 1955* (New York, 1955), pp. 39, 44; *Statistische Praxis, loc. cit.;* Szabad Nep, August 14, 1955.

[a] Data available only for January-July 1944.

[b] Rounded figures, current official (somewhat over-optimistic) estimates.

An equally important aspect is the birth rate by order of birth. Table 9 shows that postwar Hungary has a considerably higher ratio for successive births than she had prior to the war.

Table 9. Live Births by Order of Birth, Selected Years 1936-1953
(*in per cent of total*)

	1936	1946	1951	1952	1953
1st child	32.6	37.6	41.6	39.4	37.6
2nd	21.9	25.5	26.7	27.9	28.4
3rd	14.7	13.9	13.3	14.0	15.5
4th	9.6	7.8	7.0	7.4	7.8
5th	6.5	5.0	4.0	4.0	4.1
6th	4.7	3.4	2.4	2.5	2.3
7th - 10th	8.3	5.8	4.2	4.0	3.7
11th child and over	1.7	1.0	0.8	0.8	0.6
All births	100.0	100.0	100.0	100.0	100.0

Source: Statistische Praxis, loc. cit.

While the above table offers information on the "positive" side of the population movement, Table 10 gives equally valuable information concerning distribution of deaths by age group.

Table 10. Age Specific Death Rates, 1938, 1948/49, and 1953
(*number of deaths per thousand persons in each age group*)

Age Group	1938	1948/49	1953
Under 1 year	131.3	92.5	70.7
1-2 years	23.2	8.6	6.8
2-3	7.3	4.2	2.5
3-4	4.1	2.5	1.5
5-9	2.3	1.4	0.8
10-14	2.0	1.1	0.7
15-19	3.3	2.1	1.2
20-29	4.8	3.3	1.7
30-39	4.8	3.7	2.3
40-49	7.5	6.0	4.6
50-59	14.5	11.6	11.3
60-69	33.4	26.5	29.3
70 and over	108.6	88.0	105.5
All deaths	14.3	11.5	11.7

Source: Ibid.

Infant Mortality. There has been a sharp decline in infant mortality in the postwar years, which is also true of other East-Central European countries and in line with the general advancement of medical care. Prior to 1914, the ratio of infant mortality exceeded 200 deaths for

62   **Geography and Demography**

every 1,000 live births. The list below shows the gradual decrease
between the wars to an average ratio of 110-130. In contrast to these
figures, or to the exceptional increase in 1945 (16.9), the reported
ratio of 60.7 for 1954 is remarkable.

As in the case of crude birth and death rates, the accuracy of infant
mortality statistics for single years has often been questioned. The
following figures, giving infant mortality rates per 1,000 live births,
indicate the long-range development:

Year	Infant Mortality per Thousand Live Births
1921-25	187
1926-30	172
1931-35	157
1936-40	131
1941-43	122
1944	...
1945-49	116
1950-54	74

Sources: *Magyar Statisztikai Zsebkonyv*, XV (1948), 63; *Nepegeszsegugy* (Public
Health Affairs), No. 7 (1951); *Statisztikai Tajekoztato*, No. 3 (1953); *Statistical
Year-Book of the League of Nations 1942/44*, p. 54; *Statistical Yearbook of the
United Nations 1955*, p. 49; *Statistische Praxis, loc. cit.*

For the 1950-54 period the infant mortality rate has been reported
as follows: 85.7 for 1950, 83.9 for 1951, 69.9 for 1952, 70.8 for 1953,
and—as a preliminary figure—60.7 for 1954.

Life Expectancy at Birth. The term "life expectancy at birth" indicates the average future lifetime of all individuals born in a given
year. The advancement of medical science has greatly increased the
average lifetime. The gradual increase is shown in Table 11.

Table 11. Life Expectancy at Birth, Selected Years 1900-1901—1948-1949

Year	Males	Females
1900-01	37.4	38.1
1920-21	41.0	43.0
1930-31	49.3	51.8
1941	54.9	58.2
1948-49	58.8	63.8

Sources: *Statisztikai Szemle*, III (March 1951), 202; *Ibid.*, III (May 1951), 419.

The increase is less impressive if compared to Western European countries, such as Western Germany, where life expectancy was 64.6 years for men and 68.5 for women in 1949-51. However, Hungary is slightly ahead of other East-Central European countries, except Austria (61.9 years for men and 66.9 for women in 1949-51).

Family Statistics

Parallel with the declining birth rates, the average size of the Hungarian family has decreased. In the early 1920's, the average family size was about 4.5, or 450 members for every 100 families. The 1949 census returns show that there were 357 members for every 100 families. Some 8,522,751 Hungarians lived in 2,385,112 families (94.3 per cent of the total population), while 515,469 inhabitants lived in "family factions." This term apparently refers to single persons with an independent household and without family, in contrast to 166,579 individuals who lived in "institutional households," which seems to refer to religious orders, hospitals, prisons, etc. (See Table 12.)

Table 12. Family Status and Number of Household Families by Occupational Group, 1949

Occupational Group, Active and Passive Persons	Number of Persons			Household Families	
	Total	Single	In Families	Number	Per Cent
All occupational groups	9,204,799	682,048	8,522,751	2,385,112	100.0
Farmers owning					
0-5 cadastral yokes[a]	1,727,017	54,687	1,672,330	477,868	20.0
5-10	1,386,897	18,950	1,367,938	333,161	14.0
10-25	771,215	12,464	758,751	181,001	7.6
Over 25	131,623	4,052	127,571	34,248	1.4
Agricultural workers	506,173	33,914	472,259	132,317	5.5
Nonagricultural economically independent persons	870,950	41,507	829,443	239,032	10.0
Nonagricultural salary earners	845,830	85,670	760,160	236,887	9.9
Nonagricultural wage earners	2,610,101	199,001	2,411,100	704,844	29.6
Not classified	188,414	65,215	123,199	...	...
Institutional population	166,579	165,579	...	...	...

Source: Summarized from tables published in *Statisztikai Szemle*, III (April 1951), 304-13.

[a] One cadastral yoke equals 1.42 acres.

The size of families, of course, varies according to occupational group, the largest being in the agricultural category. Table 13 shows the tabulation of these groups. Apart from the somewhat vague category of "nonclassifiable" families, the smallest family units are those of the urban-industrial population.

Table 13. Average Size of Household Family and Ratio of Family
Dependency, by Occupational Group, 1949

Occupational Group, Active and Passive Persons	Number of Persons per 100 Household Families[a]			Ratio of Dependents per 100 Families
	Total	Earners	Dependents	
All occupation groups	357	153	204	133.3
Farmers owning				
0-5 cadastral yokes	351	151	200	132.5
5-10 cadastral yokes	412	178	234	131.5
10-25 cadastral yokes	424	192	232	120.8
Over 25 cadastral yokes	395	183	212	115.8
Agricultural workers	342	138	204	147.8
Nonagricultural economically independent persons	358	142	216	152.1
Nonagricultural salary earners	330	141	189	134.0
Nonagricultural wage earners	335	144	191	132.6
Not classified	262	102	160	156.9
Institutional population	...	...	...	...

Source: As in Table 12.

[a] No attempt was made to reconcile the ratios of persons in 100 household families with the coefficient resulting from multiplying the number of families by the author's ratio.

The larger agricultural families also have an economic advantage. The ratio of earners for every 100 families is higher in this group than in any other group. The highest ratios are 192 earners in the 10-25 cadastral yoke and 183 earners in the more than 25 cadastral yoke farmers' brackets, while the lowest ratios are those of agricultural workers (landless peasants) and white-collar workers, 138 and 141, respectively, for every 100 families. This is understandable, for many of the farmer's family members work as "unpaid family workers" and therefore, are considered earners. In fact, they are earners, paid in kind.

From the point of view of the earners, another ratio can be established: the ratio of dependents for every 100 earners. According to this ratio, naturally, it is the agricultural worker who has to take care of more dependents (159 for every 100 earners), while the ratio for the landowner of 25 or more cadastral yokes is 103 for every 100 earners. The average ratio pertaining to the total population in 1949 was 134 dependents for every 100 earners living in families.

The rapid industrialization program of 1950-53 may have had a considerable impact upon the composition of families. While no official statistics have become available since the 1949 census, it may be assumed that the forced recruitment of the new industrial workers has had the following effects: (1) increased the number and ratio of earners in the worker families, by mobilizing housewives; (2) decreased the number of earners and dependents in the farmer families, from which a considerable number of workers were recruited; and (3) increased the number of single household keepers (living in "family faction"), for the housing shortage and economic misery greatly hindered the establishment of new families among the newly recruited workers.

Ethnic Groups

Ethnic statistics in East-Central Europe are seldom accurate or reliable. In an atmosphere of racial persecutions, members of ethnic minority groups often find it difficult to claim nationality other than the "official." Statistics based on the "mother tongue" are contestable, for many of the ethnic group members speak two or more languages fluently. In view of the postwar population exchange with Czechoslovakia and the expulsion of Germans, the proportion of inhabitants claiming other than Hungarian nationality is less than 1 per cent of the total population.

Insofar as the mother tongue is concerned, a semi-official Hungarian publication estimates the proportion of non-Hungarian ethnic groups at 3 per cent of the total population in 1949. This figure corresponds to private estimates, shown in Table 14.

Religious Groups

Table 15 shows the distribution of population by religious group in 1910, 1930, and 1941. No similar breakdown has been published for 1949 or for any later date.

Table 14. Distribution of Population by Mother Tongue,[a]
Selected Years 1910-1949
(*in per cent*)

Mother Tongue	1910	1930	1941	1949
Hungarian	88.4	92.1	92.8	97.0
German	7.3	5.5	5.1	2.2
Slovak	2.2	1.2	0.8	0.1
Ruthenian	0.0	0.0	0.0	0.0
Romanian	0.4	0.2	0.2	0.1
Serb and Croat	0.8	0.4	0.3	0.3
Other	0.9	0.6	0.8	0.3
Total, Hungary	100.0	100.0	100.0	100.0

Sources: For 1910-41, *Magyar Statisztikai Zsebkonyv*, XIII (1946), 48; for 1949, computed on the basis of population changes and shifts, 1939-49.

Note: Generally, nationality statistics show a lower percentage than mother tongue figures for ethnic minority groups.

[a] Figures for 1910-41 pertain to Trianon territory and are, therefore, comparable to 1949 figures, which refer to the present territory.

Table 15. Distribution of Population by Religion,[a] 1910, 1930, and 1941
(*in per cent*)

Religion	1910	1930	1941
Roman Catholic	62.8	64.9	65.7
Greek Catholic	2.2	2.3	2.5
Calvinist	21.4	20.9	20.8
Lutheran	6.4	6.1	6.0
Greek Orthodox	0.8	0.5	0.4
Unitarian	0.1	0.1	0.1
Baptist	[b]	0.0	0.2
Israelite	6.2	5.1	4.3
Other, unknown	0.1	0.1	0.0

Source: Ibid.
[a] Trianon territory.
[b] In 1910, Baptists were included in "other."

In 1941, approximately two-thirds of the population belonged to the Roman Catholic Church, while the combined membership of the Protestant churches amounted to about 27 per cent of all inhabitants. The number of Israelites was 4.3 per cent in 1941, but their number decreased drastically during the war. According to the estimates of the 1947 Annual Report of the Jewish World Congress, there were only 141,480 persons of the Jewish faith in that year. Even this number has declined in the course of 1947-49 due to emigration to Israel. Their proportion for 1949, therefore, can be taken at 1.6 per cent of the total population. The sharp decrease of this group automatically increased the percentage figures for the other denominations. In 1949, the Roman Catholic Church claimed about 68 per cent of the population and the Protestant churches 29 per cent.

Literacy

The last two decades have shown a gradual decrease in the number and proportion of the illiterate population. The proportion of illiterate Hungarians over 10 years of age, was 9.3 per cent in 1930. The same category comprised 6.0 per cent of the population in 1941. In 1949, the official census did not provide a proper basis of comparison, for it includes all persons over 7 years of age. However, these figures—5 per cent of the total population—show a declining tendency. The principles and methods introduced by the Communist government in Hungarian education for both schoolchildren and adults probably reduced illiteracy to slightly above 4 per cent in 1955.

Economically Active Population

According to the 1949 census, 47 per cent (4,325,000 persons) of the Hungarian population was gainfully occupied, i.e. economically active, on January 1, 1949. Table 16 tabulates the number and proportion of the active population prior to 1949. A tendency of gradual increase may be noted since 1910, when the active population amounted to only 41 per cent. By the end of World War I, the percentage rose to 46, due to the growth of Hungarian industry. The economic stagnation of 1930 and the sudden increase of births during the 1920's are reflected in the somewhat lower figure, 44 per cent, for 1930.

Table 16. Development of Gainfully Occupied Population[a]
Selected Years 1910-1949

Census Year	Total Population	Active Population	Per Cent of Total
1910	7,615,117	3,145,400	41
1920	7,990,202	3,653,800	46
1930	8,688,319	3,829,752	44
1941	9,319,992	4,503,117	48
1949	9,204,799	4,325,000	47

Sources: Statistical Year-Book of the League of Nations 1930/31 (Geneva, 1931), pp. 38-39; International Labour Office, *Year Book of Labour Statistics 1943/44* (Geneva, 1945), pp. 10-11; *idem, Year Book of Labour Statistics 1947/48* (Geneva, 1949), pp. 16-17; *Statisztikai Szemle*, III (April 1951), 311.

[a] Figures for 1910-41 pertain to Trianon territory and are comparable to 1949 figures, which refer to present territory.

Since 1941 was the peak year of Hungary's war industrial capacity, the high proportion of active population (48 per cent) is not surprising. However, the percentage did not decrease considerably in 1949, despite heavy war losses, migration, and population changes. The 47 per cent figure for 1949 shows the first stage of the "economic mobilization" which started in 1945, and which has been drastically furthered by the Communist economic plans. The year 1949 was the end of the Three-Year Plan, aimed at the restoration of prewar capacity. It was followed by the more expansive Five-Year Plan, and the subsequent forced recruitment of manpower apparently increased the number and proportion of the gainfully occupied population. While no official figures are available since the 1949 census, unofficial estimates set the number of gainfully occupied persons for January 1, 1952 at 4,625,000, or 49 per cent of the population.

Structure of the Gainfully Occupied Population. The report "Family Statistical Returns of the 1949 Census" offers a basis for computing the approximate number and proportion of the various occupational groups. Table 17 indicates the results of these computations for agriculture, along with the corresponding figures for 1930 and 1941. The fact that the active agrarian population is numerically the same as it was in 1930 seems to corroborate the general observation that the postwar lack of farm equipment and the increase in small peasant farms did not allow any substantial decrease in agricultural manpower until 1949.

Table 17. Distribution of Economically Active Agricultural Population, by Occupational Status, 1930, 1941, and 1949

Occupational Status	1930		1941		1949[a]	
	Number	Per Cent	Number	Per Cent	Number	Per Cent
Farmers	700,466	34.5	790,059	36.8	1,113,000	54.8
Family help	536,988	26.5	591,036	27.6	702,000	34.6
Employees	793,997	39.0	772,360	35.6	216,000	10.6
Total active population	2,031,451	100.0	2,153,455	100.0	2,031,000	100.0

Sources: As in Table 16.

[a] Figures computed from the "Family Statistical Returns of the 1949 Census" (*Statisztikai Szemle*). The proportional changes within the active group seem to justify the computation, for they clearly represent the demographic consequences of the 1945 land reform: the number of landowners increased (370,963 landless workers became new proprietors); the number of family workers also increased with the small peasant farms; and the number of (landless) workers decreased accordingly.

Meanwhile, the internal shifts among the agrarian subcategories—the increase in the number of landowners and family workers, the decrease in the number of farmhands—point to those significant changes in the social structure which followed the land reform of 1945.

The rapid industrialization program of the Five-Year Plan had shifted approximately 230,000 earners and 110,000 dependents from agriculture to industry by 1952. Considering the somewhat slower, but still considerable, expansion of agricultural production, it may be assumed that the number of persons actively engaged in agriculture was around 2,050,000 in 1952, more or less the same as before. Contrasted to the growing population of the country, this means a decline in the proportion of agricultural population. In 1930, 51.8 per cent of the total population depended on agriculture and 23.4 per cent were active in agriculture; in 1949, 49.1 per cent were dependent and 22 per cent active; and in 1952, 46 per cent were dependent and 21.7 per cent were active. This declining trend might have reached its lowest point by the summer of 1953, when the "new course" policy was introduced.

Table 18 offers a summary tabulation of the gainfully occupied population on January 1, 1949, based on the same methods of computation used for the agrarian population. No tabulation is possible for a later year.

Table 18. Distribution of Economically Active Population, by Occupational Group, 1949

Occupational Group	Total Population		Economically Active Population		Ratio of Dependents to 100 Earners
	Number	Per Cent	Number	Per Cent	
All occupations	9,205,000	100.0	4,325,000	100.0	112.9
Agricultural population					
Farmers and family help	4,017,000	100.0	1,815,000	45.2	121.3
Employees	506,000	100.0	216,000	42.7	134.3
Total	4,523,000	100.0	2,031,000	45.9	122.6
Nonagricultural population					
Employers and self-employed	871,000	100.0	381,000	43.8	128.7
Salary earners	846,000	100.0	420,000	49.6	101.4
Wage earners	2,610,000	100.0	1,214,000	46.5	115.0
Others, not classified	188,000	100.0	112,000	64.9	67.9
Institutional population	167,000	—	167,000	—	—
Total	4,682,000	100.0	2,294,000	48.9	

The 48.9 per cent given in Table 18 as economically active population includes the vague category of those living in "institutions" and may include members of the armed forces, religious orders, and working convicts. Without this group the figure would be 45.4 per cent. The official figure is 47 per cent.

Distribution of Population by Occupation. Communist statistical sources have never published any data on occupational distribution of the population, which would—in the traditional sense—be comparable to corresponding statistics of the previous years. Instead, the June 1951 issue of *Tarsadalmi Szemle* (Social Review), an official periodical of the Communist Party, published a highly propagandistic study to show the "proletarization" of society and the gradual disappearance of the "nonworking" elements up to 1949. In summary, these figures give the population distribution as follows: in 1930, 58.3 per cent of the population were in Category A (wage earners), 28.7 per cent in Category B (small producers), 10.9 per cent in Category C (capitalists, kulaks, and other nonworking people), and 2.1 per cent in Category D (others); in 1949, 48.7 per cent in Category A, 43.3 per cent in Category B, 6.9 per cent in Category C, and 1.1 per cent in Category D. See Table 19 for the population distribution by occupational group.

Since the Communist *coup d'état* of 1947, Hungary has undergone a social transformation. By 1954, at the end of the first Five-Year Plan, nearly 1,400,000 persons were employed by the nationalized industries of mining, manufacturing, construction, and in "free" handicrafts. Extensive nationalization has tremendously increased the category of "wage earners," at the expense of those in private enterprises and the free professions. Although the forced collectivization of agriculture has put tens of thousands of farmers into the category of wage earners, the consequences of the 1945 land reform are still observable: the category of "independent small producers" is still higher than it was in 1930. The "capitalist" class—in the Western sense—has been completely eliminated. If there is still a category under this title, it apparently refers to "kulaks"—small landowners who work with hired farm labor. Table 20 shows these changes.

Table 19. Distribution of Economically Active Population, by Occupational Group,
Selected Years 1910-1952

cupational Group[a]	1910	1920	1930	1941	1949	1952
riculture	1,684,400	2,126,700	2,031,451	2,153,455	2,031,000	2,050,000
ning and smelting	29,100	40,100	35,182	55,281	70,000	110,000
lustry	684,200	697,700	886,676	1,057,196	855,000	1,185,000
ade and banking	151,700	183,700	226,083	260,456	} 1,005,000	992,000
ansportation	100,800	117,600	113,289	140,286		
med forces	53,400	88,100	} 238,083	} 358,104		
blic administra-tion and self-						
mployed persons	126,400	167,700				
rvants and day aborers	192,200	155,900	236,834	201,475	132,000	87,000
hers and un-specified	127,200	76,300	62,204	276,864	232,000	201,000
Total	3,145,400	3,653,800	3,829,752	4,503,117	4,325,000	4,625,000
Per cent of total population	41	46	44	48	47	49

Sources: For 1910 and 1920, *Statistical Year-Book of the League of Nations 1930/31*, pp. 38-39; 1930, *Yearbook of Labour Statistics 1943/44*, pp. 10-11; for 1941, *ibid.*, volume for 1947/48, 16-17; 1949 and 1952 estimates based on sources listed in Table 12 and *Magyar Gazdasag-ato Intezet Kozlemenyei* (Publications of the Hungarian Economic Research Institute), issue November 15, 1954 (Supplement), U.N., *Economic Bulletin for Europe*, VII, No. 2 (August 55), 85 ff., *Tarsadalmi Szemle* (Social Review) (June 1951).

[a] In view of the available reports, no attempt was made to separate trade and banking (already tionalized in 1949) and transportation from public administration and armed forces. It can, wever, be safely assumed that figures for transportation and armed forces have grown con-erably, while the elimination of free trade and free professions has decreased the numbers for de and banking and self-employed persons.

Table 20. Distribution of the Population, by Source of Maintenance, 1930 and 1954

Group	1930		1954	
	Population	Per Cent	Population	Per Cent
Dependent on wage and salary	5,056,300	58.3	5,720,000	59.4
Independent small producers[a]	2,490,200	28.6	3,009,300	31.2
Collective cooperative members	—	—	776,800	8.1
Capitalists	953,500	11.0	58,400	0.6
Others	182,300	2.1	67,600	0.7
Total	8,682,300	100.0	9,632,100	100.0

Source: Szabad Nep, November 6, 1955.
[a] Including peasants and handicraftsmen.

III. The Government

5. THE CONSTITUTIONAL SYSTEM AND GOVERNMENT

Constitution of the Hungarian Kingdom

Hungarian constitutionalism dates from the earliest beginnings of the nation. In fact, the first constitutional act may be said to have preceded even the *honfoglalas* (occupation of the land) of A.D. 896 when the seven original Hungarian tribes made a blood-pact in which they swore to unite under Arpad, the leader of the powerful Magyar tribe. The Hungarian constitution, like that of the United Kingdom, was "unwritten" until February 1946, except for the short-lived and thoroughly discredited Communist constitution of Bela Kun (June-August 1919). The old Hungarian constitution was an agglutination of laws, privileges, and concessions, which had grown up around a very ancient core as a result of bargaining, concessions, and occasional unilateral acts on the part of the monarch or the nation.

The first significant constitutional development after the blood-pact came in A.D. 1000 when Hungary became a Christian monarchy. Vajk, a descendant of Arpad, had himself baptized Istvan (Stephen) and ruthlessly converted his whole nation, thereby determining Hungary's cultural and political orientation toward the West. As a reward, Pope Sylvester II sent a golden crown for his coronation and an apostolic cross to signify the monarch's stewardship over ecclesiastical matters. The Royal Crown was an important element in the constitution, and it has enjoyed both a legal and a mystical hold over the Hungarian people down to modern times.

The promulgation of the *Aranybulla* (Golden Bull) by King Endre II in 1222 marked a turning point in Hungarian constitutional development. The provisions of the document and the events leading up to its issuance have features surprisingly similar to those of the Magna Charta, which preceded the Bull by only seven years. Each was the result of coercion applied against a weak and corrupt monarch by a powerful and hostile gentry; each proved to be the first significant check on autocracy. While many of the provisions of the two documents were substantially the same (some of those in the Golden Bull were even more democratic in form), the Hungarian version did not exert a strong democratic influence, as did its English counterpart.

The deterioration in the legal and social status of the Hungarian "unfree" peasantry illustrates this. Their conditions were among the worst in Europe and they attempted several unsuccessful armed rebellions. Their most serious effort took place in 1514 under the leadership of Gyorgy Dozsa, but like the others it was brutally crushed. As a result, Istvan Werboczy, a Hungarian legal theoretician of the sixteenth century in a codification called *Tripartitum Opus Juris Hungarici,* defined the status of the common people as wretched taxpayers (*misera plebs contribuens*) without any political rights. Under this concept, the peasants were at the complete mercy of their masters. It was not until 1764 that the peasants' status was legally improved by Act of Parliament. In actual practice, except for the short period 1848-49, their condition did not change much until the end of World War II.

Werboczy's dictum boomeranged against him and his class during one of the numerous Turkish military adventures against Hungary. The disaster suffered by the Hungarians in the Battle of Mohacs (1526) was in part due to the resentful peasantry, who were reluctant to fight against the Turks. The subjugation of the Hungarians at Mohacs resulted in the partition of Hungary into three segments: the Turks retained the central plain of Hungary; the Hapsburgs were able to put a portion of western Hungary under the control of the Austrian Empire; and Transylvania was allowed to retain an important measure of autonomy, although it had to pay tribute to the Turks. When the Turks were finally driven out in the seventeenth and eighteenth centuries, the Hapsburgs took over and remained the rulers of Hungary until the end of World War I.

During this long period of foreign rule, Hungary succeeded in maintaining its language and constitution. Symbolic of this attitude of resistance was its refusal to accept Emperor Charles VI's Pragmatic Sanction (extending the royal line to female members of the Hapsburgs) until 1723, ten years after Austria had done so. Even then, Hungary accepted only after Emperor Charles had agreed to respect Hungarian constitutional principles and to take the "royal oath" as king of Hungary.

The nineteenth century proved the period of Hungary's boldest

moves toward constitutional development and national liberty. Count
Istvan Szechenyi's books of biting criticism of his own class initiated
the movement toward reforms. Beginning in 1840, the Hungarian Parliament (which continued a limited existence under the Hapsburgs)
adopted a series of far-reaching reforms, among which were measures
abolishing the feudal privileges and aiming at a democratic transformation. Although the Hungarian revolution of 1848 led by Lajos
Kossuth failed and Kossuth was exiled, his ideals have lived and he
remains a national hero of Hungary.

Hungarian nationalist zeal continued to smolder, and under the
leadership of Ferenc Deak the Hungarian nobility won for itself the
Compromise of 1867, which established the Dual Monarchy. Under
this arrangement, the Austrians and Hungarians were each recognized
as separate autonomous nations, albeit with the same monarch. Certain
matters, such as foreign affairs and defense were to be jointly managed, but each nation maintained constitutional independence over its
domestic affairs. The Compromise sustained the feudal class structure
and perpetuated the differences between the privileged and underprivileged classes. With the beginning of Hungary's industrialization, a
new underprivileged class, labor, emerged alongside the peasants.

The end of World War I resulted in Hungary's long-sought total
severance from Austria and the Hapsburgs. The brief postwar regimes
of the revolutionary democrat Mihaly Karolyi and of the ruthless
Communist Bela Kun were wiped out without a trace by Act I of 1920,
which nullified all acts of the two radical governments. However, after
the unsuccessful attempt of Charles IV to recapture his throne in 1921,
Hungary enacted a law banishing the House of Hapsburg. The problem
of choosing a new king was shelved by the election of Admiral Miklos
Horthy as Regent; hence the anomalies of an "admiral without a navy"
and a "kingdom without a king."

The nation returned to its thousand-year-old constitution. Instead
of adjusting itself to modern social conditions, the government expended most of its energy in inveighing at home and abroad against
the Trianon Peace Treaty, under which it lost 71.4 per cent of its
prewar territory (including Croatia), containing 63.5 per cent of its
population. Despite so-called electoral and parliamentary reforms, Parliament continued to be dominated by the magnates, gentry, and
bureaucrats.

A combination of Hungarian claims, political and military pressure,
and cessions of territory awarded and promised by Germany and Italy
brought Hungary into World War II on the side of the Axis. While the
country was being devastated in the Soviet counteroffensive of 1944,

the Germans occupied Hungary and in October deposed Horthy from the Regency because of his decision to surrender to the Allies. Control of the government was given to Ferenc Szalasi, head of the Nazi Arrow Cross (Nyilaskereszt) Party, under German supervision. It was under such inauspicious circumstances that the "thousand-year constitution" approached its end. Although formally it remained in force until January 1946, for all practical purposes it was abrogated simultaneously with the termination of Horthy's regency.

During the entire period of its existence, the old constitution played a significant role in the survival of Hungarian political institutions and national customs, despite almost continuous foreign domination. It was in defense of constitutional reforms, for example, that Hungarians were incited to rise against the Hapsburgs in 1848, and although the revolution fell short of its goal of complete independence, Hungarian perseverance accounted for the Compromise of 1867, whereby Hungary retained autonomy over domestic affairs in accordance with its own constitution. This very stability, however, became a fault. Inflexible adherence to the old constitution became a fetish. The various far-reaching social changes of the nineteenth and twentieth centuries had very little effect, thereby seriously retarding progress.

The promulgation of the new post-World War II constitution featured the abolition of such institutions as the monarchy and the upper chamber, and drastically revised the old system of local government.

Democratic Constitution of 1946

Hungary was among the first of the "liberated" East-Central European countries to promulgate a new constitution (January 31, 1946). After slightly more than three years, however, this constitution, democratic in structure and spirit, was replaced by a Communist document of an entirely different character. The key to the difference is easily discernible from a brief consideration of political developments leading up to each constitution.

After the deposition on October 15, 1944 of Regent Miklos Horthy, the Commander in Chief of the Hungarian Army, General Bela Miklos, under orders from Horthy, surrendered to the Soviet Union. Under Soviet tutelage, Miklos established a Provisional National Government at Debrecen in December 1944. A Provisional National Assembly was formed on the basis of a five-party coalition, the Hungarian National Independence Front consisting of the Smallholders', Social Democratic, National Peasant, Citizens' Democratic, and Communist parties. The

Smallholders, a moderate group, were the most popular, but were without government experience. On the other hand, the Communists, banned in Hungary since 1920, lacked popularity but, in comparison with the other party groups, were organized, tightly disciplined, and backed by the Soviet Union. During the period of the Provisional Government, the Communists, although maintaining only numerical plurality in the National Assembly, were able to achieve political power.

A three-member Supreme Council of State was created to fill the gap created by the elimination of the Regency and served as collective head of the state. The Provisional Assembly adjourned on December 22, 1944, delegating "interim" powers to the Political Committee and Cabinet, subject to approval by the Assembly. After the armistice and the end of the war (April-May 1945), the Provisional National Government established its seat in Budapest.

In September 1945, the Assembly convened again to approve a number of measures submitted by the Cabinet. One of these was an electoral law which made universal suffrage a reality and paved the way for what were commonly described as "the freest elections which have ever been held in Hungary." The outcome of these elections (November 4, 1945) was decisive in determining the character of the Constitution of 1946.

For the elections, a four-party coalition (the Hungarian National Independence Front minus the Citizens' Democratic Party) was maintained, each party preserving its separate identification. The Communists were confident that the elections would bring them a majority vote and undisputed power over the coalition and government. Their hopes, however, were not realized. The government coalition won an overwhelming majority (over 98 per cent of the total vote), but within the coalition the Communists suffered a disastrous defeat, receiving only 17 per cent of the vote. The Smallholders, with 57 per cent, emerged as the leading party, while even the Social Democrats, with 17.4 per cent, squeezed in ahead of the Communists.

In view of the election results, it was agreed to give the Smallholders half of the eighteen Cabinet seats, four each to the Communists and Social Democrats, and one to the National Peasant Party. A bitter fight ensued over the Ministry of the Interior. The Smallholders were aware of the importance of controlling the police, a function of that ministry, but were unable to resist Communist demands for this key post. Under increasing Soviet pressure, they grudgingly agreed to the appointment of the Communist Imre Nagy, who was replaced shortly afterward by the notorious Laszlo Rajk. The prime ministry was given to Zoltan Tildy, a Smallholder, with Matyas Rakosi, Secretary General of the Communist Party, and Arpad Szakasits of the Social Democratic Party, as Deputy Prime Ministers. Ferenc Nagy, a Smallholder, was made President of the National Assembly and thereby presided over the Supreme Council of State as well; Monsignor Bela Varga (Smallholder) and Laszlo Rajk (Communist) filled the other two positions in the Council.

The first order of business for the newly elected National Assembly was the preparation of a new constitution, since theoretically the prewar constitutional monarchy was still in effect. The leaders of the coalition parties held a series of conferences in January 1946 and drafted a document of decidedly Western orientation. This document was adopted by the National Assembly on January 31, 1946 as the Constitution of Hungary.

The most important feature was Article 2, which declared that "Hungary is a Republic," thus ending the monarchy. The Hungarian people were declared sovereign, exercising "the power of legislation by way of the National Assembly" (Article 1).

The Constitution dealt with the rights and duties of the President of the Republic, who was to be elected by the unicameral National Assembly for a four-year term. He had the power to send bills back to the Assembly for reconsideration, but was required to give his approval if they were sent to him a second time. The Prime Minister was to be selected by the President in accordance with the principle of parliamentary majority. The rights of citizens were summed up in the Preamble, corresponding roughly to the United States' Bill of Rights, which listed as the "natural and inalienable rights of man" such concepts as "personal freedom, free expression of opinion, free exercise of religion, right of assembly and association, right of personal security, work, and dignified human livelihood."

These rights, however, fell victim to the Communists' "counteroffensive against all signs of reaction." In June 1946, only five months after the constitution was promulgated, serious inroads were made.

For example, the right of assembly and association was rendered meaningless by the Minister of the Interior's acquisition of arbitrary power to dissolve political associations. Loose application of a law on the "defense of Hungarian democracy" infringed on the provision pertaining to free expression of opinion by making it a criminal offense to "propagandize against the republican form of government, against any race or religion, against the equality of all citizens, and against infringement of civil liberties."

Rise of the Communists

The Communists' determination to gain political power was not dampened by the election results. Taking cognizance of their failure at the polls, they decided to eliminate the opposition, beginning with the Smallholders, their chief obstacle. (For details of the campaign against the Smallholders see Chapter 6, "The Party and Political Organizations.")

The most important factor in their favor was the backing of the Soviet Union. Soviet interference was exercised chiefly through usurpation of functions by the Soviet chairman of the Allied Control Commission, the joint Allied occupying agency. In addition, the Soviet Union exerted direct pressure through the physical presence of Soviet occupation personnel.

The decisive Communist blow against the Smallholders was aimed at Ferenc Nagy, who had become Prime Minister in February 1946. In May 1947, while he was on vacation in Switzerland, the Communists accused him of implication in the "conspiracy" to re-establish the Horthy regime. Nagy was forced to resign. By May 31, the Cabinet was reorganized, with left-wing Smallholder Lajos Dinnyes as Prime Minister and Minister of National Defense, while another left-wing Smallholder, Erno Mihalyfi, was appointed Minister of Foreign Affairs.

One of the prerequisites of the adoption of a Soviet-type constitution is the existence of a virtual single-party system. Although the Communists unquestionably dominated the Hungarian state apparatus by 1948, they still lacked absolute control. It was to secure such control that the Hungarian Independent People's Front was established at the beginning of February 1949. It combined all the government parties (by then reduced to the Hungarian Workers [Communist], Smallholders, and National Peasants) with the former opposition Radical and Independent Democratic parties. The Front also included in its membership mass organizations, such as the National Council of Trade Unions and the Hungarian Federation of Democratic Women.

The final step before the promulgation of a new constitution was the election held on May 15, 1949, the third in the postwar period (a second election took place in 1947). It was a "single list" election, i.e., there were no alternatives to the list of government candidates. The National Assembly convened on June 8 and adjourned eight days later.

Thereupon, a special constituent committee chosen by the new National Assembly and headed by Rakosi worked out a draft constitution. Rakosi presented the draft constitution on August 17, after a lengthy introduction. It was approved without a single change the next day after a "debate" in which a few short speeches filled with encomiums of the new regime were delivered.

The Communists designated August 20 as a national holiday, Constitution Day. This date had been traditionally celebrated by the people of Hungary as St. Stephen's Day in commemoration of the country's first king. Its expropriation for Communist propaganda purposes added a final ironic touch to the success of the tactics by which an initially insignificant Communist minority disposed of the opposition and succeeded in seizing all the implements of power in a traditionally anti-Communist and Western-oriented country.

PRINCIPAL FEATURES OF THE COMMUNIST CONSTITUTION OF 1949

In contradiction to the 1946 Constitution, which was designed to establish a republic along Western democratic lines, the principal feature of the 1949 Constitution was the establishment of a "People's Republic" (Article 1) on the Soviet Communist pattern. Hungarian Communist constitutional theory must always be seen within the framework of actual practice. The chief function of the constitution and laws apparently is to act as a collection of legalisms to which the government can refer when it suits its purposes. In the final analysis, the seat of decisive power is not in the formal government described in the Constitution, but in the highest echelons of the Hungarian Workers' (Communist) Party, if indeed not in the Communist Party of the Soviet Union.

Two factors make a "People's Republic" according to Communist theory. First, such a state must wholeheartedly take upon itself the spreading of Soviet Communist theory and practice. In other words, it must adopt as its own the goals and methods of the Soviet Union. Second, it must undergo an immediate socialistic transformation in which the Soviet Union is the model. Thus, in effect, current Soviet institutions must be adopted to whatever extent the historical (political, cultural, social, and economic) background of the country in question permits.

The Western and Soviet-type constitutions offer little basis for comparison. Though both deal with the form and organization of the state and government, with powers and limitations of the government, and with basic rights of citizens, their functions are entirely different. In the West, it is usually believed that the general welfare is best promoted by leaving to parties and individuals a broad range of activity within some very general limitations. The duty of the state is to serve its citizens, and the constitution is designed to restrict the powers of the state and to defend the rights of all citizens. Soviet theory, on the other hand, holds that the constitution is part of a superstructure set on an economic base. The economic base has decisive influence on the superstructure, but the superstructure has relatively less effect on the base. Hence, the status of the individual and of the state is determined by the economic base and not by the constitution.

The Hungarian Constitution of 1949 did not establish a "People's Republic," but rather formalized it. Rakosi announced the existence of the Hungarian People's Republic six months before the promulgation of the Constitution (*Szabad Nep* [Free People], February 1, 1949). Furthermore, in his speech to the National Assembly introducing the draft constitution, Rakosi, imitating Stalin's speech on the Soviet Constitution of 1936, announced that "the draft constitution is the registration and setting down in the form of law of what we have already struggled for and turned into reality."

The Soviet Union's role is prominently featured in the text of the Hungarian Constitution. The Soviet Union is mentioned by name in the Preamble three times for its "unselfish help" in liberating and rehabilitating Hungary and for providing experience for the march "toward socialism." This expression of gratitude to the Soviet Union is a feature of all the constitutions of the captive countries promulgated since Tito's defection in June 1948. Only Bulgaria, the one captive nation whose present constitution antedates the Yugoslav break with the Cominform, omits this specific reference to the Soviet Union.

A comparison of the Soviet and Hungarian constitutions shows that every article of the latter is inspired by the former. Differences exist but only where they follow from the theoretical assumption that the Soviet Union "has achieved socialism," while Hungary has not. For example, Article 5 of the Soviet Constitution states that socialist ownership of the means of production has been "firmly established." In the Hungarian version, Article 4 states that only the "bulk of the means of production" is state owned. The same article also notes that the aim is to "dislodge the capitalist elements and consistently build a socialist system of economy."

The dominant position of the Communists is constitutionally recognized by Article 56, in which the Hungarian government is said to "base itself on the organizations of the class-conscious workers." Among these organizations, the Hungarian Workers' Party (official name of the Communist Party in Hungary, since it merged with the Socialist Party), as the "advance guard" of the working class, is by inference assigned the leading role in the nation's economic, political, and social affairs.

A typical distinction between the Hungarian and Soviet constitutions is that in the former "every worker" is granted the right to education (Article 48), while in the latter all "citizens of the Soviet Union" have that right. Since the Soviet Union allegedly has already achieved socialism and eliminated the former "exploiters," all its citizens are presumed to belong to acceptable social groups. In Hungary, where socialism is not yet considered to have been achieved, capitalists and kulaks must be excluded from benefits. For the same reason, Hungary "strives to apply . . . the socialist principle 'From each according to his ability, to each according to his work'" (Article 9), while in the Soviet Union this principle is said to have already been "applied" (Article 12).

Article 2 of the Hungarian Constitution defines Hungary as a "state of workers and working peasantry." The corresponding article in the Soviet Constitution (Article 1) defines the Soviet Union as a "socialist state of workers and peasants." Again the difference is accounted for by the explanation that Hungary has not yet achieved socialism, and is only at the "dictatorship of the proletariat" stage. The qualification "working peasantry" alludes to the noninclusion of "exploiting" kulaks. Likewise, power is said not to belong to the people as a whole, as it theoretically does in the Soviet Union, but only to the "working people." On the assumption that Hungary has not yet achieved socialism, the state is assigned the task, in Article 3, of "organizing the forces of society for socialist construction."

Article 10 assigns to the unicameral National Assembly the role of the "highest organ of state authority," which "elects" members of the Presidential Council, Council of Ministers, and the Supreme Court. Interpretation of the Constitution is left to the Presidential Council under Article 20, which states that the Presidential Council "may annul or modify any bylaw, decision, or measure . . . if it infringes on the constitution." Paragraph 3 of the same article empowers the Presidential Council to "dissolve any local organ of government the activities of which infringe on the constitution." In practice, the Council of Ministers, the administrative branch, is the dominant government agency, and it is in this branch that the leading Communists concentrate.

The Hungarian Constitution requires a two-thirds vote of the National Assembly for the adoption of an amendment (Article 15). Although the Constitution does not indicate how amendments should be proposed, an account of a typical amendment to Article 24 indicates that in practice the process is not very complex. The amendment, which added a number of ministries to those listed in Article 24, was proposed by a member of the National Assembly. It had gone into effect *de facto* in January 1952 (*Magyar Kozlony* [Hungarian Gazette] January 6, 1952), and the National Assembly gave it *de jure* ratification more than five months later (*Magyar Kozlony*, June 6, 1952).

COMMUNIST GOVERNMENT

The National Assembly and the Presidential Council (Presidium)

The highest organ of the state administration under the Constitution of 1949 is formally the National Assembly (Orszaggyules), one of the functions of which is to "elect" from among its own members the Presidential Council, the collective head of state equivalent to the Presidium in the Soviet Union. These two bodies are theoretically more powerful than any of the others due to the principle of legislative supremacy. However, this principle remains in the realm of pure theory. It conforms fully to Lenin's doctrine requiring the state machinery to function as a transmission belt and tool for implementation of policies adopted by the Communist Party. Orthodox Communist ideology repudiates energetically the constitutional doctrine of separation of powers. State power under communisim is one and indivisible because it consists of a dictatorship not of the proletariat, as it claims, but of the Communist Party.

The National Assembly, which is composed of 298 representatives and 155 alternate representatives, elects its speaker, two deputy speakers, six recorders, four standing committees (Legal, Foreign Affairs, Economic and Financial, and Cultural) and one temporary Mandate Examining Committee to check credentials of representatives after elections. Included within the National Assembly's sphere of competence is the nominal right to regulate the structure, functions and limitations of the other central government organs as well as to elect their top members.

The Presidential Council was introduced into Hungary under the Constitution of 1949 and acts as a collective head of state in place of the single president, regent, or king of previous Hungarian regimes. Its members, consisting of a President, the Vice Presidents, a Secre tary, and seventeen other members, are elected by and from members of the National Assembly and are retained in office at the pleasure of that body; they are responsible to, and must render an account of their activities to, that body. (For list of members of Presidential Council, see page 412.)

Constitutionally, the Presidential Council has broad powers. It most clearly illustrates the principle of unity and indivisibility of powers by holding executive, legislative, and judicial functions. Its duties include the formality of signing and promulgating parliamentary acts (Article 16); issuing the writ for a general election; convening the National Assembly; concluding and ratifying international treaties; appointing diplomatic envoys, higher civil servants, and military officers; receiving credentials from foreign envoys; and exercising the prerogative of mercy. It also nominates members of the Council of Ministers for election by the National Assembly.

In addition to exercising these functions, the Presidential Council has the power to exercise all legislative functions (except constitutional changes) when the National Assembly is not in session. All such enactments are legally binding, but must be submitted to the National Assembly at its next session. It should be noted that no stipulation is made that Presidential Council's decrees require approval; the Constitution states only that such decrees "must be submitted" to the National Assembly. The distinction, however, is merely academic, since the National Assembly, so far as is known, has given rubber-stamp approval to all measures submitted by the Council. In fact, the bulk of Hungarian legislation follows this procedure, since the National Assembly is rarely in session. This makes parliamentary discussion unnecessary and permits efficient legislative activity in totalitarian fashion. Two rights not publicly exercised thus far by the Presidential Council are its right to annul or modify any bylaw, decision, or measure introduced by central or local government agencies if it infringes on the Constitution or is detrimental to the interests of the working people, and the power to dissolve any local organ of government for the same reason.

Although the constitutional functions of the Presidential Council appear impressive, in practice it does not play an important policy-making role in the government. An indication of its subservience in this respect is the fact that its president since August 14, 1952 has been Istvan Dobi, a former leading member of the Smallholders' Party. The award of this post to a nominal non-Communist is an indication of the relative unimportance of the Presidential Council in general and of its president in particular.

Central Executive Organs

While the formal system of government is based on the principle of unity of powers under pretended legislative supremacy, in practice the Council of Ministers, the top administrative organ, is the dominant government agency. Its status does not derive from the Constitution, which subordinates it to both the National Assembly and the Presidential Council, but to concentration within it of leading figures of the Hungarian Workers' Party and to its administrative control of all political, economic, social, and cultural activities.

Within the framework of Party directives, the Council of Ministers has official responsibility for authority over every aspect of state activity. One Communist author accurately described the Council as the "motor of all state work that . . . translates Party policy into practice." It is only nominally subordinate to the National Assembly, and the latter's constitutional power to interpellate the Council is meaningless in practice. Members of the Council of Ministers, unlike those of the Presidential Council, need not be members of the National Assembly. (For list of members of Council of Ministers, see page 413.)

The constitutional functions of the Council of Ministers are to direct the work of the ministries and their subordinate organizations, to ensure the enforcement of laws and decrees with the force of law passed by the National Assembly and the Presidential Council, respectively, and to ensure the fulfillment of economic plans. Like the Presidential Council, it may annul or modify bylaws, decisions, or measures of any government agency that "infringe on the Constitution or are detrimental to the interests of the working people."

Law No. 1 of 1950 assigns to the Council of Ministers supervision of the work of local councils as well as responsibility for establishing rules concerning local government administrative procedure (now implemented through its Secretariat for Local Councils). Article 29 of the Constitution further authorizes the Council of Ministers to change the various local and regional administrations. Under the Constitution, the Council may deal with any matter concerning central administration either directly or through any of its members; it also may place within its jurisdiction any branch of central administration and may create special agencies for that purpose. The Council of Ministers constitutionally has the right, along with the Presidential Council and members of the National Assembly, to initiate legislation; in reality, the Council of Ministers virtually controls legislative drafting and initiation. Other formal functions acquired by the Council of Ministers include appointing certain officials (e.g. vice presidents of subordinate agencies, such as the State Control Center, Manpower Reserves Bureau, State Bureau of Church Affairs) and making such awards as the Kossuth prizes.

The Prime Minister, under the Constitution, presides over sessions of the Council of Ministers (usually held once a week), provides for the execution of the Council's decrees and resolutions, and directs the work of agencies immediately subordinate to it. His duties include preparation of agenda and minutes for Council sessions; supervision of redrafting decrees by individual ministers in accordance with Council resolutions and proposals; promulgation of the Council's decrees; recommendations to the Presidential Council for awards (except the Kossuth Prize, which is recommended by the Minister of People's Culture for presentation by the Council of Ministers). Since 1950, the Prime Minister has been responsible for the official gazette, *Magyar Kozlony*, appointing its editor and controlling its circulation. Finally, it is his duty to coordinate the work of the individual members of the Council of Ministers and to maintain liaison with the Presidential Council. He conducts his work through his administrative Bureau of the Prime Minister.

Deputy Prime Ministers rank beneath the Prime Minister and in his absence, the senior First Deputy performs his functions. Although they have no portfolios as Deputy Prime Ministers, they may, in addition to their work in the Council of Ministers, engage in specialized state work in the same capacity as ministers; they may also serve in simultaneous separate capacities as ministers.

While the Council of Ministers is a corporate body with collective responsibility, each member minister is responsible for his own ministry. Due to the Communist policy of total nationalization of industry and agriculture, virtually all the ministers are in effect the directors of government monopolies. The structure of the ministries is based on a "branch of production" principle, whereby each ministry has authority over all matters dealing with its branch. The Ministry of Agriculture, for example, deals with all financial, educational, planning, technical, and other aspects of agriculture. This "branch of production" structure is further subdivided into regional units when geographical problems of space or local specialization become a factor. The functions of only two of the ministries, Finance and Justice, because of their nature, regularly cut across ministry lines. The Ministry of Finance manages finances and the budget for all ministries and state agencies, while the Ministry of Justice gives legal assistance, including the drafting and editing of laws and decrees.

Ministries rely for implementation of most of their tasks on a

hierarchy of subordinate agencies roughly divided into three cate-•
gories: official organizations; economic organizations; and public institutions.

Examples of official organizations performing local administrative
tasks are institutions of arrest and detention under the Ministry of
Justice; the Hungarian Telegraphic Office under the Ministry of People's Culture; and the National Committee for Examining Stenogra-
phers and Typists under the Ministry of Education.

Three general types of economic agencies are the economic office,
the administrative organ, and the state enterprise. Although the functions and lines of demarcation between the three types are not made
clear by available sources, it appears that the economic office has some
day-to-day policy-making functions, since it may issue regulations
binding both on state agencies and on the general public. The administrative organs are comprised of trusts and associations (combines)
which direct larger and smaller state enterprises, respectively, and
participate in the implementation of economic tasks. State enterprises
hierarchically seem to be the lowest state administrative units engaged
in basic economic activities (e.g., trade, production).

Public institutions perform educational, scientific, and social welfare tasks. Universities, schools engaged in training for individual ministries, scientific institutes, hospitals, and homes for orphans are all
examples of public institutions.

In addition to the ministries, specialized agencies called "supreme
authorities" are also under the jurisdiction of the Council of Ministers.
Instead of the"branch of production," they follow a "functional" principle—that is, they cut across the lines of several ministries or organizations; they are therefore not subordinated to any one ministry. Thus,
the Hungarian Ministry of Sciences, one of the "supreme authorities,"
for example, directs all scientific work, regardless of the field of specialization. Some of these agencies, such as the National Planning
Bureau and the Central Statistical Bureau, deal with economic matters; others, such as the National Committee for Physical Culture and
Sports, are concerned with large-scale social matters.

Local Government

Centralized control of the government extends to the three levels of
local government represented by popularly elected local councils. Despite extension of local autonomy by revision of the law on local councils and a 1954 amendment to the Constitution (*Szabad Nep*, August
19 and September 22, 1954), the Council of Ministers continues to

exercise ultimate and decisive authority over the local councils' administrative offices; the National Assembly, and in particular the Presidential Council, have ultimate authority over the councils themselves. These central agencies may, in fact, annul or modify any bylaw, decision, or measure issued by local committees and councils of government, not only if it "infringes on the constitution," but even if it simply is considered "detrimental to the interests of the working people." It may dissolve local agencies for the same reasons.

Prior to the summer of 1953, supervision of local council administration was exercised by the Minister of the Interior. His replacement by a Secretariat for Local Councils, subordinate to the Council of Ministers, and the appointment of its director with the rank of Deputy Minister were announced on August 9, 1953.

Perhaps the best definition of the role of the local councils was supplied by Matyas Rakosi, when, in an address before the National Assembly on August 17, 1949, he paradoxically explained their status as "not only autonomous organizations, but at the same time the executive organs of central power." Their actual function is to effect mass participation in government activity based, in the final analysis, on Party policy, and their importance lies in their closeness to the population.

The present system of local councils was established by the Constitution of 1949, but actual adoption was delayed until after the reorganization of territorial administrative divisions in 1949 and 1950. At that time, the number of counties was reduced to nineteen through the merger of small splinter counties lying along Hungary's borders and the readjustment of the three counties bordering on Lake Balaton to form only two. The main reason for the revision was to simplify the county administrative organization by creating counties of approximately equal size and population.

Structure of Local Councils. The current local council system was originally set up after the promulgation of Law No. 1 and Decree No. 143 of May 1950; these basic edicts were revised by legislation in 1954 (*Szabad Nep*, August 19, 1954). There are three levels of local councils. The top level comprises councils of the nineteen counties, the city of Budapest, and other large cities; Budapest and the large cities are given county status in structural relationships because of their concentration of population. The councils are directly under the supervision of the Presidential Council. On the second level, subordinate to county councils, are the councils of districts and large towns. On the lowest level, subordinate to the district councils, are the councils of the villages and small towns. Also on this level are the councils of the precincts of the cities and large towns, despite the absence, in the case of Budapest and the large cities, of an intermediate level.

Members of the local councils were first appointed, pending popular elections, by the National Council of the Hungarian Independent People's Front, a Communist-dominated amalgamation of all legal political parties. On June 15, 1950, the nineteen county councils and the Budapest Metropolitan Council met for the first time to elect their executive committees and officers. On August 15, 1950, local councils were also formed in the districts, precincts of Budapest and Miskolc, towns, and villages for the same purpose. Popular elections of the local councils for terms of four years were first held on October 22, 1950 and for the second time on November 28, 1954. As in elections to the National Assembly, citizens are given the choice of voting for or against a single list of front (now called Patriotic People's Front) candidates.

The number of members in the councils is determined by the council immediately superior to the one in question (the Presidential Council makes the decision for the counties, Budapest, and the other large cities), and the number of executive committee members is determined by the councils electing them. At the end of 1952, there existed 3,253 local councils on all levels, an average of more than one council for every 3,000 Hungarian residents; in all probability, the ratio of councils has increased since then.

The precise relationship of the local councils to local branches and agencies of the central government has never been given. Article 64 of the 1954 law stipulates that the Presidential Council is to issue detailed regulation on this matter upon the proposal of the Council of Ministers. However, the local councils are given the authority to supervise all state organs (except those of the armed forces) dealing with the maintenance of social, cultural, health, and work regulations. At the same time, the civil police organs (under the control of the central government) are required to submit reports at the meetings of the council and their executive committees concerning public security conditions.

The functions of the councils on all three levels are essentially the same, each level taking its cue directly from the central government. Directives from the central government filter down until they reach the councils on the lowest level. The net result is local implementation of central directives which, by taking into consideration local differences, is designed to create an efficient administrative structure.

Organs of the Local Councils. The most important part of a local council is its executive committee, which is elected by the council at its first organizational session; it is presided over by a president, who is assisted by one or more vice presidents and a secretary. The executive committee has local control of the administrative apparatus and has the same type of relation to the local council that the Council of Ministers has to the National Assembly—theoretically subordinate but actually dominant. On the two top levels, the executive committee is supported in its work by a secretariat and a number of specialized administrative organs with paid staffs. Executive committees on the lowest level do not have secretariats or specialized administrative organs if the quantity and complexity of their tasks do not warrant.

In an effort to improve the efficiency and to intensify the activities of local government, provision is made for checking and counterchecking the officials and the work of local councils.

One of the devices of the regime for checking the work of the executive committees was the establishment of permanent committees. These are elected by the local councils on all three levels and are considered their auxiliaries in the same sense that the specialized administrative organs are for the executive committees. Like sections, the permanent committees are established according to function; the number of members varies, but must be not less than three.

Civil and Religious Rights and Privileges

Chapter VIII of the Constitution, entitled "The Rights and Obligations of Citizens" (Articles 45-61), contains the Hungarian Communist version of a bill of rights. Like Articles 118 to 133 in the Soviet Constitution of 1936, the enumerated rights are impressive if taken at face value, but have little in common with daily practice, which has emphasized the "obligations" of citizens to the detriment of their "rights."

In the chapter on "The Rights and Obligations of Citizens," three articles (Articles 59-61) are devoted to defining the "obligations." These include the "obligation to defend the so-called property of the people, assure social assets, increase the economic strength of the state, raise the living standard and cultural level of workers, and strengthen the people's democratic system." Military service and defense of the country are regarded as the "honorable duty of all citizens"; treason, violation of the military oath, desertion to the enemy, espionage, and any kind of activity weakening the state militarily are "subject to the severest penalties of the law."

It would appear that the chief function of the Soviet-type bill of rights is to serve as a propaganda device; the Communists quote it to convince any who might doubt the advantages and benefits of life in the "People's Republic."

Despite constitutional platitudes, the Hungarian record has been notoriously deficient with respect to observing Article 2 of the Peace Treaty (February 10, 1947), whereby the government pledged itself to "take all measures necessary" to promote the enjoyment of human rights and to refrain from discrimination because of "race, language, or religion."

Hungarian breaches of civil and religious rights are not accomplished by legal measures alone. A wide variety of extra-legal devices are also employed for the purpose of subordinating the individual to state interests.

Hungarian electoral rights were modified by Laws No. 8 of 1945 and No. 22 of 1947, but did not produce sufficiently satisfactory results for the Communists. Consequently, they resolved this problem in 1949 by presenting voters with a single list of candidates. The list was restricted to members of the Communist-dominated Independent People's Front, a combination of all the government parties together with some mass organizations.

The new voting procedure provided two ways of casting the ballot. If the voter approved the list, he dropped the ballot unmarked into the box. If he disapproved, he exercised his right to a "secret ballot" by marking the ballot, thus revealing to the ballot committee his opposition to the regime. The national elections held on May 17, 1953 followed this same pattern.

Complete suppression of criticism of the government is attained by means of a wide variety of measures. For example, Article 1 of the General Section of the Criminal Code, Law No. 2 of 1950, stipulates that "every act which offends or endangers the political, social, or economic order of the Hungarian People's Republic or its citizens is an act hostile to society." Another law, so loosely worded as to be applicable to any criticism of governmental policy, is Law No. 5 of 1950, On the Defense of Peace, which makes liable to fifteen years' imprisonment anyone "who incites to war, or otherwise expresses or advances war propaganda."

Although Article 56 of the Constitution guarantees the right to organize, the practice has been to tolerate only Communist-inspired front organizations such as the National Council of Trade Unions (SZOT), the Hungarian Federation of Democratic Women (MNDSZ), and the Federation of Working Youth (DISZ). By making use of Article 4 of the Peace Treaty, which required dissolution of all organizations of a "fascist type" and all organizations conducting propaganda "hostile to the United Nations," the Communists effectively liquidated non-Communist organizations.

Article 45 guaranteeing the right to remunerative work is curtailed when it conflicts with state interests. Typical is Decree No. 6,660 of 1948, On the Dismissal of Employees Displaying an Anti-Democratic Attitude, which stipulates that an employee may be fired even for advancing true "facts" if they "arouse contempt against the democratic order." Another edict, Decree with the Force of Law No. 4 of 1950, On the Defense of Economic Planning, subjects to imprisonment anyone who "finishes his work late, faulty, or incompletely." Paragraph 48 of the General Section of the Hungarian Penal Code establishes "corrective labor" for a period up to two years with a wage reduction of one tenth to one fourth for minor labor infractions.

Especially discouraging for the member of a condemned class or group is the fact that the stigma can never be entirely removed. Decree with the Force of Law No. 2 of 1952, for example, defines a kulak as a person with an estate over 35.5 acres or an income of 350 gold crowns derived from landed property, or one who paid agricultural development levies in 1949. Once so classified, the unfortunate kulak and his family are doomed to permanent inferior status, regardless of any efforts to conform and to comply with governmental directives. Discriminatory legislation against people who fall within the framework of this definition is frequent. A typical example is Decree No. 90 of 1952, which forbids kulaks to slaughter cattle unless they maintain over twice as many live cows as are required of cooperatives. Characteristic also was the warning issued in a *Szabad Nep* article on January 20, 1952 against compromise with the so-called "sweet kulaks," the ones who conscientiously try to obey all the laws.

Article 54, guaranteeing freedom of religious worship means no more than the other constitutional guarantees. The whole question of religious rights is closely connected with the Communist drive to relegate the churches to the role of Party front organizations as a first step toward liquidation. The Catholic Church, because of its numerical superiority and world-wide organization, is the chief religious target of the Communists. A wide variety of suppressive measures have been employed against churches with varying amounts of success. A revealing and typical indication of government control over the Protestant churches was the appointment for the first time of a government official (Deputy Minister of People's Culture Erno Mihalyfi) as Universal

Lay Superintendent of the Lutheran Church (*Nepszava* [People's Voice], April 19, 1952). This was a clear violation of Article 54 of the Constitution, which established separation of church and state.

The Judiciary

The years 1953 and 1954 produced significant developments in the Hungarian legal system, concluding a Communist drive begun in January 1945 to sovietize the system. The impetus was given by the "new economic policy" of July 4, 1953, which had as one of its planks the "consolidation of legality" (i.e., a promise to operate within a specified legal framework. The Cabinet abolished police jurisdiction for petty offenses (Decree with the Force of Law No. 16 of 1953), ostensibly to curb the arbitrariness of law enforcement agencies and to ensure just and legal treatment for all citizens. For the first time, the Cabinet appointed a Soviet-type Prosecutor General (Decree with the Force of Law No. 13 of 1953), as provided in Articles 42-44 of the 1949 Constitution. The Cabinet also reorganized the structure and composition of the judiciary through passage of Law No. 2 of January 1954, and eliminated summary court procedure. In an attempt to ease the harshness of previous Hungarian Communist justice, the government also issued a wide amnesty (Decree with the Force of Law No. 11 of 1953) and ended the prewar institutions of police internment and banishment from certain areas (Resolution No. 1,034, issued July 26, 1953).

Under these measures, the Military Prosecutor's Office and the court system, including the Communications and Military Courts, were unified under the Prosecutor General's Office and the Supreme Court, respectively. Administrative supervision of the regular courts was left solely to the Minister of Justice, in line with Soviet practice, while the Communications Courts and the Military Courts in addition are believed to have been placed under control of the Communications and National Defense Ministries, respectively.

The Communists have also made important encroachments in the field of civil law, e.g., by the establishment of a Solicitor's Bureau in the Ministry of Justice under Decree No. 4,071 of June 4, 1949. The Bureau was authorized to intervene, allegedly in the public interest, in any civil proceeding relating to property rights if it involved statutes enacted prior to December 22, 1944 that "in their spirit or provisions are in contradiction with the aims of the Hungarian people's democracy," or if the findings of the court were based upon an interpretation even of current regulations that "does not correspond with the funda-

mental legal principles of the Hungarian people's democracy." The
Solicitor's Bureau was absorbed by the Justice Ministry by Decree with
the Force of Law No. 46 of 1950, but its operations have been continued. This, in effect, permits the government to reopen all civil cases
in which it is dissatisfied with the decision. Legal development in Communist Hungary, as in all the orbit countries, has been to restrict the
scope and importance of civil law and to enlarge criminal law. Such
matters as marriage, family relationships, inheritance, and personal
property matters remain under civil law.

Court System. The Constitution of 1949 redefined along general
lines the juridical system relative to functions, structure, appointment,
and trial procedure (Articles 36 to 41).

Appointment of Eric Molnar, member of the Party's Central Committee and formerly Minister of Foreign Affairs, as the first president
of the newly constituted Supreme Court, was announced in *Szabad Nep*
on July 26, 1953; he was subsequently replaced by Jozsef Domokos,
former State Prosecutor, as announced in *Szabad Nep* on October 31,
1954. Full enactment of the new judicial system was achieved by Law
No. 2 of January 1954 on judicial organization (*Jogtudomanyi Kozlony* [Legal Science Review], Nos. 1-2, pages 4-11, and *Szabad Nep*,
January 23, 1954).

The functions of Hungarian courts, as outlined in Article 41 of the
Constitution, are to "punish the enemies of the working people, protect and safeguard the state's economic and social order and institutions and the rights of workers of the people's democracy, and educate
the workers to observe the rules of socialist life." This provision re-
nounces the principle of "equality before the law" and openly pro-
claims a bias in favor of the working class and the interests of the state.

The structure of the Hungarian court system is outlined in Articles
36, 37, and 39 of the Constitution and elaborated in Law No. 2 of
1954. According to published 1954 budgetary accounts, the courts
now have a total of about 4,000 personnel, of whom some 1,000 are
judges; no breakdown on how judges and other personnel are divided
among the various courts has been released.

The courts of general first resort are the District Court, the Budapest Municipal Precinct Courts, the Municipal Courts of other cities
administratively independent of districts, and the Juvenile Court of
Budapest. The general court of appeal is the County Court, including
the Budapest Metropolitan Court. The County Court also handles specified first instance cases. Special courts administer justice in first
instance military and communications cases (see below). The Supreme

Court, the top organ of the unified Hungarian judiciary,[1] is the court of appeal for cases tried in the first instance by county and special courts. The Supreme Court also handles specified first instance cases and important first instance cases submitted to it by the Prosecutor General.

Professional judges of the County (and Budapest Metropolitan) Courts are organized into specialized criminal and civil benches (*kollegium*). The Supreme Court, in addition to these two benches, also has military and communications benches. The benches on both levels supply judges to serve on three-member panels or divisions (*tanacs*) as needed, probably in some sort of systematic sequence. The District Courts do not have benches.

The Supreme Court's Council of Principles, established by Decree No. 4,338 of December 1949, was abolished by the new law. The council's functions had been to issue "directives on principle" and "decisions on principles," dealing respectively with interpretation of government decrees for future court guidance and with invalidation of judgments rendered by courts in the past. Under the new organization, there is an eleven-member Presidential Council (not to be confused with the legislative Presidential Council described above), consisting of the president and vice presidents of the Supreme Court and presiding trial judges appointed by the President. It acts on behalf of a plenary session of the Supreme Court and deals with "decisions on principle" (which now embrace matters formerly dealt with as "directives on principle" as well); proposals for these "decisions" may be made by the Prosecutor General, the President of the Supreme Court, and the Minister of Justice.

Under the new law, the Prosecutor General and the President of the Supreme Court may protest to the Supreme Court against court decisions. The President of the Supreme Court is further authorized to take under review any case in no matter what court or state of process; in exceptional circumstances, he may even transfer cases to Supreme Court jurisdiction.

The Hungarian Supreme Court therefore in one respect is theoretically more powerful than that of the United States. Unlike the latter, it is not restricted to reviewing cases submitted before it, but may intervene on its own initiative in any case where it sees fit (this power is probably exercised, but no instance has been reported). At the same

[1] As originally provided in Article 36 of the Constitution, there was an intermediate appellate stage of High Courts (*felsobirosag*) between the County Courts and Supreme Courts; the High Courts, however, were abolished by Law No. 4 of 1950 (December 10) as geographically inconsistent with the pattern of administrative divisions followed by the judiciary.

time, following from the principles of legislative supremacy and unity of powers, the Hungarian Supreme Court does not have the right to pass on the constitutionality of laws and decrees.

Special courts, formerly independent of the regular court system, are now subordinated to the Supreme Court. According to Law No. 2 of 1954, there are now only two types of such courts, the Communications Courts and Military Courts; because of their limited competence they are not divided into specialized benches.

The Communications Courts, newly established, adjudicate crimes connected with telecommunications and railroad, highway, air, and water transport facilities; they were probably created, as in the other countries in the Soviet orbit, because of the critical importance of these facilities and their susceptibility to sabotage. Crimes committed to the detriment of the regular operation or safety of highway transport or telecommunications, however, may be tried before either the Communications Courts or regular courts at the discretion of the Prosecutor General's Office.

As specified in Article 20 of Decree with the Force of Law No. 31 of December 11, 1951 and a similar Decree No. 6 of February 20, 1952, the Military Courts have exclusive jurisdiction over civilians indicted for political crimes, espionage, and crimes against army property or affecting national defense, as well as over war prisoners and members of the army, the security forces, the civil police, regular civil defense organizations, fire department personnel, customs officers, and employees of institutions of detention.

The district-level courts, and Budapest Juvenile Courts, as established by Decree with the Force of Law No. 46 of 1950 and Decree No. 177,600 of 1950, appear outside the scope of the 1954 law, since no reference to them has been made. According to the 1950 edicts, only first instance cases that would normally (for adults) be tried in District Courts are referred to Juvenile Courts, while more serious cases are tried in the regular County Court.

Assignment of first instance cases to District Courts, County Courts, or the Supreme Court is based on the seriousness of the charges; it is not clear whether there is a strict standard upon which the assignment is automatically made or whether there is only a loose standard, with the actual decision for the assignment left to the prosecutor. It is known that the Prosecutor General is authorized at his own discretion to initiate or transfer trials of first instance cases to the Supreme Court; the Supreme Court is authorized to do the same after a review which it may itself initiate.

Cases of first instance in all courts, including the Supreme Court, are normally heard by one professional judge and two people's assessors, although they may also be heard by three professional judges, as when the Supreme Court's military bench is called on for a first instance case. All cases of appeal are heard by three professional judges. The elimination of people's assessors from appeal trials is occasioned by the fact that appeals are usually determined on questions of law, which makes technical competence mandatory.

People's assessors (lay judges of approved social origin) are enjoined from having legal training precisely in order to minimize "formalism" in first instance court decisions. Although Communist apologists like to equate people's assessors with Western jurymen, the two are not comparable. Jurymen are generally limited to rendering verdicts of "guilty" or "not guilty," while people's assessors potentially have the upper hand in all aspects of first instance hearing by virtue of their majority over the single professional judge.

Article 39 of the Constitution specifies that all judges are to be "elected." Under the new law, the president, vice presidents, professional judges, and people's assessors of the Supreme Court are to be "elected" (i.e., appointed) to five-year terms by the National Assembly; the presidents, professional judges, and people's assessors of County and District Courts are "elected" to three-year terms by their respective County and District Councils (local governments) on the basis of recommendations by the Minister of Justice. The president, professional judges, and people's assessors of special courts are appointed to three-year terms by the Presidential Council on the joint recommendation of the Minister of Justice and another minister competent from the standpoint of the special functions assigned. Both professional judges and people's assessors can be recalled by the organ "electing" them on a proposal by the Prosecutor General in case of criminal charges or by the Minister of Justice for other reasons.

Judges (including people's assessors) are theoretically independent and subject only to the law, although they are required to report to the organs "electing" them and to the people. (Actually, they are subject to a great degree of control by the Prosecutor General and the lower-level prosecutors.) All citizens are eligible to be judges or people's assessors if they have no police record, are over 23 years old, and have electoral rights.

Prosecutors' Offices. The top organ of the new judicial system is the Prosecutor General's Office, headed by a Prosecutor General, who, on the Soviet model, is "elected" by and responsible to the National Assembly and not to the government; his term of office, according to

Article 43 of the Constitution, is six years. This office, was filled on July 4, 1953 by Dr. Kalman Czako.

There are two levels below the Prosecutor General's Office: the prosecutors' offices in the nineteen counties and city of Budapest and the prosecutors' offices of the districts, large cities, and the Budapest municipal precincts. The chiefs of these offices are appointed to five-year terms by the Prosecutor General, according to Decree with the Force of Law No. 13 of 1953.

Qualifications for prosecutors, investigators, and other employees of the prosecutors' offices specified in the decree include faultless behavior from a political and moral point of view, vigilance against "enemies of the people" and other criminals, and relentlessness in dealing with law violators (*Szabad Nep*, July 30, 1953). It is significant that these eligibility requirements do not include any kind of legal education.

The function of the office as outlined in Decree with the Force of Law No. 13 are far-reaching. The Prosecutor General and his subordinates are independent of all other central administrative and local government organs and are charged generally with ensuring uniform application of the laws, protecting the state and social order as well as "socialist property," and prosecuting all kinds of crimes harmful to the order, independence, and security of the state. In addition, they are charged with the protection of the legal interests and the following "constitutional rights" of citizens: political, work, and dwelling and other personal property rights (*Szabad Nep*, July 30, 1953).

The decree also lists more specific functions that require the Prosecutor General and his subordinates to check the legality of decrees, resolutions, directives, and other measures issued by the ministries, various authorities, enterprises, institutions, and other organs of state administration, and to see that officials and other persons do not violate the law. In addition, they are supposed to ensure the legality of investigations; ensure the quick disclosure of criminal actions; and institute criminal proceedings against "enemies of the people's republic," looters of social property, racketeers, and other criminals. At the same time, however, the decree notes that they must take care that no one should be held criminally responsible or deprived of his personal freedom illegally and without cause, and that everyone should be free of harassments, illegal restrictions, and improper deprivation of civil rights.

Another, and highly significant, function of the office is to check the courts relative to correct application of the law; the prosecutors may appear in both civil and criminal courts and must protest "illegal" sentences and decisions. In pursuit of this end, they may ask for information or investigations, or may themselves carry on investigations to learn whether the law or the "legal interests" of the state or citizens have been violated.

Government agencies, if notified by a member of a prosecutor's office of a protest against their measures, must carry out an investigation within eight days. If the head of the agency fails to examine the complaint within the appointed time, he is compelled to suspend the execution of the measures. If the agency considers the complaint unwarranted, the relevant documents must be forwarded to superior authorities for inspection. The Prosecutor General may protest against the decision of the superior authority at the competent ministry or the Council of Ministers. If a prosecutor states that the law has been violated, he may initiate either criminal or disciplinary procedures in accordance with the nature of the offense committed.

Finally, the prosecutors' offices are instructed to note all complaints relating to violations of the law sent in by workers or public organizations. This function appears to overlap that of the Bureau of Reports in the Public Interest, established as an organ of the State Control Center by Law No. 2 of June 6, 1952 to provide a government channel for citizens to inform on each other. Since the latter part of 1953, Communist officials have been giving the populace special encouragement to use this facility and have voiced satisfaction with the rising number of informers. Law No. 1 of January 1954, On Expediting Reports by the Population, served notice on government officials to pay closer heed and act more expeditiously on these complaints and at the same time extended legal protection to informants.

In carrying out his functions, the Prosecutor General is authorized to participate in deliberations of the Presidential Council and the Council of Ministers. The county, city, district, and Budapest municipal precinct prosecutors have analogous participatory rights at sessions of the local councils (governments) and their executive committees. They maintain permanent liaison with the police, the courts, institutions of detention, "social organizations," and directors of the more important factories and farms (*Szabad Nep*, August 2, 1953).

The Military Prosecutor's Office, as defined in Decree with the Force of Law No. 13 of 1953, is now included in the regular civilian prosecutors' organization; it is believed that the Military Prosecutor is now appointed by the Prosecutor General, as is the practice in the Soviet Union. Formerly, military functions had been outside the regular civilian prosecuting organ (Law No. 63 of 1948). No special staff of prosecutors appears to have been created for the Communications

Courts (see above); regular prosecutors apparently have jurisdiction over these special courts.

Criminal Court Procedure. Significant changes in Hungarian criminal court procedure, basically regulated by Law No. 3 of May 22, 1951 for regular criminal trial procedure and Decree with the Force of Law No. 31 of December 11, 1951 for military criminal trial procedure, were produced in 1953 and 1954. Law No. 2 of 1954, while basically dealing with judicial structure, introduced the Soviet-type pre-trial session into Hungarian criminal jurisdiction (Article 23). Decree with the Force of Law No. 16 of 1953 abolished police court jurisdiction for petty offense cases, and finally, a resolution of the Council of Ministers, tersely announced in the official Communist daily, *Szabad Nep,* on March 11, 1954, abolished summary jurisdiction.

After a crime is reported to the police or prosecutor, four main stages of procedure are followed: investigation, pre-trial session, court proceedings, and implementation.

Under present procedure, as specified in Law No. 2 of 1954, the court holds a pre-trial session, which has been made a prerequisite to an open trial because formerly a "large percentage of cases ended with a verdict of not guilty at open court trials." Only those cases are referred to public trial in which convictions may reasonably be expected. Open court trials are regarded by the Communist government as implementing that portion of Article 41 of the Constitution which assigns to the courts the task of "educating the working people." In practice, this means making examples of transgressors of "socialist justice."

Under such procedure, public trials are usually formalities. The trial is presided over by a professional judge, who is the President of the Court, and both he and the two lay members actively participate in questioning the parties in the case, witnesses, and experts. An important function of the President is to keep the proceedings from wandering from the pattern set at the pre-trial session. The verdict and sentence are reached by majority decision.

The military criminal code is embodied in Law No. 62 of December 30, 1948, and military criminal trial procedure is roughly the same as civilian.

Appeals from verdicts of District Courts may be made to County Courts; those from first instance County Courts, as well as the special courts, to the Supreme Court. Normally, there is no third instance appeal (i.e., from second instance County Courts to the Supreme Court), except by the state. First instance court decisions may be appealed by the accused in his own favor or by the prosecutor either to the advantage or detriment of the accused. Appeals often result in harsher sentences for the accused, particularly in political trials.

As previously noted, the Prosecutor General and the Supreme Court are each given wide latitude in initiating actions on cases even while still in process at lower levels. The Prosecutor General is authorized to check the "legality" of all cases and decisions, and the Supreme Court to review cases. Cases may even be transferred to the jurisdiction of the Supreme Court when considered sufficiently important.

The Bar. Although Article 40 of the Constitution guarantees the right of the accused to defense counsel and Article 49 of the Law on Criminal Trial Procedure makes this mandatory in case the defendant is subject to more than five years in prison, the role and effectiveness of the lawyer has been reduced and curtailed. One method has been to persecute lawyers who consistently undertake the defense of "enemies of the state." Recently, for example, an article in *Szabad Nep* of May 14, 1954 asked that "energetic action" be taken against lawyers who file "unfounded petitions in the service of kulaks and institute law suits which lack any legal basis." Government inspectors, furthermore, periodically inspect lawyers' offices to check their practice from the standpoint of "socialist legality."

The political reliability of prospective law school applicants, as of all college and university enrollees, is ensured by acceptance only of persons who give proper answers to an "entrance examination" (Decree No. 1,015 of 1952). As specified in Decree No. 4,302 of 1949, the graduate law student must gain three years of practical legal training under the supervision of the Minister of Justice in a court, prosecutor's office, or law office. One of these years may be spent with a government agency other than a court. If the trainee then passes an examination, he is declared eligible for the bar.

The statutes regulating the lawyers' chamber or bar are based on Law No. 4 of 1937, but with certain modifications. Law No. 1 of 1947 and Law No. 29 of 1948, for example, established so-called self-government and reorganized the central organ and appeal forum of the bar, the National Committee of Lawyers' Chambers. Actually, the lawyers' chambers and their national committee are under the control of the Minister of Justice. Persons admitted to the bar are required to take a loyalty oath to "the Hungarian People's Republic, its people, and its Constitution" (Decree No. 13,400 of 1950).

Although many Hungarian lawyers outside Budapest are still practicing privately, possibly as many as 3,500, the government encourages them to join so-called lawyers' work collectives, patterned after Soviet legal aid offices, by granting them tax benefits and giving them government assignments. The director and other officers of the work collectives are chosen by a special committee of the local lawyers' chamber. Fees are pooled and distributed according to the amount of standardized work norms completed. As of April 1953, there was a total of only 61 such communities in operation (20 more were being organized) with a membership of 716; the overwhelming majority of lawyers did not belong, and 79 District Court headquarters were reported without any branch organization.

To replenish the ranks of the professional judiciary with Communist-indoctrinated personnel, an accelerated Academy for Criminal Judges and State Prosecutors was established under the supervision of the Minister of Justice on August 6, 1949 by Decree No. 4,181. Candidates who complete a four-month pre-training course in social sciences are eligible for the one-year course at the academy.

Professional judges previously had been required to have an average of eight years of primary and secondary schooling, four years of law school, and an additional four years of practical legal experience in a law office or court. Since the decree, only a total of 16 months of legal training is necessary.

Judges, lawyers, and people's assessors are instruments of the Party; decisions are rendered from the point of view of prohibiting deviations from the current Party line rather from the formal law. Laws and decrees are used as a convenient set of legalisms to be referred to only to the extent that they accord with current Party directives and policy. Control over lawyers and judges is so tight that there is little opportunity for them to stray from their assigned roles; people's assessors, who wield majority rule in first instance trial cases, are encouraged to vent hatred against defendants, especially if charged with antistate activities.

6. THE PARTY AND POLITICAL ORGANIZATIONS

Political Trends, 1800-1918

In the first half of the nineteenth century, Hungary was politically still far behind the countries of Western Europe. The intransigence of the Hapsburg Monarchy was largely responsible for this, especially since it regarded the French Revolution of 1830 as a signal to strengthen the *status quo*. However, there were other factors as well.

The fact that Hungary had still not developed any large-scale industry and commerce had serious results beyond economic dependence on Austria. Hungary had most of the attributes of agricultural backwardness, and lacked a middle class. The middle nobility, a numerous class of landowners who managed their own farms and were concerned in their own interests, provided the cohesion necessary for concerted political action. The magnates, the leading members of Hungarian society, on the other hand, lived in Vienna, totally unaware of the problems of management. The inflation and slump in agricultural prices following the Napoleonic Wars left them in a confused, helpless state, unable to adjust to the new situation.

The two remaining classes were the minor nobility and the peasantry. The minor nobles were economically little better off than the peasants, although their pride often made them oppose reforms which would have benefited them and the peasants. However, Lajos Kossuth, the Hungarian nationalist leader (1802-94), swung them into the Hungarian revolutionary movement. The peasants, on the other hand, were too deeply mired in their own economic troubles to display any political consciousness. Even such measures of reform as had been taken weighed on them. For example, if new roads were built, they had to supply the labor. In the absence of industry, there was no significant working class until relatively late in the nineteenth century.

The founder of modern Hungarian political consciousness was Count Istvan Szechenyi (1791-1860). After studying the economic and political situation in England and France at first hand in 1815, Szechenyi applied his knowledge to Hungary and exposed the superficiality and meaninglessness of the sole political concept about which his class, the privileged nobility, concerned itself, *extra Hungariam non est vita* (there is no life outside Hungary). He blamed the nobility's prejudice, conceit, and laziness for Hungary's backward condition in three famous essays, *Hitel* (Credit, published in 1830), *Vilag* (Light, in 1831), and *Stadium* (Stadium, in 1832), and demanded an overhaul of feudal relationships. Under his influence, Buda and Pest were connected by the famous Chain Bridge, which not only laid the foundations for making Budapest a great capital city (at that time Pozsony was the capital), but also was responsible for an important blow at the nobility's traditional and jealously guarded tax exemption (established by the Golden Bull of 1222), since everybody, regardless of class, was required to pay a toll for use of the bridge. One indication of his concern for raising the quality of Hungarian scholarship is the fact that Szechenyi contributed a full year's income for the founding of the Hungarian Academy of Sciences in 1825.

The underlying difference between Szechenyi and the other Hungarian political reformers of that day was that he wanted to establish reforms "from within." Miklos Wesselenyi and Lajos Kossuth held the Austrian court responsible for all Hungary's troubles, but Szechenyi insisted that economic, social, and political reforms could and should be carried out within the framework of the Hapsburg Monarchy. He thus met opposition from both sides. His own magnate class opposed him as one hostile to their class interests, while the "liberals" opposed him for not including an independence-from-Austria policy in his program.

Szechenyi was unable to win mass support for his program. The role of popular leader was filled by the fiery nationalist, Lajos Kossuth, a member of the middle nobility, who became a legendary figure. Kossuth gained wide popular support for his political program through his inflammatory editorials in *Pesti Hirlap* (Pest Journal), which he founded in 1841 after release from political imprisonment. Parts of his reform program followed along the same lines as Szechenyi's. The chief difference, aside from the question of Hungarian independence, was that Kossuth wanted to achieve his goals through the middle and minor nobility (with support from the magnates), while Szechenyi relied almost exclusively on the magnates.

In 1848, the outbreak of the revolution in Vienna frightened

Emperor Ferdinand I into granting sweeping concessions to the Hungarians, resulting in the establishment of the first independent autonomous Hungarian Cabinet, the approval of which was required to validate the monarch's decrees whenever they affected Hungary. Count Lajos Batthyany was appointed Hungary's first responsible Prime Minister.

Austria, however, attempted to weaken Hungary's position by encouraging and supporting the anti-Hungarian national minorities. Moreover, when hostilities broke out between Croatia, led by Joseph Jellachich (Ban of Croatia), and Hungary, the Austrians abolished the March reforms adopted by the Hungarian Diet, thus paving the way for the Hungarian Revolution of 1848. In order to put down the revolution, the Austrians found it necessary to appeal for aid to Tsarist Russia, in the spirit of the Holy Alliance; Russia's General Ivan Paskievich then turned the tide against Hungary.

Under the lead of Prince Schwarzenberg and General Julius Haynau, Austria dealt ruthlessly with Hungary. Many Hungarian leaders, including Batthyany, were executed, while others including Kossuth were forced into permanent exile or imprisoned. Hungary was stripped of a sizable portion of its territory by the recreation of autonomous entities out of Transylvania, Croatia, and the Port of Fiume, and the establishment of a new autonomous Vojvodina in southern Hungary. For eighteen years following the fateful uprising, Hungary was ruled by a police state bureaucracy. The only significant feature of 1848 retained was the formal liberation of the peasants from feudal burdens.

Three political groupings made themselves felt after 1849. The Old Conservatives, representing the magnate point of view, based their platform on the constitution as it existed in 1847. They sought autonomy, but within the framework of the Austrian Empire. Another group, whose spokesman was Ferenc Deak (1803-76), conducted a campaign of "passive resistance" against the Austrian administration. Its platform was based essentially on Count Szechenyi's reforms, which had been adopted in March 1848. The third group was confined to émigrés forced into exile by the Austrians. Its program was based on the Hungarian Declaration of Independence (patterned after that of the United States) and proclaimed at Debrecen in April 1849. The leader of this group was Kossuth, then an exile in Turkey. The émigrés tried to foment pro-Hungarian sentiment against the Austrians throughout the world.

Austrian intransigence was finally shaken after military setbacks suffered at the hands of Italy and France in 1859, and Prussia and

Italy in 1866. These setbacks, together with Deak's persistent pressure, forced Austria to consent to the Compromise of 1867, under which each nation retained domestic independence, albeit with the Hapsburg dynasty as monarch over each; certain "common affairs" (foreign affairs, defense, and finance) were jointly managed.

The new situation presented Hungarians with an opportunity to develop politically. Unfortunately, they failed to seize the opportunity. Instead of concentrating on real issues, political debates were devoted to arguing for or against the Compromise of 1867. Deak's party, in power 1867-75, was opposed chiefly by Kalman Tisza's moderately left Resolution Party, whose chief plank was opposition to the Compromise. Returning émigrés provided the inspiration for an Independence Party fighting for Kossuth's ideals. Kossuth himself never returned to Hungary and never renounced his Declaration of Independence.

Tisza came to power in 1875 after he abandoned his anti-Compromise stand and created a "fusion" with Deak's tottering party to form the Liberal Party. He remained at the helm of government from 1875 to 1890, despite unpopularity due to his regime's neopotism and corruption, by means of a restricted franchise: only about 6 per cent of the population voted. Restrictions of franchise were based on a rather high minimum amount of taxes paid and on a minimum of formal education. His outstanding accomplishment was maintenance of government stability, enabling Hungary to play an active role in the Dual Monarchy. Unfortunately, neither Tisza nor his successors in the Liberal Party made significant contributions to the solution of economic, social, cultural, or nationality problems. For the thirty years of its existence (1875-1905), the Liberal Party obscured issues by limiting its concern to artificial legal points posed by the Compromise.

The Liberal Party's successor was a coalition based primarily on the Kossuth Independence Party. Kossuth's son Ferenc, however, proved more flexible than his father and accepted the Compromise of 1867. Both the coalition government and the government of the National Labor Party which followed it, retained an extremely conservative outlook, apparently oblivious of Hungarian needs.

In the last decade of the nineteenth century, agrarian socialist movements, non-Marxian in character, began to appear, supported by the peasants, who though technically freed of feudal obligation, found themselves still subject to oppression and exploitation. The aim of the movement, reflected by such organizations as the Federation of Agrarian Workers, was to establish individual small estates. Count Sandor Karolyi, member of one of the nation's most prominent families, was particularly active in the field of help for the peasants. He initiated the establishment of farmers' cooperatives in Hungary, inspired and backed the Central Credit Society to satisfy peasant credit needs, and was instrumental in the creation of farmers' mutual insurance cooperatives and of the *Hangya* (Ant), a marketing and distributing cooperative network.

At the same time commerce and industry began to be established in Hungary. The textile, agricultural produce, sugar refining, distilling, leather tanning, and even the steel and electrical industries gained a foothold. A working class emerged from landless peasants seeking to supplement their meager farm wages. Among them a feeble beginning was made in the direction of adopting a social democratic Marxian platform.

At this time, the Jewish question was also brought into sharp focus. Consisting mostly of refugees from southwestern Russia, the Jewish population rose sharply from 75,000 to 1,000,000 between 1785 and 1914. Since commerce was looked on with contempt in the still essentially feudalistic Hungary, Jewish industrial entrepreneurs and bankers were very successful and Jewish tradesmen had no difficulty in setting up grain and wheat businesses in rural centers near large estates. They were resented later as their prosperity became apparent. The first anti-Semitic wave hit Hungary in the 1880's, but never attained the same proportions as in Austria. As a rule, Jews willing to accept Magyar assimilation were not persecuted.

With respect to the nationality problem, the Hungarians were regarded by the minority elements as they themselves regarded the Austrians, as a nation of ruthless oppressors. The Hungarian ruling class displayed a singular lack of understanding in dealing with this problem. Thus, the Nationality Bill of 1868 drafted by Ferenc Deak and Jozsef Eotvos was denounced both by the Hungarian gentry for being too liberal and by the national minorities for not going far enough. The bill provided for equal rights before the law, with Hungarian the sole official language, while the minorities clamored for territorial autonomy. The Educational Act of 1879 embittered the minorities still more by making Magyar language instruction compulsory, and the Act of 1907, nominally aimed at extending free education, made the teaching of Hungarian a requirement for schools seeking state subsidies.

From the nineteenth century on, nationalistic sentiments in Central Europe intensified. Feelings between Hungarians and Austrians, on the one hand, and between Slavs (both in and out of the Hapsburg Empire) and Hungarians, on the other, became increasingly strained. Austria tried to play the Slav minorities off against each other. While many Slav and Romanian elements gave expression to their hostility through passive resistance, others participated in ultra-nationalistic secret societies.

The magnates and middle nobility, the leading political elements, gradually lost their supremacy as their wealth, power, and prestige declined. A new element, composed of city merchants, industrialists, intellectuals, peasants, and the rapidly growing industrial labor force began to endanger the old order.

World War I had a mixed effect on Hungary. After more than four centuries of struggle against foreign domination, the yoke was finally lifted: the Hapsburg dynasty's connections with Hungary were severed and Hungary became completely independent. As one of the defeated nations, however, Hungary was forcd to yield 71.4 per cent of its territory and 63.5 per cent of its population to Romania, Czecho-slovakia, Yugoslavia, and Austria. This national catastrophe was made even worse by the fact that many ethnic Magyars—estimates run as high as over one fourth of the total ethnic Magyar population—were included in the transferred areas.

Political Parties, 1918-1945

After two unsuccessful post-World War I uprisings, the democratic revolution of 1918 and the Communist terror of 1919, Hungarian politics settled down under the Horthy regency to the prewar pattern of unconstructive argumentation. Whereas prewar political discussions concerned themselves chiefly with the value of the connection with the Hapsburg dynasty, postwar political discussions centered upon the territorial and population losses suffered by Hungary through the Peace Treaty of Trianon (1920).

The electoral reform of 1922, drafted by Prime Minister Count Ist-van Bethlen, modified the universal suffrage act of 1920 and became a decisive factor. The new law represented a step backward and provided for a secret ballot in towns and cities, but for open voting in the rural areas. In this way, the peasants and laborers, the numerically predominant elements, were effectively throttled by the old ruling noble and magnate classes, and the government party was never seri-ously threatened by effective opposition. Parliamentary representation was a reliable index of the bias of the electoral law; the representatives of the party in power were selected on the basis of personal friendship and cooperation with the government's ministers. Under this arrangement, the party remained free of insurgents and consistently retained a hard core of 150-200 votes in the lower chamber out of a total of 230-250.

This government party never became a party in the broad sense of the term. It consisted of a conglomerate coalition without a clearly defined set of principles or organization. Its name varied: United Party, Party of National Unity, and Party of Hungarian Life. Behind the veneer of old Hungarian parliamentary institutions and formalities, the representatives of these parties gave their votes to the government in exchange for government support of individual and class interests. The result was a conservative and stable government; Count Istvan Bethlen, for example, retained the prime ministry from 1921 to 1931, a period which Hugh Seton-Watson described as one of "peaceful stagnation."

The loyal parliamentary opposition consisted essentially of three parties with a small parliamentary representation. The Smallholders' Party, led by Istvan Nagyatadi-Szabo, entered the government coalition as early as 1920, and following the death of Nagyatadi-Szabo in 1924, merged with the government party. A new Independent Smallholders' Party was then formed by Zoltan Tildy and Ferenc Nagy, who persuaded Gaston Gaal, a well-known agrarian-political expert to assume leadership. During the war, one of its prominent members, Endre Bajesy Zsilinszky, emerged as an outstanding spokesman and a hero of anti-Nazi resistance; he was executed in December of 1944.

The National Liberal Party also had some influence. It was led by Karoly Rassay, a political author and public figure of some distinction. As its name implied, the party followed a moderate left-of-center policy and reflected liberal middle-class opinion. Its members consistently put themselves on record against the authoritarian behavior of the government between the years of 1921-38. It was forced to succumb in the face of rising totalitarian anti-Jewish tendencies after Bela Imredy's assumption of the prime ministry in 1938, and eventually it was reduced to one or two members in the Diet.

The third opposition group was the Social Democratic Party, which had a Marxist but clearly anti-Communist program. It was handicapped by the traditional conservative makeup of the peasantry. The government, moreover, clearly stipulated that the Social Democrats were not to try to influence the peasantry under threat of liquidation of the party. They were therefore confined to the industrial areas of Hungary and succeeded in gaining leading influence and control in the trade unions. Their efforts in printing popular newspapers and periodicals in the Hungarian capital helped their cause. They also possessed a well-knit organizational structure, experienced leadership, and connections with European Socialist parties.

The last elections of the interwar era were held in May 1939 and resulted in a change in the parliamentary balance. Encouraged by Hitler's gestures toward Hungary, a group of 43 Hungarian Nazis won parliamentary seats; of these, 28 were members of the *Nyilask-eresztes* (Arrow Cross) movement led by Major Ferenc Szalasi. The movement consisted mostly of unorganized workers and lower middle-class urban elements. Anticipating German intervention, they stirred up discontent and in general tried to pave the way for German conquest. Their demagogic program stressed land reform, but its main feature was anti-Semitism. Despite factional strife, the Arrow Cross movement achieved a position of formidable influence by infiltrating the administration and the armed forces.

In addition to the efforts of the Hungarian Peasant Union, the Smallholders, and the Social Democrats to counter the Arrow Cross, an attempt was made by the "village explorers," a group of young writers who later referred to themselves as the March Front perpetuating the ideals of the 1848 Revolution. They undertook a careful investigation and analysis of rural life in Hungary and presented the results as proposals for profound social reform. On the basis of their studies, they also branded Arrow Cross agitation for land reform as demagoguery. Unfortunately for Hungary, the March Front did not emerge enough to act as an effective counterfoil to the nation's growing totalitarian tendencies.

The Arrow Cross movement was strengthened by Mussolini's and Hitler's concessions on the return of former Hungarian territories. Southern Slovakia, Ruthenia (Carpatho-Ukraine), and Northern Transylvania were annexed to Hungary in 1938, 1939, and 1940, respectively; in 1941, Germany returned the former Hungarian territories attached by the Trianon Treaty to Yugoslavia in exchange for the right of troop passage through Hungary into Yugoslavia. The Hungarian Army, which had traditionally been pro-German, exerted pressure on the government, and Hungary entered the war against the Soviet Union in June 1941 after an alleged Soviet air raid on Hungarian territory.

The government Party of Hungarian Life resisted complete Arrow Cross encroachment until German occupation in 1944, when the Hungarian Minister in Berlin, Dome Sztojay, was called upon to head a puppet government. The Sztojay government put Hungary fully behind the German war effort, dissolved all legal opposition elements, and unleashed a program of persecution and deportation of the Jews. Horthy, still Regent of Hungary, made an unsuccessful effort to counter the pro-German trend by dismissing Sztojay on August 29, 1944, attempting to surrender to the Allies (October 15), and even negotiating with underground organizations to defend Budapest against German retaliatory measures. Instead, the Germans banished Horthy from Hungary, and through force of arms established an Arrow Cross government in Budapest under Szalasi. The Arrow Crossites added a bloody page to Hungarian history during their short reign (October 1944-February 1945).

At the same time the Soviet Army supported the establishment of a coalition Provisional Government based on the four underground parties (Smallholders, Social Democrats, National Peasants, and Citizens' Democrats) banned by Sztojay, plus the Communist Party (banned since 1920). General Bela Miklos, who had surrendered to the Soviet Army with some of his troops, was made Prime Minister of the Provisional Government, a post he held until the first postwar elections in November 1945.

The Communist Movement, 1918-1944

Hungary is the only country in the Soviet orbit to have experienced a Communist dictatorship prior to World War II. From November 1918 to August 1919 Hungary served as a crucible of world revolution, which later had two points of significance. First, the terrorism of the Bela Kun regime during this early experiment alienated a Hungarian nation whose historical traditions were already antithetical to communism. Second, some evidence has been amassed to show that post-World War Communist strategy in all the captive countries was partly guided by this Hungarian experiment, and several policy decisions were made by modifying and correcting what the Soviet leaders regarded as the mistakes in that experiment.

In the turmoil following the collapse of the Austro-Hungarian Monarchy and the declaration of the democratic revolutionary (Karolyi) Republic in Hungary, which proclaimed general franchise, land reform, and peace, a small band of prisoners of war repatriated from Russia and a few left-wing dissident Social Democrats formed a new revolutionary party in Budapest on November 21, 1918. The new group studiously avoided any semblance of nationalism and called itself "Party of the Communists in Hungary." Its leader was Bela Kun, a former Transylvanian journalist, who had been taken prisoner on the

Russian front during the war and had participated in the Bolshevik seizure of power in Russia. He arrived in Budapest in November 1918, and immediately set to work organizing a disciplined nucleus for the purpose of repeating the Bolshevik *coup* in Hungary.

The steadily deteriorating international situation played into Communist hands. On March 20, 1919, the Karolyi government was informed by the Budapest representative of the Allied and Associated Powers that additional Hungarian territory would have to be turned over to Romanian and Czechoslovak military occupation and that the new line of demarcation was to be regarded as a political frontier. Unwilling to accept responsibility for the loss of national territory, the Karolyi government withdrew from power. On the evening of March 21, 1919, a Revolutionary Governing Council of the Dictatorship of the Proletariat was set up. Two days later, public posters announced the dictatorship of the proletariat. Thus, the establishment of this dictatorship was not the result of internal social or political development or of the forceful displacement of a previously established government by a determined Communist minority, but rather the direct outcome of external developments.

Beset by passive resistance at home, invaded by the armies of its neighbors, and proscribed by the Great Powers, the Hungarian Communist regime could not endure. On August 1, 1919, the dictatorship of the proletariat collapsed and its commissars, led by Bela Kun, fled across the Austrian border and eventually to the Soviet Union. A Social Democratic government, which took over the direction of affairs, lasted only five days, when it was thrown out of office by a counter-revolutionary military *coup*. For the next quarter century, Hungarian Communists were to remain underground, engaging in illegal activity.

The work of the illegal Hungarian Communist Party was directed by a Central Committee, some of whose members lived abroad. The primary Communist cells were limited largely to the towns, mining districts, and camps of seasonal construction workers in southeastern Hungary. The greatest number of Communist cells was in Budapest.

An important segment of Party work consisted in the printing and distribution of illegal Communist publications. Police raids on Party presses and on Communist meeting places resulted in the arrest of some members. Afterward, the Communists organized Party seminars in prison, occasionally converting prisoners. Another important type of Party work consisted in organizing strikes. The Communist faction within the trade unions, known as the Trade Union Opposition was primarily concerned with this type of activity. The great building workers' strike, which began in Budapest on August 1, 1935 and in which 10,000 workers participated, is considered largely the work of the Trade Union Opposition.

During the interwar period, while the Party was illegal, Communist activities were concentrated in the Greater Budapest industrial area; in the industrial-mining region northeast of Budapest (Salgotarjan, Diosgyor, Miskolc) and in the southwest (the Pecs area); and among the seasonal construction workers of the so-called "stormy corner," an area east of the Tisza River adjacent to the Romanian border.

The Party sent contingents to Spain during the Civil War. The Rakosi Battalion of approximately 1,000, many of them recruited abroad from among the exiles, was a part of the International Brigade and suffered about 400 casualties.

Between the signing of the Nazi-Soviet Pact on August 23, 1939 and the opening of hostilities between Germany and the Soviet Union on June 22, 1941, the Hungarian Communists assumed a neutral attitude toward World War II. Incidentally, the Horthy government was also neutral and exchanged convicted Communist leaders, including Rakosi, for 1,849 Hungarian banners captured by the Tsarist Army. As in other countries, Communist resistance to the Germans began after June 1941 and took the form of illegal pamphlets and sporadic acts of sabotage.

Until September 1944, the underground activity of the Hungarian Communists went under the name of the Hungarian Peace Party. As such, the Communists participated in the formation, in May 1944, of the so-called Hungarian Front, a resistance organization composed of the five above-mentioned illegal antifascist parties and the newly formed Catholic People's Party. This was a "people's front," the germ of the postwar coalition government, of which the Communists formed the most disciplined nucleus. Their representatives on this body were Laszlo Rajk and Gyula Kallai.

In September 1944, the pseudonym "Peace Party" was abandoned, and the name Hungarian Communist Party was adopted. A handful of Communist guerrillas started partisan warfare in the Salgotarjan coal basin at the approach of the Soviet Army. In the meantime, Communist ranks were being reinforced by agents dropped by parachute or smuggled across the lines. Under the aegis of the invading Soviet Army, the Party came out into the open, first in eastern Hungary, and then, successively, in Budapest and the rest of the country. In the Provisional National Government formed in December 1944, Communist delegates received three portfolios out of twelve. The long period of illegal Party work was over.

COMMUNIST SEIZURE AND CONSOLIDATION OF POWER, 1944-1955

When the Soviet Army arrived on Hungarian territory in the autumn of 1944, the only organized and well-disciplined political group in Soviet-occupied Hungary was the Communist Party. The leaders, a handful of 1919 Communist exiles and "converted" POW's of World War II, numbered probably fewer than 3,000. Since the spring of 1945, however, the original hard core had been reinforced by recruits from the poorest strata the agricultural population, who received such small plots in the land reform program that the introduction of cooperatives held no terror for them, and from the ranks of the political police (about 5,000 to 10,000 individuals), who knew that their survival depended upon the continuation of the Communist regime. Even with the inclusion of these late-comers, however, a free estimate of the hard core of Communist support in Hungary could not be placed higher than 200,000, or roughly 1 or 2 per cent of the population.

From the very beginning, Soviet occupation authorities gave the Hungarian Communists strong support, making food rations available only for holders of Communist membership cards, providing jobs for Party members, and extending political amnesty to former members of Hungarian Nazi organizations who joined. On several occasions, Party functionaries visited concentration camps for the "small *Nyilas*" (rank-and-file members of the Arrow Cross Party) and circulated membership applications with a promise of liberation and immunity from punishment upon signature. In this manner, the ranks of the Communists were filled to a considerable extent with former Nazis. In addition, the occupation authorities provided the Party with motor vehicles, thus greatly facilitating its organizational activities, particularly at the time of the first postwar national elections in 1945. The Communist Party was also enabled to set up armed units, equipped partly by the Soviet Army and partly by Hungarian military authorities acting under Soviet pressure.

During the eight years that elapsed following its admission to the government in December 1944, the Party gained complete control by gradually extending its sway over every phase of state and national life. The rise of Communist hegemony in Hungary is vividly illustrated by the parliamentary election results and by Communist representation in the successive legislatures and Cabinets. In the first postwar elections (1945), although held in the presence of the occupying Soviet Army, it was able to poll only 797,040 votes (16.9 per cent of the total). This was the lowest percentage of Communist votes in any election in the captive countries following the war. In the national elections of 1947, in spite of terrorism and grossly fraudulent practices, the Party was able to raise its electoral strength to only 1,113,050 votes (22.3 per cent of the total). In 1949 and 1953, after the absorption of the Social Democratic Party, the Hungarian Workers' (Communist) Party did not put up a separate ticket, but ran on a common slate with other Communist-dominated pseudo-parties. Through this maneuver, the Communist-designed Independent People's Front (Workers' Party, Smallholders, National Peasants, Independent Democrats, Radical Democrats) was able to claim in 1949, 95.6 per cent of the vote and in 1953, 98.2 per cent. In the fall of 1954, the Independent People's Front was superseded by the Patriotic People's Front, which dropped the non-Communist political parties.

In the first postwar Cabinet (formed on December 22, 1944), Communists held three portfolios out of twelve. After the rebuff suffered by the Communists in the 1945 elections, the ratio of Communists in the Cabinet weakened to four out of eighteen (November 15, 1945), and was maintained at this level until September 24, 1947, when it rose to five out of fifteen. By December 10, 1948, after the merger of the Communists and the Social Democrats into the Hungarian Workers' Party (June 12-13, 1948), the ratio was ten out of fifteen; of the ten Workers' Party Cabinet representatives, eight were former Communists and two were former Social Democrats. By December 1953, Workers' Party representation increased to sixteen out of the twenty posts. In the present Cabinet, all posts are held by Workers' (Communist) Party members or crypto-Communists.

The growth of Communist representation in Parliament shows a similar curve. After the elections of 1945, 70 Communist deputies (17.1 per cent) were assigned seats in the legislature; after the elections of 1947, 100 (24.4 per cent). After the elections of 1949 and 1953, only Communist and Communist-selected deputies were seated, and opposition was suppressed.

The Elections of November 4, 1945

The elections of November 4, 1945 were held under the Provisional Government, composed of a five-party coalition. The coalition, called the Hungarian National Independence Front consisted of the Smallholders', Communist, Social Democratic, Citizens' Democratic, and National Peasant parties.

The Communists made various efforts to gain advantages for themselves at these elections. Through their powerful advocate, Lieutenant

General V. P. Sviridov, the Soviet chairman of the Allied Control Commission, the Communists attempted to persuade the popular Smallholders' Party to accept a single electoral list for all parties in the coalition. Similarly, they attempted to effect a merger with the Social Democrats.

Although they were rebuffed in these maneuvers, the Communists took no immediate countermeasures. They did succeed in maintaining the old Provisional Government coalition (minus the Citizens' Democratic Party), although individual party identification within the coalition was retained. The Citizens' Democratic Party at this time entered the opposition, along with the Radical Party. The Communists were confident of polling a majority, because of their organization, discipline, and Soviet Army support. The apparently limitless funds at their disposal enabled them to wage a campaign far superior to those of their rivals. In addition, the leading role played by Communist Minister of Agriculture Imre Nagy in the execution of the land reform was calculated to draw votes from the largest element in the nation, the peasantry.

Instead of victory, however, the Communists captured only 17 per cent of the votes, suffering overwhelming defeat, although the coalition as a whole received 96.7 per cent of the votes. The Smallholders, who received 2,687,000 out of a total of 4,721,000 votes, emerged as the leading party. The Communist reply to these results was to launch "a counteroffensive against all signs of reaction." This involved a relentless, systematic drive to terrorize, outmaneuver, and liquidate all opposition parties.

Liquidation of the Smallholders

Since the Smallholders were in the majority and the greatest obstacle to the Communists, they were the first to experience the latter's liquidation processes. In view of their own minority status, the Communists had to lean heavily on their Soviet protectors in order to achieve this goal.

Early in 1946, the Communists induced the Social Democratic Party and the National Peasant Party to join with them in a "leftist bloc" against the Smallholders. This, in effect, was the creation of a coalition within a coalition, the Hungarian National Independence Front. The Communist explanation was that the Smallholders represented "reaction." At the same time, the Communist-controlled Trade Union Council, abetted by the Communist Minister of the Interior, instituted mass violence against the Smallholders. In these ways, the Communists succeeded in persuading twenty-two Smallholder members of the National Assembly to resign from their party and to form another party, the Freedom Party, led by Dezso Sulyok.

Communist pressure was thereafter intensified; they staged "popular" demonstrations against the Smallholders, blaming them for all Hungary's woes, including the runaway inflation. By June 1946, the Smallholders' position had so deteriorated that their leader, Prime Minister Ferenc Nagy, was ready to resign. However, the Communists were aware of Nagy's popularity and realized that such a move would hurt their own political prospects; they therefore made a quick tactical change and became conciliatory. As a result, Nagy felt that the situation was stable enough for him to attend bilateral conferences in Washington and London prior to the forthcoming peace parley. While he was away, tension flared up again, with the arrest of a Smallholder member of the National Assembly, and a climax was reached after two Soviet soldiers were killed in Budapest.

When Nagy returned to Budapest, he found that both he and his Smallholder colleague, President Zoltan Tildy, were under sharp fire from their own party for not breaking with the Communist-controlled coalition. Nagy stressed the necessity of preserving the coalition as long as the Soviet army of occupation remained, even though he was no longer under any illusions concerning Communist intentions.

The Communists dealt their Smallholder adversaries a serious blow shortly before Christmas 1946, when Communist General Palffy Osterreicher, head of the Army's political squad, began making arrests in connection with an alleged conspiracy against the Republic. The alleged conspirators were accused of trying to re-establish the Horthy regime and to nullify the land reform. Pressure not to interfere was exerted on Nagy by General Sviridov and later by General Kondratov, Soviet head of the Military Division of the Allied Control Commission, who threatened the Premier with MVD (Soviet police) intervention.

Indiscriminate attacks on Smallholders made obvious the purpose of the "conspiracy" charges. Minister of Reconstruction Endre Misteth was the first Smallholder of Cabinet rank to be arrested. Thereupon, many Smallholder members of the National Assembly were accused and forced to surrender their immunity. Even the General Secretary of the Smallholders' Party, Bela Kovacs, was attacked by the Communists as a "conspirator" (February 15, 1947). Although he cleared himself of these charges, he was arrested again on February 25, 1947 by Soviet authorities on grounds of espionage against the Soviet Union. He has not been released, and is reportedly still under house arrest. The

Communists succeeded in splitting the Smallholders by decimating their ranks in the wake of "conspiracy" charges and by exerting pressure on them to purge their own ranks.

The "conspiracy" trials, however, did not end the Communist drive against the Smallholders. On April 10, 1947, a Communist-inspired bill establishing a so-called United Cooperative was forced through the National Assembly. A similar bill in 1946 had foundered upon the Smallholders' resistance. The bill enabled the Communists and their fellow travelers to take over 56 per cent of the administrative positions in the rural cooperatives. The issue provided still another opportunity for attacking the Smallholders, this time because of insufficient enthusiasm for the project.

The *coup de grace* was delivered to the Smallholders in May 1947, when Prime Minister Nagy, on vacation in Switzerland, was implicated in the "conspiracy" for which Kovacs had been arrested. This ended the last vestige of independence in the Smallholders' Party, and many of its prominent members had to flee the country. Nagy himself remained in exile.

The Election of August 31, 1947

The Communists had *de facto* control of the government, but felt that they were in a position to get *de jure* control by means of new national elections. Despite their maneuvers and manipulations, they felt the need of a number of additional guarantees of electoral success.

First, they exerted pressure on Dezso Sulyok's "Freedom Party." After Minister of the Interior Rajk's charges of fascism and a series of "spontaneous" mob demonstrations, the "Freedom Party" dissolved itself on July 22, 1947.

Another safeguard was the electoral law (Law No. 22. of 1947), which was forced through the demoralized opposition on July 24. The law in effect gave the newly created Communist-controlled National Front—the old four-party coalition plus one of the former opposition parties, the Citizens' Democratic Party (which left the Front before the 1947 elections)—the power to withhold recognition from parties, to disqualify candidates, to remove citizens from the voting lists, and to enable Communist supporters to engage in plural voting. Furthermore, the coalition reaped extra votes by determining the means of apportioning residual votes in counties and by manipulating the 60 supplementary seats on the so-called national slate.

The Communists sought additional assurance of electoral success by

allowing the formation of a number of new opposition parties. Besides
the two opposition parties of the 1945 elections, four new ones were
permitted on the 1947 ballot (Democratic People's, Independence,
Independent Democratic, and Christian Women's Camp parties). This
served to split the opposition.

In the campaign that preceded the elections, the Communists took
advantage of the opportunities afforded by the electoral law. Mob
demonstrations were staged. The chief target of this organized terror
was Zoltan Pfeiffer's Hungarian Independence Party, which was
rallying the anti-Communist vote. (Three months after the elections,
the Hungarian Independence Party was dissolved and Pfeiffer fled to
the West.) The Social Democratic Party, which was replacing the
battered Smallholders' Party as chief rival to the Communists in the
coalition, also received violent treatment. So rough was the election
campaign that the United States and Britain as occupying powers
issued a joint note (August 18, 1947) protesting especially the arbitrary disfranchisement of thousands of Hungarian citizens.

By these tactics, the Communists succeeded in getting more votes
than any other party. On the other hand, the four-party coalition which
won 98.2 per cent of the votes in 1945 could muster only 61 per cent
in 1947. Within the coalition, however, the loss, as might have been
expected, was mostly at the expense of the Smallholders in favor of
the "leftist bloc."

Absorption of the Social Democrats

Since the election results showed the disintegration of the Smallholders' Party, Rakosi keynoted the next Communist move, "to strike
a decisive blow against hostile hordes hiding in the Social Democratic
Party." After the elections, the Social Democratic rank and file re-
volted against its left-wing leadership. Demands were made that Rajk
(Communist) be replaced as Minister of the Interior by a Social Democrat. The left-wing Social Democrat, Arpad Szakasits, maintained his
leadership, however, and permitted continued Communist dictation.
The right wing of the Social Democratic Party was disposed of in
November 1947 when its veteran leader, Karoly Peyer, was accused
with thirteen others of espionage in much the same manner as many
Smallholders had been the preceding year. Peyer had already fled
from Hungary.

In January 1948, twenty-seven well-known anti-Communist Social
Democrats were purged by the left-wing leadership. Purges in the
Social Democratic Party continued. Finally, in March, a meeting was

called to discuss a merger with the Communists. The annual Party Congress which convened that month began with a purge of thirty-seven important members. The decision to merge was confirmed, and the merger was carried out on June 13, 1948. By this act, the Communist-dominated Hungarian Workers' Party obtained votes which could not have been won by the Communist Party as such.

Is should be noted that the Social Democrats posed less of a problem to the Communists than did the Smallholders. Two factors were apparently responsible for this. First, the Social Democratic following was never as large as the Smallholders'; second, because of the Social Democrats' tight party discipline and the principle of "workers' unity," the Social Democratic rank and file was predisposed against "deserting" the other "working class" party. Although the majority of the Social Democrats wanted to retain their independence, Rakosi's support from the left wing, led by such figures as Szakasits and Ronai, kept the Social Democrats in line.

With the merger, any chance of organized Social Democratic opposition was effectively ended. The formation of the Hungarian Workers' Party, to be sure, did not signify the end of purges. The next step, to remove unreliable former Social Democrats, took place in January 1949 within the framework of a general purge of the Party, when 178,589 members, or 18 per cent of the total membership, was expelled.

The Elections of May 15, 1949

With the Smallholders and Social Democrats eliminated, the Communists had no reason to doubt the results of the elections of 1949. Still, Law No. 9 of 1949, which abolished the franchise of those who had been under political arrest and those under "police surveillance" for political reasons, was enacted on April 8 as insurance. This law, as well as all other laws dealing with electoral matters, was made meaningless by the creation of the Hungarian Independent People's Front in February 1949. The Front was a combination of all existing parties, both government and opposition, and of mass organizations, such as the Trade Union Council and the Federation of Democratic Women.

Thus, the election held on May 15, 1949 was a "single list" election. In the so-called campaign prior to the election, instructions on how to vote "yes" were repeated over all media of communication. To vote for the candidates on the list, one merely had to fold the ballot and hand it unmarked to the chairman of the polling committee. Those who voted against the government signified their intention by using a "secret" booth provided for the purpose. The leading Communist theoretician, Jozsef Revai, cynically noted the purpose of the new type of ballot: "We do not deny that the question of a joint list is a question of power. The joint list in fact serves the purpose of preventing the possibility of undermining and shaking the power of the working class" (*Szabad Nep,* April 17, 1949).

To ensure a good turnout, agitators spurred the people to the polls. The government, as expected, won an overwhelming victory with 5,479,000 votes out of 5,731,000 or 95.6 per cent of the total; 165,000 persons voted against the list and 87,000 votes were invalidated on technical grounds (*Magyar Nemzet* [Hungarian Nation], May 18, 1949).

The Elections of May 17, 1953 and the People's Front

The elections held on May 17, 1953 followed the same pattern as those of 1949. An electoral law enacted in December 1952 lowered the voting age limit from 20 to 18, the purpose apparently being to increase the total number of voters for the single list. In this connection *Szabad Nep* of January 18, 1953 announced the preparation of a new list of eligible Hungarian voters.

Nominations of candidates were made ostensibly by mass organizations, in factories, machine-tractor stations, state farms, army units, and other organizations. The names chosen were submitted to county electoral committees, which selected the number required to make up the county list. The various county lists were then submitted to the National Electoral Committee for approval or revision.

As expected, the Hungarian Independent People's Front won an "overwhelming victory." Of the eligible voters, 98 per cent participated; of these, 98.2 per cent (6,256,653 voters) voted in favor of the front; 61,257 voters, or about 1 per cent, voted against the list; while 52,609 voters, or about .8 per cent, cast invalidated ballots.

Even nominal recognition of the non-Communist political parties was ended when the Hungarian Independent People's Front was supplanted by another Communist-dominated coalition, the Patriotic People's Front, which held its first congress on October 23-24, 1954. The new Front, while it embraces virtually all organized Hungarian groups and associations, does not include the non-Communist political parties, which no longer have even a vestigial existence. The local and regional elections of November 28, 1954 were held under the auspices of the new Front.

HUNGARIAN WORKERS' (COMMUNIST) PARTY

Organization

The changes in Party organization introduced at the Nineteenth Congress of the Communist Party of the Soviet Union in October 1952 and those brought about in the Soviet Union after the death of Stalin in March 1953 were reflected in the measures taken at the Third Congress of the Hungarian Workers' (Communist) Party (May 24-31, 1954), including a revision of the Party's organizational statutes (published in final form in *Szabad Nep*, June 1, 1954). Many of the changes had, in fact, already been effected by the Party's Central Committee in June 1953. The principal changes included scrapping the "cult of personality" in favor of "collective leadership" to conform with the new situation in the Soviet Union after Stalin's death; intensification of Party discipline to effect better implementation of new policies; and enlargement of the powers of the Central Committee's Political Committee (Politburo).

The Hungarian Workers' Party is organized in the form of a pyramid, the base of which is formed by basic organizations or cells, which graduate in rank toward the peak symbolized by the Party's Central Committee. Cells, which have a minimum of three and a maximum of 300 members, are organized in plants, districts, villages, agricultural producers' cooperatives, farms, offices, institutions, and in the armed forces; each cell must be approved by a higher Party organ. Where the organization has over 300 members, it is broken into smaller cells to keep the primary units compact and their members intimately connected with each other. The duties and functions of these cells include the whole range of Party activities on the local level.

The parent coordinating organizations of cells are the local Party establishments in municipal precincts (except Budapest precincts), villages, plants, offices, and institutions; every two years they must hold a Party conference for all members of the cells within their jurisdiction, where they elect the members and alternates of their Party committees, which in turn elect from among their own members, 5- to 7-member executive committees. The number of committee secretaries (up to three) is determined by the Central Committee. Party committees must meet at least every other month.

Next in rank to the cells and local organizations are the district, municipal, and Budapest precinct organizations, which also hold Party conferences for all the members in their respective regions every two years. The conferences elect the members and alternates of their respective Party committees and "debate" and criticize Party committee reports.

The Party committees of districts, certain towns designated by the Central Committee, and Budapest precincts elect 7- to 11-member executive committees for the coordination and direction of their cells and organizations, as well as three Party committee secretaries who are simultaneously members of the executive committee. The first secretary must be confirmed by the Central Committee.

Between Party conferences, the Party committees on this level direct the work of their respective Party organizations and control the execution of Party resolutions. They also assume responsibility for the accomplishment of economic plans.

The district Party committee directs village Party organizations. It is charged with the development of political "enlightenment" work in agricultural machine-tractor stations, producers' cooperatives, and state farms, as well as among individual peasant farmers.

The Party conferences of the districts and designated towns elect delegates to the county conference convened every two years, while the Budapest Party conference elects delegates to the Budapest conference (Budapest is always given county status in both Party and government because of its large population).

The county and Budapest Party committees, which must meet at least every three months, elect 9- to 11-member executive committees to coordinate and direct the daily activity of their subordinate organizations; they also elect their three secretaries, who are simultaneously members of the executive committees and must be confirmed by the Central Committee.

Special provision is also made in the Party's organizational statutes for the establishment of Party units in the Communist youth organization, the nation's armed forces (including police), railroads, ministries, local government councils, and mass organizations (e.g., trade unions, Federation of Democratic Women). Through such extensions of its control, the Party assures itself monolithic dominance over virtually everyone.

The leading organ of the Party in theory is the Central Committee. It directs the work of the Party during the period between national congresses and represents it in its relations with other parties, organizations, and state institutions. The Central Committee is supposed to meet once every three months and is responsible to the national congress, which elects its membership. The Central Committee elects from its own members: (1) a Political Committee (Politburo) which directs and leads the Party, theoretically only between sessions of the Central

Committee; (2) a Party Secretariat, the task of which is to ensure and control the execution of resolutions of leading Party organs; and (3) a First Secretary of the Central Committee, who in practice is dictator of Party and state. In addition, the Central Committee appoints the head of the editorial board of the Party's press. A special arm of the Central Committee is the Central Control Commission. The duties of this security unit are watching over the political behavior, moral integrity, and loyalty of Party members; waging a relentless battle against corruption and all forms of undisciplined, anti-Party, factional, and "un-Partylike" activities; and guarding against infiltration of the Party by enemies of the people and elements injurious to the interests and morals of the working people.

Another arm of the Central Committee is the Central Revision Committee. Its functions, similar to those of its regional and local counterparts, are to assure correctness and speed in the management of the Party's central organs and to control the finances of the Central Committee and the central enterprises of the Party. (For list of Party leaders, see page 410 ff.)

The highest deliberative organ of the Party in theory is the National Party Congress, which must be convoked by the Central Committee once every three years. It may convene an extraordinary congress on its own initiative and is required to do so on the petition of one third of the Party's members. The delegates to a congress, ordinary or extraordinary, are elected at Party Conferences in proportion to the number of Party members and candidates of the respective Party organizations. (The Third Party Congress was held May 24-31, 1954.) The functions of the congress are to "debate" and criticize the reports of the Central Committee and Central Revision Committee, approve or modify the Party program and organizational statutes, and prepare Party policies, tactics, and organizational directives. It also elects and determines the number of members and alternates of the Central Committee and Central Revision Committee. In practice, the Party Congress, like the National Assembly, is a rubber stamp for the directives of the Party leadership. It approves all such directives without serious debate or objection, and is little more than a transparent facade of Party "democracy."

Membership

Membership in the Party as of May 1954 was reported to be 864,607 (810,227 members and 54,380 candidates), or about 9 per cent of the population. In the winter of 1944/45, in the early days of the Soviet occupation, there was only a handful of Communists in Hungary. Party membership at the end of February 1945 was 30,000. By the end of May 1954, this had risen to 150,000; by March 1947, to 650,000. On the eve of the forced merger of the Social Democrats and Communists in May 1948, the Communist Party claimed to have 6,242 local organizations with a total membership of 884,000. When the merger was formalized on June 13, 1948, the membership of the resulting Hungarian Workers' Party was estimated as high as 1,500,000.

Less than three months after its founding, an official ban was placed upon the admission of new members; this ban remained in effect until November 1949, and during this time a drastic purge was carried out in Party ranks. By February 1951, the number dropped to 862,114 of which the age distribution was as follows:

Age Group	Number of Members	Per Cent
Under 24	111,493	12.9
25-35	243,646	28.3
36-50	320,613	37.2
Over 50	186,362	21.6
Total	862,114	100.0

New membership drives after the Second Party Congress (February 1951) brought the number up again so that membership in October 1952 was about a million, despite the disclosure by the Central Committee in March 1952 that persons under 24 would not be admitted as Party candidates, but must join the Federation of Working Youth instead. Following a Party census in October 1952, complaints were made of the inadequacy of the admissions program in general, and of the necessity for tightening screening procedures in particular. Thereupon, orders were issued for the exchange of all Party cards beginning in January 1953. As a result some 20,000 were removed from the Party.

An individual desirous of becoming a Party member must first prove himself "worthy" during a candidacy of at least six months. He must then submit a written request for admission to the directorate or secretary of the cell at his place of work or residence. The request must be supported by written recommendations from two members who have been in the Party at least one year each, and have personally engaged in joint work with the candidate for at least six months. Recommendations are not made lightly since those giving them are held responsible for any shortcomings subsequently displayed by the person recommended. In regard to members of the Federation of Working Youth, one of the two Party recommendations may be substituted by one from a Federation committee on the district, municipal, precinct, or factory level. A members' meeting of the cell concerned determines the admission of new Party candidates and members upon proposal by its directorate; this must then be confirmed by factory committees authorized by the district, municipal, precinct, or Central Committee.

Members' records are frequently reviewed. The criteria for the decision as to whether membership may be retained include class origin, political attitude before and since the inception of the regime, behavior at one's place of employment, participation in Party work, seniority in membership, political training, payment of Party dues, and extra-Party activities in the so-called mass organizations. In the words of one of its leading functionaries, "the Hungarian Workers' Party will become a crystal clear party in every respect, and even more so, the vanguard of the working class, of the Hungarian working people." For this reason, 90 per cent of the Hungarian working people will not be admitted to Party membership.

Communist-Controlled Political Organizations and Mass Organizations

The creation of mass organizations is one of the means by which the Hungarian Workers' Party ensures participation of the people in its program. Whereas the Party is theoretically the "elite" of the proletariat, the mass organizations are its followers and offer the only organized political activity open to most citizens.

The Patriotic People's Front, which superseded the Hungarian Independent People's Front on October 24-25, 1954, embraces in addition to the Hungarian Workers' Party, all mass, religious, social, cultural, academic, and scientific societies. Unlike its predecessors, the new Front organization dropped from its ranks the non-Communist political parties. While it is controlled by the Party, the new Front pretends to be independent; it allegedly initiates important legislation and sponsors all candidates on the single-list election ballots.

Particular mass organizations are created on the basis of such factors as age, sex, or occupation. The Party coordinates and directs all their activities in order to guarantee vigorous support for its goals. Three such organizations are the National Council of Trade Unions (SZOT), the Federation of Working Youth (DISZ), and the Hungarian Federation of Democratic Women (MNDSZ).

The trade unions embrace most industrial workers and act as a school for communism. Their function is to increase production and to aid in the allocation of the labor force. A detailed description of the Communist trade union movement can be found in Chapter 13, "Labor." The task of the Federation of Working Youth is to strengthen the Party and train youth in accordance with Leninist-Stalinist doctrine. The primary functions of the Federation of Democratic Women are to enlist as many women as possible in the service of the Party and to channel them into industrial and agricultural employment.

Federation of Working Youth and Pioneers

In an effort to gather all the youth into one mass organization, a nominally non-Party but Communist-dominated organization, the Hungarian Democratic Youth Federation was established after the war. Most of the other youth organizations were not taken in by this ruse. In the summer of 1946, however, Laszlo Rajk, then Minister of the Interior, following the intervention of the Soviet chairman of the Allied Control Commission, liquidated youth organizations of a religious character, such as the Catholic and Calvinist youth organizations. By the end of 1947, all youth organizations sponsored by parties other than the Communist were disbanded and even the Hungarian Democratic Youth Federation was replaced by the People's Federation of Hungarian Youth. The only other youth organizations then permitted to function were the Federation of Young Trade Unionists and the United Federation of Peasant Youth.

On February 10, 1950, Matyas Rakosi announced the creation of a youth organization similar to the Komsomol in the Soviet Union; this was achieved through the unification of the other youth organizations.

On June 17, 1950, the Constituent Assembly of the Federation of Working Youth met. At that congress, its objectives were defined:

> The Federation of Working Youth must stand on the ideological basis of Marxism-Leninism; we cannot allow alien and hostile ideologies to gain influence. . . . The Federation of Working Youth is a non-Party mass organization led by working youth. . . . Its main field of operations is the village. One of its chief aims is to foster the building of socialism in agriculture. . . . Key directives are work! study! fight! teach! Our youth organization will not allow clerical reaction to continue its traitorous subversive activities under the guise of religion . . . we must continue to fight against the subversion of right-wing social democrats . . . against agents of Tito's fascist gang, against remnants of the landowning capitalist classes, against the kulaks.

After this congress, organizational activity was greatly intensified in order to make this a real mass organization. At the Second Congress of the Hungarian Workers' Party in 1951, Istvan Hidas, member of the Party's Central Committee, announced the incorporation of the Federation of Working Youth within the framework of the Party. The Federation thus became the official youth organization of the Party and was launched along the road of the Komsomol.

On June 17, 1951, the first anniversary of the Federation, *Szabad Nep* disclosed that it had 620,000 members, of whom 170,000 were from Budapest. A subsequent membership drive raised membership to 659,000 by June 1952. On March 1, 1952, Istvan Kovacs, member of the Party's Central Committee, announced that the Party in the future would transfer all members under 24 years to the Federation and would prescribe that Party committees relinquish its 24- to 26-year-old cadres to it, which Kovacs now referred to as the "prime auxiliary force" of the Party. In this way, membership increased by another 110,000 to 120,000, while at the same time membership in the Party decreased by the same number. By May 1954, however, the number of youth organization members dropped to 577,000.

On June 28, 1952, Mihaly Farkas, the Minister of Defense and member of the Party's Secretariat expressed his dissatisfaction with the membership drive in the Federation. He noted that of the total of 1,812,000 Hungarian youths, only 35 per cent had enrolled, an increase of but 39,000 over the year before (this does not, of course, take into account the members being transferred from the Party).

Distribution of the Federation of Working Youth membership in per cent, according to trade, was reported by Farkas as follows:

Category	Per Cent
Workers	36.4
Farmers' cooperative group members	4.9
Individual farmers	12.0
"Intelligentsia"	1.8
University and college students	15.8
High school students	5.8
Others	23.3

Of the 4,930 cooperative farms in Hungary, only 1,038 had Federation organizations.

Hungarian children from six to fourteen are admitted to the Pioneer movement. Just as the Party assures replacements for itself through the Federation, so the Federation seeks to assure reserves through the

Pioneers. The November 15, 1951 issue of *Szabad Ifjusag* (Free Youth) directed an appeal to the basic organization "to create the closest contact with the Pioneers. . . . Let [Federation] committees hold discussions of the work of the Pioneer troops."

The purpose of the Pioneer movement is to indoctrinate the children with Marxism and prepare them for army training. The number of students attending the general schools in Hungary in 1952 was 1,213,251, of which 906,648 belong to the Pioneer movement. The number of Pioneer organizations in Hungary amounted to 6,487.

The Federation of Working Youth has also assumed the political direction of university youth, and is active in all classes and university departments. The Hungarian Communist press described the main task as the fight to attain excellent scholarship. It appears that the Party seeks to recruit its intellectual cadres from the ranks of the university and middle school students, but so far, despite the great mass of students, has not succeeded in attracting sufficient students of the proper caliber.

The Party has also entrusted the Federation with special assignments relating to the organization and teaching of youth. On September 15, 1951, the Communist press published the Federation program of political indoctrination. First came the political circles, in which some 100,000-120,000 students from 12 to 15 years of age were enrolled during the school year 1951/52. Sessions of political circles, lasting nine months, deal with biographies of Stalin and Matyas Rakosi, with the Five-Year Plan, and with federation bylaws.

For students from 15 to 17, there are two-year political schools. Study material at these schools includes "the discussion of the Party's internal and external policies and of the basic principles and questions relating to socialist construction." Special study circles are set up for youths of "bourgeois reactionary" origin and those whose progress is not deemed satisfactory. In the latter, Stalin's life has been the sole subject of study. In the school year 1951/52, they were attended by 50,000 students.

Hungarian Federation of Democratic Women

The Hungarian Federation of Democratic Women was founded in 1945. It was represented as an independent women's movement, but has been under Communist control from the start.

Until the spring of 1948, the various political parties organized separate women's movements, but after the formation of the Hungarian Workers' Party, the Hungarian Federation of Democratic Women was the only active women's movement. After the First Congress of the Hungarian Workers' Party in June 1948, the Federation was officially declared one of the mass organizations of the Party; it is also a member of the International Women's League, the federation of all Communist-controlled women's organizations.

Until 1949, the Federation was not active in factories and offices, since women were organized in trade unions. By mid-1949, all other women's organizations had been dissolved, and the Party resolution adopted in August 1949 called upon the Federation to organize women in factories and offices. It soon built up a national network, and organizational groups, teams of agitators, and people's educators were formed in cities and villages. In 1948, approximately 2,000 and by the end of of 1951, 5,634 groups were active. The number of members in 1949 was approximately 400,000; in December 1950, 647,000; and by the end of May 1952, 1,000,000. By 1954, the number had dropped to 560,000.

The Party aims at increasing membership. At the Third Congress of the Women's League held on May 24-25, 1952, two goals were outlined: to recruit more members, and to urge the members to step up their tempo of work.

The May 20, 1951 issue of *Szabad Nep* published an order of the Council of Ministers to increase the number of women workers in industry and agriculture. The measures now being effected, though primarily connected with worker recruitment, also aim at forcing mothers to leave the family circle and to place their small children in nurseries. The Federation has been designated by the state to execute this program.

7. STATE SECURITY

In its application to the Communist-controlled "people's democracies," the concept of national security requires complete redefinition. The classical conception of national security, by which is meant the security of a nation from the danger of foreign subjugation, cannot be unequivocally applied to Hungary, since the term implies the existence of national sovereignty. Because of the status of the People's Republic of Hungary within the Soviet orbit, one can speak of national security only in the sense of the security measures instituted by the regime for the perpetuation of its own power and in response to the military requirements of the Soviet bloc as determined by the Soviet Union.

The most salient feature of the dictatorship imposed upon the people of Hungary is the universal sense of insecurity. If the masses of this totalitarian society are insecure and afraid of the arbitrary and omnipotent state, its leaders are extremely apprehensive lest hostile elements penetrate the fabric of the state machinery. To prevent such penetration and to guard the newly created institutions of popular democracy, the rulers of the People's Republic of Hungary have not only established an apparatus of terror and surveillance, but have also set up a tightly knit network of propaganda and indoctrination to gain the allegiance and loyalty of their subjects. The primary objective of this complex system of political and police control is to absorb the entire population within the framework of the new regime.

With certain minor exceptions to fit local conditions, the pattern pursued by the Hungarian Communists was similar to that followed by their counterparts in most of the countries now in the Soviet orbit. Hiding behind the facade of parliamentary democracy, they managed gradually to infiltrate the entire network of government. Acquiring control over the Ministry of the Interior and thereby over the chief instrument for the seizure of power, the police force, the Communists soon transformed themselves from a ruling minority into a dominating majority. This process was facilitated by systematic Communist infiltration of the parties composing the government coalition, which were converted into docile instruments of political domination.

Once in a position to wield absolute power, the Communists began a concerted action for the elimination of the opposition. The intensity and scope of the drive against the opposition kept pace with the phases of Hungary's conversion into a people's democracy. During the first stage, when great stress was laid upon the preservation of the external forms of parliamentary democracy through the support given the bogus government coalitions, the drive was concentrated primarily against the most vocal opponents of the regime. In the summer of 1947, the systematic liquidation of all organized resistance was begun. The simplicity of the technique employed was matched only by its cruelty. Members of the opposition were accused of conspiring with certain "imperialist powers" to overthrow the "working people's government" and to bring an end to the regime of popular democracy. Conditioned to confess and denounce themselves publicly in "people's courts," they were condemned in accordance with "proletarian justice."

While all organized resistance has been eliminated, the instruments of suppression have by no means been abandoned or lessened. In fact, terror has become the content of the totalitarianism installed in Hungary as well as in the other captive countries.

The all-pervasive apparatus of the institutionalized terror consists of a closely knit and hierarchically arranged network of organizations which see that the activities of all citizens conform to the interests of the regime. At the summit, directly under the immediate supervision of the hierarchy of the Hungarian Workers' (Communist) Party and of the Soviet Union, are the police, the secret police, the intelligence branch of the Communist Party, and the secret control board. On the lower levels, are the many informers, tenants' committees, and social controllers, who supplement the machinery of terror.

Aside from these organizations and institutions of a supervisory, punitive, and secret character, the security of the state is further bolstered by (1) legal measures; (2) the armed forces of the People's Republic of Hungary; and (3) Soviet Army units stationed in Hungary under the pretext of "safeguarding the lines of communication with the Soviet troops in Austria."

Legal Measures

The principle of class justice aiming at the preservation of the present state structure has been so developed that anyone daring to show opposition to the regime can be silenced. The series of protective laws (beginning with Act No. 7 of 1946) calls for the death penalty or life imprisonment for forming, joining, or even supporting any organization that aims—even by peaceful means—at changing the existing form of government. Heavy sentences are applicable to those who "incite" against the state, its basic institutions, or against individuals or groups "because of their democratic or republican" convictions. Thus, these provisions can be and are applied against those who criticize Communist leaders or the Party.

Similar all-pervasive measures protect the "people's economy." Since the nationalization of industry, making the "tools of production" state property, a new category of "crimes" has emerged: those committed against the people's economy. To a great extent, "labor discipline" falls under this category, for "any action or omission which injures or endangers the economic order" is to be severely punished as provided in a number of laws, among others the Penal Code (Act No. 2 of 1950), Decree No. 4 of 1950 on the Penal Defense of Planned Economy, and the so-called Labor Code (Decree with the Force of Law No. 7 of 1951). Many "petty crimes" have thus been reclassified as major ones directed against the Communist economy.

In contrast to the heavily accentuated political and economic crimes, "common criminals" receive a certain lenience. This is not strikingly reflected by the text of the new laws, the Penal Code (Act No. 2 of 1950) and Criminal Procedure (Act No. 3 of 1950), but by the courts' interpretation of the law.

During the "Stalinist era" which is customarily identified with the prime ministry of Matyas Rakosi, there was a tendency to transfer a large part of criminal procedure from the courts to the administrative (police) agencies, which were given the power of direct interference and control over the detention (internment) and punishment (forced labor) of certain political and economic offenders. The "new course" regime, as represented first by Prime Minister Imre Nagy (1953-54) and in a somewhat revised form by Andras Hegedus (1954———), appears to have been anxious to retain the cloak of "legality" and has deprived police authorities of their punitive powers.

The Police

With the liberation of Hungary from Nazi domination, the primary aim of the Communists was to achieve control over the Ministry of the Interior and thereby over the police forces. Their efforts were successful early in the postwar period, thanks primarily to the decisive support received from the Soviet authorities and the Soviet Army.

The police forces available immediately after the debacle of 1944-45 were meager and disorganized. Most of the members of the Hungarian police left their units, preferring the safety of obscurity, while others fled to the West, fearing the consequences of past deeds. Public order was maintained by civilian committees, so-called national committees, acting under the command and supervision of the occupying authorities, and in many cases dominated by the Communists. Some of these Communists had recently emerged from prisons and years of political obscurity and were to form later the nucleus of the new Hungarian Police.

Once the Ministry of the Interior was firmly in their hands, the Communists' main concern was to transform the police into an efficient and loyal instrument of the Party. This process involved purging unreliable elements and replacing them with trustworthy Party members. In order to ensure the continued loyalty of the police, the Party leadership has provided material, cultural, and psychological benefits and has developed a complex but highly integrated system of controls which penetrates every aspect of police life.

This system is composed of a political and an executive punitive arm. The former, consisting of Party and Communist youth organizations in the police apparatus, is designed to achieve the allegiance of the police forces through propaganda and indoctrination; the latter, consisting of the security organs of the Hungarian secret police is designed to ferret out disloyal elements in the force.

Every Communist serving in the police forces is a member of a Party cell and subject to Party discipline. The political organs of the police forces are guided in their work by the directives of the Central Committee of the Hungarian Workers' (Communist) Party. Each member of the police forces is subject to two hours of political indoctrination daily. The nature and content of the lectures vary with the political climate prevailing on the domestic or international scene. The daily lectures are supplemented by "wall newspapers," movies, posters, and libraries, which are well stocked with propaganda material and whose walls are adorned with portraits of Hungarian and Soviet Communist leaders. The purpose of all these devices is to achieve total integration of the police into the machinery of the new regime.

While no means are spared for the conversion of every policeman into a loyal servant of the new regime, the Party leadership has not neglected to set up safeguards against deviationist or subversive elements. The police corps, being a sensitive bulwark of Communist power, is subjected to particularly close scrutiny. Agents of the secret police and of the intelligence branch of the Communist Party, serving as the eyes and ears of the dictatorship, are on a permanent lookout for enemies of the regime within the police corps.

From the administrative-organizational point of view, the new Hungarian Police has been remodeled in accordance with the provisions of Decree No. 274,000 of 1949 B.M. There is one national state police system, without separate local or municipal police organizations. The country is divided into nine police districts with headquarters in the following cities with district numbers in the following order: (1) Greater Budapest, (2) North Budapest, (3) Szekesfehervar, (4) Szombathely, (5) Pecs, (6) Szeged, (7) Szolnok, (8) Debrecen, and (9) Miskolc.

Each police district is headed by a police chief, assisted by two deputy police chiefs. While the entire police corps is carefully screened for political reliability, particular emphasis is placed upon the absolute devotion of the police chiefs and their deputies. They are selected from among the most trusted members of the Party and are expected to place the interests of the state above all other considerations.

From an organizational point of view, each police headquarters is divided into departments, sections, subsections, offices, and technical departments. The police chief and his deputies are appointed by the Minister of the Interior, and the heads of the various departments and offices are nominated by the police chief.

Although some latent dissatisfaction probably exists, the police forces have on the whole served the regime loyally. Short of a radical change in domestic affairs or in the international situation, there is no reason to believe that they will act differently in the future, for the ultimate power to which the police and all other Hungarian organizations are subject is the might of the Soviet forces.

The Secret Police

In the power structure of the regime, the secret police is the most efficient and best-organized department, constituting a virtually independent state within the state. While it is directly subordinated to the Party leadership, the secret police is outside the onionlike structure of the Communist hierarchy, serving as an omnipresent and all-pervasive force that permeates the entire texture of society. Its representatives are everywhere, keeping the population under careful surveillance to ensure "loyalty" to the regime. They are ably assisted by a mass of Party diehards, tenant committees, informers, and "spies upon spies" who complete the system of institutionalized terror.

While every citizen is carefully watched for antistate activity, those employed in the more sensitive areas of the government apparatus are subjected to a particularly close scrutiny. For these and all others in whom the secret police has an interest, a special dossier is maintained. Anyone connected with the government or any agency or factory, deemed sensitive from the point of view of national security, must obtain clearance by the secret police.

The effectiveness of the techniques employed by the secret police in carrying out its tasks is matched only by its cruelty. While the inviolability of the person and the home are constitutionally guaranteed, no one is immune against the secret police. Arrest of the individuals deemed undesirable by the Party is usually performed at night, a procedure designed to strike terror into the heart of the victim as well as into the population as a whole. The arrested individual is held incommunicado for a long period before he is brought to face his accusers. The primary task of the examiner is to extract a confession of guilt, for which purpose he uses a variety of methods ranging from simple persuasion to physical violence.

The personnel of the secret police is recruited from among the most trusted members of the Party. As is the case with the regular police, the Party leadership has embarked on a series of measures designed to keep the personnel contented and loyal. These range from an elaborate system of material and psychological incentives to extensive courses of political indoctrination and Party supervision. While the pay, food, quarters, and cultural advantages of the rank and file have been continually improved, remuneration for the services rendered by professional agents of the secret police is particularly lucrative. The psychological compensation derived from being representatives of the state within the state, and thus above the tribulations of everyday life, is an additional factor.

Hand in hand with these material and psychological inducements, the Party leadership has set up a network of safeguards against emancipation of the secret police from the machinery of external controls. The Party has spared no efforts to ensure the complete subordination of the secret police to the Party organization. Although every member of the secret police is a member of the Party, Party functionaries are appointed to watch over the loyalty of the members of the force. Special agents of the intelligence branch of the Hungarian Workers' (Communist) Party supplement the machinery of supervision.

In addition to these complex safeguards erected against deviation within the secret police, the Party has also established an intricate network of political indoctrination. This consists of intensive courses in Marxism-Leninism and daily lectures on the domestic and international political situation. Both supervisory and the political-propaganda machinery operate under the direct guidance of the Main Political Section of the Frontier Guard and Internal Security Services, which is subordinated to the Central Committee of the Hungarian Workers' Party. The representatives of this branch attached to the secret police operate under special directives of the Central Committee and are required to cooperate closely with the Party committees of the districts in which they are stationed. This cooperation is crystallized in joint Party meetings, in which the work performed within the secret police is periodically discussed.

While the danger to the Party leadership inherent in the power acquired by the secret services cannot be minimized, its explosive capacities are stifled by virtue of the fact that both the Party and the secret police are subordinated to Soviet control. The genesis of the present secret police can be traced back to the period immediately following the Soviet occupation of Budapest. Gabor Peter, established at the request of the Communist Party a special Political and Public Order Affairs Department of the Hungarian State Police, which is formally attached to the Central Police Authority. However, shortly after Laszlo Rajk became Minister of the Interior in March 1946, the Department was separated from the Central Police Authority and placed officially under the jurisdiction of the Ministry of the Interior. In September 1946, the Department was thoroughly reorganized and its personnel purged. From this date, hiring of new personnel has been handled not by the Ministry, but by the Party. Applicants for the secret police are referred to the cadre representative at the Department who formally recommends them, and the Minister then makes the official appointment. Following this overhaul, the Department was renamed State Security Department and its leadership strengthened by the nomination of Lieutenant Colonel Janos Kovacs as deputy to Gabor Peter. With fifteen years' experience as an officer of the Soviet secret police, Kovacs renders a special service in the gradual reorganization of the secret police along the lines of the MVD. In December 1949, following the purge of Laszlo Rajk and the official establishment of the regime of "people's democracy" (August 1949), the State Security Department was separated from the Miinstry of the Interior by virtue of the Cabinet Decree No. 4,353 of 1949 (268) M.T. Amalgamated with the Frontier Guard units of the Hungarian armed forces, which were previously under the jurisdiction of the Ministry of Defense, the secret police was renamed State Security Authority (AVH).

Under the Decree of 1949, the AVH is theoretically subordinate to the Council of Ministers, which exercises its authority through one of its members. The primary responsibility of the AVH, according to Article 3, is to defend the political, economic, and social organization of the People's Republic and to discover the enemies of the working people. Since the working people in Communist terminology are identified with the Party, the primary function of the secret police is to safeguard the interests of the Party.

The AVH and its organs are under the direct command of the chief of the AVH, who is appointed to and recalled from his post by the Presidential Council (Presidium), acting upon the recommendation of the Council of Ministers. While personnel attached to the AVH with the rank of lieutenant colonel or higher are appointed by the Presidential Council acting upon the recommendation of the minister responsible for police affairs, the right to appoint personnel below the rank of lieutenant colonel is left to the chief of the AVH.

Though the leading hierarchy of the AVH is chosen from among the most reliable members of the Party, they are by no means immune from periodic purges. Thus, for instance, Gabor Peter, one of the "Muscovites" who as head of the secret police was among those most responsible for the establishment of a people's democracy in Hungary, was accused of antistate activities, purged, and sentenced (March 1954) by the Supreme Military Court to life imprisonment. His chief aides, including the former Minister of Justice, Gyula Decsi, and fifty police officers were also arrested and sentenced to long prison terms. Shortly before Peter's purge, the AVH, following the general pattern pursued in the Soviet sphere, was again placed under the jurisdiction of the Ministry of the Interior (autumn 1953) and divided into two separate sections: the Internal Security Organ of the Ministry of the Interior, and the Frontier Guard of the Ministry of the Interior.

Units of the AVH are composed of both professional and recruited personnel. Upon the expiration of three years of service, recruited personnel may re-enlist or apply for acceptance into the professional corps. While the Frontier Guard units are composed almost entirely of recruited personnel, the officers and some noncommissioned officers belong to the professional corps. The chief of the AVH is the deciding authority on appointment of all personnel.

The uniforms and ranks of the members of the AVH correspond to those of the armed forces. In order to distinguish the members belonging to the two formations, the personnel of the AVH are required to wear special identifying insignia. Those serving in the units of the internal security services must wear a blue ribbon around their peaked caps and blue shoulder straps. From a structural and functional point of view, the AVH is divided into 17 divisions. Each division has well-defined tasks to perform. The primary function of the First Division is the general direction of internal political life. At first, it concerned itself with the elimination of opposition parties by planting subversive elements in their midst. With this task fulfilled, it now concentrates on maintaining a "vigilant" lookout against all dangers to the regime from within and without the Party. This division also handles the reports regularly submitted by the local offices of the AVH.

The Second Division deals with the surveillance of foreigners, both diplomats and private citizens. It keeps a close check on their contacts for possible later use in fabricating spy charges, and severely curtails their freedom of movement.

The Third Division has control over religious affairs, which it maintains through infiltration of ecclesiastical institutions and through regular attendance of religious services by informers. Minutes taken at sermons and signed by Party witnesses are transmitted to this section as a matter of routine.

The Fourth Division is entrusted with the task of transforming all youth organizations along Communist lines.

The Fifth Division's main concern is the infiltration and surveillance of high-ranking officers' groups and of remnants of the former aristocracy.

The Sixth Division keeps a close check on the ministries by means of informers within each ministry who are in a position to ascertain whether Party policies are being followed faithfully.

The Seventh Division investigates suspicious elements referred to it by the other divisions.

The Eighth Division deals with cases based on denunciations and thus is the secret police in the eyes of the general public. Prosecution of former Arrow Cross members, volkbundists, and war criminals rests with this division.

The Ninth Division supervises the activities of social organizations, keeps secret files on all political and Party figures (these files contain, among other material, detailed biographical data with special emphasis on transgressions, minor criminal activities, and sex deviations) and handles the installation of hidden microphones and recorders, operation of photographic laboratories, etc.

The Tenth Division is the depository of records of all former Nazis, Arrow Cross members, volkbundists, and other members of former rightist parties.

The Eleventh Division supplements the work of the Eighth Division.

The Twelfth Division handles the economic and transportation affairs of the secret police.

The Thirteenth Division is in charge of passports (before November 1946 these were under the jurisdiction of the Budapest Central Police Authority). One of the men at the head of this division, Antal Weller, was in the service of the MVD for over ten years.

The Fourteenth Division deals with secret police organizational and personnel matters, including all disciplinary problems.

The Fifteenth Division, the so-called "invisible division," arranges security measures on behalf of the President of the People's Republic and of the Cabinet ministers.

The Sixteenth Division, under which all 17 District Committees of Greater Budapest operate, may be considered the eyes and ears of the AVH. It directs infiltration and supervision of all social, political, and ecclesiastical organizations, educational and scientific institutions, and centers of amusement and entertainment.

The Seventeenth Division is entrusted with preventing economic sabotage and is given considerable latitude in the interpretation of this mission. It works closely with the different economic ministries supervising the fulfillment of the economic plans.

Material concerning the strength and composition of the AVH is virtually nonexistent. Unofficial sources, however, reveal that at the time of the merger of the AVH with the Frontier Guard units, the latter were composed of 15 battalions which were to be reorganized along with the reorganization of the Hungarian armed forces. The job was entrusted to a certain Laszlo Piros, whose first concern was purging the ranks of unreliable elements and their replacement with faithful servants of the regime.

The problem of recruiting the new officer corps was eventually solved through the establishment in Budapest of a new military academy named after Marshal Voroshilov. This school, operating entirely under Soviet methods, is geared to graduate about 200 candidates annually. While two-thirds of those completing a two-year course are commissioned with regular units of the secret police, the remaining third receives further training for intelligence and counterintelligence work.

An examination of eyewitness accounts by escapees reveals that the discipline within secret police units is quite good. There have been relatively few instances of unorthodox behavior and few defections to the West.

The terror seems to have eased somewhat in the post-Stalin period. Though security measures have been taken to assure the continuance of the regime, two official amnesty orders were issued in April 1955 (one relating to those imprisoned or accused inside the country, the other pertaining to exiles). This is the fifth amnesty granted by the regime since 1945, but its importance is emphasized by the fact that it is the first one to relate to political, rather than criminal prisoners. According to *Szabad Nep* of April 3, 1955, it calls for the

> . . . cancellation of punishment and abandonment of criminal proceedings against those who did not take a leading position in the reactionary regime before the liberation, and who, it may be supposed, will become useful working members of our society when amnestied. These persons will be amnestied for criminal acts against the State regardless of the degree of punishment, provided that they did not act with hostile intent or were obviously influenced by delusive hostile propaganda. The amnesty will also be extended, under certain restricting conditions, to other criminal acts of a general nature, as well as to criminal acts of a military character, provided that the person involved was not sentenced to more than one year in prison, or if it may be presumed that a prospective sentence will not extend to a longer period.

As a result of this amnesty and especially following the implementation of the directives of the Twentieth Congress of the Communist Party of the Soviet Union regarding the question of the "personality cult," scores of political prisoners were released and/or rehabilitated, in some cases posthumously. Among these were many high-ranking church officials (Jozsef Groesz), Social Democrats (Anna Kethley, Arpad Szakasits, Gyorgy Marosan), and Communists (Laszlo Rajk, Janos Kadar, Gyula Kallai). According to the Minister of Justice, Erik Molnar, about 11,398 persons had been released from prison by a "rehabilitation commission" appointed early in 1956.

Simultaneously with the easing of police terror, a revolt, hitherto confined to the intellectuals, has become discernible. At the meeting of the Petofi Youth Club on June 27, 1956, Tibor Dery, a writer, publicly demanded that " an end be made of this present regime of gendarmes and bureaucrats." Though such an expression of "freedom" could not have taken place earlier, the regime seems to have the situation under control. The leaders of the intellectual revolt, Tibor Dery, Tibor Tardos, and Sandor Lukacsi, have been, along with 164 other members, expelled from the Communist Party. The tightening of curbs has been more apparent since the unsuccessful revolt of the workers at Poznan, Poland. Indeed, in his outline of the program for the Party, Erno Gero, the new Prime Minister succeeding Rakosi on July 18, 1956 declared "while Hungary still has its enemies, there will be 'no second

Poznan' here." The Hungarian government has taken precautionary measures and instructed the authorities and Party leaders "decisively and firmly to combat all attempts aimed at dissolution of the structure of the state and loosening of the discipline of its citizens."

The Paramilitary Organization

Like all totalitarian regimes, the government of the People's Republic of Hungary places special emphasis on the development of youth and paramilitary organizations. Though the organization of the Hungarian youth was rather haphazard in 1945, the Communists succeeded in obtaining the concurrence of the Soviet occupation forces in organizing a small group, the Guerrilla Association, under the leadership of Sandor Nogrady, who later became State Secretary in the Ministry of Defense. In the course of its short but eventful existence, total membership never exceeded 400 to 500. In 1946, the Guerrilla Friends' Association was founded, ostensibly to serve as a nonpartisan organization for the young masses of Hungary. Functionally, however, it was tightly connected with the Guerrilla Association, both having their administrative offices in the same building. The Guerrilla Friends' Association was placed under the direction of General Laszlo Solyom, who was unsuccessful in impressing upon the country the supposed nonpartisan character of the organization, both organizations were dissolved and incorporated into the Association of Hungarian Fighters for Freedom early in 1950, under the leadership of Sandor Nogrady. The aims of the new organization were revealed by one of its former secretary-generals, Istvan Kenez: "We have to train the working masses, and above all the hundreds of thousands of youths, in a Communist spirit, consciousness, and discipline. We teach them sports which make them tough, healthy, and rugged. We also aim at the participation of the individual farmer. In this way, we shall have a well-trained, reliable reserve organization for the People's Army."

In the same year, the Ready for Work and Fight (MHK) sports organization was established on the pattern of the Soviet Ready for Work and Fight organization. The MHK is founded on two broad principles: the building of a physically and spiritually healthy youth capable of fulfilling any obligation toward the "Socialist motherland"; and "applicability," e.g., the development of those branches of sport and physical education the benefits of which could easily be applied to the "building of socialism and defense of the country." Though participation in the activities of the MHK is allegedly "voluntary," every healthy and physically able boy and girl at the age of 12 becomes a member. (Those under 12 belong to the Pioneer movement.)

From a structural point of view, the MHK is organized into four groups: those between the ages of 12 and 14 belong to the "LMHK preparatory group"; those between the ages of 14 to 16 belong to the "LMHK satisfactory and exceptional group"; those who have reached 17 years of age belong to the "MHK I"; and, finally, those who have reached 18, to "MHK II." Effort and enthusiasm for the work within the MHK is maintained through the periodic distribution of achievement medals—an incentive heavily relied on in every totalitarian country.

The official booklet of the MHK, a source of directives for the leading personnel, emphasizes that the standard-bearer of the organization is the Hungarian version of the Russian Komsomol, the Federation of Working Youth (DISZ). Consequently, the leadership of the MHK organizations is composed almost entirely of DISZ members, who are under the immediate control of the Party. Particular stress is laid on the propaganda and "enlightening" work of the DISZ within the student bodies of institutions of higher learning where, theoretically, only those in the first and second academic years are obliged to take physical education.

Although those in their last years of studies are formally exempt from participation in the MHK, a Cabinet Decree (No. 285 of 1950 M.T.) provides for extramilitary training of every student. This training was begun with the spring semester of 1951, primarily to bolster the officers' reserve corps and to broaden the strata of military specialists. Chairs of military education were established by the Minister of Defense. Participation in these military courses is obligatory for all male students as well as for those girls registered in the faculties of medicine and pharmacy. In the course of training, each student must participate in military maneuvers lasting for six months, which can later be counted toward the completion of the requirements of regular military service. Upon successful completion of the course, participants are placed in the reserve with the rank of lieutenant.

The People's Army

The history of the transformation of the Hungarian Army into one of the most formidably equipped and best-trained forces within the Soviet orbit can be traced back to World War I. Hungarian prisoners of war caught in the turmoil of the Russian Revolution were exposed to the gigantic transformation taking place in that country, and some were converted by the revolutionary idea. Upon their return to Hungary, they helped to establish the short-lived Hungarian Soviet under Bela Kun's leadership. Upon the collapse of the Communist dictatorship in 1919, many of these men left Hungary for the Soviet Union, to return again with the victorious Soviet Army in 1944-45.

Under the Hungarian Constitution of the interwar period, the Army was directly subordinate to the head of the state in his capacity as Commander in Chief. While all practical military matters were handled by the Chief of Staff, the Minister of Defense, through his presence in the Cabinet, assured the Army's legitimate place in the constitutional and parliamentary system.

The idea of a nonpolitical army prevailed more or less successfully during the first fifteen years of Horthy's regime. With the gradual deterioration of the international situation and the growing influence of Nazi Germany, especially when Gombos was Prime Minister, the Army became more and more important as a factor in political life. This trend was enhanced by the fact that Germany offered the possibility of revising the provisions of the Treaty of Trianon, by which Hungary had been deprived of much territory. The officer corps as a whole craved *revanche* and was solidly opposed to any form of parliamentary democracy. It was among them that the signs of Nazi German influence first began to appear. Under a political climate favoring the preponderance of the military in government affairs, Hungary was finally drawn into the war against Yugoslavia and the Soviet Union.

The military contribution of the Hungarian Army during World War II was negligible and was more important to the Nazi war machine from the psychological and propaganda viewpoints than from the military. The only real battle in which the Hungarian Army engaged was that of Voronezh in 1942/43. Placed under the supervision of the German Second Army led by General Weichs, the Hungarian Second Army was assigned to defend on the Don a 200-kilometer line extending from Voronezh to Pavlovsk. The Hungarian Army composed of about 54 battalions with no reserves and lacking the support of tanks or planes, was rather ill equipped for this task. In the cold Russian winter, the mechanism and lubricants of the machine guns became unserviceable, and the soldiers suffered badly, as their clothing and footwear were not adequate. Sandwiched between the German Army and the Italian Expeditionary Force, the Hungarian Army lost some 90 per cent of its heavy equipment and 50 per cent of its manpower during the Russian offensive of January 1943. Retired to the Kiev area after the battle of Voronezh, the Hungarian Army was not engaged again in any significant military operations and was used primarily for policing behind the lines.

With the final surrender of Hungary early in 1945, the Soviet occupying authorities found a greatly disorganized and widely dispersed army, which they placed under the command of Janos Veres, Minister of Defense in the newly established government. As a former Chief of Staff under the Horthy regime, Veres was greatly compromised and thus ineffective against Russian demands, for the specter of arrest always haunted him.

In the wake of the Soviet Army came a small but well-indoctrinated, thoroughly trained group of Hungarian Communists who had spent the interwar and wartime period in the Soviet Union, eager to acquire power with the aid of the Soviet occupation forces and to transform Hungary into a people's democracy. Changing the Hungarian Army into an effective and reliable tool of Communist power was high on the Party timetable. As early as 1945, the Communists succeeded through the direct intervention of Voroshilov in introducing two innovations facilitating their program.

One of these was the introduction of the Soviet-style "politruk" system, under which a "political instructor" was assigned to every military commander. These political instructors were entrusted with considerable power. Their primary function was to enforce Party directives and to see that the interests of the "working people" were faithfully observed within the army units. The first group of politruks was brought along with the Soviet occupation forces under the command of a Hungarian military deserter called Janossi. Their number was rather small at the beginning, but the Communists quickly trained reliable cadres.

The second step was setting up special committees to evaluate the reliability and political behavior of every officer and officer candidate. Each committee was composed of six members, four of them representing the four government parties, one a representative of the trade unions, and one a representative of the Ministry of Defense.

The work of these committees was greatly influenced by Russian assistance. The Party's representative in supervising the work of these committees was Geza Revesz, the son of a former Hungarian POW and a Russian peasant woman. A Soviet citizen with the rank of lieutenant colonel in the Soviet Army, Revesz enjoyed the confidence of the Russians. Under his "guidance" only those officers and officer candidates received a clean bill of health who professed themselves Communists or Communist sympathizers. After he had completed this assignment, the Russians forced Revesz on the Hungarian Army, which had to accept him with the rank of general.

Through the direct aid of the Soviet occupation authorities, the Party managed gradually to infiltrate the Ministry of Defense with some trusted members. Among these were Palffy-Oesterreicher, who later became chief of the political division of the Ministry of Defense; General Radvanyi, also a "Muscovite," who was given among other duties, the assignment to attend the political audiences of the Minister of Defense, especially the ones granted to the British and American members of the Allied Control Commission; Gusztav Illy, a Moscow-trained general who was named head of the personnel division, and as such was in a position to supervise military assignments.

While the cleansing of the military apparatus was initially undertaken by the committees operating under the "guidance" of Geza Revesz, systematic purging of unreliable elements was entrusted to General Palffy-Oesterreicher. Though the methods employed were not lenient, the officers' corps continued to harbor what the Communists called many "undesirable elements" at the time of the army's reorganization along Soviet lines. In fact, in his report to the Communist Party Congress in 1948, Palffy-Oesterreicher had the following to say on the purges:

> Though we have almost completely removed the openly reactionary and inimical elements in the officers' corps, we know that there are still many opportunists who continue to serve the present regime without inner conviction. There are others who hide behind a democratic mask, pretending to be just career officers. Those who hide their destructive purposes and hostile activities are even more dangerous. To unmask and remove these, an active and vigilant fight continues within the army.

A year later Palffy-Oesterreicher and his closest collaborators in the Ministry of Defense were eliminated and executed as Titoists.

As time went on, the officers' corps was gradually filled with reliable Party members of peasant or proletarian stock. The number of officers trained by the Communists is estimated at 15,000. Of these, according to General Istvan Bata (*Szabad Nep*, May 27, 1954), 52.8 per cent are of "proletarian" and 25 per cent of peasant descent. Fifty-two per cent of the generals are from the working class and 21 per cent from the peasantry. Eager to preserve their positions of prestige and power, barring any unforeseen political complications, they are unlikely to cause any trouble to the Party leadership.

Party control over the Army is maintained by a complex but integrated system of two parallel hierarchies operating independently of the military command. These are the organs of the Party and of the AVH attached to every regular army unit. While the primary aim of the former is to indoctrinate the military personnel with a spirit of devotion to the Party, the latter's function is to root out disaffection and disloyalty in the Army. Every Communist serving in the Army is a member of a Party cell and subject to Party discipline. The political work of indoctrination and agitation within the units of the armed forces is performed under the guidance and supervision of the Main Political Section of the Hungarian People's Army representing the Central Committee. Political organs within the Army are expected to maintain close contact with the Party committees of the districts in which they are stationed.

The political indoctrination of a soldier begins with his arrival at the military camp and continues throughout his army career. The nature and content of the daily two-hour lectures vary in accordance with the domestic or international climate. Attendance, although theoretically voluntary, is in fact obligatory, since the names of those absent and present are marked by Party representatives. The process of indoctrination is further carried out by continuous propaganda, "wall newspapers," posters, libraries, radio, and other media of communication. While the bulk of the political work is performed by the Party and DISZ members in the Army, the regular courses are conducted by graduates of the Rakoczi II Military Academy at Huvosvolgy.

The reorganization of the Hungarian armed forces was begun early in 1948. The integration of the new People's Army into the framework of the Soviet-controlled captive armies was facilitated by its structural transformation along the Soviet model. The uniform, rank insignia, training, military formations, etc. were changed to correspond to their equivalents in the Soviet Army. Knowledge of Russian is becoming an essential requirement for every officer and noncommissioned officer as the military terminology and instruction are adapted to those of the Soviet Union.

Though the Military and Air Clauses (Part III) of the Peace Treaties of 1947 restricted the size and striking power of the Hungarian armed forces to "meeting tasks of an internal character and local defense of frontiers," the present People's Army greatly exceeds these limitations. Article 12 envisaged a land army of 65,000 and an air force of 5,000 men, including "combat, service and administrative personnel." The Hungarian Army and Air Force was also restricted from engaging in military training or military air training (Article 14) for combat purposes.

Though data regarding the size and structure of the Hungarian People's Army are few, close scrutiny of available information provides the following picture.

The armed forces of the People's Republic of Hungary now consist of a Land Army, the Air Force, and the Danube Flotilla. All three branches of the armed forces are subordinated to the Ministry of Defense, which is now headed by General Istvan Bata. Like his predecessor, Mihaly Farkas, Bata is a Soviet citizen. He plays the same role in Hungary as Marshal Rokossowski in Poland. The head of the Air Force, Lieutenant General Sandor Hazi, and Chief of Staff Istvan Toth are also Soviet citizens.

Recruiting is done on the basis of the Military Law of 1939. Liability for military service begins at the age twenty and lasts until the sixtieth birthday. Selection of recruits in all four military districts in which the country is divided (Budapest, Pecs, Szeged, and Debrecen) is done by a mixed commission composed of military officers and Party representatives. Military service lasts for three years, and each year a new age group is called to the colors, representing about 0.75 per cent of the total population of 9,700,000. This means that the total active military personnel is about 240,000-255,000, as career and noncommissioned officers and the active reserves must be added to the 210,000-225,000 draftees. It is thus the largest army Hungary has ever had in time of peace.

According to reliable reports, early in 1954 the Army was composed of 9 infantry divisions, 2 modern mechanized divisions grouped into a mechanized corps with headquarters in Budapest, 4 artillery brigades, 9 antiaircraft brigades, 4 combat engineer brigades, 1 paratroop brigade, 1 quartermaster brigade, 1 cavalry regiment, 1 intelligence regiment, and 1 ABC battalion. These units are grouped into three army corps. Imitating the structural organizaton of the Soviet Army, each division consists of 12,000 men grouped into 3 infantry regiments, 2 or 3 field artillery battalions, and a few technical units.

The Air Force is composed of 4 fighter squadrons and the nucleus of a bombers' group. Strength is about 550 planes of the old JAK-9 and of the newer MIG-15 types.

The primary purpose of the Danube Flotilla is to support the Land Army in battles along the river. In 1954, it consisted of 2 ship divisions, 2 mine-laying battalions, 3 river-bank-protecting battalions, 1 training battalion, 1 wharf battalion, and of several "swimmers' units."

While the potential of the regular army units is being constantly improved, the government also devotes resources to atomic energy. One of the most modern atomic laboratories in Central Europe is the Central Physics Research Laboratory near Budapest, headed by Dr. Istvan Kovacs. Although data regarding the type and scope of the atomic research now being conducted is unavailable, in the light of prevailing political realities it is safe to assume that this research is under strict Soviet supervision.

The Hungarian People's Army is an instrument in the hands of the Party leadership for the perpetuation of its power and of the dictatorship. In fact, some high-ranking officers occupy leading positions in the Party hierarchy and ensure that the Army faithfully follows the dictates of the Party. Military personnel are constantly reminded that the Army is an offspring of the Party and must operate within the framework of rules and regulations set up by the Party leadership.

8. PROPAGANDA AND INFORMATION MEDIA

Pre-Communist Propaganda—Its Nature and Techniques

Hungarian propaganda between the two world wars, although largely officially inspired, was not under complete government control. The most universal interwar propaganda themes in Hungary were opposition to the Trianon Peace Treaty (June 4, 1920), under the terms of which Hungary lost about 63.5 per cent of its prewar population and 71.4 per cent of its territory; accusations that the Hungarian minority populations in the successor states (Czechoslovakia, Romania, and Yugoslavia) were being persecuted, and disavowals of outside protestations that Hungary was treating its national minorities unjustly. A typical indication of government encouragement of such propaganda was its sanction on the play-on-words interpretation of Trianon as the "three noes"; virtually all Hungarian children, for example, had to express organized opposition to the 1920 treaty by shouting *"nem, nem, soha"* (No, No, Never) at the beginning of each school day.

The principal domestic propaganda medium in Hungary (until the end of World War II) was the press. Hungarian propaganda abroad was conducted chiefly through periodicals and other publications. Educational and cultural exchanges were also designed to arouse favorable interest in and sympathy toward Hungary. Radio was the second most important domestic medium, the primary broadcast targets across the borders being the Hungarian minorities in neighboring states.

The Press

Because of Hungary's size, virtually all important newspapers were published in Budapest; the larger towns and communities had their own newspapers, but none were of political importance, with the possible exception of *Ellenzek* (Opposition) of Kolozsvar (now Cluj). Even during the identification of Hungary's interests with the Axis (until the German occupation on March 20, 1944), the Hungarian press was the most diverse and interesting in southeastern Europe and

151

had a wide reputation throughout the Continent. Hungarian newspapers had world-wide news coverage and, unlike the press of other
Axis and occupied countries, were sponsored by a wide cross section
of political interests and hence represented a broad range of opinions.
At the end of 1942, 101 daily newspapers and 1,278 periodicals were
officially registered. Despite modifying factors, the government and
government party exerted a controlling influence over the press and
other media of communication.

The press was only superficially independent, and its license to
engage in free debate was limited. The regime had various methods
for keeping newspapers within bounds. The Ministry of the Interior,
for example, was authorized to proscribe or suspend any publication
detrimental to the government or the "national" cause. In addition, a
censorship board which included representatives of all the ministries
was established to screen all material prior to publication. The press,
through a decree of October 25, 1942, was obliged to publish speeches
and statements by Cabinet ministers "in a prescribed way"; the government could prescribe the time of publication, position in the paper,
and even the type used. Still another government weapon was the
"press fund," for which it did not have to account to Parliament; even
the Social Democratic daily, *Nepszava* (People's Voice), was believed
generously subsidized from this fund. Moreover, the Hungarian Telegraphic Office, upon which the press was dependent for news, was an
official agency. Finally, the government exercised control over the
supply of newsprint.

Prior to the occupation in March 1944, the Hungarian press could
be divided into nine major categories: (1) Government; exemplified
by *Pester Lloyd*, a German-language daily, nominally independent, but
known as the government mouthpiece in foreign and domestic affairs;
most of the time it was subsidized by the government. (2) Right-wing;
Uj Magyarsag (New Hungarianism), a daily representing the extreme
right of the government party; its views were extremely pro-German,
anti-Allied, and anti-Semitic, and it received large German subventions.
(3) Right of center; *Pesti Hirlap* (Pest Journal) an independent,
strongly nationalist paper, with liberal traditions; while it expounded
territorial revisionism, it was principally a news organ, usually in accord with government policies. (4) Catholic; the two chief Catholic
papers were the *Nemzeti Ujsag* (National Newspaper) and *Uj Nemzedek* (New Generation); they expressed the point of view of organized
Catholic opinion in Hungary, which was not always identical with that
of the regime. In foreign affairs, for example, they were distinctly less
pro-German than the government press. In domestic affairs, they repre-

sented strong conservative paternalism. (5) Left of center; *Magyar Nemzet* (Hungarian Nation), the principal independent paper. It had a much higher journalistic standard than any other paper and was highly intellectual in tone. It supported the united opposition coalition and, until the German occupation, it remained the chief expression of pro-British opinion in Hungary. It was especially renowned for its economic, sociological, and historical articles. (6) Liberal; *Esti Kurir* (Evening Courier) was the organ of Dr. Karoly Rassay, the leading member of the parliamentary liberal party (Citizens' Freedom Party) and had an especial appeal for middle-class Jews. (7) Social Democratic; *Nepszava* (People's Voice) was the organ of the Social Democrats and printed contributions from all prominent party members. It carried regular reports of trade union meetings and articles on labor law, labor conditions, etc.; it also concerned itself with agricultural problems, particularly those of agricultural laborers. By the time of the occupation, the quality of *Nepszava* articles rivaled those of *Magyar Nemzet*. (As to the other democratic opposition parties, the Smallholders' Party published a semi-official daily, *Kis Ujsag* [Little Journal], while the National Peasant Party had a weekly paper called *Szabad Szo* [Free Word].) (8) Nazi; *Magyarsag* (Hungarianism) and the weekly *Magyarsag Utja* (The Road to Hungarianism) represented the Nazi Arrow Cross point of view. The latter was banned in March 1943. (9) Minority; *Deutsche Zeitung*, which published just a rehash of German propaganda, often reprinting entire articles from the German press. Its domestic news contained mostly details of the local *Volksbund* organization and speeches by *Volksbund* leaders. Papers for the Slav minorities were published by the government. The principal ones were: Serb, *Nova Posta* (Latest News) and *Nase Novine* (Our Press); Croat, *Nova Madjarska* (New Hungary); and Slovak, *Slovenska Jednota* (Slovenian Unity) and *Slovenske Noviny* (Slovenian Press).

Radio

The Hungarian Broadcasting Company, though nominally an independent monopoly not under direct government control, by 1943 had come under the strict supervision of the Ministry of Propaganda, and its director, Antal Naray, was also the director of the official Hungarian Telegraphic Office.

According to official statistics, the number of license-holders for radio receivers rose from 748,000 to 822,000 between March 1942 and

March 1943. At the beginning of 1942, the Post Office issued a questionnaire to all subscribers as to listening habits. A breakdown of the replies indicated that 44.7 per cent listened to Budapest transmissions two hours a day or less, 33.6 per cent two to four hours, and 21.7 cent more than four hours; 43.7 per cent reported listening regularly to foreign broadcasts.

The principal radio station was in Budapest (Budapest I); its broadcast strength was 120 kilowatts. Another Budapest station and six regional transmitting stations of lesser power supplemented Budapest I.

THE NATURE AND EFFECTIVENESS OF COMMUNIST PROPAGANDA

Propaganda is a major concern of Party and government officials in Communist Hungary—as in all Soviet orbit countries. Many policy decisions in Communist states reflect consideration of their propaganda effect internally and/or externally; in some decisions, propaganda effect is the chief, and sometimes even the sole, consideration involved. Party control embraces all media of communication, all government agencies dealing with propaganda, and all so-called mass organizations.

The principal Party propaganda agency is the Agitation and Propaganda Section, which is subordinate to the Central Committee and exercises direction of Hungarian propaganda at home and abroad. Communist use of the terms "agitation and propaganda" reflects an early theoretical formulation of the difference between the two terms: "A propagandist presents many ideas to one or a few persons; an agitator presents only one or a few ideas, but he presents them to a mass of people." In other words, propaganda is allegedly on a higher, more complex level and is meant to appeal to intellectuals, while agitation is on a less sophisticated level and is meant to appeal to the nonintellectual stratum of society. Except when quoting Communist sources, this technical distinction will not be taken into account, and the term "propaganda" will be used exclusively.

The most striking feature of Communist propaganda is its all-pervasiveness. When the Communists undertook a drive against "cosmopolitanism," for example, it was reflected in the arts, in the revision of history and other textbooks, in the press, on the radio, in films, etc., by emphasizing Hungarian national achievements and by removing all favorable references to other than Soviet foreign influences on Hungary. In this way, virtually all activities are forced within the framework of current Party propaganda and most persons are obliged to participate. There is a tendency, furthermore, to inject personalities into propaganda issues, apparently in order to polarize thoughts and actions for or against the regime. The not infrequent changes of Party propaganda line are usually accompanied by bitter denunciation of persons identified with the rejected line; such persons are usually forced to make a servile public recantation of their alleged errors and in many cases are purged.

The dissemination of domestic propaganda is facilitated by the relatively high literacy rate enjoyed by Hungary. This is significant because of the relative importance ascribed to printed media by Communists; the press is still the principal instrument of propaganda.

Hungarian Communist propaganda since World War II has tried primarily to induce the Hungarian people to accept the Soviet Union as friend, leader, and model and to participate vigorously in the economic and political policies advanced by the Party. During the period of June 1953—January 1955, a significant portion of Party propaganda centered also upon the "new course," the alleged purpose of which was to reduce political tensions and raise the living standards of the Hungarian populace. Currently, there seems to be a reversion to "Leninism" under which there has been a switch to "collective leadership" from the discredited Stalinist "cult of personality." In Hungary, this has resulted in Rakosi's resignation as First Secretary of the Party.

Hungary also participates in the Soviet propaganda attack against countries outside the Soviet orbit. Because of the practical difficulties encountered in dealing with unfriendly governments, the Communist countries have selected radio as their principal medium for propaganda abroad. In addition to assuming such Soviet propaganda objectives as fostering disunity and doubt in the West through fear of Germany and suspicion of the United States, Hungarian efforts have been directed toward convincing foreigners that Hungary is an independent and prosperous nation of happy people making "wondrous strides" toward abundance. Efforts are made also to convince Hungarian émigrés to return to Hungary or to act as spokesmen for the current regime.

The propaganda apparatus of the Hungarian Workers' Party has had to cope with a formidable barrier in attempting to win support for Communist rule from the people of Hungary, the overwhelming majority of whom are non-Slavic and non-Orthodox in national and religious origin and anti-Communist by tradition. The effectiveness of Party propaganda has in fact been very limited, despite more than seven years of undisputed control. While Communist press and radio propaganda, through constant repetition and full exploitation of monopoly control, has undoubtedly affected the thought patterns of even the most anti-Communist elements of Hungarian society, it is nevertheless generally regarded with boredom and indifference by the population. Most Hungarians have a higher regard for the accuracy of news items emanating from Western broadcasters than for those found or heard in the domestic press and radio. One Western observer, known for his objective and reliable reporting, recently noted that practically no one in Hungary takes seriously the controlled official press and radio, and went so far as to say that Hungarian opinion on both domestic and foreign affairs is formed in the editorial offices of foreign broadcasters.

That Hungarian film techniques, among the most highly developed in Europe before World War II, now leave much to be desired was revealed in a general critique of Hungarian films by Tibor Meray, *Szabad Nep* correspondent, entitled "The Film as an Independent Art." In it, he complained that film production was reduced to the status of "a branch of literature and a species of theater-playing. The film is an independent art . . . [which] has its own artistic peculiarities. . . ." Nevertheless, according to Meray, Hungarian films are characterized among other things by too much verbiage, schematicism, superficial depiction of personality and human nature, and overdramatization.

The Communists' propaganda failure is reflected in the grave Hungarian domestic crisis, which is a direct result of the passive resistance of a hostile populace. The failure of Hungarian propaganda abroad is reflected in the widespread disbelief and antagonism of foreigners and Hungarian emigrants, although it achieves some limited successes, particularly among the so-called colonial peoples and in some neutralist countries.

Content and Techniques of Communist Propaganda

The principal propaganda theme in Hungary since 1949 has been homage to the Soviet Union, expressed mainly as gratitude to the Soviet Union for "liberating" Hungary, for setting an example of "socialism," for leading the so-called fight for peace and for providing "generous" economic and technical assistance. Other recurrent propaganda themes include optimistic appraisals of the results of various social and economic programs; decadence of the West in general and hatred for the United States in particular; the class struggle against alleged exploiting elements, especially kulaks; exhortations to workers and peasants to increase the quantity and improve the quality of production; attacks on "clerical reaction" (i.e., religion); superiority of the Communist way of life over that of the non-Communist; and vituperative denunciation of recalcitrant "enemies of the people."

In addition to these relatively permanent themes, new ones are introduced from time to time to meet current needs. A feature of Hungarian propaganda between July 1953 and December 1954, for example, was the "new economic policy" or "new course" inaugurated by the Prime Minister, Imre Nagy. This new policy seems to have been motivated at least as much by propaganda as by other considerations. Popular morale had reached such a low ebb by the spring and summer of 1953 as to lead to widespread passive resistance, which in turn resulted in serious economic, social, and political strains. The main features of the program were promises to change the degree and emphasis from heavy industrial to consumer goods production, and concessions to peasants, including permission for free withdrawal from collective farms. There were also promises of more tolerance in religion, more regard for legal rights, and abolition of certain offensive arbitrary measures. At the end of 1954, however, there were indications that the "new course" line would be replaced by more orthodox Communist propaganda. By March 1955, Prime Minister Imre Nagy, the Hungarian official most closely identified with the "new course," was being denounced as the leader of a "right-wing deviationist" group in Hungary. It is notable that Rakosi's withdrawal from leadership on July 18, 1956 does not seem to have changed Nagy's position. Neither has there been any "rehabiliation" in this case.

The chief characteristic of Hungarian newspapers and radio programs today is their tendentiousness; this was only slightly moderated under the impetus of the "new course." Agricultural and industrial production records and competitions are featured in newspapers and on radio programs to arouse interest in these matters. Considerable space is given to reporting and commenting upon Soviet internal developments and foreign policy. News items on non-Communist countries are selected to fit the pattern of current Soviet policy. Frequent articles give invidious descriptions of the policies and practices of the Western world and pre-World War II Hungary; life under these non-Communist systems is painted in the darkest terms. Even the sports page frequently attributes Hungarian athletic achievements to communism.

Hungarian films come within the framework of Communist theory on art, which eschews "art for art's sake." Under this concept, all artistic works, including motion pictures, literature, and painting, must "educate" (i.e., indoctrinate) as well as entertain. Under the impact of the "new course," this tendency was toned down, but present indications are that this was only a breathing spell. Even during the relatively liberal "new course" period, motion pictures were imbued with propaganda. A typical example was the film *The Symbol of Life*, which is based on the story of a successful Hungarian mine rescue operation in December 1952. A review of the film in *Szabad Nep* of September 5, 1954 included the following passage:

> A genuine passion and flame permeate this film which speaks courageously and with deep dramatic force about our life. It says that in present-day Hungary a man's life is dear, that the entire people was mobilized to save the lives of the endangered miners. It is a heroic romantic epic, the heroic epic of solidarity. Its pathos strikes roots in our new life which is fed by socialist humanism.

Another important consideration in gauging the propaganda aspect of Hungarian films is the extent of Soviet guidance of the Hungarian film industry. For example, *Magyar Nemzet* on June 27, 1954 carried an article by Erno Mihalyfi, Deputy Minister of People's Culture, under the heading "Moscow Debate on the New Hungarian Films." He reported the "debate" by 50 "outstanding" film directors, cameramen, critics, and writers before a visiting Hungarian movie delegation. The Soviet group critically reviewed current Hungarian film productions, including *The Symbol of Life*, which had not yet been shown in Hungary. Mihalyfi noted that "the members of the Hungarian delegation listened happily to the [Soviet] words of appreciation and gratefully accepted the extraordinarily valuable guiding diagnoses."

Propaganda is disseminated mainly through the Party, government, and mass organizations; the propaganda machinery, however, is completely controlled by the Party.

Party

Propaganda lines are formulated by the leaders of the Hungarian Workers' Party, which in turn are guided by Soviet propaganda policies. The Party assures its dominance over public, and to a large extent private, expression in Hungary by utilizing its monolithic power status to place its members in positions of control over the various government propaganda agencies, communication media, and non-Party mass organizations. The Agitation and Propaganda Section of the Party's Central Committee administers the Party propaganda apparatus and supervises the government and mass organizational propaganda networks and media.

The Propaganda Section maintains close liaison with the editorial committees of the central Party newspaper, *Szabad Nep* (Free People), and Party periodicals. The Party's highest level publication is *Tarsadalmi Szemle* (Social Review), a theoretical monthly. It contains articles on current events and theoretical, historical, and philosophical matters, as well as book reviews and critiques of other Party publications; typical recent topics included the United States elections in 1956, problems of Party work in agricultural cooperatives, documents on the birth of the Hungarian "people's democracy," and Lenin's philosophical works. Another monthly, *Partepites* (Party Building), deals with Party organizational problems, political agitation, and Party training. *Partifoiskola* (Party College) is a publication for students, the purpose of which is officially described as overcoming errors and shortcomings through the use of criticism and self-criticism. In addition, the Agitation and Propaganda Section publishes three monthlies under its own sponsorship: *Anyag es Adatszolgaltatas* (Material and Data Supply), *Propagandista* (Propagandist), and *Nepnevelo* (People's Educator). The purpose of the first is to provide guidance for agitation and indoctrination work. It includes translations of practical and theoretical material on communism, primarily from articles in Soviet newspapers and periodicals; typical articles are devoted to international problems, construction work in the Soviet Union and the captive countries, problems of Marxist-Leninist theory, Party work, art, and science. *Propagandista* serves as a practical guide and handbook for Party propaganda workers; it is supposed to clarify propaganda lines and summarize current domestic and foreign political events. *Nepnevelo* is a less sophisticated pocket-size guide published for people's educators (discussed below) and other Party officials. It contains answers to current political questions and provides suggestions for the practical exploitation of magazine articles and guidance for the evaluation of current events.

Party members are encouraged to study Party history, ideology, and policy by self-study or by enrollment in Party schools and lecture courses. A three-year Party college was opened on September 1, 1954. Two-year Party colleges and one-year, five-month, and three-month Party schools had been in operation for some time; the number of students attending these schools, however, has not been very large. At the Third Congress of the Party (May 24-30, 1954), it was revealed that of the 864,707 Party members, 3,203 were attending various Party schools. It was stated that between January 1951 and June 1954 a total of 356 members would have completed the two-year course and that an additional 263 were enrolled as corresponding students in the two-year colleges. Between June 1948 and June 1954, 593 members were either to complete or be in the process of completing one-year school terms, 4,988 members were to complete the five-month, and 15,822 the three-month terms. At the same time, it was claimed that over 400,000 persons—of whom 15 per cent were non-Party members —were participating in Party education outside schools (*Szabad Nep*, May 25, 1954).

People's educators, similar to agitators in the other captive countries and the Soviet Union, are Party members with intensive indoctrination in Party history, ideology, and current policy and probably some training in propaganda techniques. Their task is to disseminate Party propaganda, usually through personal presentation before small groups and even by ringing doorbells. In order to improve their effectiveness, they are supposed to become well versed in local economic and other peculiarities. People's educators are frequently assigned to convince recalcitrants, by persuasion or threat, to carry out unpopular Party directives, such as attempting to induce hostile peasants to deliver production quotas to the state collection depots.

Government

Government propaganda agencies are under the eye of the Party. On the central level, control is exercised by one of the subsections of the Central Committee's Agitation and Propaganda Section.

The most important government propaganda agency is the Ministry of People's Culture, which in 1949 was given operational authority over virtually all media, including the nation's press, radio, films, theaters, museums, libraries, art, music, and theater schools and academies. However, since the replacement of the Party's leading theoretician, Jozsef Revai, as Minister of People's Culture (apparently due to illness) in July 1953, the importance of the ministry has been declining. In any case, some of its powers have been transferred to the Information Bureau, which was formerly a department in the Ministry of People's Culture but is now directly attached to the Council of Ministers. No definition of its functions other than the cryptic announcement that its purpose is to "improve informational work" has been released.

The press is by far the most important medium of mass propaganda. As of February 1, 1953, 22 dailies and 88 weeklies were published with a total circulation of more than 3,000,000 copies. It is estimated that the total number of press publications comes close to 400, if fortnightlies, monthlies, and quarterlies are included. With respect to nonperiodical publications, it was officially announced that 2,750 books were published with a total press run of 20 million copies in 1954.

The principal and most widely read newspaper is the Party daily, *Szabad Nep*; all other newspapers take their lead from it. *Szabad Nep's* circulation is now about 800,000. Its current format, adopted August 20, 1952, is modeled after *Pravda,* the newspaper of the Communist Party of the Soviet Union. The high circulation figures for *Szabad Nep* may in part be attributed to the fact that it is required reading for all Party members; in addition many non-Party members are virtually forced to buy it at their places of work or in schools. The number of *Szabad Nep* readers, and to a lesser extent those of other papers, is supplemented by "captive" listeners required to attend daily sessions in school classes, factory shops, collective farms, and army barracks or tents, where *Szabad Nep* is read aloud; it is also read over the radio.

The top government agency dealing with the press, at least until recent times, was the Hungarian Telegraphic Office (MTI), which was placed under the Ministry of People's Culture in 1950. Its jurisdiction over the following functions may now be shared with or supplemented by the Information Bureau: (1) transmission of official and semi-official news information to the domestic and foreign press and the Radio Bureau (see below); (2) transmission to these agencies of production, cultural, and other news connected with the "construction of socialism"; (3) transmission of foreign news information to the press and Radio Bureau; and (4) development of the provincial news service.

The second most important Hungarian propaganda medium is the radio. In May 1954, 1,100,000 persons held radio ownership licenses, presumably including wired diffusion receivers (piped broadcasts) installed in individual apartments or homes. There are also public loud-speakers in houses, factories, public squares, cafeterias, post offices, etc. The loudspeakers are usually connected to a reception and diffusion center equipped with a powerful wireless receiving set, an amplifier, and a microphone. In 1954 there were over 250,000 wired diffusion receivers in Hungary; their production rate of about 7,000 a month is probably greater than in any other Soviet captive nation.

The functions of the Hungarian Radio Bureau, top government agency dealing with radio, may have been curtailed or supplemented by the Information Bureau; technical radio and other electronics matters are handled by the Ministry of Communications and Postal Affairs. The following functions were assigned to the Radio Bureau in 1950:

(1) to provide program material for radio and television broadcasting stations; (2) to provide and maintain technical broadcasting equipment in collaboration with the Minister of Communications and Postal Affairs; and (3) to provide wired speakers.

The motion picture is the third most important Hungarian propaganda medium. According to the 1954 budget, motion pictures (both 35 millimeter and 16 millimeter) were shown before a total audience of 68,400,000 in 1953, and this figure rose to about 98,000,000 in 1954. In 1953, the Hungarian film industry produced eight feature films; for 1954, it planned to produce ten feature films and six short ones. The National Film Bureau was organized to handle film matters in April 1948; its functions were transferred to the Ministry of People's Culture in October 1949. The Ministry of the Interior, however, is believed to have a hand in film censorship.

Another important propaganda device employed by the government is the institution of "cultural houses" on the regional level and "cultural homes" on the local level. Control over these cultural houses and homes is exercised by the Cultural Homes Department of the Ministry of People's Culture through the executive committees of the regional and local councils and competent organs of the enterprises or trade unions sponsoring them. They present various dramatic, concert, dance, lecture, and other cultural programs, heavily tinged with propaganda. There were 2,300 cultural homes in villages, cities, and factories in 1953.

Still another important propaganda agency is the Institute for Cultural Relations established in 1949 under the joint jurisdiction of the Ministries of People's Culture and Foreign Affairs. The functions of the Institute are related to its counterpart in the Soviet Union, the All-Union Society for Foreign Cultural Relations (VOKS), and presumably there is some form of cooperation with the permanent VOKS representative in Hungary. The functions of the Institute are as follows: (1) exposition and popularization of Hungarian culture abroad; (2) exposition and popularization of the culture of foreign peoples in Hungary; (3) aid in implementing foreign cultural agreements; and (4) sponsorship of delegations to scientific and artistic conferences. The principal method for implementing these functions is the creation of so-called friendship societies at home and abroad (see below).

Patriotic People's Front

In an effort to attract mass support for and participation in the nation's "new course," a super-front organization, the Patriotic People's Front was established in August 1954. Like its predecessor, the Hungarian Independent People's Front (created in February 1949 but dormant since 1951), the new group is controlled by the Hungarian Workers' (Communist) Party and embraces the various mass organizations (e.g., Hungarian-Soviet Society, Federation of Working Youth, Hungarian Federation of Democratic Women, National Council of Trade Unions). Unlike its predecessor, the new front does not include remnants of the former non-Communist political parties but does include virtually all other organized groups. The Patriotic People's Front now embraces such diverse organizations as the Hungarian Red Cross, Hungarian Writers' Federation, National Peace Council, and the Hungarian Aeronautical Federation, as well as various religious groups; almost the entire population is thus drawn into membership.

The creation of the enlarged front came after more than a year of the Party's acknowledged "new course" failures and seems to have been motivated, at least partially, by a desire to transfer identification with these failures from the Party to the Front. It is undoubtedly an attempt to convince the population that the new Front is a genuine coalition dominated by the Party; all indications are, however, that the people are skeptical and remain aloof.

The chief function of the mass organizations in the Front is to diffuse Communist propaganda. To this end, they have their own newspapers, such as *Szabad Ifjusag* (Free Youth) and *Nepszava* (People's Voice), the daily journals of the youth organization and trade unions, respectively. Most of the religious newspapers are likewise required to operate within the framework of Communist propaganda—e.g., *A Kereszt* (The Cross), published by the National Peace Committee of Catholic Priests; *Evangelikus Elet* (Evangelical Life), published by the Lutherans; *Az Ut* (The Way), published by the Calvinists; and *Uj Elet* (New Life), published by the Jews. Specialized appeals are made to the large cultural, professional, religious, peasant, or worker groups. For example, women are urged to support current policies in order to protect the "advances" in their status effected by the present regime; academic groups are told of government interest in research activities; trade union members are told of the alleged improvement of working conditions since the Communists came to power.

One of the most important mass organizations is the Hungarian-Soviet Society, which reportedly had a membership of 1,300,000 and 8,243 branch units in February 1953. Its tasks are to diffuse pro-Soviet propaganda and to assure a cultural monopoly for the Soviet Union in Hungary. Efforts are made to accomplish this by encouraging the study of Russian (3,600 Russian-language courses were organized for 45,000 students in 1953), by printing and translating Russian books (1,100 Soviet literary works were published in 9,000,000 copies in 1945-54), and by organizing lectures, films, and exhibits on various phases of Soviet culture, and exchanging cultural and technical delegations to learn the "benefits of Soviet experience." An annual Soviet-Hungarian Friendship Month from mid-February to mid-March places special emphasis on the role of the Soviet Union in Hungary. During the Soviet Friendship Month in 1954, for example, 7,000 lectures were delivered (*Szabad Nep,* April 27, 1954).

The Patriotic People's Front as a whole appeals for unity chiefly on the basis of nationalist sentiment. A typical appeal noted illustrious chapters in Hungarian history when the nation was united under such national heroes as Janos Hunyadi and Ferenc Rakoczi II in struggles for Hungarian liberation, and called on the Hungarian people to follow in their footsteps under their present leaders. Control in both the Front and the mass organizations within it, as in other Communist political institutions, is channeled from centralized national organizations to regional and local units. Like its member organizations, the Patriotic People's Front issues a newspaper, *Magyar Nemzet* (Hungarian Nation).

Foreign Propaganda

Hungary's foreign propaganda efforts are supervised and coordinated by the Agitation and Propaganda Section of the Party's Central Committee. The principal medium employed is radio, because it is relatively inexpensive to operate and is capable of reaching a vast audience, but press publications are used as well. The information and research units of the Ministry of Foreign Affairs' diplomatic missions and of the Institute of Cultural Relations are also utilized. The general aims of Hungarian foreign propaganda include: (1) support of Soviet foreign policy; (2) portrayal of favorable economic and political circumstances in Hungary under communism; and (3) appeal to nationalist sentiments of Hungarian emigrants in an effort to induce them to return to Hungary or to become adherents and spokesmen abroad of the current order in Hungary.

Hungarian foreign broadcasts are designed to fit the over-all scheme of Soviet efforts to disseminate Communist propaganda to non-Soviet radio audiences. A new development in 1954 was the inclusion of quasi-clandestine broadcasts to North Africa, apparently as part of an intensified Soviet propaganda drive in that area. In addition to transmitting general Communist propaganda, these broadcasts exploit local conditions in the countries concerned. Typical programs to the United Kingdom, for example, may emphasize such items as Soviet bloc progress reports and assorted international comment, but also include news from Britain, British workers' demands for higher wages, and Hungarian friendship for Britain.

Dissemination abroad of Hungarian propaganda through printed media is more limited because it is dependent on the attitude of the authorities of recipient countries. For this reason, Hungarian foreign propaganda in print is generally more restrained than on radio; it usually concentrates on defending and praising Hungarian policies and institutions, and only rarely attacks those of the target country. The Hungarian government publishes in Budapest English, French, and German language editions of the fortnightly *Hungarian Bulletin*, and English and Russian language editions of the monthly *Hungary*, as well as pamphlets in various foreign languages on special subjects (e.g., speeches by leading Party and government officials); these are distributed through Hungarian diplomatic missions abroad, friendship societies, and other local Communist and pro-Communist organizations. A Hungarian language weekly *Hirek a Magyar Nepidemokraciabol* (News from the Hungarian People's Democracy) is available at diplomatic missions. Other publications extolling Hungarian products are published by Cabinet ministries and the Chamber of Commerce (e.g., *Hungarian Foreign Trade*). In addition, Hungarian diplomatic missions or subsidized agencies publish a monthly periodical, *New Hungary*, in the language of the target country.

Hungarian films are not a major factor in foreign propaganda activities; they are generally shown to foreign officials and selected audiences, while the friendship houses often try to attract a somewhat wider audience.

Another means for disseminating Hungarian propaganda is the institution of "friendship societies" formed on the general model of the Hungarian-Soviet Society. The societies maintain liaison with the Institute for Cultural Relations; orbit liaison is formalized by technical and cultural exchanges. Cultural agreements were signed between Hungary and Bulgaria, Poland, and Romania in 1948. The captive countries do not maintain friendship societies among themselves, but those between Hungary and free countries, in addition to stressing Hungarian cultural achievements, express their appreciation for the "progressive" elements (i.e., Communists and Communist sympathizers) in the local culture.

IV. Literature and Education

9. LITERATURE AND THE ARTS

Hungarian literature has a glorious past stretching over many centuries and a well-deserved place in world culture. Generally, however, it is less known than the literatures written in, for example, English, French, or German. The Hungarian language, a member of the Finno-Ugrian family, was never spoken by more than fifteen million people in any given period. Nor did adequate translations of Hungarian literary works in the more widely known languages exist until the beginning of the twentieth century. Even then, chiefly the writings of contemporary authors succeeded in breaking through the language barrier and becoming known to, and appreciated by, wider audiences. Most of the greatest Hungarian poets, novelists, and playwrights of earlier periods are still a "secret treasure" of the Hungarians.

The earliest literature in Hungarian was created, as is the case with so many other national literatures, not by individual writers but by the people, collectively, and it came down through the channels of traditional sayings, folk tale motifs, and fragments of ancient lyrics of folk songs. After the emergence of the organized state in the eleventh century, individual authors appeared on the cultural scene. With them, Hungarian literature took a new course and, following the European political, social, and cultural pattern of the times, developed as an integral part of Western Christian civilization.

The beginnings of Hungarian poetry as a conscious form of art go back to the middle of the thirteenth century and their only surviving relic, a religious poem called *Mariae Lament*, testifies to an extraordinary sense for form and beauty of language. The landmarks of poetry throughout the centuries are the humanist poet, Janus Pannonius (fifteenth century;) the soldier poet, Balint Balassi, who created a genuine new style in lyrical poetry (sixteenth century); and the first great epic poet, Miklos Zrinyi (seventeenth century). They were followed during and after the time of the language reform, which was initiated by a group of writers who created the foundations of modern literary Hungarian, by Mihaly Csokonai Vitez, Ferenc Kazinczy ("The

Reformer of the Language"), Daniel Berzsenyi, Sandor Kisfaludy, Ferenc Kolcsey, Mihaly Vorosmarty, Sandor Petofi (the greatest Hungarian lyric poet), Janos Arany (the greatest Hungarian epic poet), and Janos Vajda (eighteenth and nineteenth centuries). The twentieth century brought with it great modern poets, who distinguished themselves in practically all fields of literature—Endre Ady, Mihaly Babits, Dezso Kosztolanyi, Arpad Toth, Jeno Heltai, and others.

Hungarian prose developed from the chronicles of Anonymous (the "Nameless Chronicler" at the court of King Bela III, around A.D. 1200) through the historians and story tellers of the Hungarian Renaissance (fifteenth century), the important religious writers of the Reformation and Counter Reformation (sixteenth century), and the political writers of the period of Ottoman conquests in the sixteenth and seventeenth centuries. The eighteenth century saw the ancestor of exile writers, Kelemen Mikes (after the collapse of Prince Ferenc Rakoczi's War of Independence against the Hapsburgs), the brilliant essayists of the Age of Enlightenment, and the first novelist in the modern sense of the word, Jozsef Karman. The giants of political literature, Istvan Szechenyi and Lajos Kossuth, appeared during the decades of revolutionary intellectual and political preparations preceding the War of Liberty in 1848/49. The Hungarian novel took an unprecedented upswing in the works of the nineteenth-century writers, Jozsef Eotvos, Zsigmond Kemeny, Mor Jokai (justly known as the greatest Hungarian novelist and widely read throughout the world), and Kalman Mikszath. Important prose writers in the twentieth century are, to mention only the foremost, Geza Gardonyi, Ferenc Herczeg, Gyula Krudy, Dezso Szabo, Zsigmond Moricz, and Dezso Szomory.

After modest beginnings (early morality plays, makeshift situation comedies almost in the manner of *commedia dell'arte*, and bloodcurdling tragedies concocted mostly by "house dramatists" of traveling theater groups in the sixteenth and seventeenth centuries), drama developed, in the eighteenth and nineteenth centuries, into one of the strongest branches of Hungarian literature, with such playwrights as Karoly Kisfaludy, Jozsef Katona, Imre Madach, and Ede Szigligeti. It continued vigorously throughout the first four decades of the twentieth century, with Sandor Brody, Ferenc Herczeg, Zsigmond Moricz, Ferenc Molnar, Dezso Szomory, and Jeno Heltai.

Hungarian culture has its great twentieth-century historians, important biographers, essayists, religious writers, critics, many of whom now occupy their rightful places in the history of world literature.

It has also produced many literary lights among the younger generation. A fair number of these writers, in fact, some of the most outstanding, are living in exile today, isolated from their native country.

The postwar era of Hungarian cultural life will be considered in
four cycles, into which it can be divided: (1) the period of relative
freedom from 1945 to 1948; (2) the Communist campaign against
cultural freedom in preparation for seizure of power from 1947 to
1949; (3) with complete Communist possession of political and economic power, communization of culture after 1949; and (4) the "new
look" of sovietized Hungarian cultural life since Stalin's death in
1953.

A HOPEFUL START

The cultural climate of the immediate postwar period was honestly
and authentically characterized by the Socialist thinker and politician,
Anna Kethly, then Vice President of the Hungarian National Assembly and a victim of communism a few years later, in an article
published in the Christmas 1946 number of *Corvina: A Periodical of
Hungarian Cultural Life*:

> For years [during the war], Hungarian writers, poets, artists have
> been cut off from their colleagues on the other side of the Fascist
> curtain [and] . . . all the best intellectual values, embodied in Hun-
> garian letters, were either burned on bonfires or sent to the paper
> mills . . . by the same [Nazi-Arrow Cross] spirit which raised a
> wall of hatred between nation and nation. But, despite lying Nazi
> propaganda of staggering dimensions, we in this little country
> stretched out our eager hands for any English, French, Russian or
> Swiss-German book which chanced to find its way to us. And [when
> Hungary regained her freedom after the war] the masses of the
> people became conscious of their tasks and obligations . . . the most
> important of which is to join forces in a common effort for the good
> of mankind. As for the future, there is very little we Hungarian
> writers and artists fear. We offer our [new or newly published]
> books to a free world as our [first] contribution to the constructive
> cultural work of a new, ethical commonwealth of man liberated from
> fear.

Culturally no less significant, but politically no less naive, than this
message of faith is what the famous veteran Socialist poet and novelist
Lajos Kassak said in the Spring 1947 issue of *Corvina*: "We [writers

and artists] confidently hope that the advent of democracy has brought with it the final removal of spiritual shackles and that . . . [our] creative spirit will find a safe basis in our traditions."

Freedom and progress based on traditions, such were the auspices under which the postwar renewal of cultural life took a hopeful and promising start. However, the political idealists seem to have been sadly unaware that Moscow sought not cooperation, but conquest.

In order to get a clear picture of the period, one has to consider an official declaration issued a few years later. In his *Report on the Situation and the Tasks of Hungarian Literature,* submitted to the First Hungarian Writers' Conference in April 1951, Jozsef Darvas, Minister of Public Education, said:

> During the first years after the liberation, our cultural develop-
> ment was sadly lagging behind the rapid political and economic
> changes. Crushed in every other respect, reactionary forces still
> flourished in the cultural field. Decadent pseudo-humanism, bourgeois
> cosmopolitanism sneaked back into literature and art. Except for
> some notorious Fascists, everybody was allowed to speak and . . .
> representatives of previous oppositional bourgeois factions could
> even assume leading roles in our cultural revival, decrying, in
> defense of so-called literary freedom, the necessity of Marxist-
> Leninist-Stalinist partisanship in literature. This mortally dangerous
> trend of tolerance, which denied the sole leadership of the revolu-
> tionary working classes in cultural matters, was the quartermaster
> of the most rotten, counter-revolutionary Western outlook.
>
> The [Communist] Party followed a magnanimous policy during
> those early years when it advocated the unification of all progres-
> sive national forces under its leadership. But with the political and
> economic remnants of bourgeois, capitalistic, counter-revolutionary
> resistance successfully liquidated . . . the policy of cooperation be-
> came outdated, even harmful, in the cultural field. Our creative
> culture must be coordinated with Soviet culture and subordinated
> to Marxist-Leninist philosophy as interpreted by the great Stalin.
> This is a decisive, and final, development, and all those who oppose
> it must vanish from the cultural scene.

When these words were uttered, literature and all other branches of cultural creation had already been shackled, for soon after Hungarian culture began to breathe freely again, a clandestine war on its freedom was launched by the Communists under the direction of a cadre of Moscow-trained Hungarian intellectuals. This war was marked by dithyrambic praise for Soviet and Hungarian Communist literature and art, and savage criticism of everything non-Communist. This campaign of ridiculous adulation and almost insane vilification was too obvious to mislead any intelligent man. The non-Communist intelligentsia, the overwhelming majority that is, dismissed it as blatant propaganda, noisy but ineffective; the politically undecided strata remained unimpressed. Hungarian literature and art were, at that time, still enjoying what appeared to be genuine freedom.

Writers and publishers were feverishly at work to help the country fulfill its task in Europe's cultural life. Out of some two hundred prewar publishing firms, forty-five had resumed activities by the end of 1945, and they were joined by fifty-one new publishers. Parallel with their efforts, a nation-wide drive was launched to recover all prewar publications that had been spared by the destruction of war, and it took hardly a year from the end of hostilities before a first postwar general catalogue of Hungarian books was published.

During the first eight months after the war, 72 writers published 87 volumes of memoirs, diaries, and documentary reports, all dealing with the war, the Nazi-Arrow Cross terror, and the German occupation of the country, the battles for various regions and towns, the siege of Budapest, and what was generally called the liberation by the Russians. Based on personal experiences, these books, collectively, are an authentic record of the darkest and most fateful era in Hungarian history.

One of the most impressive of these works is a brilliantly written volume of recollections by Miksa Fenyo, a distinguished author of the older generation. His *Az Elsodort Orszag* (Stormswept Land) is comprehensive, profound, and candid in its critical evaluation of the Hungarian tragedy in World War II. Another important work is the three-part documentary history of the sufferings of Hungarian Jewry from 1939 to the end of the war, written by the well-known newspaper editor Jeno Levai: *Fekete Konyv* (Black Book), *Feher Konyv* (White Book), and *Szurke Konyv* (Gray Book). A crushing indictment of Nazi cruelty, it is at the same time a monumental protest against genocide. *Pince Naplo* (Cellar Diary) by the noted writer Lajos Nagy, and *Egy Szemtanu Naploja* (Diary of an Eyewitness) by the popular novelist Sandor Torok, offer graphic descriptions of life in wartime Budapest during the horrible months of Arrow Cross terror and the Russian siege.

Among the rest there are the works of Communist writers, freely printed, published, distributed, and read in Hungary for the first time since 1919, such as *Igy Kezodott* (It Began Like This) by Andor

Gabor, *Itelet Ejszakaja* (Night of the Judgment) by Gyula Hay, and *Tizenhat Ev Fegyhazban* (Sixteen Years in Prison) by Zoltan Vas. All these books presented plain and unconcealed Soviet propaganda to the Hungarian public, which accorded this first salvo of Communist literature an interested and tolerant reception.

Up to the end of 1946, a flood of new novels swamped the Hungarian literary scene, but the number of significant works was comparatively small. Perhaps the most notable of the postwar novels in this first cycle is Gyula Illyes's *Hunok Parizsban* (Huns in Paris) not dealing, of course, with the German occupation of the French capital, but with the lives of self-exiled Hungarian writers and artists who sought between the two world wars spiritual freedom, success, and happiness in the intellectual and art center of Europe. An absorbing autobiographical novel of exceptional beauty, Illyes's book was listed by *Corvina* as the best seller of 1946/47. (The first place on the best seller list of foreign books translated into Hungarian was occupied by Erich Maria Remarque's *Arch of Triumph.*) Illyes, one of the most versatile Hungarian men of letters of this period, the leading poet and an excellent novelist, playwright, and essayist, is politically as questionable as he is eminent as an author. While not adverse to political opportunism, Illyes is today what might be called a problem child of the present Hungarian regime.

Another type of problem child is Tibor Dery, a veteran Communist writer and, at times, the literary showpiece of the regime. Occasionally repenting and recanting publicly, he has not accepted blindly the literary dictates of the Party. His long-heralded and widely publicized first postwar novel, *A Befejezetlen Mondat* (The Unfinished Sentence), was as much a disappointment as were his other novels.

An unusually gifted writer of the younger generation, Ferenc Karinthy, is another problem child, not of the regime or the Party, but of literature itself. The son of Hungary's greatest modern satirist, Frigyes Karinthy, who was an outstanding poet, philosopher, and novelist, Ferenc Karinthy achieved instantaneous and well-deserved fame with his first novel, *Szellemidezes* (Conjuring the Ghosts). Dealing with the intellectual and emotional development of a sensitive young man, the novel is devoted in great part to the memory of the writer's famous father, his endless struggles with his family, his friends, and society, his financial troubles, controversial ideas, and constant fluctuation between pettiness and grandeur. Written in a brilliant prose and as profound as frank in its psychology, this book secured Karinthy a prominent place among the most significant contemporary young writers. Unfortunately, his later novels and short stories have not approached this level.

The literary production of the home-coming Muscovites offers a sad spectacle. The works of Sandor Gergely, Andor Gabor, Gyula Hay, and Bela Illes (to mention only the more prominent names) seem to be translations of Soviet-Russian originals into Hungarian; even the prose sounds alien to the Hungarian ear. No matter how much advertised by the Communist Party and hailed as masterpieces by the commissars of literature, the literary works of the Muscovite writers have proved a complete and dismal failure.

Two excellent writers of peasant origin, Pal Szabo and Peter Veres (who appear to be reliable, if not enthusiastic, fellow-travelers) have had considerable literary backgrounds. A relative newcomer to Hungarian letters, the brilliant writer Kalman Sandor is a Communist and one of the main literary chroniclers of the infamous Bela Kun episode of 1919. All three have contributed several remarkably good and interesting volumes to contemporary literature.

However, the early literary harvest does not reveal important new talent in adequate numbers. With a very few exceptions, young writers seem to have been only preparing for their grand entrances which never materialized. The time was too short, or the Communist pressure too violent and frightening.

To summarize the first cycle, let us turn for a moment to some rather instructive facts and figures.

The last official book catalogue of the Hungarian Publishers' and Booksellers' Association for the years 1937-40, issued in March 1941, lists 24,141 titles. It indicated the number of titles then available at publishers and in bookstores. The first comprehensive, but not complete, postwar book catalogue issued by the same body early in 1947 for 1946, lists only 9,310 titles. The next catalogue, published early in 1948 for the year 1947, lists 17,110 titles, indicating an almost 90 per cent increase in the sum total of books printed in Hungarian. This last "free" catalogue has not been followed by a comprehensive, or even more extensive, list of "communized literature" or of Hungarian books still in circulation after the Communists took over. From 1949 on, only occasional brief book lists have been issued by the Book Division of the Ministry of People's Culture. One of these lists, undated but distributed in 1951, enumerates 228 titles.

The following comparative data concerning books published are limited to poetry and fiction, yet the trend they reveal is characteristic of all categories of publications, including scientific and technological literature.

	1937–40	1946	1947
Poetry, including anthologies and collected works			
Authors, total	260	214	378
Hungarian	244	174	323
Anglo-American	1[a]	7	9
German	3	8	10
French	3	7	9
Italian and Spanish	2	4	4
Russian	—	2[b]	4
Other, including the classics	7	12	19
Titles, total	323	323	665
Fiction, including volumes of short stories			
Authors, total	700	992	1,206
Hungarian	392	512	641
Anglo-American	152	170	197
German	67	94	102
French	40	76	95
Italian and Spanish	15	31	36
Russian	10[c]	36[d]	51[e]
Other, including authors active			
before A.D. 1800	37	73	84
Titles, total	1,107	2,121	2,706

[a] Shakespeare's *Sonnets.*

[b] Pushkin's *Evgeni Onegin* and a book of verse by Mayakovsky.

[c] In addition to works of the great Russians of the nineteenth century, 2 volumes by Ilja Ehrenburg and one volume each by Alexej Tolstoy and Sergey Tretyakov.

[d] The classics of the nineteenth century were limited to 9 volumes by Tolstoy Dostoevski, Gogol, Gorki, and Goncharov. The rest, 31 writers with 55 volumes, are contemporary Soviet authors.

[e] In addition to the five classics mentioned above, 46 Soviet writers represented by 141 volumes.

The undated (Communist) list enumerates the following items of poetry and fiction:

	Authors	Titles
Hungarian[a]	63	89
Russian[b]	59	97
Anglo-American[c]	10	11
German[d]	6	10
French[e]	9	11
Italian and Spanish[f]	2	2
Other[g]	5	8
Total	154	228

[a] Of the 63 writer-members of the Communist-controlled Writers' Association, 46 are Party members, 14 are non-Party member fellow-travelers, and 3 are "independent" Communist sympathizers.

[b] With the exception of Tolstoy and Dostoevski (each represented by one volume), all Soviet writers.

[c] Howard Fast, 2 volumes; one volume each by Shakespeare, Shaw, Dreiser, Thackeray, Chaucer, Dickens, Poe, Steinbeck, and Jack London.

[d] Goethe, Schiller, Heine, Gottfried Keller, Thomas Mann, Stefan Heym.

[e] One volume each by Racine, Moliere, Balzac, Hugo, Merimee, and Zola; 2 volumes each by Aragon and Elouard, and 1 volume by Vercors.

[f] Dante's *Divine Comedy* and Cervantes' *Don Quixote.*

[g] In addition to the *Iliad* and the *Odyssey* and a volume of Aristophanes' comedies, books of one Czech, one Romanian, and one Chinese Communist writer.

By the time of the publication of this fragmentary list, Hungarian cultural life had been completely sovietized. All publishing firms had been taken over by the state or dissolved, and the industry concentrated into the hands of a dozen or so state-owned, and Party-controlled, companies.

THE COLD TERROR

The tactics of the early Communist campaign against literary freedom proved a failure. On the level of letters, the frantic efforts to glorify Communist, and discredit non-Communist, literature converted few people; on the ideological level, discordant statements of leading Communists caused resentment and considerable confusion in the ranks of the Party. Unequivocal policy, strict coordination, direct and aggressive action were deemed imperative by the Communist leadership to escape complete defeat. The true face of Communist culture showed itself clearly for the first time. It meant the end of the Communist underground warfare on cultural freedom and the beginning of the "cold terror."

By the middle of 1947, two important organizations in the literary field were almost entirely in the hands of the Communist Party, the Writers' Federation, and the Division of Cultural Policy of the Prime Minister's Office. In the beginning, the Federation was a free body of writers, a guild rather than a union, but subsequent to its domination by the Communist minority, it assumed the role of the highest politico-literary tribunal. By granting or refusing membership on orders from the Party, the Federation decided who was or was not to be considered a writer and admitted to public literary life. At the same time, the Division of Cultural Policy, which was in control of distribution of printing paper, decided which book might, and which one should not, be published.

Another weapon of the Communist cold terror was intimidation, both direct and implied. Early in 1948, Hungarian literary life was preparing to celebrate the hundredth anniversary of the War of Independence by a solemn and large-scale book festival. The long list of publications included novels by two Hungarian authors, one of them living in France and the other in the United States. As soon as these titles were announced by their publishers, *Szabad Nep* (Free People) wrote "It seems to us ill-advised, even dangerous, to publish books by writers whose . . . absence we consider sufficient proof of their hostility to the new [Communist-dominated] Hungary and all she stands for." In conclusion, *Szabad Nep* added a direct threat by saying,

"Publication of such books—no matter whether good ones or, as we are inclined to presume, trash—might easily get their thoughtless, if not downright reactionary, publishers in trouble." At that time, *Szabad Nep* was the official organ of the Party and not, as yet, of the regime. Even if only by mistake in the Division of Cultural Policy, printing paper had been allotted for the publication of some non-Communist books, including the two novels referred to above, which of course were bitterly attacked by Communist critics. The Book Festival of 1948 was the last occasion Hungarian publishers could show some independence and act against the "good advice" of such a powerful agent as the official daily of the Communist Party.

Coincidental with the last free, or relatively free, book festival, all elements of the Communist cultural storm troops were deployed in a final offensive against literary freedom or, as Marton Horvath, a leading Communist termed it, "literature of a defunct era." Gyorgy Lukacs, the Hungarian Grand Old Man of Marxist philosophy and a Nestor, even if not a boss, of Hungarian Communist cultural life, wrote in the May 1948 issue of the monthly *Forum:* "It was the historical mission of the Hungarian Communist Party to liquidate the rotten [cultural] compromises of a whole century and the [cultural] treason of a people and a nation. . . . It is the Party whose perseverance, inexorableness, and ideological purity brought about a radical and complete break with the past and created such moral and mental atmosphere as was necessary to our cultural rebirth and our magnificent start to build our future."

In the October-November 1948 issue of the so-called independent periodical *Valasz* (Answer), the fellow-traveler, formerly Nazi sympathizer, Peter Veres assailed "Western, and particularly American, literature" as "poisonous filth which the reborn nations of Europe [the Soviet captive countries] must reject with disgust." In the August 1948 issue of *Forum,* Gyorgy Paloczi-Horvath, who himself was to become a victim of communism a year or two later, called contemporary American literature "a gigantic howl of a dying civilization" and "neo-sadistic rubbish written by manufacturers of best sellers and read by psychopaths."

These are merely a few examples picked from hundreds of articles about literature, theater, music, and the arts. Simultaneously, the public was flooded by a corresponding amount of enthusiasm for Communist culture and Russian literature. Supervised by the state and directed by the Hungarian Politburo, literature was transformed into the joint business of regimented writers and the Book Division of the Ministry of the People's Culture.

Total Eclipse

Whereas in the Soviet Union communization of culture took more than a decade and a half, the cultural revolution was accomplished in less than two years in Hungary. Hungarian Communists followed the Moscow pattern and ruthlessly applied Soviet methods. The sketch of translation into practice is as follows:

1. "Revolutionary break" with "bourgeois" civilization and establishment of "proletarian hegemony" in culture.

The meaning of "proletarian hegemony in literature" has been discussed more often, perhaps, than that of any other Communist literary dogma. A clear definition was offered by Tamas Aczel, favorite of the regime and one of the few Hungarian recipients of the Stalin Prize:

> On the one hand, writers hailing from non-proletarian strata must free themselves from the sentimental ties which might bind them to their backgrounds. Proletarian ideology must pervade their thinking and they must become aware of the inevitable necessity of being melted socially, emotionally, and intellectually into the proletariat. On the other hand, the writer's interest must be centered exclusively on the life and struggles of the proletariat.

Whatever "proletarian hegemony in literature" may mean, one thing is sure. This forced limitation of the writers' interests and, consequently, the shrinking of their treasury of themes (which should be life at large) have, in fact, proletarized Hungarian literature and reduced it to pauperism.

2. "Respectful adherence to progressive [national-cultural] traditions" but "complete liquidation of all bourgeois cultural trends," such as cosmopolitanism, idealism, romanticism, naturalism, and "other ridiculous or obnoxious 'isms'" as well as "their artificial and esoteric ways of expression." Adoption of "socialist realism and its artistic but simple styles, originally created and easily understood by the masses of the people."

A spectacle both ludicrous and frightening is the Communist "respectful adherence to progressive traditions." This sanctimonious movement of self-justification attempts to appropriate for the Communist cause all great writers and artists of both the distant and the more immediate Hungarian past as "predecessors" or "heralds" of communism, and "spiritual ancestors of Marxism."

From the sixteenth-century soldier-poet Balint Balassi (reclaimed as a "fighter for peace" whose "struggle [against the Turks] to defend his landed estates was essentially identical with the self-defense of landless peasantry") to the famous contemporary novelist, Zsigmond Moricz (who died in 1942 and was characterized in 1952 by Minister Revai as "one of those few great Hungarian writers whose hatred of, and contempt for, the [then] ruling classes coupled with his critical realism and humanistic optimism made him a harbinger of socialist realism"), there is hardly an important figure in the history of Hungarian culture who was not claimed as their own by the Communists. The dead could not defend themselves against Communist "revaluation," and the living who could have defended them were either cautiously silent, had been brutally silenced, or were living abroad in exile.

Jozsef Darvas stated "Under the firm direction of the Party, all bourgeois trends had been squeezed out of our rejuvenated literature and their place triumphantly occupied by socialist realism. . . . Soon, no other writer can exist in Hungary but a socialist-realist one, and nobody can become a socialist-realist writer but he who is a Marxist."

3. Rejection of "all shades of objectivism" and acceptance of [Communist] partisanship in culture. Embodiment of culture as a whole into the fabric of Marxism-Leninism-Stalinism and subordination of all creative activities to "the inexorable logic of dialectic materialism."

In his speech at the Writers' Conference, Jozsef Revai said: "I want to make one point clear, Comrades. It is a good thing, indeed, if a writer has literary talent, but talent in itself will not make a good writer. A good writer must be a good Marxist in the first place. Our whole culture must be based on Communist philosophy and grow organically out of dialectic materialism." As a result, the minds of writers and artists were thrown into further and, it often appeared, hopeless confusion.

4. Complete isolation from Western civilization and its "sinister influence," and recognition of the "superiority to all other national cultures" of Soviet-Russian culture.

Against a background of anti-Western cultural propaganda of unprecedented vehemence and viciousness, a high was reached in Soviet adulation and a low in self-humiliation and self-debasement. A new vocabulary of flattery was developed. "At long last, we have a friend and teacher of monumental magnitude and unsurpassable perfection to whom we can look for help and [cultural] guidance" (Jozsef Revai). "We stand agape in silent awe before the magnificence of Russian civilization and Soviet culture" (Jozsef Darvas). "We cannot create such heroes [in our literature] as can the Soviet writers because our development lags far behind Soviet life and literature" (Jozsef Darvas). "We all, Hungarian writers, will have to work hard and learn much, very much, I even might say *all*, from our Russian colleagues before we shall be able, not to compete with them but, at least, prove their worthy pupils" (Marton Horvath). If Communist political policy is out to infect whole nations with paranoia, Communist cultural policy is certain to afflict them with an inferiority complex.

According to a book list enumerating "the important publications" in 1952, of 277 titles, 162 were works of Russian writers, 91 of Hungarians, and 24 of writers from other Soviet orbit countries. The entertainment magazine *Szinhaz es Mozi* (Theater and Movie) on one day in October 1952, noted that, out of 14 Budapest theaters, 6 were performing Hungarian and 8 Russian plays. During the same week, 4 new Soviet pictures were shown in 17 movie theaters, 5 Soviet documentaries in 22, 2 Hungarian feature films in 4, and one Italian film in one movie house. Of 71 neighborhood movie houses, 56 featured one Russian picture and 38 Russian double features.

Step by step, both the spoken and written language became infested with Russian words and phrases. Russian-tinted expressions have spread in the popular language; writers appeared the more proud (or feel the more secure) the more Russian words they used; and it was only on very rare occasions that the timid voice of a linguist or philologist could be heard in defense of the purity of the national language. In 1951, the official publisher of the Party brought out a new dictionary of foreign words, with definitions and explanations literally translated from a similar Soviet publication.

Despite the Marxist viewpoint that permeates his work, elderly Gyorgy Lukacs is one of the important aestheticians and cultural philosophers of Hungary. Jozsef Revai and Marton Horvath are two outstanding literary figures among the theoreticians, ideologists, and critics, mass-produced in the factories of Communist culture. Both are brilliant writers. Blindly obeying the dictates of Moscow, Revai has dominated the Hungarian cultural scene during the period of communization and can be considered mainly responsible for the ruthlessness and the success of the process. His volumes on the poets, Endre Ady and Sandor Petofi, and his political and cultural-theoretical works are of value. Marton Horvath is the official spokesman of the Party in cultural affairs; however, his intellectual influence will hardly survive Communist rule in Hungary.

The oustanding poet of the period is the non-Communist Gyula Illyes whose enigmatic human and political attitude might, and most probably will, be subject to criticism from a great variety of angles later, but whose place as a poet is firmly established among the great representatives of Hungarian poetry. Of less significance, yet of genuine talent, are the poets Lajos Konya, Ferenc Juhasz, Peter Kuczka, and Laszlo Benjamin, all of proletarian origin and, perhaps with the exception of Juhasz, all ardent Communists. Fanatical Communists but minor, if much publicized, poets of some merit are Geza Kepes, Lajos Tamasi, Gyorgy Somlyo, and Zoltan Zelk. They all write in a popular style, currently termed "the people's simplicity," which has a definite leaning toward folk song. The language of some of them is colorful and interesting; their imagery, however, is strictly limited by their Communist outlook. Their works, unlike those of Illyes, will fade into oblivion. The rest of contemporary Hungarian Communist poetry is inconsequential.

The conspicuous lack of at least one outstanding and important novel testifies to the risks and difficulties of being a novelist in Hungary today. Many voluminous works, especially trilogies, were published and yet all such efforts are mediocre at best. The Muscovite Bela Illes's vast novel, a trilogy, *Karpati Rapszodia* (Carpathian Rhapsody), is a piece of coarse Communist propaganda and a pale imitation of Tolstoy's long novels. Tibor Dery's two trilogies have hardly anything to add to the reputation of their author, although, in part, they offer some interesting fragments of contemporary history. In addition to Ferenc Karinthy, younger novelists of some promise are Tamas Aczel, Istvan Soter, Sandor Nagy, and Istvan Kamjen. The peasant writers Pal Szabo and Peter Veres, and the veteran Socialist writer Lajos Nagy and Kalman Sandor (all mentioned previously in another connection), are still the leading, most successful, and most valuable representatives of contemporary fiction. Even though blatant Communist propaganda, their works are readable and, perhaps, less liable to be forgotten than most other works of fiction of the period.

Drama sank to an unprecedentedly low level after 1948. Of a vast number of plays presented, only a few can be qualified as stageworthy, and only three as outstanding. Two written by Gyula Illyes, *Az Ozorai Pelda* (The Ozora Example) and its companion piece *Faklyalang* (Flame of the Torch), are brilliant and moving historical dramas set against the background of the 1848 War of Freedom. The third play is Kalman Sandor's *A Harag Napja* (Day of Wrath), an unequivocally propagandistic but, for all that, excellent dramatization of some episodes of the Bela Kun adventure.

The New Look and After

The changes that were expected to follow Stalin's death began to materialize in the cultural field after the Hungarian administration was reorganized in July 1953.

The official literary weekly *Irodalmi Ujsag* (Literary Journal) complained that, "according to the opinion of the public, the products of our new literature are not sufficiently attractive and interesting," and went on to say that "despite some tremendous achievements of our cultural revolution," more and more young people can be seen in the streetcars reading "withered old copies of favorite novels of former times." The root of the trouble, *Irodalmi Ujsag* declared bluntly, is that "life, its real conflicts and characters" are invariably missing in the works of new writers, who are "desperately trying to substitute 'pre-fabricated literary elements' in their works for the riches and genuineness of life which can be acquired through personal experience only" and who think that "ideological discourses can replace a striking plot and good characterization."

A month or two before, the writer of such an article would have been ruthlessly liquidated. Even more astounding was the opinion, voiced in the daily *Magyar Nemzet*, that "an entire generation is growing up before our very eyes, young people who never read anything written by Kosztolanyi, Babits, Krudy, Frigyes Karinthy, Ferenc Molnar, Brody, Hunyady, and other great writers. [All these are twentieth-century non-Communist writers, with Molnar a special earlier target of Communist hatred.] This arbitrary sifting of our modern literature is bad literary policy. If the books of these authors are out of print [as they were, indeed, because the copies still on stock had been sent to the paper mills a couple of years earlier] they should be republished forthwith."

As if at the stroke of a magic wand, a storm of accusations, counter-charges, and self-incrimination broke loose, with everyone busy seeking the causes of what no longer appeared to be "the victory of Communist culture," but the "predicament of Hungarian culture." Writers openly accused themselves of being "mechanical copyists" of the Soviet literary pattern "unfit to be adopted uncritically," or for having "bowed to political considerations to the detriment of their literary beliefs."

At the same time, frank criticism spread from literature to general conditions and, in particular, to the communized economic life of the country. Officially encouraged to investigate and criticize the socialist system of industrial production and socialized agriculture, writers reported in prose and poetry alike on the "unholy situation" they discovered in every walk of life. In a long short story, Peter Veres, seething beneath a calm and polished surface, disclosed corruption, impotence, bureaucracy, neglect, and other ills in the management of agricultural cooperatives and state farms. Lajos Konya, one of the "official" poets of the regime accused himself of "blind optimism and faith in the Party" which made him suppress "certain doubts" and the realization of "deep-rooted conflicts between my party and my people." He concluded that he himself was responsible "for having seen the trouble without warning the country and its leaders." Peter Kuczka, another of the regime's favorites, wrote in a long poem:

> ... we both are guilty, Comrade,
> [of silent consent to, or enthusiastic support of, the mistakes of
>   the preceding administration]
> You as boss of the district and I as a poet.
> And now, the result of it is that your harvest is a failure
> And I'm hardly able to write poems. ...

A great number of young writers went to factories and collective farms to report with indignation on the inefficiency of government-appointed leaders, the ignorance of Party secretaries, the slackening of production and productivity, the growing diffidence and discontent of the workers and the people at large. In the light of these disclosures, the whole Communist experiment of the past years appears to have been a gigantic failure. Zoltan Kodaly, one of the greatest composers of our age, who had wrapped himself in silence—compulsive, of course, and endured with patience and great dignity—declared in a public debate: "Culture cannot be taken over ready-made, the way one moves into a vacant apartment or buys some furniture or clothes. Culture cannot be acquired but through learning by generation after generation."

While discussion and dispute shifted from private to public affairs, some banned literary works were quickly "revalued" and reissued; for example, Jozsef Erdelyi, a poet of exceptional talent who sold out to the Hungarian Nazis ten years earlier, was officially forgiven and welcomed to "the renewed community of writers." Jozsef Revai disappeared from the public scene and little was known about his activities or whereabouts. Many writers, artists, and scientists, conspicuously neglected during the previous few years were awarded substantial prizes. The slogan of the day was freedom. But, as some eight years before, once again, the new freedom did not last long. The disillusionment that followed was all the more cruel.

On March 15, 1954, *Szabad Nep* in a keynote article unexpectedly came out with the new Party line. The paper declared that, during the past few months, "the critical voice of literature more often than not degenerated into hostile agitation against the State," that the "general trend of pealing alarm" was as unfounded as obnoxious, and that the Party would instantly put an end to all such "misuse or exaggeration of literary freedom and independence by the enemies of the people and their irresponsible dupes." A long list of do's and don'ts for a renewed regimentation of culture was issued, but the sound of the resolution was remarkably muffled, its wording elaborately cautious. Literary errors to be avoided were defined as "bureaucratism," "servile imitation of the great Soviet literature," and "schematic representation of our new life [under the Communist rule] as a perfect idyl." Also, "literary freedom" was still mentioned as one of the "fundamental tenets and goals of socialist culture." And while the policy declaration designated the "fight against all hostile cultural trends" as one of the "paramount and imperative creative duties" of the writer and artist, forgiveness and consideration was promised to "all those honest, gifted, and useful workers of culture who, occasionally, had strayed off the path of the people but sincerely wish to return to it."

This ambiguous policy line, vindictive and dictatorial on the one hand and vague and wavering on the other, was received with markedly mixed feelings by the cultural world. Perhaps the very fact that dissenting or reserved opinion could be recorded publicly was of some significance. The new literary Party line was rapturously hailed by the Muscovites and their closest followers, but criticized with remarkable openness by even some Communist writers. True, a new wave of loyalty declarations swept the country, and most of the recently readmitted writers were promptly ousted from the literary scene again, but the new about-face seemed not quite complete. Writers who had been loudest in their criticism of the previous period were more moderate in their repentances, recantations, and self-criticisms than before. And the great majority of writers and artists qualified their appreciation and acceptance of the new Party line by reiterating their firm belief in the necessity of "constructive freedom," "independence from any particular cultural influence," "creative connections with the whole of world literature," and "recognition of the writer as the spokesman of the nation's conscience."

All this might be interpreted as a sign of the craving of even those Communist writers and artists who had not sold out irretrievably to Moscow for some measure of national independence and cultural freedom, and the determination to retain it once they had achieved it.

The post-Stalinist intellectual "thaw" in Soviet art and literature was echoed by a ferment of intellectual unrest in Hungary. When in 1953 the Party admitted the bankruptcy of Hungarian literature and called for a "new spirit," Hungarian writers became bolder and bolder. Such poets as Peter Kuczka and Laszlo Benjamin again celebrated nonpolitical romance in their verse, and the novels of Tibor Dery, Tamas Aczel, and Aron Tamasi began to put literary craftsmanship above Communist propaganda. Many of the black-listed works of the roughly 600 writers proscribed in 1951 reappeared in the bookshops, and some were newly reprinted. The "writers' revolt" which dominated the cultural scene from the latter half of 1955 reached a climax when Sandor Lukacsi launched a violent attack on Matyas Rakosi during the April 13, 1956 meeting of the Hungarian Writers' Federation, to be followed by the denunciation of the Stalinist section of the Party and a demand for the end of "this present regime of gendarmes and bureaucrats" by Tibor Dery and Tibor Tardos at a subsequent meeting of the Petofi Youth Club. It was later revealed that at a closed meeting of the Writers' Federation on November 10, 1955, Tibor Dery, Zoltan Zelk, Tamas Aczel, and other writers had submitted a joint memorandum protesting cultural measures taken by the Party Central Committee, and Gyula Hay, Tibor Meray, and their supporters had assailed Party guidance of literature in the name of literary freedom.

The subsequent resignation of the "Stalinist" Rakosi signified a sop to Tito and an attempt to follow the new leadership of the Soviet Union in their campaign of de-Stalinization rather than a beginning of any true cultural and political freedom in Hungary. In the spring and early summer of 1956 Sandor Lukacsi, Tibor Derdy, Tibor Tardos, and over one hundred other rebelling intellectuals were successively expelled from the Hungarian Communist Party, and writers and artists were warned by Erno Gero, Rakosi's successor as Prime Minister, that "there will be no second Poznan here." The predominant role of writers, artists, and other intellectuals in the October 1956 revolt is dealt with in a later chapter.

THEATER, MUSIC, AND THE ARTS

While the preceding sections dealt mainly, if not exclusively, with literature, the word *culture* was used in many places where, perhaps, the word *literature* might have been more specific. This was done to make the reader realize that the theories and practices applied to literature were also adopted for other areas of culture.

The theater, music, and art have gone through the same development as literature during the past decade. Initially, they enjoyed comparative freedom; subsequently, they were subjected to Communist encroachment; after the Communist *coup*, they were "communized"; and developments in the post-Stalin era have been similar to those in literature. Therefore, only a brief account of the specific problems concerning the theater, music, and art is given here.

Theater

The theater proved remarkably resistant to infiltration and "cold terror" and, in the beginning, defied all attempts to turn it into an organ of Communist propaganda. Unlike the state-owned National Theater, which had been run by Communists since its reopening after the end of World War II, all private theaters showed independence both in program policy and in handling casting problems. No third-rate play could be forced upon them merely because it was a Soviet play; no mediocre actor could expect leading parts in their productions merely because he was a Party member. In addition to the works of Hungarian playwrights, contemporary American, British, and French plays were staged at private (although mostly state-subsidized) theaters in superb performances. The reward was a theater boom during the first years after the war.

A well-nigh permanent crisis, sometimes admitted but more often denied by the cultural commissars, ensued on two levels when the Communists gained complete control of the theater, which was plunged into hopeless chaos. Management was entrusted to unqualified Party members, an ambition-ridden actress or a politically successful stage-hand. Well-trained ensembles were disrupted and new ones improvised on a political basis. The final word in casting belonged to the local Party Secretary. Communist partisanship held the reins at the offices of the director and the dramatist. Some Budapest theaters managed to maintain an artistic level, but the majority rapidly sank to that of provincial dilettantism.

Amateur theater, operating mainly in the newly built Homes of the People's Culture, was encouraged and supported by the state, and strenuous efforts were made to stimulate the interest of peasantry in the theater, both by sending star performers to the provinces to play on permanent local stages and by organizing troupes which toured the country. The results of these policies were predetermined by the fact that the peasantry as a whole was preoccupied with its struggle for survival.

Like literature, the theater is haunted by endless discussions, theoretical and political disputes, and conferences. It wrestles hopelessly with problems in the deadly atmosphere of a sterile, destructive philosophy and an oppressive, alien civilization.

Music

Musical life seems to have suffered the least damage by communization. Of course, it is ruled by a Muscovite dictator and has been subjected to regimentation of varying severity; it has not been free from long-winded, fruitless ideological disputes (the only result of which were, as a rule, an occasional "purging" of a composer for having "deviated" from the Party line or questioned the supremacy of Soviet music, and a prompt recantation by the "culprit"). Yet, on the whole, neither composers nor performers have been bothered more than is usual under a Communist regime. Hungary's excellent concert artists perform throughout the country, and on rare occasions and after careful screening, are even allowed to appear abroad.

A great number of fine pieces, from piano sonatinas to great symphonies and operas, have been produced by many excellent older and some younger composers. A definite shift from instrumental to vocal music is discernible, perhaps because the texts set to music could more easily testify to the composer's "adherence to socialism." The general trend in composition, certainly not invented, but energetically fostered, by the Communists, inclines toward folk music or, with the favorite word of the day, "the people's music," and the simplification of musical forms. Simplicity of melody ("which anybody can whistle at first hearing") is a rule. "Modernism," which includes, on various occasions, every style followed by any composer picked by the commissars to be purged, is sin, but a well-chosen title of any piece, "Faith in the People," for example, or "Cantata of the Revolution," or any other combination of the verbal props of socialist realism, such as the Party, the Soviet Union, communism, the proletariat, the "Peace-Fight," or the builders of socialism will secure official success. Contemporary Western music is rarely heard in concerts and recitals, nor is it on the curriculum of music schools; but the whole country is flooded with Russian music, from Tchaikovsky and Shostakovich to the most insignificant Soviet composers.

Mass-singing is much favored; besides some excellent choirs, amateur choruses were organized by the thousand all over the country, a proper way, indeed, to popularize music. The Budapest Opera is rela-

tively good and the Budapest Symphony Orchestra is still one of
Europe's leading orchestras.

The situation could, perhaps, be best characterized by a much-
quoted quip by Zoltan Kodaly, world-known Hungarian composer.
When asked by a journalist what, in view of the then latest Soviet line
in music, was his "policy for the People's Choirs Movement," Kodaly
replied, "One mustn't sing falsely." Despite the Communist rule,
Hungarian musical life has managed so far, by and large, to avoid
singing falsely.

The Arts

The architectural style of the regime is a lame and dull neo-
classicism, exaggeratedly monumental and strictly nonfunctional, as
officially adapted by, and servilely copied from, the Soviet; it is over-
decorated with synthetic folk motives.

Painting and sculpture, which experienced a marvelous revival
during the first few years after the war, were as brutally crippled by
Communist regimentation as they were cruelly hit by the annihilation
of the moneyed middle classes. Creative artists became dependent
upon the authorities to a much larger degree than writers or musicians,
and more directly so. Their position was similar to that of the theater,
with one important difference: the earning strata were not only not
interested in buying works of art, but also were not encouraged to become interested. The patrons of the arts were the state and its various
public organizations. The state has proved a rather magnanimous art
patron in its singular and exclusive position. Most of the artists have
not had to go hungry (and some favorite artists live almost in luxury),
so long as they serve their master obediently.

There are still some painters and sculptors who create great works
of art, destined to survive the sad age in which they were created.
As a foreign observer has put it, "they simply can't go wrong, whatever
they do." It is due to these artists that contemporary art in Hungary,
as a whole, could not be wrecked beyond repair by Communist rule.
But the majority, and particularly the young artists, fell victims of
"socialist realism," and for what little it is worth, Communist artistic
tastes. Art cannot evade the scrutinizing eyes of the Party. With all
modern schools and styles execrated as "reactionist bourgeois pseudo-
art" and forbidden, Hungarian art under communism has dropped to
a degree to the petty bourgeois, late Romantic manner of the 1870's
and 1880's, sweetened by "socialist optimism," featuring happily smil-
ing faces in large-size genre pictures, carefully selected and often

doctored historical scenes, and heroic statues. Favorite themes are "The Leader Among People," "The Factory," "Party Meeting," "Home Builders," "Harvesters," "Socialist County Council in Session," "Communist Youth," "Men of Our New Army," "The Builders of Socialist Future," and the like: men and women of the proletariat and peasantry, content with life, determined, optimistic,strong, handsome. This is socialist realism—even if rather far from both true realism and reality—in art. Such themes are repeated *ad nauseam* by the regime's "accepted" artists, the frustrated and frightened art clerks of communism.

10. EDUCATION

Since the Middle Ages, Hungarian education has paralleled the cultural-educational development of Western and Central Europe. In the early days, the free exchange of ideas was fostered by attendance of many Hungarian students at the universities of Paris, Padua, Bolo-ogna, Cracow, and Vienna. For centuries, education was vested in the hands of the Catholic Church, and after the Reformation the Protestant churches also played a leading role. Many Protestant students attended such great Protestant universities as those at Leyden, Utrecht, Oxford, or Geneva. This church domination, from the Renaissance to the middle of the nineteenth century, made Hungarian education unique among the educational systems of Europe. The churches' role in educational matters stemmed from the centuries of Turkish occupation, which resulted in the division of the country, and the influence of the Hapsburgs. Since elementary schooling was the most neglected sector of the educational field, the illiteracy rate was relatively high until the 1860's, although lower than that of Italy, Portugal, or Spain. Secondary and higher education was under the direction of the Catholic teaching orders such as the Jesuits, Piarists, Order of St. Paul, Cistercians, Benedictines, and Premonstratensians, as well as the Calvinist, Lutheran, and Unitarian churches.

The most important step toward expansion of the educational system and public schooling took place following the Compromise of 1867. The chief architect of the modern Hungarian educational system was Jozsef Eotvos, a great statesman and philosopher of the nineteenth century, who proposed Law No. 37 of 1868, which introduced compulsory elementary education and expanded secondary schools. The law provided for a six-year *nepiskola* (public school) on an elementary level, equivalent to the American grammar school. After this school, a student was to attend the *ismetlo iskola,* a three-year school where seven hours a week were spent recapitulating the main subjects of the grammar school. One-year practical vocational training schools were also instituted. However, the school system beyond the elementary grades lacked organization and was not properly executed. Therefore, compulsory education for the 6 to 15 age group remained rather theoretical.

Law No. 37 of 1868 established three general types of secondary schools: (1) the Gymnasium, an eight-year school of humanities, offered preparation for higher education in universities and colleges (comparable to junior and senior high school in the United States). The Gymnasium-type educational system was further developed by Law No. 30 of 1883, which created two types: a Gymnasium with classical subjects, and the Realgymnasium, emphasizing natural sciences and modern languages. (2) The *Polgari iskola*, a four-year higher elementary school designed to give craftsmen, farmers, etc. a better education. After completing this school, one could pursue studies in the Gymnasium only upon passing an entrance examination in certain subjects. (3) The vocational high scchool, usually a four-year course, attended mainly by students from the higher elementary schools.

The enactment of Law No. 46 of 1908 represented another important development, introducing free education on a grammar school level.

In the nineteenth century, beside several academies, Hungary had three universities, two in Budapest and in Kolozsvar, and a Technical University at Zagreb. At the turn of the century, a university was founded in Pozsony and another at Debrecen. Following World War I and the Trianon Treaty, the University of Pozsony moved to Pecs and the University of Kolozsvar to Szeged; the Academy of Forestry and Mining, formerly at Selmecbanya, was transferred to Sopron. Universities enjoyed a considerable degree of autonomy until the end of World War I. Although during the interwar period some inroads were made by the government, theoretical autonomy still existed.

Kuno Klebelsberg, Minister of Education, 1922-31, made great progress in extending the Hungarian educational system. Under his ministry, elementary education was greatly improved by enforcing the laws on compulsory attendance at grammar schools, as well as by the establishment of a network of rural schools for the farm population, who found it difficult to send children to village schools. This system aimed at establishing small rural schools accessible to the major farmsteads and manors. In the field of secondary education, progress was achieved by doubling the number of higher elementary schools and increasing the number of high schools. Klebelsberg also introduced an extensive scholarship program to further higher education. Hungarian institutes were established in a number of European cultural centers and grants-in-aid in foreign universities were provided.

The next important step was the enactment of Law No. 20 of 1940, which extended compulsory elementary schooling to eight years. The eight-year curriculum was composed of four lower (junior) and the four upper grades. To replace the unsuccessful practical vocational training school, a forty-day course was introduced in the ninth year. Unfortunately, the outbreak of World War II greatly hindered transition to the new system.

Parallel with the reforms in elementary education, a new type of secondary school was introduced in 1939: the eight-year vocational high school, providing a general education in the humanities and vocational training both in theory and in practice. Agricultural, commercial, trade, and industrial high schools were established, and within industry further specialization could be achieved in heavy industrial, textile industrial, and leather industrial schools.

After Klebelsberg's school reforms, Hungarian educational policy favored the middle class, particularly children of civil servants. For a short time, this might have had certain practical advantages, but in the long run it considerably deepened the sharp class differences. It became more and more difficult for children of workers and peasants to obtain advanced education.

Another unfortunate step was the enactment of Law No. 25 of 1920 and No. 14 of 1928, the so-called *numerus clausus* restrictions which limited admission of Hungarian citizens of Jewish religion to universities and colleges. As a consequence, a great number of young talented Hungarians were forced to seek higher education outside of Hungary.

BEFORE WORLD WAR II

Primary and Elementary Education. Kindergartens were provided for children from 3 to 6 years old. Parents were obliged to send their children to a kindergarten, unless they could properly care for them at home or elsewhere. About one fourth of the children attended kindergarten.

School attendance was compulsory from the age of 6 to 15. Elementary schools (grammar schools) were attended by all children from 6 to 12; theoretically, the age limit was 14 years of age during World War II. Religion was a required subject, and attendance at school religious service was compulsory. No teacher could have a class of more than 80 pupils (the average was under 50), but many village schools had only one teacher and one classroom.

Continuation schools were provided for children from 12 to 15 who did not pursue studies in a secondary school. In winter, the students attended these schools two days a week, seven hours a day, and in summer for one four-hour day a week. Most teaching was done by elementary school teachers; larger communes had special elementary agricultural schools, with special staffs. In the towns, there were also industrial and commercial apprentice schools for employees between the ages of 12 and 15. In 1937/38, there were 395 such schools, of which 160 were state, 101 communal, and 101 denominational.

Secondary Education. There were four kinds of secondary schools: lower secondary schools; Gymnasia; technical secondary schools; and training colleges for elementary school teachers. The lower secondary schools or "higher elementary schools" offered a four-year course for students 10 to 14 years of age who were not going to college; their standard was lower than that of the Gymnasia.

The Gymnasia provided the bulk of secondary education. Their eight-year course ended with the "matura," an examination which alone qualified a student for the university. The curriculum emphasized the humanities and was nonelective for the first five years, with Latin and German among the obligatory subjects. There were then three choices: a classical course with Greek and Latin; a modern course with an additional modern language (French, Italian, or English); and a scientific course, geometry and chemistry replacing Latin. In 1937/38, there were 38 Gymnasia, principally denominational, with 75 Real-gymnasia (scientific course), and 47 secondary schools for girls, for there was no coeducation in secondary schools.

Technical secondary schools offered a four-year course for students from 14 to 18 years of age. These schools were partly an outgrowth of the commercial high schools and agricultural schools and partly new industrial schools. In 1937/38, there were 18 technical secondary schools.

Training colleges for elementary school teachers were also under the secondary education system. Offering a four-year course for students from 15 to 18, they were generally connected with an elementary school since no religious group could found a training college if it did not also maintain elementary schools.

Higher Education. There were six universities in Hungary, all maintained by the state, and their graduates received the title "Doctor."

The Peter Pazmany University of Budapest, founded in 1635, comprised faculties of law and politics, medicine, Catholic theology, and arts. The arts course prepared teachers for secondary education and covered both science and arts subjects. The Istvan Tisza University at Debrecen had faculties of law, medicine, Calvinist theology, and arts. The Francis Joseph University at Szeged, which was renamed Miklos Horthy University in 1940, contained faculties of law, medicine, and liberal arts. The Erzsebet University at Pecs had law, medicine, and liberal arts faculties. A university faculty for Lutheran theology was located at Sopron. The Jozsef Nador Technical and Business University in Budapest comprised five faculties, each with two divisions: general engineering and architecture; mechanical engineering and chemical engineering; mining and forestry; economics, commerce, and public administration; agriculture and forestry.

In 1936, there were fifteen Catholic bishopric seminaries, three Calvinist colleges, one Lutheran college, and one Unitarian college (in Transylvania), as well as one College of Rabbinical Studies. These colleges were equivalent to the theological faculties of the universities. Three law colleges were run by the churches, but the students had to take their doctoral examinations at the law faculties of the universities. Agricultural colleges, some of them for special vocational training, and the so-called "popular agricultural colleges," maintained by the Ministry of Agriculture, offered inexpensive agricultural training. In Budapest, there were also the Academy of Music, the Academy of Fine Arts, the Academy of Applied Arts and Crafts, and the Academy of Dramatic Arts.

Adult Education. Committees for adult education were set up by municipal authorities. They received grants-in-aid from the Ministry of Education and were under its supervision. These committees provided all types of courses from reading and writing for illiterates to lectures on topics of general knowledge.

Minority Schools. The minority schools were based on a school law enacted in 1923, providing that a commune with an overwhelming majority of the same linguistic minority, or the parents or guardians of at least 40 children of school age, might ask for minority instruction in state and communal elementary schools. They could choose among the following types of schools: (1) all instruction given in the minority language, with Hungarian an obligatory subject; (2) some subjects taught in Hungarian, and others in the language of the minority; and (3) all instruction given in Hungarian, with the minority language as a subject.

In the mid-1930's, most of the minority schools were of the first two types. The German minority had 47 and the Serbian 17 of the first type; there were 372 German, 53 Slovak, and 64 other minority schools of the second type. However, many schools attended by children from linguistic minorities were purely Hungarian. There was no secondary education in a minority language.

The situation changed when Hungary began her territorial "re-acquisitions," and a slightly different policy, dependent on political considerations, was pursued toward each minority.

Number of Schools. According to *Hungary: Basic Handbook,* in 1937/38, of 1,140 kindergartens, 404 were state, 476 were communal, and 183 were denominational (174 were Catholic). Of the 6,899 elementary schools, 1,287 were state, 826 were communal, and 4,633 denominational (2,856 were Catholic, 1,079 Calvinist, and 349 Lutheran). Of 397 secondary schools, 160 were state schools, 101 were communal, and 101 denominational (80 were Catholic). Elementary education was compulsory and in the public schools there were no fees. Consequently, illiteracy declined rapidly and was as low as 4 per cent of the population over six years in 1941 (see Chapter 4, "The People").

Youth Movements. In 1928, the chief youth movement, Levente (Young Champion) was founded. As it was designed to evade the disarmament clauses of the Treaty of Trianon, it appeared to be a physical- and health-training program. However, it openly became a pre-military organization, mainly under the command of retired and active officers. Membership for all boys between the ages of 12 and 21 was obligatory. There was also a girls' Levente, but membership in it was voluntary. Although university students had no Levente, they had sports clubs and military training clubs. The Levente and other youth organizations were permeated with nationalist spirit and teaching.

UNDER THE COMMUNISTS

The Communists attach great importance to the education of youth, which they take to be synonymous with the free molding of the human personality. Although their pedagogy has from time to time changed, both in theory and practice, in Hungary, certain general principles have remained constant, though the stress has at times shifted:

1. Young people are the property of the Communist state, which must control and direct their development both in and outside the school. The influence of all other competing factors, such as religion and the home, are to be eliminated as much as possible.

2. Instruction in all fields of learning has to end in mastery of the doctrines and historical perspective of dialectic materialism. In a sense, the success of each citizen depends on the degree to which he has been able to acquire this knowledge. However, the study of Marxism-Leninism is not a separate part, but permeates the whole curriculum, for pharmaceutical studies, as well as musical or agricultural training, are based on it.

3. Even more important than the acquisition of ideological knowledge is the student's ability to understand the organization and methods of the Party. Such education, which is political in the most comprehensive sense of the word, is continually being changed and is carried on principally in youth organizations functioning outside the school (Pioneers, Federation of Working Youth, etc.), which are important in complementing the schools.

4. Whereas Western schools strive to inculcate general knowledge in the student before specialization, the emphasis of Communist education is on specialization. Instruction in subjects dealing with general problems is relatively neglected, or at least it is equated with the study of Marxism-Leninism and Party tactics.

5. The young people must be taught to appreciate that the Communist world community precedes national consciousness. They must be aware that they are militant members of a world-wide youth organization aimed at the overthrow of capitalistic governments and the introduction of a new world order. Youth conferences, uniting the Communist youth of the entire world and exchange of students serve this purpose.

6. Students are completely isolated from the West and Western ideals. The groundwork for this was prepared by the proponents of Hungarian National Socialism preceding and during World War II. The Communists fear that contact with Western ideas will endanger their control over the youth. One of the manifestations of this effort is insistence on the thesis that young people in the Free World, especially in America, are brought up in an atmosphere of barbarism, ignorance and anxiety.

7. The school is the main channel of political and cultural Russification. The Soviet Union is the supreme authority in every segment of life and learning; it is the country where everything existing in Hungary in an imperfect state has achieved realization.

8. The elimination of all differences between the education of boys and girls. The mechanistic psychological doctrine of the Communists does not take into consideration the special requirements or inclinations of women, whether at work or at school. They have few girls' schools, and only then in places where coeducation would not be feasible, but even here the curriculum is the same as in coeducational schools.

Since the "new course" began in June 1953, a certain relaxation in a few educational principles has appeared. There has been a retreat in the denationalization endeavor, for more emphasis is laid on patriotism and the historical past. No attempt is made to increase the number of girls in schools for courses preparing for jobs in heavy industry, building, and the like, although the principle of identical education for boys and girls is maintained. The regime has also realized that under the current educational system, acquisition of general knowledge is almost impossible.

Changes in Educational Administration. Until 1948, education had been under the jurisdiction of the Minister of Religion and Education. At that date, religious policies were transferred to the State Office for Church Affairs, cultural affairs outside the school became the charge of the Ministry of Culture, and the educational system, which was nationalized, came to be administered by the new Ministry of Education. In 1952, when emphasis on broadening the system of higher education was very strong, a Ministry of Higher Education was created. However, this was abolished at the beginning of the "new course" in the summer of 1953, when the entire educational system again came under the jurisdiction of the Ministry of Education.

The budget of the Ministry of Education amounts to about 4 per cent of the state budget. In the 1954 budget, the Ministry of Education received a sum of 2,234.6 million forints (about 191 million dollars, at the official exchange rate). Of this amount, 634.8 million forints were destined for institutions centrally maintained by the Ministry itself, while 1,595 million forints were to be turned over to local councils. The educational budget of 1954 represented a 235.2 million increase over expenditures in 1953.

Educational System

Primary and Elementary Education. Nurseries are the first link in the process of education. They accept children up to 6 years old. Many nurseries are directly attached to plants and work places, while others serve districts of a community and are controlled by local councils (soviets). According to data released by the Hungarian government, and Communist data can be distorted according to current requirements, for the science of statistics is officially described as a "Party science," there were 2,072 nurseries in 1952/53.

In 1945 (Degree of August 16, 1945), all types of primary schools were replaced by the compulsory "general school," offering an eight-year study program. With this readjustment, the curriculum of the lower half of the secondary schools was incorporated into the curriculum of the "general school"; at the same time, new specialized studies were introduced. Practical execution of this change was completed by 1948. However, much remains to be done to achieve its purpose. A resolution of the Council of Ministers made public on August 3, 1954, states: "The system of general schools must be developed, if possible, by 1960, in such a fashion that, as a result of the extension of specialized training, every pupil in the upper grades may benefit from specialized training. . . . Wherever the number of children is small, central schools shall be organized for the education of children attending the fifth through eighth grades, in which conditions necessary for the conducting of specialized training must be sustained."

According to the second Five-Year Plan (1956-60), 4,100 elementary school rooms are to be built, approximately twice as many as during the first Five-Year Plan.

Secondary Education. The lower half of the curriculum of the Gymnasium has been incorporated into the program of the "general schools." In addition, less than one fifth of Communist secondary schools have classical curricula, opposed to the former two-thirds, and the trend is still moving in favor of vocational, specialized schools. In the school year 1945/46, the Realgymnasia were discontinued and replaced by Gymnasia of natural sciences. The collective name for all Gymnasia is "general Gymnasium"; in its program, specialization has been highly developed. Among the vocational secondary schools, there are general mechanical, farm, milling, construction, textile, electrical, chemical, lumber, foundry, mining, and transportation industrial schools. Table 1 gives a percentage of secondary school types in prewar and Communist Hungary. In 1937/38 the secondary schools numbered 285, and in 1953/54 they rose to 441.

With the "new course" the trend was somewhat reversed, and the regime feels that more propaganda efforts must be displayed in favor of Gymnasia. The second Five-Year Plan specifies an 11 per cent increase in the number of students in the first grade of the Gymnasia.

However, it also calls for a 35 per cent increase in the technical secondary schools.

Table 1. Types of Secondary Schools, 1937/38 and 1953/54
(in per cent)

Type of School	1937/38	1953/54
General Gymnasia	56.1	43.0
Industrial	2.2	27.0
Agricultural	1.5	6.0
Economics (business)	22.1	14.0
Normal (teachers')	17.2	7.5
Teacher training institutes for nursery schools	0.9	2.5
Total	100.0	100.0

Sources: *Statisztikai Szemle* (Statistical Review), No. 1 (1954).

Higher Education. As a result of joint application of the two main Communist pedagogical principles, (1) the widest possible extension of the school system and (2) specialization, the number of institutes, academies, and universities has grown considerably. Most of the institutions established before Communist rule are still in existence. However, the academies of law have been discontinued, and most religious seminaries and academies have either merged or have been closed. The Communists have added the following institutions: Academy of Heavy Industry, at Miskolc; Academy of Industrial Chemistry, at Veszprem; Academy of Transportation, at Szolnok; Architectural Academy, at Budapest; Agricultural Academy, Trade School (Academy of Domestic Trade), and Lenin University (until 1954, Lenin Institute), at Budapest; Academy of Agricultural (Agronomic) Engineering, at Godollo. Communist terminology calls all these schools "universities"; however, they provide higher education within a narrowly circumscribed branch of knowledge. Several were created by detaching one of the schools or departments from Budapest University. In 1950, the Catholic Theological Department was separated from the University of Budapest (formerly Peter Pazmany University, now Lorant Eotvos University) and the Evangelical Theological Department from that of Pecs. On the other hand, the Budapest Language School and Bookkeeping School, institutes of higher learning, were created by the Communists, the former in 1951 and the latter in 1952. The Academy of Education opened in Budapest in 1950 was discontinued in 1952. The agricultural schools of Keszthely and Magyarovar, which had previously functioned as secondary schools, were raised to the rank of academies in August 1954. In 1953, the number of institutions of higher learning in Hungary reached 31. Without doubt, there has been an increase in higher education, but one has to take into consideration the statistical juggling with school types achieved by converting secondary schools into academies and universities.

Apprentice Schools, Workers' Schools, Evening Courses. The lowest link in the chain of vocational schools is the training of industrial and commercial apprentices. The training of apprentices was, first of all, obligatory. Since it was difficult to find a sufficient number of industrial apprentices, especially in the building, mining, and heavy industries, the Communists endeavored to recruit "volunteers." It was one of the tasks of the local councils to induce a certain percentage of village young people to choose industrial apprenticeship. Its hermetic nature was a secondary characteristic, since most of the recruits were placed in state hostels, which sometimes formed a whole town or settlement, as at Mohacs, Gyor, Sztalinvaros, or the Rakosi Works on Csepel Island. Third, most of the apprentices engaged in productive work from the outset.

Industrial apprenticeship was in such ill repute by 1953 that the government was forced to regulate its status. The resolution of the Council of Ministers on this subject, published in *Szabad Nep* (Free People) on May 21, 1953, provided that pupils receive free working clothes, uniforms, underwear, shoes, equipment, and textbooks. Those accommodated in hostels receive free room and board. The others receive free lunch on workdays and school days. About 50 per cent of the apprentices live in hostels run by the state. In addition to payments in kind, apprentices are entitled to cash allowances. Those employed in the iron industry, for instance, receive anywhere from 30 to 110 forints monthly (about $2.50 to $9.40, at the official exchange rate).

Another important instrument of regular specialized training is the workers' school, created for adults who could not get a grammar or high school diploma and who are obliged to work while attending school. These schools existed before 1945 as schools for adult education. Since then, however, they have been expanded and transformed into institutions for the re-education of persons of peasant and working-class descent.

The lowest form of workers' school is called "the workers' general school"; it is completely free and open to all workers. Workers' general high schools, which function in many Gymnasia and technical schools, admit persons over seventeen who have graduated from a general school and are gainfully employed.

Somewhat similar in nature to workers' schools are the courses, on a secondary level, leading to workers' diplomas, which entitle their holders to register in institutes of higher learning. Possessors of workers' diplomas enjoy special privileges at universities and colleges.

In 1951, the first correspondence school was founded in Budapest. Courses are now offered on both secondary and college levels. In the first year, 6,400 students, including those pursuing preparatory studies, were enrolled in correspondence courses. Of these 44.5 per cent studied engineering. In Budapest, a so-called free university has been founded, named after the famous modern Hungarian poet, Attila Jozsef; it is affiliated with Budapest University. During the second semester of the academic year 1954/55, it had 4,300 students, 60 per cent of whom were white-collar workers; the number of manual workers enrolled was only 500.

Enrollment. In 1952/53, there were 3,785 nursery and kindergarten teachers, while the number of pupils in nurseries was 144,000 in 1954. Since there was a great need for more nursery school teachers, one-year courses were opened in several parts of the country in April 1954.

With the "general school" becoming compulsory, the number of pupils in primary education increased. In 1937/38, the number was 1,096,650; in 1952/53, it reached 1,196,043. According to Communist data on general school statistics, there were 24,273 teachers in 1937/38 and 40,156 teachers in 1952/53. Communist statistics, however, are not comparable with prewar data because of the basic changes in the entire school system.

In changing to the new system, the small number of available teachers of special subjects presented a serious obstacle. In the former elementary schools, the teacher was permitted to teach every subject. In the upper grades of the general school, this system could have been introduced only at the expense of professional competence, for teachers' colleges did not train primary school teachers in more advanced studies. Besides, the Bolshevist ideal of specialization required that special subjects be taught by teachers who majored in those subjects. Many courses have been initiated on the district, county, and national level to instruct former elementary school teachers in special subjects. These courses do not always fulfill their purpose because ideological indoctrination consumes a great amount of time to the detriment of pertinent material. Older teachers, suspected of reactionary tendencies, were not allowed to teach subjects regarded as crucial by the Communists, such as history, literature, and sociology.

Table 2 gives the number and proportion of teachers of special subjects in general schools.

Table 2. Teachers of Special Subjects, 1950/51-1953/54

Year	Teachers of Special Subjects	Per Cent of Total
1950/51	7,500	20.5
1951/52	9,300	24.5
1952/53	10,100	25.3
1953/54	11,900	27.8

Statisztikai Szemle (No. 1, 1954) gave the enrollment in secondary schools as 52,349 for 1937/38 and 165,000 for 1953/54. This indicates the regime's emphasis on secondary education, and the creation of vocational schools has contributed greatly to the increase in pupils. While the enrollment in the first year of secondary schools was 13,200 in 1937/38, it reached 44,800 in 1953/54. The same issue of *Statisztikai Szemle* states that "in the school year 1953/54, more than 20 per cent of our children received secondary school training, compared to 5 per cent in the school year 1938/39." During the second Five-Year Plan, 130,000 pupils are expected to graduate from secondary schools (excluding night courses). With the increase of students, the number of secondary school teachers also increased. In 1954, they were estimated at 7,500.

Table 3 gives a general picture of the increase in the number of pupils and teachers in Hungary between 1949 and 1954.

The enrollment in institutions of higher learning has increased from 11,747 in 1937/38 to 53,000 in 1953/54. According to Gabor Tolnai, chief of the university affairs section of the Ministry of Education, there has also been a shift in the enrollment figures of the various university faculties (see Table 4).

In the academic year 1951/52, the shift in favor of engineers (34.0) and the decline of lawyers (3.8) was even more marked. The situation has apparently not changed much in recent years. Under the second Five-Year Plan, the regime hopes to graduate 40,000 or more engineers, economists, physicians, and educators. Table 5 gives the number of students in institutions of higher learning. Percentages for 1952/53, using as a basis 1951/52, are 143.9 for specialized institutions, 124.3 for others, and a total of 131.4.

Table 3. Educational Services, 1949–1954

	Units							Coefficients	
	1949	1950	1951	1952	1953	1954		1949	1954
	(in thousands)								
Teachers in nurseries	4.3	5.3	3.2	3.8	...	4.3	Children per teacher	23	33
Pupils in nurseries	99	106	121	130	...	144	Nursery pupils per 100 in age group	...	25
Teachers in elementary education	36.5	36.4	38.4	39.9	42.7	46.1	Pupils per teacher	31.2	26.0
Pupils in elementary education	1,144	1,248	1,205	1,197	1,204	1,208	Per 100 of age group, 6 to 14	...	97.5
Teachers in secondary education	...	6.2	5.9	6.2	7.0	7.5	Pupils per teacher	...	...
Pupils in secondary education	93	107	122	139	154	162	Per 100 of age group, 14 to 18	11.8	20
Day classes	82	96	108	119	130	121 ⎱	Per 100 of all secondary school pupils	88	75
Evening classes[a]	11	11	14	20	24	41 ⎰		12	25

Source: U.N., *Economic Bulletin for Europe,* VI, No. 2 (August 1955), 99.
[a] Includes correspondence classes after 1951.

Table 4. University Enrollment, by Faculty, 1938/39 and 1949/50

| Faculty | Per Cent of Students | |
	1938/39	1949/50
Law	37.5	9.1
Education	20.3	22.1
Medicine	13.2	15.1
Engineering	9.6	28.9
Agronomy	9.1	8.1
Economics	6.2	9.5
Art	2.7	5.0
Pharmacy	1.4	2.2

Source: *Tarsadalmi Szemle* (Social Review) (November 1950).

Table 5. Number of Students in Universities and Academies,
1950/51, 1951/52, and 1952/53

Year	Specialized	Other	Total
1950/51	9,712	19,663	29,375
1951/52	13,384	23,525	36,919
1952/53	19,272	29,234	48,500

Source: Statisztikai Tajekoztato (Statistical Bulletin), No. 3 (1953).

In the beginning, the Communists declared that there was no need for lawyers because justice was achieved by the will of the people. Therefore, the bulk of the students shifted from the study of law to engineering. However, the Hungarian leaders during the post-Stalin era realized the disadvantages of overemphasizing engineering. Mrs. Gyulay-Barna commented as follows on the disproportionate distribution of students in various university departments in an article entitled, "Before the New Term" (*Kozneveles* [Education], November 1, 1953):

> This year, we must see to it that enrollments are well balanced in the various departments. Last year, far too many students enrolled in the chemical and electrical engineering departments. . . . At the technical universities, more students must be induced to enroll in civil engineering . . . mathematics and physics, and at the agricultural colleges and academies, in agronomy.
>
> Efficient informative work must be carried on in order to induce students wishing to continue with their studies to choose agronomy, mining, engineering, or law as their career.

According to the second Five-Year Plan, the number of freshman in universities and colleges in 1960 should be 20 per cent higher than in 1955. Within this percentage, the number of technical (engineering) universities must be 40 per cent higher.

Scientists, Scholars, and the Academy of Sciences

The training of scientists and scholars has been rendered largely independent of university professional training courses. Preliminary stages to the doctorate are "aspirantship" and "candidacy." Doctors' degrees in the new system are granted only to persons whose erudition, scholarship, and political reliability are outstanding. Members of the various professions do not as a rule hold any one of these three titles. Scientists and scholars who have been granted "aspirantships" become members of an exclusive class who live apart and devote their time to their specialties. They are relatively highly paid as their minimum monthly salary is fixed at somewhat above 1,000 forints (about $85.00, at the official exchange rate).

The Hungarian Academy of Sciences, founded in 1830 as the supreme authority in science and scholarship, has retained its high place under Communist rule. It formerly had three branches: philology and belles-lettres; philosophy, sociology, and history; and mathematics and natural sciences. In 1949, when the Academy was reorganized, its scope was broadened to include biology and agronomy, medicine, and technical sciences. All the members and officers of the Academy were previously elected by the members themselves. Now the president or secretary-general, as well as other important officers, are appointed by the state, and naturally the election of members is under government supervision.

The Hungarian Academy of Sciences is not an institute of learning. Not affiliated with any college or university, the Academy carries on research and sponsors, edits, and publishes scientific books and periodicals. In recent years, the Academy has published two types of works. The first deals with specialized or abstract and often abstruse scientific problems, while the second has been launched to promote the study and understanding of science on a popular basis and in a terminology that may be easily mastered by wide masses of people. The publication of books belonging to this second category has been increased lately, and in this sense we may speak of the educational role of the Academy.

Religious Education

Before 1949, religion was a compulsory subject in primary, secondary, and special schools. As early as 1947, the abolition of the compulsory character of courses in religion was under study, and in mid-1949 elective (so-called facultative) religious education was introduced by the Communists and regulated by decrees issued in 1949 and 1950. However, this "free" or elective religious education existed in name only, and the decrees made the following specification: only those children could receive religious education whose parents requested it of the school authorities before the beginning of the academic year, and until 1953, had also to notify the Local Councils. Teachers of courses in religion were not appointed by church authorities, but by government authorities at the recommendation of church officials. They could be dismissed if, in the opinion of the government, the teacher showed an antagonistic attitude toward the People's Republic or its institutions. The religion teacher had to submit a curriculum on the basis of textbooks approved by official authorities, from which he was not allowed to deviate. Classes in religion could be held only after the last school period and only in the school building. The teacher was forbidden to hold any meeting or gathering outside the official periods.

Despite these restrictions, most parents expressed a desire to have their children receive religious instruction.

During the first half of 1948, about 40 per cent of the primary and secondary schools were operated by the Catholic Church, 18 per cent by the Protestant churches, and only 42 per cent by the state or other organizations. According to statistics of February 1, 1947, 463,405 students were taught by 3,597 Catholic secondary school teachers and 10,022 Catholic public school teachers in 3,148 parochial schools. In certain educational fields there were more church schools than state schools; for example, of 58 teachers' colleges, 14 were maintained by the state and 44 by the churches, 32 by the Catholic Church alone. Only a small fraction of student homes or boarding schools were state owned, the rest being administered by the churches.

After 1945, the demand to register children in parochial day and boarding schools was greater than ever before. It was impossible to satisfy this demand, even though between 1945 and 1948 several boarding schools on the secondary school level were created. In the scholastic year 1947/48, parents sought to register 20 per cent more children in Protestant and parochial schools than could be accommodated. Indicative of the popularity of Catholic schools was the request in 1945 by the workers of the industrial center, Csepel (referred to by the Communists as "Red Csepel") for establishment there of a Benedictine Gymnasium. The Gymnasium functioned until the secularization of schools on June 16, 1948.

In 1948, the Catholic Church lost all its educational institutions; in 1951, after the signing of an "agreement" with the state, eight secondary schools were restored. The Protestant churches, which had signed an agreement with the state in 1948, were allowed to keep a few secondary schools. (See Table 6.) The number of Catholic, Protestant, and Jewish schools demonstrates impressively what the Communists have done to education by religious groups.

Table 6. Religious Schools, 1947 and 1954

Denomination	1947	1954
Catholic[a]	3,148	8
Calvinist[a]	1,057	4
Lutheran[a]	359	1
Jewish[a]	39	—
Eastern Orthodox[b]	15	—
Total	4,618	13

[a] Primary, secondary, vocational, and special schools.
[b] Elementary and grammar (general) schools.

There was no Catholic university, but the faculty of Peter Pazmany University of Budapest, an autonomous university founded in 1635 by Cardinal Pazmany, was chosen in such a way as to give pre-eminence to Catholic education even in lay subjects. Similarly, Protestantism had a decisive influence at Debrecen University. The churches also maintained several institutes of higher learning, such as the law schools of Eger (Catholic) or Kecskemet (Protestant). A significant proportion of university students were accommodated in student homes or boarding schools maintained by the various churches. In 1945, there were three Catholic, one Calvinist, and one Lutheran institution of higher education; by 1954 there were none.

The Communists also interfered with theological seminaries in order to reduce the supply of young clergy to replace the old and in order to be able to control their training. Table 7 indicates the plight of religious seminaries.

The state requires the teaching of dialectic materialism in seminaries. Examinations in theology must be held in the presence of an official delegated by the state. The decree of the Ministry of Defense that abolished the exemption of priests and seminarians from regular service in the Hungarian Army and made the grant of exemptions a discretionary right of the Minister of Defense was also aimed at obstructing the exercise of the priestly vocation and the education of seminarians. Archbishop Grosz, in an interview with foreign correspondents on June 9, 1956 (*The New York Times*), stated that seminaries were operating "in accordance with church regulations" and that the 500 novices now being educated "meet our needs under given conditions."

Table 7. Number of Theological Schools, 1945 and 1955

	1945	1955
Department of Catholic Theology of Budapest University	1	—
Catholic seminaries	22	7
Catholic School of Philosophy (Jesuit, scholastics)	1	—
Department of Theology (Reformed Church) of Debrecen University	1	—
Seminaries of the Reformed Church	3	2
Department of Theology (Evangelical Church) of Pecs University	1	—
Lutheran Seminaries	—	1
Jewish seminary	1	1
Total	30	11

Party Education

In 1951, the Academy of Marxism-Leninism was opened in Budapest, connected with the Faculty of Letters of Budapest University. The principal subjects taught are the foundations of Marxism-Leninism, political economy, dialectical and historical materialism, Hungarian history, comprising the history of the Hungarian labor movement and the Communist Party, and the Russian language. The institution aims at forming leaders for the Party, for government organizations, and for professional unions. Those of the graduates who have obtained a teaching certificate become instructors in institutions of higher learning, which without exception are obliged to give courses in Marxism-Leninism.

An active organization in Party educational work is the Federation of Working Youth (DISZ). When a student leaves school, he is subjected to ideological indoctrination by members of the organization, which is under the direction of the Hungarian Workers' Party. The Pioneers, a Communist organization that embraces all children from 7 to 14 years of age, is under the supervision and control of the Federation.

Marxist-Leninist night schools have been set up in Budapest. They aim at the education and indoctrination of workers and peasants or persons of working-class or peasant background.

Educational Policy

At the outset the Communists endeavored to create, especially from the children of workers and farmers, a great number of new experts, as Minister of Education Tibor Erdey-Gruz put it, "in order to complete the process of [postwar] reconstruction and start the process of building socialism." The stress was laid on expansion and specialization in schools of secondary and higher education to the neglect of primary education. The first resolution on education (April 12, 1950) of the Communist Party stated that the greatest shortcomings of secondary schools were that they had not yet been completely professionalized and specialized, and therefore did not directly train the students for vocations. A year before, the message of the Minister of Education, who asked for the passage of a law establishing an Economic and Technical Academy (Law No. XIX/1949) stated: "In the interest of promoting the success of the economic Five-Year Plan, it is necessary to improve the economic and technical professional training on a high level; [the task] of training an adequate number of technicians, adjusted to the necessities of individual fields primarily of economic life, who are entirely familiar with the different specific trades and will be suited to fill leading positions, urgently needs to be accomplished." General knowledge was considered superfluous.

With the "new course," the emphasis began to shift. On July 4, 1953, Prime Minister Imre Nagy observed:

> As far as training the new intelligentsia is concerned, our educational program has become unbalanced. We have pressed the development of college education at great sacrifice. Now we must be more conservative in this field too. We must not build castles in the air. We must devote far more attention to our public schools. Their investment allocations must be increased, as well as the number of schools, classrooms, teachers, in order to ensure the best possible conditions for the elementary education of the young Hungarians [who are] our hope for the future. It must be admitted that . . . we have grievously neglected elementary education.

Matyas Rakosi, First Secretary of the Central Committee of the Hungarian Workers' Party until June 1956, in his speech before the Third Congress, quoted in *Szabad Nep*, May 25, 1954, maintained that since the cultural needs of the Hungarian people have vastly increased, first of all the "foundations of education," i.e. the general schools, must be broadened and consolidated. Education began to be looked upon as a chain which started with the general schools and ended with the university. The essence of the new education policy, which was confirmed at the Third Congress, may be summarized as follows:

1. The immediate main goal is the improvement and extension of the general schools.

2. In primary, secondary, and higher education, emphasis must be on the standard of education, not on the number of pupils; the "quantitative" stage must now be followed by the "qualitative" stage in the development of education.

3. It is still important to ensure a majority of working-class and peasant pupils; however, ability must be given priority over social origin. In other words, priority must be given to pupils who will benefit most from education, who will be the most useful to the regime.

4. Technical training is not enough; students must also be given a general education.

5. More attention is to be given to "national culture" and "patriotic education."

Under a Communist government, educational policy must always go hand in hand with political and economic policies. In Hungary, it has become more liberal, and in general there is a scaling down in quantity and a scaling up in quality in the educational plans. It seems that the Communist leaders have become aware that education is a process where neither norms nor "socialist competitions" can be successfully applied.

Russification

The study of Russian is compulsory in all types of schools, beginning with the upper grades of general school and continuing through the university. Numerous Russian professors lecture at Hungarian universities. Special instruments of the Russification are the Gorki Institute in Budapest and the Russian Institute of Budapest University; the latter founded in 1947, was reorganized under the name of Lenin

Institute (Lenin University since 1954). Before the "new course," Pavlov and Makarenko were the greatest authorities in the realm of pedagogy. While Makarenko still remains a great authority, Pavlov's pedagogical teachings have lost their significance as dogma, although remnants of Pavlov's experimental psychology are slipped into pedagogical literature, often in connection with Makarenko's teachings. On the list of recommended books published in each issue of *Kozneveles* (Public Education), works by Soviet scholars are in overwhelming majority. In many classes there are Russian clubs, and students are encouraged to exchange letters with Russian boys and girls. Since the introduction of the "new course," however, a certain reserve has been observable on the part of the authorities in applying unrestrained Russification. The number of Russian classes has been somewhat reduced, and Party resolutions at times object to the fact that Soviet methods have been "slavishly adopted" and the teaching of national culture neglected. Loyalty to and "love for" the Soviet Union still figure prominently in school teaching. However, it is evident that there is a reaction against the pressure of Russian influence on Hungarian education.

V. The Economy

11. NATIONAL INCOME AND ITS DISTRIBUTION

CONCEPTIONAL DEFINITIONS AND PROBLEMS

The total value of the income and product of a country can be established either by the summation of the incomes accruing to the factors of production during, say, a year (income approach), or by the summation of the expenditure on the national product created during a year (product or expenditure approach). As distinct from the measurement of the two basic flows indicated above, a third way consists in the summation of the value added (or of the incomes originating) industry by industry, building up to a total covering the economy as a whole (income by "industrial origin," computed from the output or income side). These approaches should yield the same total after certain adjustments. The variations of this total from year to year and the shifts in the share of its components indicate both the performance of the economy as a whole and the ways in which its various parts are related to one another.

Numerous conceptual and statistical problems are involved in the definition of "incomes" and "national product" and, hence, in the establishment of national income computations. In the case of Hungary, three types of data are available: (1) two sets of data for the interwar years, one excluding and one including estimates for some specific services; (2) planned estimates for the "period of reconstruction" up to 1949, as well as official estimates of actual income data up to 1947/48; (3) official percentages on the increase and distribution of income for the period of the first development plan, 1950/54, and various estimates derived from these percentages.

The first set of prewar data has been computed by Frigyes von Fellner.[1] In the Fellner approach, national income is defined as the

---

[1] Frigyes von Fellner, "Le Revenu National de la Hongrie Actuelle," *Bulletin de l'Institut International de Statistique*, XXV, No. 3, p. 367 ff.; von Fellner, "Das Volkseinkommen, Seine Statistische Erfassung und sein heutiger Stand in Verschiedenen Laendern," in *Der Internationale Kapitalismus und die Krise, Festschrift fuer Julius Wolf* (Stuttgart, 1932).

aggregate net value of all material goods produced during a year, valued at factor cost (i.e. excluding indirect taxes, but including subsidies). The national income also includes net income from abroad. It excludes all services of business which are not connected with material production, as well as the services of government. The underlying assumption is that these services do not yield "new products."

The second set of data for the prewar period has been computed by Matolcsy and Varga.[2] Their approach rests on a broader definition of national income, which is defined as the value of all material goods as well as of some services, valued at market prices. However, only such services as housing and entertainment are included in these computations, while all professional, personal, and government services are treated as "overhead cost for maintaining the economy" and excluded as such from total national income. This same approach has been used in the early postwar years for computing the planned development of income for the Three-Year Plan, up to 1949.

The Marxist methodology as it has evolved in the Soviet Union and been adopted by Hungary underlies the official income computations since 1949. It postulates that the national income includes only the income created in the production of material goods and of "productive services" valued at market prices, i.e. prices including the "turnover tax," which is essentially a sales tax. (In the West, national income is generally valued at factor cost, i.e. excluding indirect taxes.) Material production has the following branches: agriculture; industry; construction; transport and communications (in Hungary, transport includes passenger transport, which Soviet computations exclude); trade and catering; and miscellaneous. The services not directly related to production and distribution, e.g. nearly all personal and government services, are not included in national income. Essentially, the Marxist approach is similar to the Fellner approach, however, the former evaluates the national income at market prices, the latter at factor cost. National income is computed from the side of production. The gross annual product is computed as the sum of the gross output (including duplications) in all the above-mentioned sectors of "material production." The total is readily obtained by multiplying quantities produced times market prices, for each enterprise and for each sector. This total, in turn, is broken down into (1) cost of production *(c)*, i.e. cost of materials and fuels as well as depreciation allowances;

---

[2] M. Matolcsy and S. Varga, *The National Income of Hungary 1924–1925—1936–1937* (London, 1938).

(2) wage bill and contributions to social security (v); and (3) "surplus value" (m) absorbed by the state in the form of the turnover tax and by the enterprises as "profit." The total $c + v + m$, while used as a key element in planning, is actually of very doubtful use as a measurement of the performance of the economy from one year to the next, since it disregards the fact that certain outputs of an industry are inputs of another. Actually, official statistics in all East-Central European countries make a rather abusive use of the indices of the total final product, along with the national income figures as the measurement of the rate of development of the national economy.

From the total $c + v + m$, net material product is obtained, in its turn, by the subtraction of c and, hence, by elimination of duplications is given as equal to $v+m$.

National income is divided (distributed) into a consumption fund (c) and an accumulation fund (A). The first comprises the outlay on consumer goods and material services of the population as a whole (personal consumption) as well as the material consumption of institutions, e.g. hospitals, state administration, armed forces, etc. (social consumption). Evidently, C is larger than v, since new redistribution of means occurs in the broader framework determined both by all the **transactions on** goods and services and by the budget. Accumulation, which is correspondingly smaller than m, is equal to gross fixed invest-**ment (i.e.** including expenditure on capital replacements, but not on repairs) plus changes in inventories and work in progress, plus surplus on the balance of payments.

The shares of accumulation and consumption are officially released in percentages. Sometimes, the data on capital formation are released in "plan prices." The data on income are usually released in percentage increases from one year to the next. They are based on computations in current prices and sometimes in "comparable prices." Up to 1949/50, income data were in 1947 plan prices; from 1950, presumably in 1949 plan prices. The income series that can be constructed from these data often rest on uncertain ground, as much of the information released is often unclear concerning coverage and concerning comparability from year to year.

DEVELOPMENT OF NATIONAL INCOME

The Three-Year-Plan estimated that the national income of Hungary, computed in 1947 plan prices, would rise from a low of 14.7 billion forints in 1946/47 to 25.7 billion in 1949/50. The increase was to range from a level corresponding to 65 per cent to 114 per cent of prewar income. Data on the progression up to 1947/48 indicate that the targets set were met. The first Five-Year Plan, 1950-54, scheduled the increase of the net national income (material product only) to 163, on the basis 1949 equals 100. Available data indicate that the actual increase ranged from some 38 billion forints (at 1949 prices) to 57.5 billion, or to the index number 151. On the basis that each preceding year equals 100, the yearly rates of increase during the first Five-Year Plan were 1950, 116; 1951, 118; 1952, 104; 1953, 107; 1954, 99.

By using a crude conversion factor derived from the two data for 1949[3]—at 1947 and at 1949 prices—the income for 1938, 1946/47, and 1947/48 can be estimated at 1949 prices. (See Table 1.) It can be inferred from the data thus obtained that on the basis 1938 equals 100,[4] the national income increased to 124 in 1949 and 176 in 1954, after having reached the peak of 189 in 1953. During the Three-Year Plan, the per capita income related to the low level of 1946/47 rose in 1949 to 187. During the first Five-Year Plan, the per capita income, computed on the basis 1949 equals 100, rose to 144. The ratio of the two indices—per capita income related to total income —fell constantly throughout the period, given the population increases. Using the same conversion factors, we can link both series on per capita income. From these data, the increase of per capita income on the basis 1938 equals 100 would appear to have attained the index number 120 in 1949 and as much as 173 in 1954.

The increases in total material product over the period of the first Five-Year Plan imply a compound rate of growth of over 11 per cent up to and including 1953 and of 9 per cent per annum including 1954 —with the highest increase registered in 1951 (18 per cent) and the lowest point (−1 per cent) in 1954, following the decisions taken during the "new course" period, which placed a somewhat greater emphasis on the production of consumer goods and a more lenient attitude toward the private farming sector. The "new course," in general, represented a lessening of the proportion of investment so as to channel more of the national income into those goods and services which would raise the standard of living.

---

[3] This conversion factor is 1.417 forints of 1949 for one forint of 1947. Applied to the preliminary estimates of the income for 1950 at 1947 prices (as derived from official percentages), namely 31.6 billion, it would give a slightly higher income for the same year at 1949 prices, namely 44.8 billion forints. For the 1950 income at 1947 prices, *Az 5 Eves terv Masodik evenek feladatai* (The Tasks of the Second Year of the Five-Year Plan) (Budapest, 1951), p. 38.

[4] In 1937/38 and in 1938/39, the national product reached the highest prewar level, as the economy recovered from the low level of 1932/33.

Table 1. Estimates of the National Income in "Comparable Prices,"[a]
1938 and 1946/47–1954

Year	Actual Figures at 1947 Plan Prices (in billion forints)	Actual Figures at 1949 Plan Prices (in billion forints)	Index of Income at 1949 Plan Prices (1949=100)	Population in Thousands	Income per Capita (in forints)	Index of Income per Capita (1949=100)
	1	2	3	4	5	6
1938	21.6	(30.6)	(80)	8,980	(3,407)	(83)
1946/47	14.0	(19.8)	(52)	9,093	(2,177)	(53)
1947/48	19.1	(27.0)	(71)	9,205	(2,933)	(71)
1949	26.8	38.0	100	9,289	4,090	100
1950		44.0	115	9,378	4,691	114
1951		52.0	136	9,459	5,497	134
1952		54.0	142	9,537	5,662	138
1953		58.0	152	9,632	6,021	147
1954		57.5	151	9,749	5,898	144

Sources: Column 1, *Jelentes a haromeves terv elso everol* (Report of the First Year of the Three Year Plan) (Budapest, 1948), p. 188, and [Z. Vas] in *Szabad Nep* (Free People), March 4, 1950 and *For a Lasting Peace, for a People's Democracy*, March 17, 1950; column 2, U.N., *Economi Bulletin for Europe*, VII, No. 2 (August 1955), 87; column 4, U.N. Statistical Office, Departmen of Economic Affairs, *Demographic Yearbook 1952*, fourth issue (New York, 1952) and *Ne Hungary*, V, No. 5 (July-August 1955), 4; columns 3, 5, and 6, author's computations.

[a] 1947 and 1949 Plan prices. Figures in parentheses are recalculated on the basis of 194 planned prices.

STRUCTURAL CHANGES IN THE NATIONAL INCOME

Let us now see what these high rates implied as far as investment and actual consumption were concerned. The data on the planned structure of income for the period of the Three-Year Plan reveals essentially a tendency toward a methodic, but rather modest, increase in the share of industry, namely, from an estimated 29 per cent in 1938 to 32.9 per cent in the product of 1949/50. In contrast, the relative share of agriculture was scheduled to fall from 30.2 per cent in 1938 to 25.0 per cent in 1949/50, while the other sectors were to maintain, with small variations, their respective positions. (See Table 2.)

In reviewing the plan figures given in Table 2, it should, however, be noted that they are based on computations at 1947 Plan prices, i.e. on a set of prices in which the relationship between industrial and agricultural prices had been shifted in favor of the former. Hence, the relative share of agriculture in 1938 appears smaller, while that of industry appears larger, than previously.

Table 2. Planned Structure of Income, by Sector,
1938 and 1946/47—1949/50
(*in per cent*)

Year	Agriculture	Mining	Manufacturing	Handicrafts	Commerce	Housing	Other	Total
1938	30.2	2.5	29.0	14.3	9.8	3.0	11.2	100
1946/47	26.9	4.3	27.9	14.0	9.5	4.4	13.0	100
1947/48	26.9	3.7	30.6	13.2	9.4	3.5	12.7	100
1948/49	25.4	3.4	32.2	13.4	9.5	3.1	13.0	100
1949/50	25.0	3.3	32.9	13.4	9.6	2.8	13.0	100

Source: Computed from "The Hungarian Three-Year Plan," *Hungarian Bulletin* (Budapest, 1948).

The data on actual results for two years of the Three-Year Plan and for all the years of the first Five-Year Plan again reveal the familiar trends of fall in the relative share of agriculture and growth of the relative share of industry. (See Tables 3 and 4.) However, these statements call for certain qualifications. The share of agriculture appears to have dropped sharply during the first Five-Year Plan, as a result both of a further shift in prices in favor of given industrial commodities in 1949, and of a substantial drop in output in 1952. In 1949, approximately half of the total population was dependent on agriculture, while in 1954 probably not more than 44 per cent. The ratio of the percentage of income to percentage of population dependent on agriculture (computed at 1949 prices) dropped from .38 in 1949 to .32 in 1954, a sign of a fall in the productivity per capita in this sector. The share of industry appears clearly overemphasized,

Table 3. National Income by Origin, 1946/47-1953[a]
(*in per cent*)

Year	Agriculture	Mining and Manufacturing[b]	Building	Other	Total
1946/47	28.6	45.0	2.8	23.6	100
1947/48	26.7	47.1	2.6	23.6	100
1949	20.5	46.1	3.9	29.5	100
1950	18.9	49.3	4.8	27.0	100
1951	18.1	51.5	6.0	24.4	100
1952	12.2	59.3	6.6	21.9	100
1953	15.0	56.6	6.4	22.0	100
1954	14.3	58.6	5.4	21.7	100

Sources: For 1946-48, *Jelentes a haromeves terv elso everol;* for 1949-54, based on U.N., *Economic Bulletin for Europe, loc. cit.,* p. 87.

[a] The underlying data for 1946/47 and 1947/48, at 1947 Plan prices; for the other years, at 1949 Plan prices.

[b] Including handicrafts.

Table 4. Growth of Net Material Product, 1949-1954
(*in billion Plan forints*)

Sector	1949	1950	1951	1952	1953	1954
Agriculture	7.8	8.3	9.4	6.6	8.7	8.2
Mining and manufacturing	17.5	21.7	26.8	32.0	32.8	33.7
Building and construction	1.5	2.1	3.1	3.6	3.7	3.1
Other branches of material production	11.2	11.9	12.7	11.8	12.8	12.5
Total	38.0	44.0	52.0	54.0	58.0	57.5

Source: U.N., *Economic Bulletin for Europe, loc. cit.,* p. 87.

since it includes handicraft production which in 1946/47 and in 1947/48 represented about 10.0 and 8.9 per cent, respectively, and mining, previously counted separately. During the first Five-Year Plan, much of the handicraft production was integrated in the "socialist sector"; private handicrafts as such fell to insignificant proportions. The share of the socialist sector in the net material product increased from 53 per cent at the beginning of 1949 to some 73 by the end of the plan. According to the Central Bureau of Statistics, the socialist share increased from 53 to as much as 81 per cent in 1954. The data given by the Bureau of Statistics for 1954 were revised subsequently. Thus, Andor Berei, the president of the National Planning Office, stated in a report to the Hungarian National Assembly on the 1956 Plan that the share of the socialist sector in the national income "reached 73 per cent in 1955 and will reach 74.5 per cent in 1956."

An indirect check on the consistency of the income and output figures might be obtained by considering the fluctuations in the contribution of each sector from year to year (see Table 5). The net value of agricultural output marked the highest increase in 1951 (120) and reached its lowest point in 1952 (85). It should be noted that these figures closely parallel the data on the gross value of crop raising and animal husbandry. The figures of gross output are, for these years, on the basis 1949 equals 100: 1950, 105.8; 1951, 123; 1952, 93.2. The gross output in 1954 is given as 12 per cent above 1949, i.e. "approximately the same level as in 1938." With perhaps the exception of 1951, the level of output in agriculture has thus remained either at the 1938 level or below it.

The officially revised data of the gross output of industry give, on the basis 1949 equals 100, the following progression throughout the

Table 5. Fluctuations in the Sector Contribution to the Net Material Product,
1949-1954
(1949 = 100)

Sector	1949	1950	1951	1952	1953	1954
Agriculture	100	106	120	85	111	105
Mining and manufacturing	100	124	153	183	187	192
Building and construction	100	140	206	240	246	206
Other	100	106	113	105	114	111

Source: Computed from U.N., *Economic Bulletin for Europe, loc. cit.,* Table 3, p. 87.

plan years: 1950, 119; 1951, 148; 1952, 184; 1953, 207; 1954, 231. While these indices are parallel with the corresponding indices of net output up to 1952, they diverge sharply from them from 1953 on; this might express the upward bias of the gross indices as new products enter the stream of production. As can be seen from Table 5, building registered a spectacular increase up to 1953 and a slight fall during the "new course." All other material production remained, by and large throughout the plan years, at the same level as in 1949. The relation between net income from "industry" (mining, manufacturing, and handicrafts) and employment (Table 6) reveals that the increase in the former was essentially due to a large increase in the labor force rather than to an increase in productivity. The latter even fell below the 1949 level in 1950 and registered modest increases in 1951 and 1952; the average for the whole five years was but slightly above the 1949 level. The inability to lift productivity from the low levels of 1949 was due, among other things, to the influx of unskilled workers into industry and is a phenomenon that can be observed in other planned economies of the area.

Table 6. "Productivity" in Industry, 1949-1954

Year	Net Output of Industry (in billion forints)	Labor Force (in thousands)	Net Output per Capita (in forints)	Index (1949 = 100)
	1	2	3	4
1949	17.5	490	35,714	100
1950	21.7	610	35,573	99
1951	26.8	690	38,840	108
1952	32.0	800	40,000	112
1954	33.7	885	38,079	106
1953	32.8	900	36,444	102
1950-54 (average)	29.4	777	37,837	106

Sources: Columns 1 and 2, U.N., *Economic Bulletin for Europe, loc. cit.,* p. 87; columns 3 and 4, author's computations.

INCOME, GROSS CAPITAL FORMATION, AND MILITARY EXPENDITURE

The United Nations study "The Economy of Hungary, 1950-1954" (*Economic Bulletin for Europe*, August 1955) has put together, from a variety of sources, the data on both gross and net capital formation. If we relate the former to the data on net income, we obtain a series coinciding with the figures given in Hungary as representing the shares of "capital expenditure." The gross capital formation represents some 25 per cent of the total income during the long-term plan period (i.e. 67.0 billion forints out of 265.5 billion). This was a far higher percentage than the ones planned or actually reached during the previous period and clearly indicates the strenuous pace set for the economy as a whole. (See Table 7.)

Table 7. Capital Formation in "Comparable Prices" as Related to Income, 1938 and 1946/47–1954

Year	Gross Fixed Capital Formation		Net Capital Formation	
	Billion Forints	Per Cent of National Income	Billion Forints	Per Cent of National Income
	1	2	3	4
1938	1.3	5.9		
1946/47	.5	3.5		
1947/48	2.1	10.5		
1949	6.8	17.9		
1950	9.5	21.6	6.5	14.7
1951	13.0	25.0	9.8	18.8
1952	16.0	29.6	13.2	24.4
1953	17.0	29.3	15.0	25.8
1954	11.5	20.0	9.4	16.3
1950–54	67.0	25.2	53.9	20.3

Sources: Column 1, for 1938–48, *Jelentes a haromeves terv elso everol*; columns 1 and 3, U.N., *Economic Bulletin for Europe, loc. cit.,* p. 88; columns 2 and 4, author's computations.

The figures, net of depreciation, indicate that the actual rate of capital formation was equal to 20 per cent of the national income. The highest net investment seems to have been reached in 1953 (25.8 per cent); the lowest, in 1954 (16.3 per cent).

The capital-output ratios (i.e., ratios of investment to income, showing the increment needed in the former in order to bring about an increase in the latter) for the whole period of the first Five-Year Plan during the "new course" in 1954, 24.0 per cent of the total budgeted were of the order of 3.4, computed with a year lag (i.e, investment in, say, 1949 as related to increment in income in 1950). The ratios were very low at the beginning of the Plan, 1.3 and 1.1, and high subsequently, 6.5 and 4.0.[5]

During the first Five-Year Plan, emphasis was heavily placed on new productive investments. The ratio of new investment to capital repairs was approximately 84:16; the ratio of productive to non-productive investment (excluding administration) was probably 70:30. Table 8 shows gross fixed capital formation by sector for the plan period.

Table 8. Gross Fixed Capital Formation, by Sector, 1949–1954
(*in billion Plan forints*)

	1949	1950	1951	1952	1953	1954
Heavy industry (including building industry)	...	3.7	5.9	7.3	7.9	4.3
Light industry	...	0.3	0.4	0.5	0.5	0.5
All industry	2.6	4.0	6.3	7.8	8.4	4.8
Agriculture	0.5	0.9	1.4	2.2	2.2	2.5
Transport	1.1	1.9	...	...	...	1.1
Trade	...	0.3	0.3	0.3	0.4	0.3
Housing	0.7	1.4	1.4	0.5	1.1	1.3
Schools, hospitals, public buildings, etc.	...	1.0	...	...	...	1.5
Gross fixed capital formation	6.8	9.5	13.0	16.0	17.0	11.5
Capital repairs	1.0[a]	1.1	1.3	2.3	3.6	4.1
Gross fixed capital formation and capital repairs	7.8[a]	10.6	14.3	18.3	20.6	15.6

Source: U.N., *Economic Bulletin for Europe, loc. cit.,* p. 88.
[a] Estimate.

A comparison between total budgetary expenditure (see Table 9) and both investment (i.e. fixed investment at current prices) and military outlay stresses the heavy drain of these combined expenditures, which are both subtracted from consumption (see Table 10).

---

[5] Both the planned and the actual capital-output ratios are low, compared to non-orbit countries. Although any generalization is risky, this may be in part attributed to the direction of investment, namely, concentration on producer goods and partial suppression of the demand for private housing.

Table 9. Budget[a] Expenditure, 1949–1954

| Year | National Enterprises and Their Administration | Government Expenditure | | | | Total Expenditure |
		Administration	Defense	Other	Total	
		(in billion forints)				
1949	4.8	0.5	1.8	2.2	4.5	9.3
1950	11.6	1.0	2.6	4.8	8.4	20.0
1951	18.0	1.4	4.1	6.0	11.5	29.5
1952	26.2	2.2	5.9	8.2	16.3	42.5
1953	31.7	2.0	7.4	10.2	19.6	51.3
1954	28.7	1.9	7.3	10.0	19.2	47.9
		(in per cent)				
1949	51.60	5.37	19.35	23.68	48.40	100.00
1950	58.00	5.00	13.00	24.00	42.00	100.00
1951	61.01	4.74	13.89	20.36	38.99	100.00
1952	61.64	5.17	13.88	19.31	38.36	100.00
1953	61.79	3.89	14.42	19.90	38.21	100.00
1954	59.91	3.96	15.24	20.89	40.09	100.00

Sources: Budget Reports; "The Economy of Hungary 1950-1954," p. 97; U.N., *Economic Bulletin for Europe,* VII, No. 1 (May 1955).

[a] Drafts.

Table 10. Ratio of Gross Fixed Investment to Total Budgetary Expenditure
and to Military Expenditure, 1949–1954

| Year | Total Budget (in billion forints) | Defense | | Fixed Investment | | Ratio of Defense to Fixed Investments |
		Billion Forints	Per Cent	Billion Forints	Per Cent	
1949	9.3	1.8	19.3	3.3	35.4	54.5
1950	20.0	2.6	13.0	7.2	36.0	36.1
1951	29.2	4.1	13.9	11.7	39.6	35.0
1952	42.5	5.9	13.9	15.5	36.4	38.0
1953	51.3	7.4	14.4	19.0	37.0	38.9
1954	47.9	7.3	15.2	11.5	24.0	63.3

Source: Computed from the Budgets.

As can be seen from Table 10, the budgeted expenditures for defense and fixed investment were maintained together at a high level up to 1954. The relative share of defense fell from 19.3 in 1949 to 13.0 in 1950, but then started to increase quite methodically. The data available on actual expenditure indicate that in 1953, 16.7 per cent of the total went for defense. The relative share of fixed investment reached its peak in 1951, 39.6 per cent, and its lowest point during the "new course" in 1954, 24.0 per cent of the total budgeted expenditure. The ratio of military expenditure to defense indicates a sharp increase in 1954. In 1953, this ratio was substantially smaller.

The budget covers both expenditure on the national economy and government expenditure proper (see Table 11). If we contrast these two types of expenditure, the following trends become apparent: the share of expenditure on national income tended to increase, as related to all other expenditure, from about 52 to around 60 per cent. On the other hand, about half of all other expenditure went to administration and defense, with the share of the latter increasing from year to year. Actually, it is impossible to estimate accurately the proportion of military expenditure, since certain military allocations are concealed under other headings.

Table 11. Pattern of Budget Expenditure, 1949–1954
(*in per cent*)

Category of Expenditure	1949	1950	1951	1952	1953	1954
Expenditure on the national economy as per cent of total budget	51.6	58.0	61.0	61.6	61.8	59.9
Government expenditure excluding national economy	100.0	100.0	100.0	100.0	100.0	100.0
Administration	11.1	11.9	12.1	13.5	10.2	9.9
Defense	40.0	31.0	35.6	36.2	37.8	38.0
Total administration and defense	51.1	42.9	47.7	49.7	48.0	47.9

Source: Computed from the Budgets.

INCOME AND CONSUMPTION

During the Three-Year Plan, the share of private consumption was to be "stabilized" at around 73 per cent of the national income.[6] The reduction as related to 1938, when the share of private consumption was over 80 per cent of the net national product, was attributed, among other things, to the increase in both the shares of investment and of national liabilities (reparations). The sharp contrast between the early goals in the division of the net material product and its

[6] This refers to the share of private consumption in the net material product; a larger distribution occurs, however, in the broader framework determined by the budget and by all transactions on goods and services.

actual distribution during the first Five-Year Plan is apparent from Table 12.

Table 12. Share of Personal Consumption in National Income,
1938 and 1946/47—1949/50
(*in per cent*)

Three-Year Plan[a]		Five-Year Plan[b]	
Year	Personal Consumption	Year	Personal Consumption
1938	80.5	1950	62.0
1946/47	73.2	1951	56.0
1947/48	72.4	1952	56.0
1948/49	72.8	1953	58.0
1949/50	72.9	1954 (plan)	70.0

Sources: "The Hungarian Three-Year Plan," p. 28; for 1950-54, U.N., *Economic Survey of Europe in 1954* (Geneva, 1955), p. 40.
[a] All planned figures at 1947 Plan prices.
[b] Actual data at current prices, 1954 Plan.

In 1949, the per capita income was approximately 120 per cent of the prewar level (see Table 1). The per capita income (net material product) available for private consumption was, however, somewhat lower than the prewar level.[7] During the first Five-Year Plan, the share of private consumption fell to 56-58 per cent of the net material product up to 1953. It was scheduled to rise to 70 per cent in 1954, after the introduction of the "new course." It appears from an official declaration made during the "new course" period that the standard of living fluctuated around the low level of 1949 almost throughout the first Five-Year Plan. An increase in this standard by some 15-18 per cent was officially claimed toward the end of 1954, but the economy had "difficulties in sustaining even this increase."[8] As the "new

[7] Assuming that the share of private consumption was of the order of 65 per cent of the 1949 income, per capita available for private consumption could be estimated at less than 2,700 forints, compared to 2,740 in 1938.
[8] Thus, Imre Nagy wrote in 1954: "[The old economic policy] did not take into account the human being, the society. It narrowed down the meaning of the term "socialism" to a maximum increase of iron and steel production, to over-industrialization. According to computations, the standard of living rose, from 1949 until the middle of 1954, by about 15 to 18 per cent. Is it too much or too little? In this connection one must take into account the following: from 1949 to the end of 1953, national income, even according to corrected data, rose by about 60 per cent. In these circumstances the rise in the standard of living cannot be considered exaggerated. If this increase can be supported by our economy only with difficulty, the explanation is not that we have set ourselves exaggerated tasks in the June [1953] resolutions, but that the instructions—increased production, reorganization, increase of agricultural production, all of which would have made a firm foundation for the raising of the standard of living—have not been implemented." *Szabad Nep* (Free People), October 20, 1954. Actually, the computations of the then Hungarian Prime Minister were optimistic and were based on higher increases in total income than existed.

course" resolutions were only partially implemented and the increased needs of investment and defense were again advanced against the available means, the claimed increase of the "new course" in the standard of living had rapidly evaporated by the turn of 1955.[9] Thus, the expansion in total product has not brought about an increase in the level of consumption per capita, which has again fallen to the low level of the pre-Five-Year Plan period. The post "new course" slogan became not an increase in the share of consumption, but a further increase in output, which allegedly could "alone assure the supply of goods . . . demanded by higher living standards" (*Szabad Nep*, January 1, 1955).

With regard to the pattern of consumption, available data indicate, as can be expected, a substantial increase in expenditure for food and clothing—making up to between 70-80 per cent of the consumer expenditure, compared to some 50 per cent before the war (see Table 13). The high increase in the expenditure for food—from 40 per cent of consumption expenditure before the war to 57 per cent or more in 1953—was officially attributed to increases in the prices of a narrow and poorly supplied free market to which the townspeople had to turn after 1951.

Table 13. Structure of Consumer Expenditure, Prewar, 1950, and 1953
(*in per cent*)

Commodity Group	Prewar	1950	1953 (Second Half)
Food	40.0	53.0	64.0
Clothing	9.0	15.0	16.0
Heat and light	8.0	8.0	5.0
Rent	23.0	7.0	4.0
Household goods	2.0	2.0	1.0
Other (including alcohol and tobacco)	18.0	15.0	10.0
Total	100.0	100.0	100.0

Source: U.N., *Economic Survey of Europe in 1953* (Geneva, 1954), p. 64.

[9] A Resolution of the Central Committee of the Communist Party, condemning the article of Imre Nagy, quoted above, after affirming that the standard of living had effectively increased in 1954—"real wages per capita, by 15 per cent and real income of the peasantry by even more"—adds: "Inasmuch as our country's economic forces have not developed satisfactorily in the recent period, the higher living standards of the working people *do not rest on a firm, solid base*." Cf. On the Political Situation and Tasks of the Party. Resolution of the Central Committee of the Hungarian Working People's Party, in *For a Lasting Peace, for a People's Democracy*, March 11, 1955.

Concluding Remarks

During the first Five-Year-Plan, there was, according to the figures presented above, a substantial expansion of the net material product, namely, about 50 per cent over 1949. This expansion was roughly as great in Hungary as in neighboring Czechoslovakia and Poland. Per capita income increased by 44 per cent, but the amount available for personal consumption remained by and large stationary. Given the renewed emphasis on investment versus consumption, the official policy tends to continue these trends during the second Five-Year Plan, which started in 1956.

While there is a broad consensus among economists that international income comparisons are of a limited accuracy and can be quite misleading, the tradition remains strong in favor of the presentation of such figures. As far as Hungary is concerned, it can be estimated, on the basis of the data presented above, that per capita income increased in current dollars[10] from a level of $224 in 1938 to some $268 in 1949 and $387 at the close of the first Five-Year Plan. The last figure remained substantially below the corresponding per capita figures of the more developed captive countries of Czechoslovakia and Poland.

---

[10] For 1947 forints, the U.N. equates $1.00 to 10.745 forints. See U.N., *National and Per Capita Incomes, Seventy Countries—1949*, Statistical Papers, Series E, No. 1 (October 1950). Using the conversion factor derived from our Table 1, $1.00 can be equated to 15.225 forints of 1949.

12. AGRICULTURE

INTRODUCTION

Agriculture, based primarily upon extensive cultivation of cereals and secondarily upon animal husbandry, has traditionally been the main economic activity of Hungary. In the interwar period, half of the population was dependent upon agriculture, which produced, on the average, some 40 per cent of the national income and contributed as much as 70 per cent of the value of total annual exports. Under Communist economic management, which stresses industrial development and maintains a variety of depressant agricultural policies, the importance of agriculture has significantly diminished. The Communist regime is proud that in 1951 the contribution of industry to national income exceeded that of agriculture. This development is primarily due to the regime's emphasis on industrialization at the expense of agriculture, which in the best postwar year, 1951, produced only 95.1 per cent of the 1938 level.

In many respects, Hungary occupies a position midway between the advanced agricultural economies of Western Europe and the agriculture of the Balkans. In the interwar period, the average yield of the most important crops was higher than in the Balkans and the Iberian peninsula, but considerably below that in Hungary's northern and western neighbors, Austria, Czechoslovakia, and Poland. The same midway position characterized the density of livestock (and hence the availability of natural fertilizers), the degree of rural overpopulation, the use of machinery, and, in general, the application of advanced agronomy.

The pattern of land use (see Table 1) of Hungary's total area[1] demonstrates the unusual dominance of arable farming, which utilizes about 60 per cent of all land, and the small proportions both of permanent meadow and pastures (16-17 per cent) and forest land (around 12 per cent).

[1] Acreage figures given in this report are in hectares, usually calculated from Hungarian statements in terms of cadastral yokes, a measure equal to 0.576 hectares, or 1.42 acres. One hectare equals 2.47 acres.

Table 1. Land Use, Selected Years 1937/38—1951/52
(*in per cent*)

Type	1937/38	1945/46	1948/49	1949/50	1951/52
Agricultural land					
Arable	60.4	60.2	58.0	59.2	58.5
Gardens and orchards	1.3	1.4	1.4	1.6	1.6
Vineyards	2.2	2.3	2.5	2.6	2.6
Permanent meadow	6.9	6.9	6.4	6.6	...
Permanent pasture	10.4	10.2	10.0	10.2	...
Total	81.2	81.0	78.3	80.2	...
Forest and woodland	11.9	12.1	12.4	12.4	12.4
Reed bank	0.3	0.3	0.3	0.3	0.3
Built-up and waste	6.6	6.6	9.0	7.1	...
Total	100.0	100.0	100.0	100.0	100.0

World War II had two main effects on Hungarian agriculture: the temporary acquisition of much land under Hungarian rule before World War I; and a significant setback, affecting primarily animal husbandry, as a result of military operations on Hungarian territory and the policies of the Soviet occupation authorities. The four areas acquired by Hungary just before and during World War II were predominantly agricultural and added greatly to Hungary's agricultural potential and balance. Military operations hampered fall planting in the Great Plain in 1944 and spring planting in Transdanubia in in 1945. Operations in those years and for several years after were hampered by destruction, by removal by the Soviet Army of farm machinery and equipment, and by severe losses of animal draft power. The livestock losses also caused serious deprivation in the use of natural fertilizers at a time when lack of materials and disorganization of industry prevented an increase in the manufacture of artificial fertilizers. The inclusion of live animals, meat, and other agricultural products in the reparations imposed upon Hungary by the Soviet Union and, to a lesser extent, Czechoslovakia and Yugoslavia, added an unusual burden to the task of reconstructing Hungary's agricultural economy.

DEVELOPMENTS BEFORE THE COMMUNISTS

The most significant developments in Hungarian agriculture before the takeover by the Communist regime were those connected with Hungarian agriculture's particular social problem, the prevalence of large estates and the existence of a large class of landless and land-poor peasants.

Post-World War I Land Reform

In the pre-World War I Hungarian kingdom, almost half of the agricultural land (43.9 per cent) was in large estates of 115 hectares and over. Moreover, the land reform of 1920 had a very limited effect. This reform, which applied to only 6 per cent of the agricultural land, was purposely limited in scope by a belief on the part of its promoters in the efficiency and greater investment propensity of the large agricultural units. Thus, no upper limit was set for private land ownership. In practice, an upper limit of about 1.7 hectares per family was established for allotments. On private estates, only holdings over 576 hectares were expropriated without compensation. In all, 552,000 hectares were taken over; 415,000 hectares were distributed to almost 390,000 beneficiaries; the average allotment per beneficiary was thus about 1.06 hectares. Of the beneficiaries, about 185,000 had been landless and about 113,000 had been dwarf and small holders. The insignificant effect of the 1920 land reform is seen in the fact that in 1930 holdings of 100 hectares and over still accounted for about 41 per cent of all land. In the same year, about 300 families owned as much land as 1.4 million families (about 12 per cent of the total in each case). In 1935, Hungary surpassed any other country in the lower Danube Basin in the proportion of dwarf holdings, large gentry farms, and giant farms, but had the smallest proportion of medium-sized peasant farms (see Table 2).

Table 2. Landholdings, by Size, 1935

	Farms		Land	
	Number	Per Cent of Total	Thousand Hectares	Per Cent of Total
Dwarf farms (under 2.88 hectares)	1,440,750	76.1	1,103.2	12.0
Small farms (2.88–5.76 hectares)	204,471	10.8	853.5	9.2
Medium-sized peasant farms (5.76–57.6 hectares)	232,744	12.3	3,005.6	32.4
Large peasant and gentry farms (57.6–576 hectares)	12,485	0.7	2,041.6	21.9
Giant farms (576 hectares and over)	1,560	0.1	2,272.8	24.5
Total	1,892,010	100.0	9,276.7	100.0

Another striking feature was the high number of landless (787,000) and land-poor (552,000) peasants. This "rural proletariat," as Table 3 shows, amounted in 1930 to about two-thirds of the total agricultural labor force, a larger proportion than in any other country of the lower Danube Basin. Including dependents, this "rural proletariat" probably amounted to 2,200,000 persons. About a half of Hungarian agriculture was worked by family labor on owner farms; the other half was worked by hired labor on large owner or tenant farms. Although tenancy flourished on both small and large farms, by 1930, 90 per cent of all landed peasants were full owners. The number of landless peasants was reduced during the 1930's by further land resettlement and movement to cities, but in 1941 this group still numbered about 746,000.

Table 3. Landless and Land-Poor Peasants, December 1930

Category	Number	Per Cent of Total
Agricultural workers[a]	787,000	38.7
Land-poor peasants[b]	552,000	27.2
Total	1,339,000	65.9
Total agricultural labor force	2,031,000	100.0

[a] Hired physical labor, including tenant laborers.
[b] With holdings of less than 0.576 hectares (1 cadastral yoke).

Land Reform After World War II

In one of its first moves, the provisional Hungarian government on March 15, 1945 passed a sweeping land reform. This reform contained features which the Communists, who were members of the coalition government, designed with two purposes in mind: first, to win the support of the largest groups of peasants, or at least to weaken their resistance, while early moves toward socialization were proceeding elsewhere in the economy; and, second, to prepare the ground for later moves toward socialization of the countryside.

Under the terms of the land reform, large estates of more than 576 hectares were confiscated without compensation. Holdings between 57.6 and 576 hectares were reduced to 57.6 hectares, except in the environs of Budapest, where in practice the maximum holding allowed was about 29 hectares. Payment was to be made for expropriated land. Exceptions were made for working peasant proprietors, who were allowed to retain up to about 115 hectares, and members of the anti-German resistance during World War II, who could retain up to about 158 hectares. Churches, municipalities, and village communes were allowed to retain the standard maximum of 57.6 hectares. Forests received separate treatment: all forests above 5.8 hectares were na-tionalized. Those of 5.8 to 57.6 hectares became community, village, or municipal property, while individuals could retain up to 5.8 hectares. Holdings left intact could keep sufficient farm equipment, livestock, buildings, and other equipment to work the farms, with agricultural cooperatives absorbing the excess, either for cooperative use or dis-tribution to cooperative members.

The maximum plot for distribution was 8.6 hectares, with about 1.7 hectares additional for gardens and vineyards. Peasants who had participated in the short war against Germany could obtain a maximum of 14.4 hectares, plus as much as 2.8 hectares in gardens and vine-yards.

In all, a little over 3.2 million hectares, about one third of the country's land area, were seized in the land reform. About 43,000 farms were confiscated, and payment was made for about 85,000 holdings. Of some 700,000 original claimants in 1945, land was finally distributed to about 642,000 families, who received an aggregate of almost 1.9 million hectares, or an average allotment of just under 3 hectares. The remaining 1.3 million hectares was retained for public use.

Table 4 indicates the breakdown of expropriated land by type of land use. This land contained a much larger proportion of forest than the national total (see Table 1). These forests constituted the major portion of land taken over by the state and communities, the remainder being composed largely of meadows and pastures. Most of the ex-propriated arable fields, gardens, and vineyards were apparently dis-tributed to individuals.

Table 4. Land Expropriated in 1945 Land Reform, by Type of Land Use

Type of Land	Area (hectares)	Per Cent of Total
Arable	1,658,369	51.4
Gardens	24,224	0.8
Vineyards	26,522	0.9
Meadows	198,797	6.1
Pastures	316,834	9.8
Forests	809,977	25.1
Other	190,673	5.9
Total	3,225,396	100.0

The breakdown of distributed land by type of beneficiary shows that the 371,000 former landless recipients (farm servants and agricultural laborers) constituted the largest group numerically. Except for small groups of professional agriculturists and forest employees, the landless elements also received the largest average allotment, 3.4 hectares, which elevated them into the ranks of small holders, or at least into the upper brackets of dwarf holders. The next largest group was composed of about 214,000 dwarf holders, who, on the average, received allotments sufficient to raise them to the class of small holders. The third largest group, the 33,000 small holders received sufficient land to elevate them to medium-sized peasant holders.

Table 5 presents a comparison of the farm-size distribution in 1947 with that in 1935, with special emphasis on the great bulk of individual holdings in the categories below 57.6 hectares.

Table 5. Comparative Distribution of Holdings, 1935 and 1947

Category	Number of Farms (per cent of total)		Area of Farms (per cent of total)		Average Size of Holdings (hectares)	
	1935	1947	1935	1947	1935	1947
Dwarf farms						
0–2.88 hectares	76.1	68.1	12.0	17.9	0.75	1.15
Small farms						
2.88–5.76 hectares	10.8	18.8	9.2	21.1	3.80	5.00
Medium-sized peasant farms						
5.76–11.52 hectares	7.6	8.5	12.6	17.3	8.06	9.16
11.52–28.8 hectares	3.9	3.4	13.5	14.7	17.00	19.12
28.8–57.6 hectares	0.8	0.7	6.3	8.1	39.00	50.11
Total	99.2	99.5	53.6	79.1		
National average					2.65	3.57
Large peasant and gentry farms						
57.6–576 hectares[a]	0.7	0.5	21.9	12.8	162.70	124.50
Giant holdings						
576 hectares and over[b]	0.1	—	24.5	8.1	1,463.00	1,268.40
Total	100.0	100.0	100.0	100.0		
National average					4.87	4.48

[a] In 1947, these were mostly large state holdings.
[b] In 1947, these were all state holdings; none were in private hands.

The post-World War II land reform considerably reduced, but did not entirely eliminate, inequalities in size of landholdings. The total number of farms increased by about 175,000, the largest increase being within the group of small farms (2.88 to 5.76 hectares). The dwarf farms decreased somewhat in absolute numbers and in proportion to the total number of holdings, but the area of such farms increased considerably, both in absolute and relative terms. Although the area of these farms remained small, most of these holdings were near urban centers and were owned by industrial laborers and craftsmen who did not depend solely upon them for their livelihood. The average size of the bulk of individual peasant farms, those below 57.6 hectares, increased appreciably, with the largest absolute increase registered by the small group at the top level of medium-sized peasant farms.

From the economic point of view, the main problem posed by the land reform was the reduction of yields produced for the market, caused by the dissolution of productive large and giant farms and their replacement by peasant subsistence farms. The establishment of new farmsteads by the formerly landless and land-poor peasants also increased capital requirements at a time of great capital stringency.

COMMUNIST AGRICULTURAL POLICIES

Communist agricultural policies, in force since 1948, have had two interrelated goals:

1. To secure agricultural commodities at low prices for distribution by state channels to the growing urban industrial population and for export. It was important for the Communist program that peasant purchasing power not restrict government plans for industrial investment or exert inflationary pressures.

2. To ensure social and administrative control by the regime over the peasants.

The principal means of implementing the first goal has been fixing compulsory deliveries to the state. This wartime practice was continued and increasingly adapted to Communist purposes by extension to a greater number of agricultural products and to a larger proportion of total production, and by widening the gap between delivery prices and market prices. The second goal called forth a host of policies, chief among which was the inauguration in 1948 of a drive for collectivization and elimination of the influence of prosperous individual peasants, who were branded "kulaks." Basically, the purpose has been to convert the Hungarian peasantry into a rural proletariat, completely dependent on state and collective institutions, deprived of ownership of the means of production (land, livestock, major farm buildings, machinery), and hence unable to exert influence on production or marketing policies. The interrelation between the two principal goals is best illustrated by the application of the compulsory delivery system, which became increasingly discriminatory in the effort to control the most prosperous peasants and to force less prosperous ones into various types of collective farm groups.

Communist policies for the development of agriculture were incorporated in the state planning system. In theory, they placed great stress on: (1) mechanization, which was to compensate for the removal of labor from the countryside to industry; (2) a shift of emphasis to industrial crops, which was supposed to reduce Hungary's dependence on cereal production; (3) irrigation, which was to open regions in the semi-arid parts of the Great Plain for rice cultivation; (4) afforestation, which was to help resolve the drought problem and to increase Hungary's marginal forest reserves; and (5) introduction of advanced agronomy, which was to overcome the backwardness of Hungarian agriculture. In practice, all phases of agricultural work—cropping pattern, plowing, sowing, harvesting, threshing, animal husbandry—were subjected to minute direction by administrative order, which sought to plug loopholes left by the application of the compulsory delivery system.

Communist agricultural policies have been the least successful aspect of the entire Hungarian economic program since 1948. With the possible exception of irrigation and afforestation, on which some progress has been reported, agricultural development has at best stagnated, and in many respects deteriorated. The principal cause of this failure has been the bitter and determined opposition of the peasantry to the government's agrarian policies, expressed either directly, in resistance to collectivization and defiance of regulations concerning cropping and deliveries, or indirectly, in negative reaction to the lack of incentives inherent in the regime's policy. Both production and marketing have been depressed by the regime's social goal, which dictated discrimination against the most productive elements in the countryside.

A further cause of the failure in agriculture has been the low priority assigned to agriculture in investment. The government's agricultural development program even in the initial plans was subordinate to industrialization. In the implementation of the plans between 1948 and 1953, agriculture consistently received the lowest priority. Scarce building materials were assigned predominantly to industry, and planned mechanization was neglected when industrial production assigned higher priority to capital goods for export or further industrialization. Agriculture remained a distinctly limited field for private investments, because the government was trying to force the independent peasants into collective farms, and the few independent peasants with financial reserves were not disposed to invest, in view of the grim future facing independent farming. Labor, attracted by expanding industry and discouraged by the limited opportunities in agriculture, left the countryside. The result was a labor shortage in agriculture and a poor showing by the new collective farms, which were supposed to attract the independent peasants.

The government did not achieve its principal agrarian goals. By mid-1953, only a little over one fourth of the arable land had been included in collective farming groups, and peasants with the most skill and experience remained outside. Collection authorities still had to combat all kinds of evasion, and the degree of control the government had achieved over marketing agricultural commodities meant less as production, hit by droughts in 1950 and 1952, stagnated or declined. Thus, agriculture failed to provide the degree of support needed for the industrialization program.

This situation provided one of the strongest incentives for the government to adopt, in mid-1953, a revised economic policy, reducing the stress on industrialization and promising greater concentration on agricultural development. During the first eighteen months under this "new course," the government made significant concessions to the peasants, reducing delivery quotas, canceling arrears both for deliveries and taxes, allowing mass withdrawals from the collective farms, and replacing compulsory deliveries, in the case of some commodities, by a system of pre-contracting on terms more favorable to producers. However, it failed to increase agricultural investments or to improve agricultural performance. Part of the difficulty was caused by bad weather (an unusually cold winter, and rains and flood at harvest time in 1954), but more important was the uncooperative attitude of the peasants, who did not trust the government. At the end of 1954, the government had neither found a successful formula for solving the ills that beset its agrarian program, nor had it basically changed its goal.

Producers' Cooperatives

The development of producers' cooperatives, modeled on the Soviet kolkhozes, is shown in Table 6. This also lists the state farms, which together with the producers' cooperatives, comprise the "socialized" sector of agriculture, as distinguished from agriculture still in the hands of peasant proprietors.

Table 6. Development of Agricultural Socialization, 1948–1954[a]

| | | Producers' Cooperatives | | | |
| | | Households | | Members | |
Date	Number	Number	Average per Cooperative	Number	Average per Cooperative
1948 June					
Nov./Dec.	200				
1949 March	398			7,862	(20)
June/Sept.	510–560			10,522–12,907	(21–23)
Dec.	(1,400)			39,577	(28)
1950 June	1,520	46,000	(31)		
Aug./Oct.		50,000–59,000			
1951 Feb.	2,500				
May	4,250	200,000	(48)		
Nov./Dec.	4,500–4,652	230,000–236,000	(51)	350,000	(75)
1952 Aug./Sept.					
Dec.	5,315	318,500	(60)	446,900	(85)
1953 March	(5,315)	340,000	(64)		
Oct.	(5,315)			(515,000)	(97)
Dec.	4,677			263,070	(56)
1954 May		200,000		250,000	

[a] Figures without parenthesis are as given in various official or quasi-official Hungarian reports. Those in parenthesis are calculations or approximations based on other figures in the table, or estimates based on indirect official references.

| Producers' Cooperatives | | | State Farms | | Total Socialized Sector[b] | |
| Arable Land | | | Arable Land | | Arable Land[c] | |
Hectares	Per Cent of National Total	Average Hectares per Cooperative	Hectares	Per Cent of National Total	Hectares	Per Cent of National Total
			34,560	(0.7)		
(22,000)	(0.4)	(110)				
(131,400)	(2.4)	(94)	230,400	(4.3)	(361,800)	6.7
(378,000)	7.0		(324,000)	6.0	(702,000)	13.0
(432,000)	8.0	(173)	(324,000)	6.0	(756,000)	14.0
(702,000)	13.0	(165)	(378,000)	7.0	(1,080,000)	20.0
(842,400)	15.6	(185)	(486,000)	9.0	(1,328,400)	24.6
(972,000)	18.0		(540,000)	10.0	(1,512,000)	28.0
(1,303,800)[d]	24.6	(245)	684,140	12.7	1,987,940	(37.3)
(1,404,000)	26.0		(712,800)	13.2	(2,116,800)	39.2
(1,080,000)	20.0	(231)	(702,000)	13.0	(1,782,000)	(33.0)
979,000	18.0		(675,000)	12.5	(1,654,000)	(30.5)

[b] Aggregate of state farms and production cooperatives.

[c] Where acreages are calculated from given percentages, or vice versa, the calculation is based on an assumed national total of 5.4 million hectares of arable land, as derived from data in Table 1, applied to the total land area of Hungary.

[d] Official Hungarian sources give the acreage as 1,435,329 hectares, which implies too large a national total for arable land and also appears inconsistent with other figures in the series. For purposes of this table, it is assumed that the percentage is correct, but the given acreage an error, and the acreage is calculated as in the other cases.

As shown in the table, the producers' cooperatives grew by fits and starts, and several periods of intense activity may be identified, followed by lulls, which in 1951 and 1952 were determined by legislation forbidding the formation of new cooperatives between early spring and late fall. Several reasons explain this unsteady growth: (1) preoccupation of local government and Communist Party officials with consolidation of the new, often loosely organized groups after a big drive; (2) the desire to allow agricultural operations to proceed without the disruption attendant upon a collectivization drive; and (3) the need for a breather for the outraged and resentful private peasants who, the government seemed to hope, would forget about the threat to their future and fulfill their duty as producers.

Collectivization was launched by legislation in the fall of 1948 authorizing the establishment of three types of producers' cooperatives, each with its own model statutes. The three types are distinguished by the degree to which operations are carried out jointly, the extent to which private property rights are retained or submerged, and the mode of payment for work or production. Type 1 is the lowest form; only plowing and some sowing are carried on jointly, with each member gathering his own harvest and paying his share of common expenditures out of the proceeds. Type 2 is the intermediate form; the members perform *all* work collectively and, after the deduction of operating expenses, share in the net income proportionate to the size of the land contributed. As in Type 1, Type 2 collective farmers still retain private property (land, livestock, implements, buildings) for their own cultivation and use. Type 3 is the highest form, with landholdings and even draft animals pooled, and payments made only on the basis of work performed. In all three types, it was provided that each member should retain a household plot of 0.86 hectare. The authorities have favored Type 3, since it is the closest to the Soviet kolkhoz. In the beginning, the peasants formed this type, as the early producers' cooperatives were primarily formed by landless peasants on land leased from, or otherwise provided by, the state. The subsequent division between the three types is not known in detail, but Type 3 has remained dominant.

Producers' cooperatives were originally formed as adjuncts to existing rural cooperatives. In May 1950, legislation was adopted providing for so-called "self-governing independent production cooperatives" to be formed from producers' cooperatives that had become large-scale enterprises, uniting at least 30 families and owning an area of at least 300 hectares.

In the first year of collectivization activity, the landless peasants and new dwarf holders and small holders created by the land reform comprised more than 91 per cent of the membership of the producers' cooperatives. It was not until the fall of 1952 that the so-called middle peasants (identified as those holding between 4.6 and 14.4 hectares) were forced to join the producers' cooperatives in sizable numbers by various financial and moral pressures. So-called kulaks (generally speaking, peasants owning more than 14.4 hectares, but from time to time including lesser landholders accused of opposition or capitalist tendencies) were barred from joining producers' cooperatives after the first stage. They were found to have a harmful influence on the spirit the government was trying to instill into the new cooperative peasants. The "kulaks" were blamed, whether justifiably or not, for inspiring their poorer cooperators with what the government termed "capitalist mentality," a set of traditional peasant ambitions that played havoc with cooperative rules and regulations and led to the disbanding of some groups.

A quick reversal in the march toward collectivization came after the new Prime Minister of the post-Stalin period, Imre Nagy, announced, as part of the new policy toward agriculture promulgated in July 1953, the right to disband or withdraw from the producers' cooperatives. The response of cooperative members to this offer apparently caused the government to rue its generosity, for by the time the enabling decree was published in October, the rights of disbandment and withdrawal had been hedged with so many requirements and restrictions as to make these steps very difficult. In brief, the decree allowed producers' cooperatives to remain in existence if as much as 10 per cent of the membership so chose, and saddled those withdrawing with heavy debt burdens, part of which could only be paid by relinquishment of some property brought into the cooperative.

Nevertheless, the reversal was striking. Between October and December 1953, about 12 per cent of the groups disbanded outright, total membership was reduced by almost 50 per cent, and arable landholdings were reduced about 20 per cent, compared to the spring of 1953. For the most part, those withdrawing were middle peasants who had only recently joined the cooperatives, bringing, along with their superior experience in agricultural pursuits, hope for more efficient cooperative performance. Their departure, with apparently less of their land than they brought, left the cooperatives land rich, but short of both labor and skills. A few months later, the cooperatives were obliged to lease parts of their holdings for cultivation by private peasants on a share-cropping basis, thereby reviving shades of a past which the Hungarian Communists declared buried five years earlier.

In spite of attempts during 1954 to revitalize the producers' cooperatives by a variety of concessions and inputs of material and equipment, in every case more generous than those offered to individual peasants, the producers' cooperatives appeared to lose more ground during that year. A revised set of model statutes for producers' cooperatives, adopted in the fall of 1953, had dropped the requirement of three years' membership before withdrawal and guaranteed the right of any cooperative member to withdraw after fall work, upon six months' advance notice. The figures in Table 6 suggest that some, at least, were able to withdraw even before May 1954, while in the fall of that year about 2,900 more members withdrew.

In September 1954, an attempt was made to entice some former members back into the cooperatives by offering them postponement and eventual dissolution of the debts to the state arising out of their withdrawal, but there was apparently only minor response. At several times during 1954, announcement was made that 20,000 peasants had rejoined, but this number is small compared with the more than 250,000 members who had withdrawn in 1953. At the end of 1954, it was announced that during the last six months of that year, about 14,000 peasants with an aggregate of a little more than 9,000 hectares had joined the cooperatives, indicating that even such a moderate step forward depended on a reversion to the former concentration on landless or land-poor elements. Only 2,000 of the recruits in the latter half of 1954 were industrial workers responding to the government's "back-to-the-land" appeal.

Throughout the five-year collectivization period, complaints were voiced constantly about the poor performance of the producers' cooperatives, and decrees were passed periodically to strengthen them. Addressing the Third Congress of the Hungarian Workers' Party in May 1954, Matyas Rakosi, former Prime Minister and Party Secretary, boasted that "several hundred" of the producers' cooperatives were already successful groups with "efficient, careful management, high income, discipline, diligence and the well-being of its membership to be set as examples to the rest." This, of course, leaves more than 4,000 producers' cooperatives, the bulk of Hungary's socialized agricultural establishment, apparently unsuccessful. Toward the end of 1954, other spokesmen stressed the need to raise the living standards of cooperative members to the level of an average independent middle peasant. On New Year's Day 1955, hope was expressed by the press that during the coming year 500 more producers' cooperatives should reach the level of minimum viability already attained by Rakosi's "several hundred." Thus, as of early 1955, rural socialization in Hungary could be pronounced a failure qualitatively as well as quantitatively, and even its proponents appeared somewhat dubious about its future. In spite of this, the regime doggedly pursues its course of socializing agriculture, and the widely publicized resolution of June 1955 gave the goal of at least 50 per cent "socialized" by 1960.

State Farms

State farms, agricultural estates operated directly by the state with wage labor, were originally formed in 1948, mostly of former Crown Lands, very large estates, lands belonging to banks and other enterprises taken over by nationalization, and the lands of "model" farms set up during the post-World War II land reform. In addition to the state ownership principle, state farms differ from producers' cooperatives in that the workers have no privileges of free marketing of surpluses, although some of the surplus is distributed as wages-in-kind. Workers on state farms may have household plots, but they are limited in size to 0.288 hectare.

The development of state farms is shown in Table 6. Their holdings increased considerably faster than planned, owing to the increase in "offerings" to the state of land by "kulaks" and "hybrid industrial workers," who were especially hard pressed by the regime. In 1952, the regime inaugurated a policy of restricting such land "offerings" to specific months and refusing to take land from which outstanding taxes and delivery quotas had not been met. The decline in the holdings of state farms after the announcement of the policy revision in 1953 apparently arose from the new practice of leasing state reserve lands for cultivation over fairly long periods to individual peasants.

State farms, often cited by Communist leaders as the highest type of socialized agriculture, were supposed to be models of advanced agronomy and high productivity. Specializing in livestock, bread grains, sugar beets, maize, and flax, they have indeed provided a large proportion of market surpluses. Their production belongs to the state, but their performance in productivity has been disappointing to the regime. Among the shortcomings have been the lack of managerial skill—managers often being appointed, as in industry, because of their political reliability, rather than technical and administrative experience—and extreme fluctuation in the labor force, which has been poorly paid and badly housed. On the average, state farms have operated on a deficit, financed by heavy state subsidies.

Machine-Tractor Stations

Even before the onset of collectivization in 1948, the regime took steps toward the creation of central depots for agricultural machinery, which were considered a decisive element in the drive to restrict kulaks and to promote agricultural socialization.

The land reform decree had transferred the more costly agricultural machinery of the large estates to the farmers' cooperatives. Later decrees authorized the government to requisition tractors and other large machinery still in private hands. Beginning in 1947, the sale of agricultural machinery was forbidden to private persons. Some central machinery depots were established in 1946 to serve the "model" farms, but the machine-tractor stations themselves were formally established in 1948 (see Tables 7 and 8).

Table 7. Stock of Machinery at Machine-Tractor Stations, 1949–1954

	1949	1950	1951	1952	1953	1954
	(in units)					
Stations	221	361	368	364	364	312
Stock of machinery	*(in thousands)*					
Tractors	3.5	6.7	8.8	9.7	10.7	12.7
of which plowing	...	...	...	8.2	8.2	10.3
Row-crop tractors	...	...	...	0.17	0.36	0.87
Tractor plows	3.9	...	8.8	9.2	10.2	...
Reaper-binders	—	0.38	0.99	1.6	2.1	2.2
Grain combines	—	—	0.05	0.18	0.78	...
Threshing machines	1.3	3.2	6.3	10.4	10.6	11.6

Source: U.N., *Economic Bulletin for Europe*, VII, No. 2 (August 1955), 85 ff.

Table 8. Operations of Machine-Tractor Stations, 1950–1953
(*in million hectares of normal plowing equivalent*)

	1950	1951	1952	1953
All operations	1,983	2,755	2,988	4,555
Field work	1,529	1,952	2,040	3,037
Plowing	1,141	1,531	1,527	2,295
Cooperatives	484	963	1,187	1,751
Private farms	582	317	20	149
Other	75	251	320	395
Sowing	49	67	75	140

Source: Ibid.

At first, the machine-tractor stations hired their services to producers' cooperatives at a rate 30 per cent less than that to individual peasants, but later this gap was increased to 50 per cent. Producers' cooperatives were allowed to pay in cash after they delivered or sold their crops, but individual peasants were required to pay in kind and in advance. Individual peasants who could afford payment were often denied the service, because the producers' cooperatives had priority. After the 1953 policy revision, individual peasants were allowed to pay in cash, but the preferential rates for the producers' cooperatives were maintained.

Under the second Five-Year Plan (1956-60), about 4.4 billion forints are to be invested in farm machinery (2.3 billion forints in the first Five-Year Plan) and 3.5 billion forints to improve the machine-tractor stations. (11.70 forints equal $1.00, at the official exchange rate.) State farms are to be 95 per cent mechanized and cooperatives 65 per cent within this period. One hundred new repair stations are to be established, and electrification is to be extended to all state farms and machine-tractor stations. There is to be a considerable increase in farm equipment within the planned period: an additional 19,000 tractors; 3,800 harvester-threshers; over 1,400 harvesters; over 6,000 maize combines and silage cutters; and about 1,500 sugar beet combines.

PRINCIPAL CROPS AND ACTIVITIES

Cereals

Cereals have traditionally been the main crop, accounting on the average for almost four-fifths of the arable land use, an unusually large proportion. This has been about equally divided between bread grains (wheat and rye, with wheat predominating by a ratio of more than 2 to 1) and various coarse grains, of which the most important is maize, followed by barley, oats, and millet, the last insignificant in acreage. (See Table 9.)

With regard to bread grains, the most striking phenomenon is the reduction of sown area in 1950-54, especially in the latter half of this period. In these five years as a whole, acreage of wheat and rye combined were some 15 per cent below the average for 1936-40. Thus, in spite of claims of excellent yields, appreciably above the prewar average, the total crops averaged about 88 per cent of those during the prewar period.

Table 9. Sown Areas, Yields, and Harvests
(area in millions of hectares, yield in quintals per hectare, and harvest in millions of tons)

	1936–40	1950–54	1949	1950	1951	1952	1953	1954
Bread grains								
Area	2.21	1.88	2.06	2.04	1.92	1.80	1.75	1.88
Yield	13.7	13.9	12.5	14.4	14.9	12.7	15.6	12.2
Harvest	3.01	2.63	2.58	2.93	2.88	2.30	2.75	2.30
Coarse grains								
Area	1.87	1.68	1.80	1.77	1.71	1.50	1.68	1.75
Yield	18.4	16.9	14.5	14.2	19.6	11.7	20.0	18.6
Harvest	3.44	2.84	2.61	2.51	3.35	1.75	3.36	3.25
of which Maize								
Area	1.19	1.11	1.13	1.10	1.10	1.00	1.15	1.21
Yield	21.2	18.8	14.8	15.6	22.6	12.2	22.6	21.7
Harvest	2.51	2.13	1.68	1.72	2.50	1.22	2.60	2.63
Rice								
Area	—	0.025	0.014	0.014	0.017	0.021	0.029	0.04
Root crops								
Area	0.480	0.434	0.481	0.467	0.419	0.370	0.430	0.46
Potatoes								
Area	0.288	0.241	0.285	0.290	0.240	0.220	0.210	0.2
Yield	81.0	77.2	66.0	48.7	86.9	48.7	95.6	92.1
Harvest	2.31	1.77	1.88	1.39	2.13	1.07	2.00	2.2
Sugar beet								
Area	0.049	0.118	0.106	0.115	0.117	0.115	0.128	0.1
Yield	212.0	172.1	115.9	136.6	207.5	104.3	208.6	203.3
Harvest	1.04	2.02	1.23	1.57	2.39	1.20	2.65	2.3
Fodder beet								
Area	0.143	0.075	0.090	0.065	0.061	0.055	0.092	0.1
Oleaginous crops								
Area	0.067	0.310	0.305	0.319	0.306	0.316	0.301	. .
Textile plants								
Area	. . .	. . .	0.030	. . .	0.063	0.081	0.101	0.
Tobacco								
Area	0.013	0.024	0.022	0.021	0.024	0.024	0.026	.
Yield	1.32	1.09	1.15	0.94	1.27	0.96	. . .	1.
Harvest	1.72	2.51	2.53	1.97	2.79	2.30	. . .	.
Grass fodder								
Area	0.688	0.657	0.515	0.563	0.614	0.673	0.684	0.
Field vegetables								
Area	0.035	0.067	0.040	0.50	0.055	0.086	0.080	0
Total sown area	5.46	5.25	5.40	5.44	5.36	5.00	5.05	5

Source: Ibid., p. 92.

Hungarian spokesmen attribute the decrease in bread grain acreages to the shift to industrial crops, a state-sponsored move to decrease the traditional concentration on cereals. In the later years of the collectivization drive, this decrease was also due to an increase in the proportion of fallow and uncultivated land. The government discouraged bread grain production through price policies, which made grain an unprofitable crop, even after the partial liberalization in mid-1953.

Recent statistics for the important maize crop show a declining tendency in sown area, reaching the lowest point in 1952. Since then, the regime has emphasized maize cultivation, and the sown area in 1954 surpassed the prewar level. A parallel development has been observed in yield and harvest.

Remedies proposed in 1953 to improve the inadequate supply of all cereals leaned heavily on orders to increase the yields, but also gave more consideration than before to reversing the trend toward acreage decline.

The proposal to achieve a record bread grain production without an increase in acreage was based primarily on hopes for increased mechanization of sowing, cultivation, and harvesting, as well as more widespread dissemination of advanced agro-technical knowledge. Based on past performance, when such remedies were frequently prescribed but seldom implemented, the planners appeared overoptimistic. Performance during 1954, the first year of the new plan period, dashed hopes considerably. The sown area was increased, although apparently not to the extent desired. A combination of early fall frosts and drought in 1953, coupled with unsatisfactory field work caused by the dissolution of and withdrawal from cooperatives, affected fall sowings. Rains and floods at harvest time in 1954 caused unusual losses, and it was reported that the 1954 bread grain crop was 22.4 per cent below that of 1953. Accordingly, Hungary had to import bread grains. In the fall of 1954, leading agricultural spokesmen were counseling a departure from the traditional dependence on grain for agricultural export surpluses and suggesting more concentration on specialty products, such as poultry products, wine, and high-grade seeds, for which investment requirements were light and world market prices high.

Under the second Five-Year Plan (1956-60), bread grain production is to be increased from 27 million quintals in 1955 to 30 million quintals in 1960, and maize production from 29 million quintals to 41 million quintals. The area for bread grains and maize is to increase by 6 per cent.

Rice is the only new cereal crop developed in postwar Hungary. Starting with experimental production in 1939, rice cultivation was expanded, to some extent during World War II, but mostly beginning in 1949. The acreage reached a total of 42,000 hectares in 1954, and was slated to increase to 52,000 hectares by 1956. Rice is cultivated on irrigated portions of the semi-arid region of alkaline soils in the northeastern part of the Great Plain. Possibilities for further extension of rice cultivation have been provided by the opening in mid-1954 of the first section of the Tiszalok Dam and irrigation system, on the Tisza River. Since average prewar consumption of rice was about 19,000 tons annually, the current claim that domestic production has, since 1950, provided an export surplus appears justified, in view of estimated production of 50,000 tons in 1951. Hungary now claims to be the leading rice producer in Europe.

Industrial Crops

The acreage devoted to industrial crops in interwar Hungary was increased tremendously during the postwar years, the most striking increase being in oilseeds. The sown area of oleaginous crops grew from 6,000 hectares prewar to 305,000 hectares in 1949, and acreage of textile plants and tobacco also increased. Sugar beet acreage more than doubled. This shift started during World War II under German influence, but was greatly intensified by the Communists after the war.

Planners taking stock of the agricultural situation in 1953 noted that the over-all acreage of industrial crops had increased fourfold in comparison with the "pre-liberation" period. This led to increased production of sugar and of edible oils, with output of the latter claimed as more than forty times the average for the ten years preceding "liberation."

This development was vigorously promoted by the government, which, beginning in 1945, passed several decrees making the cultivation of industrial crops compulsory on certain lands. However, disregard for the suitability of natural conditions in certain parts of the country, led to a drop in average yields for most of these crops.

In addition to the crops listed above, Hungary has begun the cultivation of several new industrial crops, the most important of which is cotton. Cultivation started on a small scale in 1949 and was gradually increased, mostly on state farms, to an acreage slightly over 46,000 hectares in 1952. The original plans called for cotton cultivation on about 113,000 hectares in 1953, when it was hoped that cottonseed production would be about 39,000 tons and raw cotton production about 16,500 tons (presumably ginned basis). Raw cotton requirements are estimated at about 30,000 tons, indicating that the planners hoped to replace about 50 per cent of the imports and to enlarge the supply of vegetable oil. The planted areas in 1950-52 considerably exceeded the schedule laid out in 1949, but acreages after 1952 have not been reported. The original 1953 plans implied a yield of raw cotton (presumably ginned basis) of about 3.5 quintals per hectare, but it is not known if these expectations were justified. The Szeged region, at the extreme south of the Great Plain, was chosen as the area most suitable for cotton cultivation.

Other new industrial crops cultivated, at least on an experimental basis, are *kenaf* (a jute substitute), natural rubber (from the *kok-sagyz* plant, imported from the Soviet Union), and peanuts. In 1950, preparations were also under way for experiments with three other fiber plants, ramie, yucca, and jute.

Prior to World War II, silk production was carried on to some extent, with an average annual cocoon production of about 338 tons in the 1934-38 period. By 1945, silk production was negligible; no production figures are available for the postwar period.

According to agricultural plans adopted in 1953, extension of the acreage of industrial plants was to cease, and the acreages of sunflower and cotton were to be reduced by unspecified amounts. This plan was accompanied by severe criticism of the practice of allocating industrial crop cultivation to unsuitable areas, and seemed to imply that cotton cultivation might have been found unsuitable to climatic conditions, even in the extreme southern portion of the country. By being more careful in this respect, providing more fertilizers, and mechanizing more stages of the cultivation of industrial crops, the planners hoped by 1956 to reverse the great decline in yields that had accompanied extension of the acreage and scheduled yields that far surpass any achieved in recent years.

Potatoes and Vegetables

Available information of the prewar and current status of potatoes and other selected vegetables is shown in Table 9. These figures illustrate the decline in potato acreage, which agricultural spokesmen have deplored for several years and which apparently could not be halted even by such decrees as that of January 1952, making potato cultivation mandatory on all farms. The reason for this decline is not known, but it may be connected with shortages of nitrogenous fertilizers and an inadequate labor supply, since potato cultivation is labor consuming and soil depleting.

Spokesmen have also complained of a failure to increase vegetable production, in spite of an increase in the acreage for these crops. During 1950-54, the average yield of onions was 96.5 quintals per hectare, compared with 98 during 1934-38, and the average yield of cabbage was 153.1 quintals per hectare, compared to 226.3 during 1934-38. However, during 1950-54, the average yield of tomatoes and paprika, which is grown both as a spice and a vegetable, increased, compared to the 1934-38 average: for tomatoes, from 102.6 quintals per hectare in 1934-38 to 113.2 in 1950-54; for paprika, from 20.9 quintals per hectare to 30.4. Vegetable prices are high because of shortages and the greater demand in the enlarged urban centers.

Plans adopted in 1953 for the 1954-56 period for the improvement of the potato and vegetable supply call for a moderate increase in potato acreage, which would still leave it about 15 per cent below the prewar acreage. Vegetable acreages, according to this plan, do not require any increase, but methods of cultivation need to be improved to provide higher yields. Among other things, it was proposed to increase irrigated vegetable acreage, then 12,700 hectares, to a little over 16,000 hectares. Hungarian agricultural leaders hoped, through these latest plans, to meet the domestic demand for fresh vegetables and to realize export earnings.

Hungary also raises the following vegetables, shown with pre-World War II sown areas in parentheses: dry legumes (peas, beans, and lentils) (40,000 hectares); melons (17,000 hectares); green peas (3,600 hectares); cucumbers (2,700 hectares); lettuce (1,800 hectares); carrots (1,000 hectares); parsley (1,000 hectares); garlic (1,000 hectares); pumpkins (900 hectares); spinach (600 hectares); and cauliflower (500 hectares).

Viticulture

Hungary has enjoyed a world-wide reputation for fine wines, especially those of the Lake Balaton region and the Tokaj district in northeastern Hungary, where an unusual quality is imparted to the grapes by the volcanic soils. Wine exports in the period 1933 to 1940 were a considerable item in Hungary's foreign trade, ranging between 19,000 and 44,000 metric tons annually.

Data on vineyard areas and grape and wine production up to 1949 are presented in Table 10. No quantitative data have been released since 1949, and it appears that vineyards have suffered from neglect attendant upon collectivization and Communist investment policies. The area in vineyards and the yields of wine have probably declined.

Throughout the period since 1948, there have been increasing complaints within Hungary of a diminution in the yield of grapes, due to the shortage of copper sulphate for combatting fungus diseases. Although export data are not available for the past five years, high-grade wines produced have been exported mainly to the Soviet Union and other Soviet bloc countries in payment for imports for the industrialization program.

Table 10. Sown Area and Yields of Grapes and Wine, Selected Years
1934-38 (Average)—1949

Year	Sown Area Bearing Vineyards (in thousand hectares)	Grape Production (in thousand tons)	Wine Yield (in hectoliters per hectare)	Wine Production (in thousand hectoliters)
1934–38 (average)	204	36.3	17.7	3,332
1942	218	46.2	19.7	3,953
1943	226	41.0	17.6	3,688
1945	231	59.1	14.6	3,135
1946	238	...	16.1	3,830
1947	219[a]	...	12.3	2,700
1948	...	...	...	3,500[a]
1949	192[b]	...	16.5	3,173

[a] Preliminary official estimate.
[b] Calculated from other figures.

In 1949, almost 50 per cent of the vineyards had been planted prior to 1918, and were badly in need of replanting. In 1948-49, it was reported that over 4,000 hectares of vineyards were destroyed and only some 2,900 planted, leaving the vast bulk of the over-age vineyards untouched. The most recent plans, announced in 1953, call for planting over 40,000 hectares of new vineyards by 1959, with the bulk of the planting to be done on private farms and on the household plots of cooperative members. This six-year program also called for the revitalization of existing vineyards, the establishment on cooperative farms of vine nurseries for growing grafting stock, and the diversion of some scarce copper supplies for use as fungicides. Since wine is cited as one of the potential export surpluses, considerably more attention will probably be paid to this branch of agriculture than in the past several years.

Fruits and Nuts

During the interwar period, fruit orchards developed rapidly and were fairly evenly distributed throughout the country—about 50 per cent on the Great Plain, 37 per cent in Transdanubia, and 11 per cent in northeastern Hungary. In 1935, there were an estimated 34.6 million fruit and nut trees in Hungary. The major varieties were plums (9.6 million); apples (6 million); cherries (4.5 million)—including both sweet and sour cherries; peaches (3.8 million); pears (2.9 million); and apricots (2.8 million). Other fruits and nuts grown in some quantity include walnuts, quinces, almonds, and hazelnuts. Orchards continued to increase after 1935 so that in 1947, even after considerable damage from the unusually cold winter of 1946/47, there were still an estimated 34 million fruit and nut trees. (For production, see Table 11.) Progress since that time is not known, but the spell of severe weather in the winter of 1953/54, followed by hailstorms in the spring of 1954, was said to have damaged considerable numbers of fruit trees.

Table 11. Fruit and Nut Production, Prewar Average and 1945–1947
(*in thousand tons*)

	Prewar Average	1945	1946	1947
Apples	32.2	15.0	20.0	45.8
Pears	23.5	5.4	8.0	11.6
Cherries, sweet	11.0	5.2	4.0	11.7
Apricots	37.2	25.0	22.4	17.8
Plums and prunes	17.3	16.5	27.3	19.7
Almonds	...	...	0.2	0.4
Hazelnuts	10.2	...	2.9	7.1

Production of some fruits (apples, sweet cherries, and plums and prunes) regained the prewar level in 1947 after serious declines, due both to wartime disruptions and bad weather. However, in 1953 spokesmen revealed that the supply of fruit during the past several **years had not been meeting demand.** They blamed this primarily on an invasion of scale insects, which had affected the fertility of the trees. The proposed remedies were to augment the stock of fruit trees, with some 15 million new trees in the period 1954-59, above regular replanting; to increase the orchard area on state farms and cooperatives by about 58,000 hectares in the six-year period 1954-59; and to provide both insecticides and facilities for their use. If this program is successful, there will be about a 50 per cent increase in the number of fruit trees, and about a 30 per cent increase in the total area devoted to gardens and orchards.

Animal Husbandry

Although secondary to cereal cultivation, animal husbandry has always been an important agricultural pursuit. Before World War II, the livestock industry (excluding poultry, fish, and game) provided about 25 per cent of total agricultural output and income, a level somewhat above that of the Balkans, but far below that of Western Europe, where the livestock industry generally provided about two-thirds of agricultural income. The principal factors responsible for its secondary position in Hungary are the low proportion of pastures and meadows and the assignment of so large a proportion of farmland to grain for human consumption.

Information on numbers of economically important types of livestock and poultry is given in Table 12.

In spite of severe losses in the final period of World War II, when numbers of most livestock were reduced by one half or more, substantial recovery has been made.

Cattle. Before World War II, cattle were kept primarily in Transdanubia. The dominant type was the Hungarian-Transylvanian breed, but this is gradually being replaced by Simmenthal and various red-checkered Berne cattle, which are better milk producers. In 1953, however, the Hungarian-Transylvanian breed was still said to make up the bulk of the country's cattle stock.

Cattle numbers appear to have come close to meeting the goal originally set for 1954 in the Five-Year Plan, but it was officially reported that the proportion of cows failed to keep pace with the growth of the total number of cattle. In 1953, new plans for 1956 called for keeping the total approximately stable, but increasing the proportion of cows. These latest plans repeated the former goal of achieving a large-scale cattle industry based primarily on cooperative herds, but also called for more individual husbandry by members. By the end of 1956, it is hoped that every cooperative farm will have a collectively owned cattle herd, but also that every individual member will have his own cow, for which purpose long-term state credits are to be provided.

According to *Szabad Nep* (Free People) of April 27, 1956, the number of cows in 1955 was 885,000, and the number should increase to one million in 1960.

In spite of low milk and butter yields, butter was a sizable export item in interwar Hungary, as relatively little was consumed domestically. Fattened cattle also constituted a Hungarian export item.

Table 12. Quantity of Livestock and Poultry,[a] Selected Years 1938–1956 (Plan)

Year		Livestock					Poultry				
		Cattle	Hogs	Sheep	Goats	Horses	Chickens	Geese	Ducks	Turkeys	Total
		(in thousand head)					*(in million head)*				
1938		1,882[b]	3,110[b]	1,629[b]	41[c]	814[c]					22.9
1940		2,068[b]	4,390[b]	1,510[b]	41[b]	865[b]	24.6[de]	2.0[de]	1.7[de]		28.3
1941	(Spring)	2,049	3,949	1,254	37	844					
1942	(Spring)	2,365	4,670	1,709	71	900					
1945		1,070[b]	1,114[b]	329[b]	58[b]	329[b]	4.9[d]	0.6[d]	0.7[d]	0.7[d]	6.2
1946											
	Spring	1,104	1,327	370	87	394					
	Fall	1,223	1,717	397		397	16.0	1.5	1.6	0.04	19.1
1947		1,639[d]	2,733[d]	488[b]	89	464[b]	28.0[d]	3.9[d]	5.0[d]	0.8[d]	37.7
1948	(Spring)	1,804	2,499	591						0.5[b]	
1949[c]		2,000	3,800	950		580					
1950	(Spring)	2,050	6,500								
1951	(Spring)	1,700	4,500								
1952	(Fall)	(2,200)	(4,828)	(1,483)							
1953	(Fall) (Plan)[cf]	(2,442)	(5,504)	(2,402)							
1953	(Fall) (Actual)	(2,236)									
1954	(Plan)[cg]	2,400	6,000	2,000							25.0
1954	(Fall) (Actual)		6,800								
1956	(Plan)[ch]	2,200	5,500	2,300			17.0	1.5	1.2	0.25	19.9

[a] Figures in parentheses are calculations based on indirect official statements. Others are cited directly in official sources.

[b] Spring.

[c] Season unspecified.

[d] Fall.

[e] Includes Ruthenia (Carpatho-Ukraine) and annexed zone of Slovakia.

[f] As planned in September 1952.

[g] As planned in 1949–50, in original Five-Year Plan.

[h] As planned in 1953.

Hogs. The most important type of hog raised is the Mangalitsa, a curly-haired, rather small breed, developed especially for lard. Before World War II, this breed comprised more than 80 per cent of the total hogs. In spite of attention given to meat breeds during the postwar period, it still comprised 70 per cent in 1953. Plans in that year called for an increase in the proportion of meat-producing hogs, Yorkshires, Berkshires, and Cornwalls predominantly, to 38 per cent of the total.

The total number of hogs, which had declined in 1945 to hardly more than one third of the prewar total, recovered rapidly up to 1950. Since 1950, quantity has varied, due to the effect of droughts and of government policies. The 1953 plans aimed to rectify some of the government's previous policy mistakes, to stabilize the total number of hogs at about 5,500, well above prewar, and to increase slaughter weights and productivity. (See Table 12.)

During the interwar period and occasionally after World War II, Hungary had an export surplus of fattened pigs, shipped primarily to nearby Central Europe. At other times in the postwar period, however, there have been extreme shortages of meat and lard.

Sheep. Sheep raising appears to have been on the decline over the past fifteen years, due primarily to the upheavals in agriculture. Before World War II, sheep were kept mainly on the large estates, and efforts on the part of the government to encourage sheep breeding by small landholders in the years just after World War II were not very successful. The dominant breed is the Merino, a fine-wool breed, which in the early postwar period comprised about 75 per cent of the flocks. Other fine-wool breeds comprised about 10 per cent, and long-wool breeds about 15 per cent. Mutton-type sheep have been raised only to a very limited extent.

Sheep flocks were reduced in 1945-46 to less than one fifth of their prewar number, but they recovered considerably up to 1952, without, however, reaching the prewar status. The Five-Year Plan goal for 1954 envisaged surpassing the prewar status in that year, and later plans have raised this goal considerably. Latest plans call for continued dominance of the Merino breed, pointing out that it is useful also as a supplier of milk. Plans no longer seek to encourage sheep breeding on small holdings, but concentrate instead on cooperatives and state farms, of which all with over 115 hectares of land are expected to have sheep flocks by 1956.

From an average total of 6,000 metric tons (greasy basis) in 1934-38, wool production dropped to 2,000 metric tons in 1947 and 1948

but reached an estimated 4,000 metric tons in 1951. In the period
1934-38, Hungary imported an average of nearly one thousand tons
of wool (greasy basis) annually. In view of the low level of postwar
wool production, it is apparent that import requirements in this period
must have greatly increased.

Horses. Hungarian horses, once famous as breeding stock throughout the world, were raised primarily on the Great Plain on large estates of the gentry and nobility, where the concentration was on sad-
dle breeds. Draft breeds (about one fifth of the total number of
horses) were raised in Transdanubia. The total number of horses
was reduced by more than half toward the end of World War II, and
since then only moderate recovery has been made. Hungarian planners
apparently intend to keep the total well below the prewar level in view
of the gradual replacement of animal draft power with mechanical
draft power. However, it is doubtful that agricultural mechanization
has yet reached a point where the comparative shortage of animal
draft power can be ignored. Also, a shortage of feed supplies probably
contributes to the current decision not to encourage an increase in
number of horses.

Poultry. Poultry raising was a minor agricultural enterprise until
about 1935, when efforts were made to organize this branch. Both
poultry and eggs became important Hungarian export items in the
late 1930's. No direct information has been given on the number of
poultry since 1947, but it is apparent from the rather modest plan
goals published since that time that they must have decreased greatly.
Plans drafted in 1949-50 for 1954 called for 25 million poultry (as
compared to almost 38 million in 1947), but this figure was apparently far from achieved by 1953, when a new set of plans placed the
goal for 1956 a little under 20 million, with only about one million of
these in collective and state farm flocks. According to the second
Five-Year Plan, 30 million poultry are to be hatched by incubators
in 1960.

Hungarian planners in 1954 placed great emphasis on prospects for
a rapid increase in export surpluses of such poultry products as eggs,
feathers, and goose livers, in order to make up for declining surpluses
of grains.

Yields. Available figures on the yields of certain animal products indicate a lower national average in the postwar period than before the
war, i.e., a prewar average of about 1,700 liters of milk per cow,

compared to about 1,500 liters in 1953. Although the regime has particularly favored the state farms as far as investment and equipment are concerned, even the planned yields of animal products for state farms have not been reached. For the state farms, the planned goal was 3,300 liters of milk per cow in 1952, but the actual amount produced was only 2,100 liters. With regard to eggs, the planned goal for 1952 was 150 per hen, but the actual number was only 60. In view of the failure to meet these goals, the planners lowered those for 1954 to 3,200 liters of milk per cow and 110 eggs per hen; it is not known whether or not the goals were reached.

Hungarian spokesmen have consistently blamed deficiencies in livestock yields on an insufficient supply of fodder. In 1947, it was reported that fodder crops were planted on 242,000 hectares, compared to 388,000 hectares before World War II. Plans in 1950 called for an increase in yield of fodder crops, but failed to stipulate any increase in area. However, later plans of 1953 called for an increased area to be devoted to fodder plants; in 1954, 432,000 hectares were to be sown in rough leguminous fodder, and in 1956, 510,000 hectares; in 1954, 97,000 hectares sown in autumn hybrid forage crops, and in 1956, 164,000 hectares; in 1954, 201,000 hectares of green silage crops, and in 1956, 248,000 hectares.

Other factors cited as contributing to the low yields of animal products are the lack of proper shelter, resulting in high losses of livestock during the winter; the low level of zootechnical knowledge of the Hungarian peasants; and the lack of adequate veterinary service.

Fishing

Fishing was not an important activity in prewar Hungary. In the interwar period, fish consumption on the average was only about 2 kilograms per capita in Budapest, and even less in the provinces. Fishing was done for the most part in small boats on Lake Balaton and in parts of the Danube and Tisza rivers, the bulk of the catch being whiting and other small fish. Cultivation of fish in ponds was practiced only on a limited scale. In this period, about 50 per cent of the total fish catch was exported.

Against considerable resistance, the government has been attempting to introduce more fish into the diet. Success has been limited mainly to supplying workers' canteens, where consumers' preference can to some extent be disregarded. There is little evidence of an increase in retail marketing of fish.

Forestry

Owing to Hungary's small forest area, forestry is of relatively minor importance to the economy, and there is little prospect for achieving self-sufficiency in lumber and wood products.

Forests comprise only about 12 per cent of Hungary's total land area, covering in all a little over one million hectares. In 1936, the Hungarian forests consisted of about 38 per cent oak, 56 per cent other deciduous trees (primarily beech), and only 6 per cent coniferous trees.

Both in the interwar period and in the immediate postwar years, Hungary was dependent upon imports for about half of the domestic requirement for timber of all types, and, as no pulpwood was produced domestically because of the scarcity of coniferous forests, all domestic pulpwood requirements had to be imported. Domestic timber production at a level equal to half of the requirements was sustained only by cuttings exactly equal to new growth, or, in some years, by a small percentage of overcutting. Details about the forest economy in the past five or six years are not available, but it appears that some improvement in the reserves has occurred through an afforestation program.

This afforestation has been launched to provide windbreaks and shelterbelts for drought amelioration on the Great Plain and to increase forest reserves. Under the Three-Year Plan (1947-49), Hungary planted 270 million saplings on about 51,000 hectares, and the Five-Year Plan (1950-54) called for the afforestation of a further 328,000 hectares. Within the latter period, plans adopted at various times stipulated as follows: the planting of 27 million saplings between the fall of 1949 and the spring of 1950, and the planting of 200 million saplings on 23,000 hectares in the fifteen-month period between October 1, 1951 and December 31, 1952. The government has claimed that in 1950 more land was reforested than in all the twenty-five years of the Horthy regime. It placed the total of saplings planted in 1950 and 1951 at 140 million. Afforestation remained a concern of the government after the adoption of the new 1953 agricultural policy. The new Five-Year Plan (1956-60) stipulates that 480,000 cadastral yokes be afforested.

13. LABOR

Historical Background

The development of Hungarian labor has paralleled the country's gradual industrialization and may be divided into four major phases: (1) the epoch of "pioneering" industrialism, 1867-1919; (2) consolidation of industrial economy and stabilization of labor movements, both economic and political, 1920-44; (3) postwar reconstruction of democratic Hungary, 1945-47, with labor a decisive economic-political factor; and (4) regimentation and exploitation, subsequent to the Communist *coup d'état* of 1947.

The conditions of industrial production and the structure of the Hungarian economy were quite different in each epoch. The transition from one phase to another was not smooth. In fact, grave political crises that led to basic economic changes mark the end of each period. The pioneering epoch came to a close at the end of World War I, which resulted in the dismemberment of the Austro-Hungarian Monarchy, and a considerable loss of Hungary's natural resources. The second phase ended with the collapse of the Hungarian kingdom at the end of World War II. Gradually increasing Soviet domination of East-Central Europe, leading to the Communist *coup* of June 1947, destroyed the democratic institutions as well as the economic balance of postwar Hungary. The new phase—Hungary's integration into the Soviet orbit—then began.

Industrialization

The industrial revolution occurred relatively late in Hungary. In fact, the Vienna government considered Hungary's place in the Austro-Hungarian Empire as an agricultural colony, the source of cheap food supplies and of raw materials for Austrian and Bohemian industry. The Compromise *(Ausgleich)* of 1867, which established the Dual

Monarchy, did not substantially change the economic role of Hungary. Except for a few mines, no large-scale industrial operation existed, and wandering journeymen and small handicraftsmen, mostly of foreign origin, were the forerunners of the Hungarian labor movement.

The change began in 1879, when Hungarian export of grain and livestock to Germany was almost paralyzed by the protective tariffs introduced by Bismarck. Government leaders came to realize that Hungary's economy was dangerously unbalanced, and a series of laws was enacted by Parliament to promote industrialization. The period of 1879-84 marks the beginning of industrial development.

At the turn of the century, 16.9 per cent of Hungary's population depended on industrial production, while an additional 1 per cent depended on mining. In 1910, the ratio of the same categories had risen to 20.1 per cent and 1.2 per cent, respectively.

Under the Treaty of Trianon in 1920, Hungary ceded large mineral deposits, whose loss immediately affected industrial production. A relatively better situation prevailed in manufacturing, for the Trianon territory comprised the more industrialized regions, with 2,385 industrial establishments of the former total of 4,851. The total effect, however, was a decrease in the ratio of industrial population to 19.9 per cent by 1920. Under the pressure of the agrarian "surplus" population, the trend toward industrialization soon resumed its course: by 1930, 23 per cent of the population depended on mining and industry. The ratio increased to 25.4 per cent in 1941.

World War II gave further impetus to industrial expansion. During the years 1938-43, mining and manufacturing increased considerably. The proportion of small handicraftsmen was about 50 per cent of the total number of persons engaged in industrial production. Among the East-Central European countries, Hungary was second to Czechoslovakia in degree of industrialization.

Hungary entered the war in 1941, and in 1944-45 the closing phase of the war brought serious devastation. From 80 to 90 per cent of the industrial establishments sustained damages, and 40-50 per cent of the industrial machinery was destroyed. In addition, high reparation payments in industrial goods were required by the armistice agreement. Therefore, the rapid restoration of prewar production capacity became a vitally important task of the democratic coalition government. After 1947, the Communists placed heavy emphasis upon industrialization.

The structure and strength of the Hungarian labor force is given in Table 1, which reveals the serious setbacks suffered after the wars and the expansion of manufacturing industry at the expense of handicrafts.

Table 1. Labor Force Employed in Mining, Industry, and Handicrafts,
Selected Years 1910–1946

Occupation	1910	1920	1929	1938	1943	1946
Mining and Smelting						
Employees	...	...	2,646	2,897	4,795	4,000[a]
Workers	...	...	35,863	41,782	59,090	53,378
Total	29,100	40,100	38,509	44,679	63,885	57,400
Manufacturing Industry						
Employees	...	...	43,642	53,364	92,128	71,571
Workers	...	...	235,004	288,512	391,838	237,489
Total	226,695	173,331	278,646	341,876	483,966	309,060
Small Handicrafts						
Artisans	125,029	107,051	143,177	189,214	192,900	181,243
Journeymen	151,043	94,226	194,914	147,154	171,200	96,328
Apprentices	87,896	66,627	81,368	68,313	68,600	49,352
Total	363,968	267,904	419,459	404,681	432,700	326,923
Total, Industry	590,663	441,235	698,105	746,557	916,666	635,983
Total, Labor force	619,763	481,335	736,614	791,236	980,551	693,400

Sources: Statistical Year Book of the League of Nations 1930/31 (Geneva, 1932),
pp. 38–39; Central Statistical Bureau, *Magyar Statisztikai Zsebkonyv* (Hungarian
Statistical Pocketbook) (Budapest, 1947, 1949), XIII (1946) and XV (1948).
[a] Estimate.

Table 2 shows the shifts of employment which have occurred within
the manufacturing industry between 1938 and 1946.

Table 2. Employment in Manufacturing Industry, 1938, 1943, and 1946
(*in per cent of total labor force in manufacturing*)

Industry	1938	1943	1946
Iron and metal	17.6	16.0	22.5
Engineering	14.0	28.8	20.3
Electric power	2.4	2.0	3.9
Stone, earthenware	10.3	8.0	6.7
Wood, bone	4.4	4.0	2.3
Leather, rubber, bristle	3.6	2.6	2.7
Textile	22.1	14.3	15.5
Clothing	3.5	2.7	1.9
Paper	1.9	1.9	1.3
Food	11.8	10.6	12.1
Chemical	5.7	6.5	7.9
Printing and reproduction	2.7	2.6	2.9
Total	100.0	100.0	100.0

Source: Dezso Elekes, A Mai Magyarorszag (Hungary Today) (Budapest, 1947)
pp. 227–31.

As of 1940, approximately 21 per cent of the handicraftsmen were engaged in the clothing industry and 19 per cent in the building industry. The various services—hotels, barber shops, etc.—employed 17 per cent of all handicraftsmen, and 14 per cent were engaged in the food industry. The 7 per cent of handicraftsmen active in the engineering field, as well as the 6 per cent engaged in the iron and metal industry, consisted mostly of workers in independent repair shops, village blacksmiths, and the like. The rest represented a great variety of small enterprises, ranging from small printing shops to highly developed art crafts of weaving and earthenware.

Since the early 1880's, Hungary has gradually changed from an agrarian country to a mixed agrarian-industrial one. Accordingly, the number and proportion of the industrial labor force has constantly grown, with an increasing emphasis on manufacturing industry. At the time of the Communist seizure of power, Hungarian labor had already become a major factor in the nation's economy.

Labor Organizations

Hungarian trade unionism started around 1870, parallel with the first industrial expansion. Earlier attempts, such as the caterers' union in 1835, had no significance. In 1862, the formation of the first important union, the bookprinters' union, was registered. This was followed by the tanners' union (1867), the hatters' union (1874), the glassworkers' (1881), and clothing workers' (1892). The watchmakers, jewelers, and chemical workers became unionized in 1897. The first "white-collar union," that of commercial employees, was founded in 1900. At that time, total union membership was approximately 10,000. The great masses of building workers, iron, steel, and metal workers, textile workers, etc. raised the membership rapidly, and in 1907 it reached 150,000. In 1917, the total number of unionized workers was 215,000.

Naturally, the Hapsburg Monarchy did not sympathize with trade unionism, particularly because Hungarian trade unions were closely affiliated with the Social Democratic Party. Drastic measures, bitter fights, and temporary setbacks marked the period that ended with the collapse of the Hapsburg Monarchy. The democratic revolution of 1918 gave great impetus to union membership, which reached a record 721,000. At that time, the unions were already highly centralized; a Central Secretariat had been set up in 1904 by the Third Trade Union Congress, and the bargaining power—both political and economic—

was vested in the Trade Union Council, representing the national federations of the various craft unions.

The democratic Hungarian Republic was overthrown by a Communist *coup* in 1919. The trade unions displayed an explicitly anti-Communist attitude during the short-lived Communist dictatorship, and therefore had to be "tolerated" by Admiral Horthy's counter revolution that followed in November 1919. However, the semidictatorial methods of "cold" oppression enabled the Horthy administration to cut the activity as well as the membership of the unions to a minimum until the end of World War II.

Even though Hungarian industry underwent a great expansion in this period, political circumstances prevented labor from regaining its 1917-18 strength. However, the organized force of 100,000 to 110,000 unionists played a decisive role in formulating labor legislation and wage policy, for the overwhelming majority of the nonunionized workers supported the unions' actions.

Besides those trade unions identified as "free trade unions" or "Social Democratic unions," there were some Christian Socialist labor federations and also fascist labor organizations. Unfortunately, there are no detailed statistics available concerning their membership figures. In 1920-22, the Christian Socialist federations registered some 100,000 members, but the figure soon decreased to 20,000, in spite of government favoritism and the general political trend. In the 1930's, the so-called Organization of Vocations and the National Center of Labor emerged, representing extreme rightist political ideas. Neither of these organizations played a significant role, but in 1939 both claimed a membership of 10,000. While the Christian Socialist federations cooperated in most labor matters with the trade unions, the extremist organizations went their own way.

Prewar trade unionism had an excellent reputation and great appeal. Union membership was not obligatory. Neither were there "closed shops" of any kind. The list below shows the yearly membership figures of the Hungarian trade unions, prior to the Communist seizure of power.

Prior to the end of World War II, there were 31 national craft unions federated in the Trade Union Council. After the war, a great number of new craft unions were established to unionize workers, such as railroadmen, public and municipal employees, postal and telegraph workers, and firemen, who had not been permitted to unionize. A large number of white-collar unions were also chartered. In fact, the Communist Secretary-General of the Trade Union Council, Istvan Kossa, encouraged the formation of new unions, for the newly established organizations offered greater opportunity of infiltration than the traditional ones.

Year	Membership	Year	Membership	Year	Membership
1901	9,999	1917	215,222	1933	111,561
1902	15,270	1918	721,437	1934	111,783
1903	41,138	1919	214,908	1935	112,165
1904	53,169	1920	152,441	1936	112,669
1905	71,173	1921	152,577	1937	108,500
1906	153,332	1922	202,956	1938	102,000
1907	142,030	1923	176,401	1939	110,000
1908	102,054	1924	127,526	1940	108,000
1909	85,266	1925	125,024	1941	106,000
1910	86,478	1926	126,260	1942	104,000
1911	95,180	1927	127,422	1943	102,000
1912	111,966	1928	124,378	1944	102,000
1913	107,486	1929	110,704	1945	10,140[a]
1914	51,510	1930	88,870	1946	936,022[a]
1915	43,381	1931	103,552	1947	1,288,095[a]
1916	55,338	1932	110,060		

Sources: Elekes, *op. cit.* p. 120; *Die Gewerkschafts und Genossenschafts Bewegung in Ungarn* (Budapest, 1928), p. 14; Hungarian Ministry of Foreign Affairs, "The Development of Hungarian Trade Unions, Their Social, Economic and Political Role," Press Release (Budapest), May 1, 1947.

Note: Figures relate to territory of the given year.

[a] Figures pertain to January 1. All other figures are for the end of respective year.

Labor Legislation

A gradual increase of labor rights and gradual improvement of working conditions characterized the period before 1947. The first labor law, the so-called Mine Act of 1854 established the 12-hour working day for adults. Other industrial branches were first regulated by Act No. 17 of 1884, which left open the possibilities for free bargaining between employer and employee. It prohibited the use of child labor below the age of 10 years and limited the working day of apprentices under 14 years to 10 hours in handicrafts and to 8 hours in factories. The average work day for adult workers varied from 12 to 14 hours, according to the industrial branch.

The provision of the law concerning free bargaining for working conditions aided the trade unions. The campaign slogan "Three-Times Eight"—meaning a social program for an 8-hour work day that would leave 8 hours for rest and 8 hours for self-education and leisure—soon became popular. The fight was resumed with vigor after World War I and, by means of successful strikes, labor achieved the 8-hour work day in many industrial branches. (Cabinet Decree No. 6,660 of 1935 M.E., later ratified by Act No. 21 of 1937.) The working hours of the various white-collar workers ranged from 40 to 48 hours weekly.

Parallel with the regulation of working hours, special legislation provided for the protection of children, juveniles, and women employed in industry. Act No. 5 of 1928 strictly prohibited the work of children and women where such work exceeded their physical strength, or endangered their health or morals. Night employment was not permitted.

After World War II, the democratic coalition further improved labor conditions and extended labor rights. Cabinet Decree No. 3,530 of 1946 abolished discrimination between laborers and white-collar workers as to working conditions. Weekly working hours were not to exceed 48, including the paid 30-minute daily lunch break. A paid vacation of 12 work days was stipulated after the first year of uninterrupted employment. This vacation was to be increased by one additional work day each consecutive year of employment, not exceeding 25 work days. Cabinet Decree No. 8,620 and No. 12,100 of 1946, as well as No. 15,500 of 1947, established that all working conditions—within the framework of the legislation outlined above—should be regulated by collective agreements between the Trade Union Council and the respective employers' organizations. In case of wage disputes, the National Wage Establishing Board, representing labor, management, and government, was the mediatory agency.

The exclusive right to maintain employment exchanges was granted to the trade unions by Decree No. 48,400 of 1946 Ip.M., issued by the Minister of Industry. The unions established and administered the network of employment offices throughout the country.

The most important achievement of labor was that of obtaining the right of "co-determination," i.e. the workers' active participation in industrial management, a much debated issue in Western Europe. Cabinet Decree No. 55,000 of 1946 authorized the trade unions to form so-called Shop Committees whose activity was extended to all questions pertaining to the terms of work, such as working hours, overtime, leave, etc.; social and cultural matters; the physical welfare of the workers; disciplinary actions, dismissal of workers; representation in the Board of Directors, joint control over the enterprise's production plans, and executive administration.

Standard of Living

A less favorable picture must be drawn with regard to real wages and the standard of living. Taking 1913 as the base year (100), the average index number for the period 1926-37 is 91.3. Only after the outbreak of World War II, during the war boom, 1941-43, did real wages come close to that of 1913.

The decline in real wages was, of course, due to various factors: the dismemberment of the economic unity of the country by the 1920 Trianon Treaty; the pressure of the agrarian "surplus" population upon the industrial labor market, particularly during the depression years of the early thirties; and government policy. Real wages did not keep pace with expanding industrial production nor with the increase of labor productivity. During the 1930's, when German labor—19 per cent of Germany's population—received 31.5 per cent of German national income, Hungarian labor—6.3 per cent of the population—received only 8.3 per cent of the national income.

The economic disaster that followed the end of World War II made all wages unrealistic until the inflation was stopped and a new currency, forint, was introduced in August 1947. Lack of reliable data prevents the computation of accurate real wage figures for this period. Nevertheless, Table 3, which gives nominal wage indices and cost of living indices, provides an idea of the economic difficulties which labor faced in postwar Hungary.

Table 3. Nominal Wage and Cost of Living Indices, 1938, 1939, and 1947

Year	Cost of Living Index	Nominal Wage Index
1938	100.0	100.0
1939	100.4	117.0
1947	185.1	129.1

Source: Frederick S. Pisky, "Standard of Living in Hungary," microfilmed MS No. 352, Library of Congress, Washington, D. C.

While the cost of living for a worker's family of four members amounted approximately to 600 forints monthly in 1947, monthly earnings of day laborers ranged from 120 to 350 forints. White collar workers' salaries were from 103 to 703 forints. Engineers earned between 217 and 869 forints. Thus the large majority of wage earners lived on an "emergency" budget, from which many items of primary importance must have been eliminated.

Labor Under Communist Rule

In the spring of 1947, a Three-Year Plan for the economic development of Hungary was prepared by the democratic coalition government. Before it could be launched, the Communists seized power. It was under the new government that on August 1, 1947, the Three-Year Plan came into effect. The plan, completed by the end of 1949, generally succeeded in reaching the production level of 1938. In terms of labor, however, 1949 output required the employment of a considerably larger force than that of 1938, mainly because of the slow increase in labor productivity and the lack of modern technical equipment.

The end of 1949 marks the beginning of a new economic policy within the Soviet orbit. Until then, the countries were exploited by the Soviet Union in a rather haphazard fashion. The introduction of the various five- and six-year plans signaled the beginning of the systematic colonization of the area, and the gradual integration of the countries into the Soviet economy. Production plans as well as production methods, labor legislation as well as the standard of living, have since been adjusted in order to conform to those of the Soviet Union.

Industrialization, with particular emphasis on heavy industrial development, was the feature of every plan introduced in the Iron Curtain countries. In Hungary, the Five-Year Plan was enacted by Act No. 25 of 1949, and came into effect on January 1, 1950. The growing demands of the Soviet Union during the period of the Korean War soon called for amendment of the original plan. At the beginning of 1951, the planned production targets were raised considerably.

From 1951 until June 1953, the ruthless drive for the fulfillment of the plan resulted in constant labor shortages, both in industry and agriculture. Forced labor was employed on a large scale, and almost every major achievement of the Communist economy was attained with the help of forced laborers.

From June 1953 until January 1955 there was a rather spectacular interlude, commonly referred to as the "new course" policy, in the Soviet Union as well as in East-Central Europe. Prime Minister Imre Nagy attempted to lessen the unbearable strain on the country's economy by putting more emphasis on consumer goods and agriculture and easing police control and political tension. The shift of emphasis, of course, resulted in local unemployment and in redirection of the workers toward light industry and agriculture. This "rolling readjustment" was, however, not completed.

With the beginning of 1955, the "soft policy" came to a sudden halt, and the official Party line resumed much of its original rigidity. Top priority of heavy industrial production, as well as further collectivization of agriculture, has since been emphasized. At the beginning of 1955, the structure of the labor force roughly corresponded to that of 1953.

Structural Changes in Labor Force

The major changes within the labor force which have accompanied the Communist industrialization program may be summarized as follows:

1. Industrial labor force nearly doubled its 1938 size. On January 1, 1953, and, generally, again on January 1, 1955, there were 2,295,000 workers and employees engaged in nonagricultural activities, excluding civil service and armed forces. The number of nonagricultural laborers was around 1,600,000. The number of white-collar workers was astonishingly high, 695,000.

Thus, labor productivity has gradually become the vital problem of further industrial expansion in Hungary. The large supplies of new industrial labor available in the earlier years are apparently exhausted, and it is officially estimated that further additions to the labor force will not exceed 2 per cent per year.

The index figures in Table 4 show the relatively slow increase, and in 1954, the decrease, of labor productivity, compared to the quantitative increase of the labor force.

Table 4. Employment and Labor Productivity in the Manufacturing Industry,
1948–1954
(1938 = 100)

Year	Employment		Labor Productivity	
	Index	Increase	Index	Increase
1948	99	—	98	—
1949	113	14	122	25
1950	127	12	149	23
1951	144	14	174	16
1952	161	12	194	11
1953	180	11	194	0
1954	196	9	179	−8

Source: Free Europe Press Research and Analysis Department, Free Europe Committee, Inc., *Relationships Between Productivity and Wages in the Satellites: Part III—Hungary* (New York, 1955).

Although low productivity may be due in part to the fact that a large part of the labor force consisted of new recruits from agriculture, the main factor was the inefficient Communist bureaucracy, burdening industry with an oversized administration. Communist leaders have revealed that the ratio of productive workers to nonproductive administration in certain industrial branches was slightly better than 2 to 1. The impressive figures of the expanded labor force, therefore, do not imply proportionally higher production.

2. The Communist economy has directed large numbers of workers to industrial production, partly from other fields of activity and partly from nonemployed persons. Until 1949, nationalization of banking, wholesale and retail trade, and most handicrafts made new manpower available for expanding manufacturing. Since 1950, the bulk of manpower has come from agriculture. Approximately 360,000 persons left agriculture before June 1953, and only 150,000 were allowed to return during the "new course." The present balance sheet indicates that about 200,000 additional persons have found employment in industry, while the rest are apparently engaged in transportation and (nationalized) trade.

From among formerly nonemployed categories, the recruitment of women is significant. Immediately after the war, the number of gainfully employed women decreased considerably. By 1951, however, the number of women in industry was roughly equal to the number in 1930, approximately 138,000. On the basis of Communist plans, it may be assumed that their number has passed the 300,000 mark. Their proportion in mining is 8 to 10 per cent of the mine labor force, while in the manufacturing industry it is reportedly 32 per cent. In transportation, communication, and service industries, the ratio must be even higher, according to the plans. The total number of women in the nonagricultural labor force at the beginning of 1955 may be estimated at 700,000 to 750,000.

3. Industrialization has greatly affected rural areas. While the Budapest region has retained its dominant position, with more than half of all industrial wage earners, the increase of industrial labor in the rural areas indicates a strong tendency toward decentralization of industry. The proportion of industrial labor in Komarom County has increased by 600 per cent since 1938; in Fejer County by 560 per cent; and in Pest-Bacs-Kiskun County by 540 per cent. Heves, Szolnok, and Baranya counties recorded increases of 480, 380, and 370 per cent respectively, for the same period. Until 1949, the main effort was concentrated on rebuilding the traditional industrial centers. During the Five-Year Plan, the traditional areas have been greatly expanded

and new ones established. Sztalinvaros (iron), Kazincbarcika (heavy chemical), Veszprem (chemical), Tiszalok (electric power), and Szeged (textile) have become sites of new labor concentration. The impact of rural industrialization on the Hungarian social structure is highly significant.

4. The Communist methods of mass production and their concept of nationalization have resulted in major shifts within the industrial economy. Large-scale nationalization, for instance, has eliminated the small trade character of the building industry and developed a highly centralized network of building construction enterprises, closely related to the manufacturing industry. To a lesser extent, food and service industries have undergone the same transformation. As a result, the number of independent handicraftsmen sharply decreased before June 1953, when there were only 44,000 self-employed artisans left, while 75,000 registered themselves as "small-trade-cooperative" members. The others were swallowed by the manufacturing industry, and there was a pressing need for village blacksmiths, repair shops, etc. This explains why the "new course" had to change the trend, and why the number of self-employed artisans has increased. (See Table 5.)

Table 5. Number of Persons Employed in Industry and Handicrafts,
1949–1954
(*yearly averages in thousands*)

	1949	1950	1951	1952	1953	1954
Industry, excluding handicrafts						
Manual workers	420	475	540	600	666	685
Other employees	70[a]	135	150	200	234	200
Total	490	610	690	800	900	885
Building and construction						
Manual workers	90	135	165	220	210	160
Other employees	5[a]	35	35	45	60	40
Total	95	170	200	265	270	200
Members of artisan cooperatives	25	30	30	50	75	95
Self-employed artisans	110	95	80	60	55	80
Workers employed in private workshops	135	75	20	10	5	5
Total	855	980	1,020	1,185	1,305	1,265

Source: U.N., *Economic Bulletin for Europe*, VII, No. 2 (August 1955), 90.

[a] Excluding about 30,000 employees in economic administration who were shown under industry and building and construction after 1950.

The manufacturing industry has tended toward concentration. In 1938, approximately 25 per cent of the workers were employed in plants with less than 100 laborers; in 1953, the number had decreased to 1 per cent. Meanwhile, the number of workers employed in plants with more than 500 workers increased from 46 per cent in 1938 to 70 per cent in 1953. Table 6 shows the emphasis on heavy industry.

Table 6. Distribution of Labor by Main Industrial Branches, 1938,
1949, and 1953
(in per cent of total labor force)

Year	Heavy Industry	Light Industry	Food Industry	Total
1938	58.1	30.5	11.4	100
1949	64.0	24.5	11.5	100
1953	68.5	21.1	10.4	100

Source: Jeno Redei, *"Ipari munkassagunk tizeves fejlodese"* (Ten-Year Development of Our Industrial Labor), *Kozgazdasagi Szemle* (Economic Review) (February 1955), pp. 121 ff.

The number of industrial employees in January 1955 roughly corresponded to that of 1953. While the number of workers in the manufacturing industry has remained almost unchanged, the number of building industry workers has declined, and the number of handicraftsmen, trade cooperative members, and food and service industry employees has increased.

Communist-Controlled Trade Unions

The structure of the Hungarian trade unions prior to World War II was based on national federations, organized according to crafts. Craft unions exercised great power in their domain, while the Trade Union Council, the central body of all unions was a representative forum. The first change was the postwar Communist reorganization of the unions, which started on the top level and influenced the lower bodies.

At the beginning of the new era, the basis of organization was still the craft union. However, the dictatorial power of the Trade Union Council overshadowed the unions and made them departments of the General Secretariat of the Council. It was in the interest of Istvan Kossa, the Communist Secretary-General, to increase the number of craft unions for a while, preventing the old and well-established unions from strengthening their influence. The course, however, was immediately reversed after 1949, and the number of craft unions was gradually reduced from 51 to 20 through centralization and mergers. In 1956, the following unions were represented in the Communist-controlled National Council of Trade Unions (formerly the Trade Union Council):

Agricultural Workers
Art Workers
Chemical Workers
Commercial and Financial Workers
Communication and Transportation Workers
Construction Workers
Construction Material Workers
Civil Service Employees
Food Industrial Workers
Iron and Metal Workers
Leather Industrial Workers
Local Industrial and Town Economy Workers
Metallurgical Workers
Mine Workers
Postal Employees
Printing and Paper Industrial Workers
Physicians and Sanitary Workers
Railroad Employees and Seamen
Teachers and Pedagogues
Textile Industrial Workers

After the seizure of power, Communist trade union leaders redefined the role of trade unions along Soviet lines. Communist leader Antal Apro, who succeeded Istvan Kossa in 1948 as Secretary-General of the Trade Union Council, specified that the trade unions' role was to intensify production, to organize work competitions, and to make secure the leadership of the Party. Trade unions have become a tool for the control of labor on local, regional, and national levels. The local bodies, the Shop Committees, once the representative organs of the workers in industrial "co-determination" have been converted into government agencies, preoccupied with the fulfillment of the Five-Year Plan. Basic trade union rights have been taken away. The right to strike was abolished by Act No. 34 of 1947. The provision of this law was replaced by Edict No. 4 of 1950 on Criminal Protection of the Planned Economy. The unions' exclusive right to maintain employment exchanges was eliminated by Cabinet Decree No. 12,400 of 1948. The so-called Labor Code of 1951 made collective bargaining an empty phrase and wiped out remnants of "co-determination." In 1952, the

National Council of Trade Unions surrendered to the government its right to determine working conditions by the Joint Resolution of the Council of Ministers and the National Council of Trade Unions on Overtime and on Work to be Performed on the Weekly Day of Rest and on Holidays.

Of course, the Communist conquerors did meet opposition in their bid for control. The leaders of the Social Democratic Party's "Old Guard," Karoly Peyer and Agoston Valentiny, fought a valiant rearguard action even after the Communist seizure of power. President of the Trade Union Council Odon Kishazi and Deputy Secretary General Miklos Vas organized resistance to Communist pressure within the Trade Union Council. Persecutions against the "Peyerists" started as early as September 1947, and the followers of another popular Socialist, Gyula Kelemen, were purged. In the spring of 1948, all those trade union leaders who resisted the Communist *coup* were removed from office by force. Odon Kishazi was succeeded as president by the fellow traveler, Jozsef Harustyak. On June 6 and 7, 1950, about 4,000 labor functionaries were arrested and sent to forced labor camps or prisons for their "right-wing socialist" convictions. According to Rakosi, these men spread ideas responsible for the undermined labor discipline, the increase of rejects in production, slackened norms, and wage frauds. Since 1950, whenever production has lagged or the workers' unrest has grown, Social Democratic influence was blamed. This has been the labor counterpart of the "clerical reaction" in educational matters, or the "kulak conspiracy" in agriculture.

Since the role of the Communist trade unions is that of the Party's transmission belt, efforts have been made to increase union membership. Accordingly, total membership rose from its January 1, 1947 level of 1,288,095 to 1,430,000 in February 1951. In December 1953, membership figures passed the 1,800,000 mark, and in May 1954, membership was 1,913,000.

The present organization of the trade union movement clearly reflects the Soviet pattern. The "highest body," in principle at least, is the National Congress of Trade Unions, which convenes every four years. During the four-year period, the National Council of Trade Unions is authorized to carry on the business. It must convene every six months to deal with the agenda prepared by the Executive Committee. As in the Soviet Union, the Executive Committee is the real central body, while the Council and the Congress are limited to granting approval of steps already taken. The heart of the machine is the Secretariat, which is composed of the President of the National Council of Trade Unions, the central secretaries (the post of Secretary-General was abolished when Secretary-General Istvan Kristof succeeded Jozsef Harustyak in the presidency), and the secretaries of the Executive Committee. In 1954, Jozsef Mekis succeeded Kristof.

Under the direct supervision of the Executive Committee are the County Trade Union Councils. Local Trade Union Committees are formed in every city, village, or community, wherever the size of membership justifies. These committees, which are also control organs, are in charge of supervising the work of the Shop Committees in their localities. The basic organs of the pyramid are the Shop Organizations, which are formed wherever the number of employees exceeds thirty, and their work is directed by the Shop Committee. Where the number of employees is less than the required thirty, a so-called Local Group is formed, whose function is similar to that of the Shop Organization.

Since the Communist seizure of power, the rank and file have been allowed to "elect" their leaders. They can vote for a single list of candidates presented by the officials. Technically, the members may vote against the list, but the leaders of such "revolts" disappear.

By Cabinet Decree with the Force of Law No. 36 of 1950, the administration of social insurance was assigned to the unions, in particular to the Shop Committees. This move tightened the government's control over the workers, since it is not the physician's diagnosis, but the Shop Committee's decision that makes the worker eligible for sickness benefits. As a matter of fact, by this measure labor lost its finest achievement. As a result of a long and persistent fight, the National Social Insurance Institute emerged in the late 1920's as one of the best social insurance systems in Europe. It was under the administration of a board composed of labor, management, and government members; each group was represented according to its financial share. The postwar coalition government extended labor's influence and withdrew from the board, leaving it under the control of labor and management. With labor represented by the Communist-controlled trade unions, the Institute has become the tool of the Party, an important instrument in the system of political coercion and economic exploitaton.

Labor Administration and Enforcement of Labor Discipline

With the transformation of the free trade unions into control organs of Communist management, labor lost its bargaining power. This is clearly reflected by the rigid provisions of Communist labor legislation.

The data on available manpower are registered with and administered by the Central Bureau of Manpower Reserves, which, according to Cabinet Decree No. 12,400 of 1948, is the sole agency charged with labor recruitment and employment exchange. By Cabinet Decree No. 8 of 1950, the Bureau is also authorized to "direct and secure the special training of the workers." Various decrees, both old and new, are applicable in cases where a person refuses to accept the job assigned by the Bureau. Act No. 2 of 1939 authorized penal action against persons "disturbing public order and security or another important state interest." Decree with the Force of Law No. 4 of 1950 and Act No. 2 of 1950 provide drastic measures for ensuring the "legal protection of the planned economy." For offenses listed as "disturbing order," "loafing," "endangering the people's economy," and the like, the persons charged may be sent to a labor camp or a prison workshop. It is impossible for the worker to ignore the regime's policy on labor mobilization. Usually, he accepts the job assigned in the hope of later changing to a more suitable assignment. However, this is difficult, for "manpower fluctuation" is practically forbidden.

In 1950 and 1951, the government issued decrees (Cabinet Decree No. 175 of 1950 and No. 23 of 1951, Labor Code, paragraph 131) which stipulated that every industrial worker must have a work book in which all changes in his employment must be recorded. Issued by the local authorities, and registered with the Bureau of Manpower Reserves, work books are considered "legal documents" and should be dealt with as "state property." Rigid rules govern their compulsory use. Both management and workers are fined or penalized severely for mishandling work books. In connection with the compulsory use of work books, the government has made it almost impossible for a worker to leave his job. Only through the Bureau of Manpower can he get a new job, and then only upon presentation of his work book. According to the terms of the Labor Code (Decree with the Force of Law No. 7 of 1951), a person shall be considered as "arbitrarily quitting the job" if he refuses the overtime work order of the management (paragraph 42), or if he declines to accept a transfer in his place of employment (paragraph 132). In any case when workers have arbitrarily left their previous place of employment, or have been dismissed on disciplinary grounds, they are given only subordinate jobs at less pay. Their paid vacation and sickness benefits are curtailed in the new place of work, according to the provisions of Cabinet Decree No. 2,000 of 1950. In some cases, penal action is taken, which may result in more serious consequences. In order to enforce the regulations, Cabinet Decree No. 161 of 1951 stipulated that management must immediately report the names of workers who leave arbitrarily or are dismissed on disciplinary grounds to the Bureau of Manpower

Reserves. The worker's right to "legal termination" of employment is restricted by the Labor Code (paragraph 30) to the following instances: (1) if the worker has reached the age when he is entitled to an old-age pension; (2) if he is judged eligible to enter high school or another institute of higher education; (3) if family circumstances or other vital reasons justify his quitting. In the last case, however, employment must not be terminated without the consent of the manager.

As a consequence of the forced manpower recruitment and the restrictions against changing the place of work, the term "collective contract" has lost its original meaning. Cabinet Decree No. 1,008 of 1951 rules that in a collective contract the management of an enterprise undertakes to provide conditions necessary to fulfill the state's economic plan, while the workers assume responsibility for fulfilling the plan. No collective contract can conflict with a law, decree, or higher official regulation. The employer is prohibited from rendering benefits to the employee above those granted by other legal provisions. Wages not covered by such "collective contracts" are established by the National Wage Control Commission, which is appointed by the Council of Ministers, under authority granted by Cabinet Decree No. 4,194 of 1949 and No. 163 of 1950. The Labor Code (paragraphs 37-43) and its implementing Cabinet Decrees (Nos. 30, 31, and 32 of 1951) establish the 48-hour working week "in general," but the Cabinet reserves the right to fix work hours as the case may require. Workers in food plants, for instance, may be required to work 56 hours per week. Workers are entitled to half an hour lunch break, which is not paid, except in the civil service. However, if the worker has been "found guilty of unwarranted absenteeism," he may not be given his lunch-time for a month (Cabinet Decree No. 1,008 of 1952). While workers have no right to refuse overtime work, paid overtime is limited to 8 hours monthly by the Joint Resolution of the Council of Ministers and the National Council of the Trade Unions issued on November 2, 1952. Between two work days, at least 6 hours' rest must be given to the workers.

Regulations on paid vacation, as enacted by the democratic coalition, have been sustained "in principle" by the Communist regime, with some restrictions. Those who leave a job arbitrarily are entitled to only half of their vacation at their new work place for a period of two years. In case of unwarranted absenteeism, the days of absence must be deducted from the annual vacation, but no wages are paid for such periods. In case of sickness longer than 3 months, a day a month must be deducted from the annual vacation. No vacation can be granted in case of dismissal on disciplinary grounds. If such vacation has already been granted, it must be repaid by the worker. Nonpaid vacation granted by the management cannot exceed one month.

Cabinet Decree No. 34 of 1950 and the Labor Code give full authority to management to handle all matters pertaining to discipline. Offenses against labor discipline are defined in terms so broad that they easily serve as a pretext for persecuting those who displease the plant manager. Such offenses include: failure to perform work properly; an attitude on the part of the worker that suggests he is opposed to the regime; violation of disciplinary regulations, and actions deleterious to the planned economy and "socialist ethics"; and conduct considered immoral or scandalous. The penalties include: verbal reproval; written reproval; fine; deprivation of "privileges," such as lunch-time, social security benefits, and vacation; demotion to an inferior position; and immediate dismissal.

Wages, Deductions, and Competitions

When Hungary's industry was chiefly under private ownership, the Communist Party accepted the traditional view of the trade unions concerning workers' salaries. The unions were then opposed to the piece-rate system of payment, under which the worker was paid not for the time he was employed but for the amount of work done. After the Communist Party gained control in 1949, the trade unions reversed their stand and "enthusiastically" accepted the piece-wage system. In the spring of 1950, piece-rate payment was introduced throughout Hungary's industrial sector, together with the regrouping of all industrial workers into new wage categories. By the spring of 1951, 56 per cent of the workers were paid by piece. Moreover, the "premium wage system" was introduced in those industrial sectors where piece-rate payment was not applicable. According to this system, workers' hourly wages were set at a low rate, and a premium, usually a percentage of the hourly rate, was paid for completing the work in less than the specified time. Thus, the workers were pressed to speed up their activity.

However, the premium wage system by no means resulted in an increase in the workers' earnings. On the contrary, there was a decrease in the average level of the wages of workers paid on an hourly basis. This fact was acknowledged in the trade union daily *Nepszava* (People's Voice) on May 9, 1951. The principal aim of both the piece-rate and the premium wage systems was to establish "socialist competition" in all branches of industry. This was accomplished by means of norms, individualized production quotas to be performed by workers in a given period (hour, shift, working week, etc.).

First, the government set wages at such a low level that workers sought to overfulfill their quotas in order to attain their former earnings. Second, the government organized special work contests for celebrating national holidays and festivals. The underpaid workers entered these competitions wholeheartedly, for they were scheduled for only a short term at a generous wage rate.

These contests called for a short-term record achievement. However, as soon as they were completed, the government raised production quotas accordingly. This action is referred to as "readjustment of the norms" and means an inevitable setback in earnings for the average worker. In order to meet his needs, he is compelled again to fulfill, and possibly overfulfill, the new higher norms. Norms were readjusted July 31, 1950, on the basis of the work performed in April 1950, when work contests set a record performance commemorating the "liberation" of Hungary (April 4), and May Day (May 1). Even the official *Nepszava* acknowledged on July 20, 1950 that "there will be a slight and temporary drop in wages." In June 1952, the norms were readjusted again. On June 11, 1952, *Nepszava* reported that the workers "pledged themselves to attain shortly their former production percentages and earnings even with the new norms."

Wages earned with such difficulty are subject to great deductions. The enterprise is entitled to deduct from the workers' wages a certain amount for faulty or wasteful production or damage caused to the enterprise. Under the law, the worker is financially responsible even for unintentional faults, in which case the amount of the deductions may not exceed 15 per cent of his monthly earnings. In case of intentional damages, the worker may be compelled to pay full compensation.

Other deductions include Party fees, trade union fees, old-age insurance fees, and payments for "peace loans." This last is a heavy burden, for the compulsory subscription to the peace loan at one time amounted to one month's salary, to be paid in 12 installments. In the fall of 1953, this was lowered to half a month's salary.

Altogether, 33 per cent of his total earnings may be deducted from the worker's wage, or 50 per cent in case of alimony. At the termination of employment, or in case of transfer, the employer must issue an affidavit attesting that the worker is not indebted to the company or stating the amount owed. Such certificates must be presented at the new place of employment, along with the work book.

Stakhanovism

To induce the workers to increase their productivity, the regime has found it necessary to set up a system of cooperative competition known as "popular movements." In joining a movement, the worker voluntarily pledges to step up his output. He is not required to take part in the movement, although his participation may be the only way he can retain his job.

The Stakhanovite movement, a system organized by the Russian shockworker Stakhanov who exceeded his norms in record-breaking fashion, is widely used in Hungary. In fact, from only 5,000 Hungarian Stakhanovites in 1949, the number jumped to 63,000 in February 1953.

Among the several Hungarian movements are the Gazda movement (named for a Hungarian shockworker), aimed at saving raw materials by reducing the number of rejects; the Nazarova movement, a contractual system, aimed at making workers responsible for their tools and machines; and the Koznietzov movement, similar to the Nazarova.

There are movements for improving methods of production (Innovation movement) and increasing production (Loy movement). The Roder movement, similar to the Soviet "experience exchange," encourages shockworkers and Stakhanovites to take over less efficient workers and show them the methods by which they can increase production and decrease rejects. Two movements concern the "voluntary" extension of working hours: under the Ten-Minute movement, the workers pledge to arrive ten minutes early to set up their tools and machines; and under the Five-Minute movement, the workers stay five minutes later cleaning the workshops. The workers are not compensated for this overtime.

In bigger plants, Stakhanovite Schools press for "outstanding" results in production. There are Schools of Reciprocal Training, Schools of Outstanding Quality Production, Raw Material and Material Saving Schools, Schools of Quick-Processing Methods, Schools of Increasing Profitableness, and so on.

A campaign of public ovation and the granting of special privileges and awards has also accompanied the popular movements in persuading workers to overfulfill their norms and comply with disciplinary regulations. The newspapers and other media publish the names of shockworkers, Stakhanovites, and other workers who have distinguished themselves as "socialist heroes." Shockworkers are given priority in leasing apartments. Their children are given preference as candidates for higher education. The regime has established certain prizes, orders of merit and other decorations, which are awarded to the best workers of science, arts, and industry. The highest award is the Kossuth Prize, which bestows upon its winner an amount ranging anywhere from 5,000 to 50,000 forints ($427 to $4273 at the official exchange rate). Frequently, the government rewards shockworkers by "electing" them members of Parliament.

Standard of Living

Shortly after the workers' uprising in East Germany, on July 4, 1953, Hungarian Communist leaders surprised the country by announcing a sudden change of economic policy. They promised relaxation of norms, readjustment of wages, and a higher standard of living. Was it the East German example that made Hungarian Communists change their minds? Or was it the Hungarian people's resistance that indicated imminent danger of open revolt? Available information on the Hungarian workers' standard of living seems to prove the latter. At the time of the economic-political change, the living standard was unbearably low, and dissatisfaction was widespread.

From 1947 to 1949, when mass persecutions and political purges followed one another, the standard of living was relatively high. Beginning in 1950, the Five-Year Plan period, conditions gradually deteriorated and by the summer of 1953 had declined to an unprecedentedly low level. The Malenkov era, short as it was, sought to counterbalance political instability by improving the standard of living. The year 1955 brought a sudden stop to this, and there are indications that there will be no major improvement of the living standard in the near future.

In 1949, according to the Final Report on the Three-Year Economic Plan, the general standard of living surpassed that of 1938 by 37 per cent. However, the figures of the Communist Statistical Bureau should not be taken at face value.

Real wages are computed on the basis of certain selected consumer goods prices, including food, clothing, and household expenses. The Communist statisticians changed the traditional method of food-basket and commodity computations by reducing most of the items considerably. The average 4-member worker family was given less bread, milk, meats, etc., providing approximately 56,000 calories per week, or 2,000 calories per day per person. The average caloric consumption in prewar Hungary was around 2,750, and in 1947 slightly above 2,500 per day per person. The "statistical change," therefore, clearly points to a deliberate reduction of per capita food consumption and to a lower standard of living. A similar reduction may be observed in clothing.

Housing conditions of the average Hungarian worker's family have always been far from satisfactory in terms of Western European standards. The generally miserable housing conditions might have been improved gradually, but World War II caused a serious delay. The siege of Budapest and other industrial cities inflicted heavy damages. Postwar housing conditions were therefore particularly bad. Communist planners, with the primary aim of industrial development, deliberately ignored the task of providing adequate housing facilities for the increased labor force. Instead, they followed the Russian system of dividing the 2-, 3-, and 4-room apartments of the nationalized apartment houses, allotting one room to a whole family. In the light of this, the relatively low indices of household expenses are not surprising.

Since many items were rationed and others not available on the market, or available only at astonishingly high black-market prices, it is impossible to compute accurate indices on real wages. Instead, the nominal wages will be shown against the total cost of food-basket, clothing, and household expenses. In fact, no wage earner, except some Stakhanovite shockworkers, has been able to provide adequately for his family since 1949. The published figures on family statistics prove that there were only 138 dependents for every 100 earners in 1949. The deliberate cut in real wages has been a successful means of manpower mobilization.

In Table 7, 1949 is chosen as a base year. According to Communist claims, 1949 surpassed the standard of living of 1938 by 37 per cent.

Table 7. Living Costs in the Weekly Budget of an Average Four-
Member Worker Family, Selected Years
1949–1954
(*in forints*)

Expenses	1949	November 1951	December 1951	1952	May 1954
Food-basket	90.36	155.85	217.75	223.06	189.61
Household	14.08	14.08	14.08	25.50	25.50
Clothing	25.56	31.49	41.41	42.72	38.45
Total	130.00	201.42	273.24	291.28	253.56
Index	100.00	154.9	210.0	224.1	195.0

Source: Pisky, *op. cit.*

Correcting the inbuilt bias of Communist statistics, the real increase was probably about 30 per cent. The chosen base year, 1938, has been qualified as 98, compared to 1929 as a base year. Computing the 1949 figure on the 1929 basis, the result is a 27 per cent increase. Computing the same figure on the 1913 basis, it yields only 4 per cent, that is, the standard of living reached by 1949 was slightly above that of 1913. At any rate, 1949 appears to have been a relatively "consolidated" year and offers a good basis of comparison for the inflationary trend of the years 1951 and 1952, and the small-scale improvements of the "new course" policy in 1954.

The tabulation above points to the rapid inflation that followed the expansion of the Five-Year Plan in 1951. The improvements initiated by the "new course" policy amounted to an average 15 per cent cut in food prices and another 10 per cent cut in clothing items. Table 8 shows the fluctuation of nominal wages. Here too there is some difficulty in obtaining accurate estimates, for the wages shown in published collective contracts call for 100 per cent work performance, yet the average worker seldom exceeds 80-90 per cent of his norms.

Table 8. Average Weekly Wage and Cost of Living of an Industrial
Worker, 1949, 1952, and 1954

(1949 = 100)

| Year | Wage | | Cost of |
	Index	Forints	Living Index
1949	100.00	156.00	100.00
1952	120.00	187.20	224.10
1954	132.00	205.92	195.00

In 1949, the average worker family's weekly cost of living was about 130 forints, covered by a weekly wage of 156 forints, therefore only 26 forints remained for transportation, tobacco, small items, and entertainment. In 1952, the weekly wage, 187.20 forints, out of which at least 15 to 25 per cent was deducted for the peace loan, rejects, etc., could not cover the food-basket price, let alone clothing, household, and other expenses. Every family was compelled to "mobilize" the housewife or another member of the family in order to meet the most pressing needs. The balance as established by the "new course," an average wage of 206 forints against 253.56 forints of costs, is still far from satisfactory. It meant, however, that families were able to buy some long needed items. With the beginning of 1955, production of consumer goods lost its priority. It is fair to assume that the increasing lack of consumer goods will be counterbalanced, a usual trick of the Communist economists, by a deliberate cut in the buying power of the public. In other words, as long as the overemphasis of heavy industry continues, real wages will not improve, and the coercion to keep the whole society mobilized will not lose its force.

14. MINING

Hungary's economy and, in particular, its industrial development have been closely connected with and largely based upon the utilization of domestic mineral wealth. Until 1919, this wealth included the fuels, metallic ores, and other mineral deposits of Transylvania, the Banat, and Slovakia, much of which were processed in Budapest, and in the Magyar core of the then Hungarian state. As a result of the territorial losses imposed by the Trianon Treaty, the mineral resources of Hungary shrank very considerably. During the interwar period, systematic surveying led to the discovery of huge resources of bauxite and less abundant reserves of oil, natural gas, and manganese ore. Since World War II, prospecting has been continued with even more energy. Under the second Five-Year Plan, 1956-60, investments for geological research will reach 2.5 billion forints, a sum surpassing that budgeted for either light industries or the food industry; three quarters of the total industrial investment are earmarked for the exploration and exploitation of sources of energy and other natural resources. Among these, mineral wealth plays a most prominent part.

These decisions reflect both the relative paucity of Hungarian mining resources and the determination of the regime to use all these resources now. By granting the highest priority to processing domestic mineral wealth, the regime plans to develop the production of many substitutes for the raw materials brought from abroad and thus to halt, or at least to limit, the increase of such imports.

In 1956, Hungary could be described as sufficiently endowed with fuels and building materials. However, with the exception of bauxite and manganese ore, there are insufficient supplies of metallic ores, and almost no raw materials for the inorganic chemical industry. More coal, oil, and bauxite deposits may be discovered, but the discovery of important metallic deposits, except for bauxite, is much less likely, since they have been sought by several generations of geologists.

Coal

Hungary has no carboniferous coal in the proper sense, but does have some Liassic black coal, the deposits of which exist near Pecs and Komlo on the southern slope of the Mecsek hills in southwestern Hungary, near the Yugoslav boundary. The reserves of this coal are estimated at about 311 million tons. The average caloric value of this coal is 6,200 calories per kilogram; this industrial-type coal can also be used as chemical raw material and for gas manufacturing, but until now the coke made from it has been too brittle to be used in blast furnaces. Experiments are being made with the Komlo mine coal to adapt it to the production of hard metallurgical coke.

All other Hungarian coals are lignites, mostly the subbituminous type, and of high caloric value; in Hungarian terminology, which will be adopted here, these coals between 3,200 and 5,200 calories per kilogram are described as brown coals, and the term lignite is reserved for very low quality coals below 3,200 calories, of which there are little in Hungary. Brown coal deposits are concentrated in four major basins. the two largest deposits are located west of Budapest in the Vertes hills, and in the region of Esztergom-Dorog, northwest of Budapest; these deposits contain brown coal of 5,000-5,200 calories and serve as the principal source of fuel for Budapest and its industries, and for the aluminum plants north of Lake Balaton. There are almost equally rich deposits of lower quality coal (4,000 calories) in the Sajo Valley in Borsod County; this coal contains a great quantity of ash and cannot be exploited by strip mines; it is used by the iron and steel and chemical industries of Miskolc and vicinity. The fourth area is the region of Salgotarjan, north of the Matra Mountains near the Slovak frontier; this coal varies in value from 3,500 to 4,200 calories and is consumed by local heavy industries. In addition to these principal basins, Hungary has two minor brown coal and three minor lignite fields; in some of the latter, the caloric value of coal hardly surpasses 2,000 calories. All Hungarian coals are also used for power generation, transportation, and household fuel.

Estimates of the brown coal and lignite reserves vary. In 1932, the Hungarian expert Haidegger estimated reserves at about 545 million tons. The geographer Geza Teleki believed in 1952 that they equaled 1,576 million tons (870 million tons certain, 346 million tons probable, and 360 million tons possible), while the eminent German geologist Friedensburg wrote in 1956 that all Hungarian coal reserves, including black coal, should reach 3 billion tons. In addition, there is in Hungary an estimated reserve of about 1 billion tons of good quality peat. Coal extraction since 1938 is shown in Table 1.

Table 1. Coal Extraction and Number of Workers,
Selected Years 1938–1960 (Plan)

Year	Hard Coal	Brown Coal and Lignite	Hard Coal Equivalent	All Coal	Workers Employed
		(*in thousand metric tons*)			(*in thousands*)
1938	1,042	8,318	...	9,348	37.1
1943	1,373	10,789	...	11,575	48.0
1945	711	3,574	...	4,285	...
1949	...	...	7,800	11,840	...
1951	1,822[a]	...	9,680	15,270	73.0
1952	2,000[a]	...	11,250	18,750	83.8
1953	2,000[a]	...	12,180	21,290	88.4
1954	2,000[a]	...	12,360	22,000	81.7
1955	...	...	...	22,270	85.0[a]
1956 (Plan)	...	...	...	23,750	...
1960 (Plan)	1955+30%	...	16,000–16,500[a]	29,400	...

Sources: For 1938 and 1943, Central Statistical Bureau, *Hungarian Statistical Annual 1948* (Budapest); all coal 1945, 1949, and 1951–54, *United Nations Statistical Yearbook*, volumes for respective years (New York, 1945–1954); all coal, 1955 and 1960 (Plan), *Szabad Nep* (Free People), April 27, 1956; all coal, 1956 (Plan), *ibid.*, February 11, 1956; hard coal estimates for 1951–52, Geza Teleki, *Coal Reserves of Hungary*, 1952; for 1953–54, Friedensburg, *Bergwirtschaft der Erde*, 6th edition, p. 463; hard coal equivalents, 1949 and 1951–54, U.N., *Economic Bulletin for Europe*, VII, No. 2 (August 1955), 95; hard coal equivalents, 1960 (Plan), author's estimates; workers employed 1938–43, annual, 1951–54, Hungarian Economic Research Institute, Publications, Supplement to the November 15, 1954 issue (Budapest); for 1955, author's estimate.
[a] Estimate.

Under the Communist regime, the rate of coal extraction doubled between the peak year 1943 and the end of 1955. Though it did not reach the high figure expected for 1954 in the revised version of the first Five-Year Plan (27.5 million tons), the rise in coal mining was thus very respectable and higher than in any previous period. This increase was due in large measure to large investments in coal mining. Under the Three-Year Plan, 380 million forints (about 32 million dollars at the official rate of exchange); one new mine, Balinka, and 32 new shafts were put into operation, from which one fifth of all coal was extracted in 1954. Under the current plan, 7.5 billion forints have been assigned to all mining, of which 5.5 to 6 billion may have been earmarked for coal mining. In 1956-60, geological surveying for coal, in the course of which 330 million tons of new coal deposits are expected to be located, will be financed by additional funds.

If these huge credits are wisely spent, coal extraction in 1960 may reach the planned figure of 29.4 million tons. The improvements in mining technique, mechanization of output, and transportation, which have already been made, will assist in the realization of this goal. On the other hand, Hungarian coal mining has met many grave difficulties since the war. The law of diminishing returns has set in in this industry.

The quality of coal extracted has been progressively deteriorating since 1948. From an average of 3,913 calories per kilogram in 1949, the caloric value of coal fell to an average of 3,432 calories in 1953 and presumably much less in 1955. Consequently, the cost of extraction rose from 1949 to 1954 by 76 per cent, and again, by an unknown percentage in 1955. The sorting of coal has been so bad that in 1953 "Hungarian railroads transported some 3 million tons of stone marked as coal . . . an average metric ton of coal contained 150 kilograms of stone" (*Szabad Ifjusag* [Free Youth], December 3, 1954). Accordingly, it seems logical to assume that the true volume of coal extracted in 1952 was about 700,000 tons less than officially claimed, and as much as 3,000,000 tons less in 1953 and in 1954. Because of constant backlogs in coal extraction and the low quality of the coal itself, power generation has been behind schedule and many industrial targets were not attained.

The shortage of mine props, which must be imported, is one of the reasons for the chronic crisis in coal mining. Other reasons, all openly discussed in the press, are inherent in the Communist economy: bad planning and bad organization, stress upon quantitative achievements, and neglect of manpower. Even if nominally better paid than other Hungarian workers, most coal miners suffer from low real wages, generally poor housing conditions, long commuting distances, and disregard of safety measures. The incidence of accidents is high, and so is the fluctuation of labor. The increase of coal extraction is due to increased manpower more than to other factors; per capita coal output under the first plan actually fell by one fifth between 1950 and 1953, and it is not certain that it rose again to its former level. Implementation of the 1960 target will depend not only on the improvement of mining techniques as planned by the regime but upon a different, and much improved, attitude toward the men who dig the coal.

Oil

Oil extraction on an industrial scale was inaugurated by the Standard Oil Company in 1937; during the last war, the oil fields were operated by a German group, which in 1943 raised extraction to

839,000 tons. After the war, the oil industry passed to a Hungarian-American company, MAORT, and was nationalized in 1948. Output remained stationary until 1952, when a new oil field was opened. Since then, extraction has been rising steadily, as can be seen from the following figures:

Year	Thousand Metric Tons
1938	42
1943	839
1949	500
1951	490
1952	590
1953	830
1954	1,190
1955	1,600
1960 (Plan)	2,000

Source: As in Table 1.

Until 1952, the principal oil field was that of Lispe, southwest of Lake Balaton near the Yugoslav frontier, from which an 8-inch pipeline goes to the main refineries in Budapest. The new field is that of Mezotur in the Great Hungarian Plain southeast of Budapest; in addition, there are ten small fields. The search for oil has been led by Soviet oilmen; the target of the first Five-Year Plan was reached on time; 1.2 million meters of new exploratory drilling is planned in the course of the current plan and 30 million tons of new oil deposits are to be located by 1960. Extraction of oil has lately surpassed the needs of domestic consumption and leaves a surplus for export.

Natural Gas

Small deposits of natural gas exist all over Hungary. Most of the deposits are in the northwest—the continuation of the Vienna oil and gas basin; some are in the immediate vicinity of the capital. The output was insignificant until very recently. Under the current plan, it is expected to rise from 543 million cubic meters in 1955 to 700 million in 1960.

Iron Ore

Iron ore deposits are located in the northeastern upland in the vicinity of Miskolc. The large surface mine, Rudabanya, is the principal source of supply, with annual production of 250,000-300,000 tons and a reserve of 31 per cent limonite of about 9 million tons. There are small deposits and low-grade ores in various parts of Hungary, as well as some pyrites in the Matra Mountains; in addition, there are large deposits of bauxites containing up to 23 per cent iron.

Manganese

Forty-two per cent manganese ore is mined at Urkut in the Bakony Forest in Transdanubia. Its extraction covers domestic requirements and probably leaves a small volume of ore for export (see Table 2).

Copper, Lead, and Zinc

Copper ore, which also includes some gold and silver, is mined in small quantities near Recsk in the Matra Mountains; 336 tons of copper were smelted from the ore extracted there in 1938, together with 178 kilograms of gold and 1,465 kilograms of silver; no data about these ores have been disclosed in the postwar decade, but there is no reason to suppose that extraction has increased. Some lead ores have sporadically been exploited (283 tons of pure content in 1929, 300 tons in 1950), and it was claimed in 1952 that enough zinc and lead ores have been discovered to supply domestic requirements.

Bauxite

Bauxite reserves are very rich and constitute up to 9 per cent of world reserves; they are second in Europe after France. They surpass Soviet reserves and probably exceed those of the rest of the Soviet bloc; they are generally estimated at 250 million tons. Bauxite occurs in many places in Hungary; the largest deposits are located in two adjoining districts near Gant in the Vertes hills southwest of Budapest and in the Bakony Forest farther southeast. The strata of bauxite are thick and lie close to the surface, which in most cases renders possible their exploitation by strip mines at very low cost. The bauxite from these two fields contains 50-63 per cent aluminum oxide, in addition to much iron and some sulphur. There are lesser deposits of poorer bauxite in the north and the south. During World War II, the control of Hungarian bauxite was of extreme importance to Germany, and extraction rose to about one million tons per year; at present this control is equally important to the Soviet Union, whose bauxite is less abundant and poorer in content of pure metal. Most Hungarian bauxite is exported to the Soviet Union, and lesser quantities of alumina are supplied to East Germany, Czechoslovakia, and Poland for further processing. Under the current plan, the search for new bauxite deposits is expected to lead to the discovery of 10 million tons of new ore. A plant will be established capable of processing low-grade bauxite.

Table 2. Iron Ore, Manganese Ore, and Bauxite Extraction,
Selected Years 1938–1960 (Plan)
(*in thousand metric tons*)

Year	Iron Ore (39 Per Cent of Fe)	Manganese Ore (25 Per Cent of Mn)	Bauxite
1938	297	16	540
1949	340	22	560
1954	390	50[a]	1,260
1955	...	...	1,290
1960 (Plan)	...	...	1,600

Sources: For 1938, Royal Hungarian Statistical Bureau, *Hungarian Statistical Yearbook 1938* (Budapest) ; iron ore, U.N., *Economic Bulletin for Europe*, VII, No. 2 (August 1955) ; bauxite 1949, *ibid.;* 1954, *Szabad Nep*, May 5, 1955; 1955, *ibid.*, January 21, 1956; 1960 (Plan), *ibid.*, April 27, 1956.
[a] Estimate.

Uranium

Uranium was discovered in 1954 near Pecs in the Mecsek Mountains and also probably on the Savo River near the Slovak frontier. Little is known about these apparently rich deposits, except that they were immediately taken over by the Russians. All uranium ore is exported to be processed in the Soviet Union.

In addition to the above metals and minerals, Hungary has deposits of fluorspar, gypsum, and talc, as well as of quartzite, glass, and foundry sand, colored and siliceous earth, and kaolin; the last is exported. There is also enough marl for cement production.

15. INDUSTRY

PREWAR INDUSTRIAL DEVELOPMENT

Industry developed in Hungary only after the Compromise *(Aus-gleich)* in 1867. The Hungarian state remained a part of the Austro-Hungarian customs area, but its government became able to foster industry by various administrative and financial measures. The Hungary of 1867-1918 was an economic unit sufficiently populous and endowed with enough natural wealth to support a relatively large food-processing and metal industry. Budapest developed into an industrial center of the Dual Monarchy, second only to Vienna.

In 1919, Hungary lost most of her mineral resources and important markets. The foundations for her industrial development thus shrank considerably. The adaptation of Hungarian industry to new political and economic conditions was difficult and took several years. Because of the paucity of raw materials, at first the industrial outlook seemed rather hopeless, but the shortage of ores led to intensified exploration and the subsequent opening of a rich manganese ore mine in 1925; bauxite deposits were located and have been commercially exploited since 1927, and oil deposits have been developed on a large scale since 1938. The discovery of new minerals led in turn to new industries in ferro-alloys, aluminum, and oil refining. An extensive textile industry was created. The food-processing industry, in particular flour milling and distilling, lost its pre-1918 markets and never recovered its prewar position. Because of its skilled manpower and transportation facilities, the Budapest metropolitan area preserved its dominant position in industry producing 62 per cent of gross industrial output in 1938; about 250,000 workers were concentrated there.

The interwar trends of Hungarian industry did not always parallel those in neighboring countries. The depression hit Hungarian industry less deeply and lasted for a shorter time than elsewhere in Central Europe; it was practically limited to producer goods industries (75,000 registered unemployed in industry and construction in 1932, and 46,000 in 1947). Metallurgy and machine building were concentrated

291

in several large enterprises, some of them state owned; in 1938, there were 109 plants employing over 500 people. Index figures of industrial production, on the basis of 1929 equals 100, dropped to 82 in 1932, and rose to 107 in 1935 and to 130 in 1937; the ascending trend was more visible in the consumer goods industry, which reached 139 in 1937. The relatively favorable development of industry, combined with the slow natural increase of population, was regarded as proof that Hungary, unlike Poland, Romania, and Yugoslavia, could in time absorb her rural underemployed.

In the statistical tables that follow, handicraft production is not included; the gross value of this production constituted about one sixth of the total and employment apparently exceeded 200,000. Tables 1 and 2 give data on industrial employment, production, and gross output of selected industries.

Table 1. Industrial Employment and Production, Selected Years 1913–1938[a]

Year	Employees (in thousands)	Gross Output (in million pengo)
1913	219	1,904
1929	244	2,867
1932	176	1,823
1936	265	2,555
1937	275	2,893
1938	289	...

Sources: Karl Geller, *Die Strukturanderungen der ungarischen Volkswirtschaft nach dem Kriege und die Stellung Ungarns im mitteleuropaischen Wirtschaftsraum* (Munster, 1938) ; Gustav Gratz, *The Hungarian Economic Year Book 1939* (Budapest, 1939).

[a] All figures pertain to Trianon territory.

Table 2. Employment and Gross Output of Selected Industries,[a] 1913 and 1937

Industry	1913		1937	
	Employees (in thousands)	Gross Output (in million pengo)	Employees (in thousands)	Gross Output (in million pengo)
Iron and metal	35.6	293	46.8	380
Machine-building	44.6	263	38.6	262
Chemical	9.8	144	14.4	273
Textiles	16.1	95	67.7	508
Leather, footwear[b]	5.8	52	9.8	107
Paper[b]	3.0	12	4.9	47
Food-processing	40.6	807	33.1	847

Sources: As in Table 1.

[a] All figures pertain to Trianon territory.
[b] Data pertain to 1913 and 1936.

After 1937, the number of employed, the sum of their wages, and the value of industrial product progressed until about 1943, when the number of industrially employed rose to 392,000. This ascending trend was due largely to the armament policy inaugurated early in 1938. Under the so-called Billion Pengo Plan of 1938, armament plants and modern and efficient plants for power, aluminum, heavy chemical, rayon, and oil industries were built; these increased Hungarian industrial capacity by about one fourth.

ECONOMIC PLANS FOR INDUSTRIAL EXPANSION

War losses reduced the capacity of Hungarian industry by a percentage variously estimated from 20 to 40 of its 1938 level. If the increase in industrial capacity up to 1943 were taken into account, the above percentages become 25 and 50, respectively, of peak capacity. Actual capacity in 1945 was about one third that of 1943. Direct war damage to Hungarian industry in 1944 was accompanied by German evacuation of much industrial equipment. In turn, Soviet authorities seized the equipment of many of the best and most recently built plants as war booty. Such equipment was dismantled and shipped to the Soviet Union, together with the reparation goods, which often consisted of machinery and industrial installations; the new plants built since 1938 were most seriously affected. In addition, some branches of Hungarian industry were declared the property of Soviet-Hungarian joint companies administered by Soviet managers; these companies were dissolved only in 1953 and 1954. A reliable evaluation of the total loss of Hungarian capital equipment under the two occupations is not available; published estimates vary between the equivalent of several hundred million and three billion dollars for German looting; it seems certain that Soviet dismantlings were much greater.

Rehabilitation of industry thus started from a point lower than admitted by the Communist regime. It began within the framework of the Three-Year Plan (August 1947—December 1949), drawn up for rehabilitation and reconstruction. Important industrial sectors had been nationalized before the plan was launched; in addition to the prewar state-owned industries and to German and Austrian property, coal mining, power stations, and five large industrial concerns which controlled three quarters of the heavy industry, were seized in 1945-46. In March 1948, all industrial plants employing more than one hundred workers were nationalized. On December 28, 1949, all enterprises employing ten or more workers were nationalized. At first, nationalization did not harm industrial productivity, and the plan itself was favorably accepted by the working class; a great release of national energy occurred, and high hopes were harbored for raising the living standard through planned economy. At the end of 1949, the industrial targets of the plan were officially declared fulfilled ahead of schedule, with the index of industrial production reaching 154.4 per cent of 1938. Four years later, this index was reduced to 137.5 per cent (heavy industry 166.3 and consumer goods industry 120.0), equal to about 110 per cent of the peak year 1943. This considerable progress was due not so much to investments, which were relatively small, as to the utilization of facilities much above their prewar level through greatly increased industrial employment. The latter rose from about 395,000 in 1943 to about 490,000 in 1949 (including mining but not handicrafts nor the construction industry).

In 1950, Hungary embarked upon the Five-Year Plan (1950-54). The new plan aimed at transforming Hungary from an "agrarian-industrial" country into an "industrial-agrarian" one; this was to be achieved through enforced development of the heavy and machine industries. In the course of its implementation, the plan became a source of controversy between two groups of Communist planners. The plan was completely recast in 1951 and in 1953. This double revision, and the adoption in 1955 of still another set of planned indices for the second Five-Year Plan (1956-60), led to repeated drastic changes in allocation of resources and to a great waste of human and material wealth.

The first version of the plan was prepared in 1949 on the assumption that the Three-Year Plan would be substantially overfilled and that, under pressure, the Hungarian economy could develop more rapidly than hitherto expected. This assumption justified the anticipated increase in industrial output by 1954 of 86 per cent, in comparison with 1949. The indices reached in 1950 seemed to confirm this optimism. Early in 1951, faced with the prospect of the extension of the Korean War, the Soviet Union demanded that all the captive governments develop their armament industries in order to supply arms shipments to Communist China and to supply modern weapons to their own armed forces. Hungarian Communists responded to this demand with more alacrity than their colleagues in other captive countries. The extremists among the Politburo members, led by Erno Gero, imposed new goals for the Hungarian economy. Industry was to triple its output by 1954, heavy industry to rise to 380 per cent, and construction to 438 per cent of 1949. Armament production targets were hidden within these steep percentages. For a relatively poorly industrialized country with few raw materials and a limited reserve of manpower, such targets were irresponsible. However, the targets were unanimously voted in the spring of 1951 by the Second Party Congress.

Such a high rate of increase in industrial output could be maintained only at the cost of a sharp decline in personal consumption. After the bad harvest of 1952, Stalin's death in 1953, and some relaxation of Soviet pressure, "moderates" led by Imre Nagy and Istvan Kovacs forced a drastic downward revision of the plan targets and more emphasis on consumer goods. Even under this "new course" policy, the planned goals of industry and construction remained high, closer to the accelerated plan of 1951 than to the original version. The results of the Five-Year Plan, published in 1955, indicate that the targets of the third version of the plan were not reached. Only a few key industrial export goods (aluminum and cotton and woolen goods) were produced at the rate prescribed by this version. Most key commodities reached only 80 to 90 per cent of their targets. The general planned and actual indices of industrial production in 1954 can be seen in Table 3.

Table 3. Indices of Planned and Actual Gross Industrial Production, 1954
(1949 = 100)

Category	Plan 1949 Version	Plan 1951 Version	Plan 1953 Version	Actual 1954
Industry[a]	186	310	265	258
Heavy industry	204	380	315	288
Light and food industry[a]	173	245	220	227
Building and construction	231	438	270	269

Source: U.N., Economic Bulletin for Europe, VII, No. 2 (August 1955), p. 86, table 1.
[a] Excluding the output of handicrafts.

Outside of Hungary, the plan was considered a failure, as it was from the formal point of view, because industrial output remained behind schedule. However, if published reports are exact, Hungarian industry nearly tripled in 1954 its peak prewar and wartime gross industrial output. Aside from new industries, such as oil refining and aluminum smelting, only a few industrial branches showed this high average rate of increase, for example engineering and machine building.

The very considerable increase in the capacity of Hungarian industry in 1950-54 was rendered possible by the development of its energy sources, i.e. coal, oil, and natural gas; however, power generation lagged behind schedule as a result of the 1951 curtailment of many basic investments in favor of armament production. The combination of armament investments in 1951-53 and the "new course" policy in 1953-54 restricted planned productivity of the engineering industry. Even so, one quarter of all industrial investment was made in engineering, which was very substantially expanded; new divisions were added in most plants, and 18 large new factories were opened, some of them in rural districts with an abundance of manpower. Several hundred types of new machinery were added to those already in production in 1949, and the range of production included nearly all industrial equipment required by the Hungarian economy; the range of machinery and equipment made for export was also widened. Even in the late thirties, Hungary's machinery exports were greater than imports; in 1953, her active balance of trade in industrial equipment was estimated at 80 to 120 million dollars, and it has continued to rise.

Launching of the second Five-Year Plan was delayed until 1956 to synchronize it with similar plans inaugurated in the Soviet Union and all European captive countries except Bulgaria. In the course of 1955, for which only an annual plan was provided, the economic principles of the "new course" were abandoned in Hungary, as elsewhere in the Soviet bloc, and the priority of heavy industry firmly re-established. During this intermediary year, industrial production rose by only 7 per cent, though much higher increases were registered for power generation, oil extraction and refining, cement production, and the manufacture of woolen fabrics and footwear.

In the annual plan for 1956, which was disclosed before the second long-range plan, stress on industrial production was increased. Investments in heavy industry were more than doubled over 1955, and gross output of heavy industry was to increase by 10.1 per cent. The foodstuffs industry was to increase output by 10 per cent, and light industry to reduce output by 4 per cent. The engineering industry was to begin the serial production of 60 more new types of machinery.

The "principles" of the second Five-Year Plan were published in April 1956. According to these, industrial production "must" increase by 1960 by 50 to 52 per cent over 1955; output of producer goods is expected to rise by about 60 per cent and that of consumer goods by about 40 per cent. In order to effect a relative reduction of raw material imports and to assure continuous supplies, production of raw materials will be increased even more than that of processing industries. Of the 78 billion forints earmarked from the central budget for new investment under the plan, industry, including mining, will receive 33 to 34 billion forints compared to 32.9 billion forints. The planned redistribution of this sum among the principal industries is as follows:

Industry	Billion Forints	
Mining	7.5	
Metallurgy	3.0	
Power generation	6.5	
Atom energy	...	
Chemical industry	5.0	
Building materials	2.0	
Engineering and machine making	3.5	
Total, heavy industry		27.5
Light industry	2.9	
Food industry	2.3-2.4	
Total, consumer goods		5.2-5.3
Building industry		1.0
Total		33.7-33.8

Source: "Principles of the Second Five-Year Plan of the Hungarian People's Economy," *Szabad Nep,* (Free People), April 27, 1956.

In addition, 2.5 billion forints will be spent on expanded geological exploration to discover new deposits of 330 million tons of coal, 30 million tons of petroleum, and 10 million tons of bauxite. Of the total sum assigned to industry, 13 billion forints will be spent on maintenance and renewal of funds. The credits assigned to housing cannot as yet be separated from those earmarked for utilities and social, health, and cultural purposes, for which another 13 billion forints has been budgeted. Two-thirds of the planned production increase will be covered by increased productivity; industrial production costs are to be reduced by about 16 per cent.

The natural resources of Hungary are to be exploited to a greater extent than ever before. In the second Five-Year Plan, three quarters of total industrial investment will be spent on discovery and exploitation of natural resources and sources of energy. This determination of the Communist planners reflects the difficulties that the Hungarian government must recently have had with imports from the Soviet Union and the captive countries of raw materials and key industrial commodities, such as coke, soda, and cellulose. If prospecting and other measures contemplated in the plan produce the expected results, the policy of the planners will be justified.

In 1956-60, as in the other captive nations, Hungarian industrial investment will concentrate on the termination of large projects initiated but not finished under the first plan and on modernization of existing plants, the equipment of many of which is obsolete; spectacular new projects will be avoided. Great emphasis will be placed on discovering and utilizing so-called hidden reserves of productivity, which abound in a centrally planned and bureaucracy-ridden Communist economy. New industrial techniques will be promoted by raising the standard of local industrial research institutes and introducing new processes from abroad. Study and imitation of Western scientific methods will be permitted. An atomic reactor modeled on the Soviet ones is under construction, and construction of the first atomic power plant will be begun, though not completed, under the second plan. Great efforts will be expended in improving the quality of industrial goods, especially of export goods to be sold outside the Soviet bloc.

What is new in the plan is recognition of the necessity of some kind of division of labor between Hungary and the other captive countries. The advantages of such division of labor have been repeatedly discussed. Until 1956, the practical results of these discussions were few and were generally limited to minor production lines, such as the alleged decision to concentrate the manufacturing of light Diesel trains in Hungary for export to her neighbors. In the new plan, Hungary's poverty in energy resources and many raw materials is recognized; therefore, Hungary will concentrate on the production of finer kinds of rolled steel, communications equipment, Diesel motors and engines, combines and tractors, drugs and medicines, and the food industry. Expansion of these industries appears reasonable for a small country with a limited domestic market but many skilled workmen and specialists.

Prospects of Industrialization

The opinion that Hungary has no future as an industrial state because of the lack of domestic raw materials is only partly correct. In reality, her fuel and energy requirements can be and actually are supplied by domestic fuels, production of which can be considerably expanded. Hungarian exports of manganese ore and bauxite can balance at least a large part of imports of other metals. Although it would be rash to rely upon the discovery of great mineral wealth, the postwar geological survey has already increased Hungary's mining resources. Hungarian agriculture produces or, under proper conditions, can produce considerable surpluses for food processing, though not enough timber or textile raw materials.

In summary, Hungary's shortages of industrial raw materials on the whole are concentrated in certain basic sectors, such as coal, iron and most other metal ores, and basic minerals for the inorganic chemical industry. Some of these raw materials are located in areas which until 1918 belonged to the Hungarian state. They can easily be transported to Budapest or the industrial northeast by the Hungarian railroad system, which is the best of its kind in East-Central Europe, or by the Danube. The same transport facilities are available for raw materials coming from distant European or overseas countries, though the inland position of Hungary often makes the cost of such transportation very high.

Of even greater importance are the social aspects of Hungarian industrial development. Hungary possesses well-trained industrial man-power, and a competent and relatively numerous group of graduate engineers and other industrial specialists. The present rapid increase of this managerial group is due as much to the desire to occupy relatively safe technical jobs as to the regime's stressing technical education.

The best program for Hungary would be the development of indus-tries depending less on volume of goods processed than on skill, and more on domestic raw materials than on bulky minerals brought from afar. Thus, food processing and general machine making will remain structurally more natural than heavy engineering and tank production. For Moscow-imposed doctrinaire and strategic reasons, based upon the proposition that what is good for the Soviet Union must be good for Hungary, natural economic lines of industrial development have been ignored by Hungarian Communists, at a heavy cost to the national economy and to living standards. This has been one price Hungary has had to pay for dependence on the Soviet Union, the ultimate bene-ficiary of the satellite system.

INDUSTRIES

Power Generation

In 1955, about 5.4 billion kilowatt-hours were produced in Hungary, equal to about 550 kilowatt-hours per capita; a small amount of power was imported from Slovakia. These consumption figures are roughly twice those of Romania, but only half those of Czechoslovakia, the Soviet Union, and France. In 1960, it is planned to produce 8.35 billion kilowatt-hours, equal to 800 kilowatt-hours per capita. This figure, if realized, will still lag far behind northwestern Europe, as well as Eastern Germany, Czechoslovakia, the Soviet Union, and Po-land.

Implementation of this plan will not be easy. Power generation is not a bottleneck, but may become one because of the extreme poverty of water power potential. Because of the high cost and long time needed for the construction of hydroelectric plants, it is unlikely that this potential will be developed within the foreseeable future. Hungary's limited coal is the basis of 98 per cent of all power now produced, and the quality of this coal has been gradually deteriorating. As a result, the high costs of power generation are mounting. The time may come within a generation when Hungary will have to import a considerable amount of power from her neighbors.

Since the war, Hungary has done a great deal for the development of power generation. In the 1946-49 period, after 1945 output had fallen to half of prewar, investment was heavy to repair war damage and to replace equipment lost through Soviet looting. About 4.2 billion forints were invested in this industry under the first long-range plan and 6.5 billion are budgeted for it in the second; the capacity of all plants is estimated to have risen from 870 kilowatts in 1949 to about 1,379 kilowatts in 1955 and it is supposed to rise by another 663 kilowatts under the current plan. This accretion will be concentrated in a few large plants, two of which, Kazincbarcika in Borsod County and Tiszapalkonya, the seat of the chemical combinat in northeast Hungary, are supposed to reach or exceed a capacity of 200 megawatts. In addition, construction of other plants totaling 632 megawatts will begin under the current plan. Power production is expected to rise by two-thirds by 1960, compared with 1955; a large part of this increase is to be achieved through better utilization of existing facilities and their reserve capacity. The following figures give the actual and planned power producton for selected years:

Year	Billion Kilowatt Hours
1938	1.40
1943	2.14
1945	0.76
1949	2.52
1954 (Plan No. 1)	4.88
1954 (Plan No. 2)	6.93
1954 (Plan No. 3)	5.10
1954 (Actual)	4.83
1955 (Actual)	5.40
1960 (Plan)	8.35

Sources: For 1938 and 1943, Central Statistical Bureau, *Hungarian Statistical Yearbook 1948;* for 1945, *Statisztikai Szemle* (Statistical Review) April 1956; for 1949 and 1954 plans, U.N., *Economic Bulletin for Europe, loc. cit.,* p. 95; for 1954 actual, *Szabad Nep,* May 8, 1955; for 1955 actual, *ibid.,* January 22, 1956; for 1960 Plan, *ibid.,* April 27, 1956.

In spite of this increase in output, electric power has constantly fallen short of demand. This is partly due to obsolete equipment in some of the old plants and partly to the high consumption of current in aluminum production (18,000 to 20,000 kilowatt hours per ton) and in ferro-alloy plants. The regime plans to reduce the specific heat consumption in generating plants from 5,000 to less than 4,000 calories.

Ferrous Metallurgy

The raw material bases for ferrous metallurgy are markedly insufficient in Hungary. Iron ore extraction is limited and cannot be greatly expanded; in 1955, less than one fifth of the pig iron smelted was made of domestic ore. In the same year, only 2 per cent of the hard coke consumed by blast furnaces was of domestic origin. The volume of iron ore and hard coke imported from the Soviet Union, Poland, and other countries approached 2 million tons; in other words, for every ton of iron made in Hungary more than two tons of raw materials had to be imported. Hungarian steel could be much more cheaply produced from imported iron, which would cut the import volume to one third. However, this solution would be contrary to regime policy. In 1952-53, there were plans for developing Hungary into an "iron and steel" country by expanding steel output in 1960 to 4 million tons, which would mean an output of at least 2.5 million tons of iron and a vast increase in coke and ore imports. These plans were abandoned under the "new course," and smaller targets have been fixed for 1960 in the second Five-Year Plan.

The iron and steel plants remaining in Hungary after 1920 had to be adapted to the new boundaries. This was more or less successfully accomplished by importing iron ore from Slovakia (under special conditions stipulated in the Trianon Treaty) and Yugoslavia; coke was imported from the Ruhr and Czechoslovak Silesia; most of these imports were cheaply transported by waterways. Between 1913 and 1938, output of iron and steel nearly doubled, but by 1938 the equipment was largely obsolescent. Technically, ferrous metallurgy made great progress by introducing the production of many high-grade steels. Primary metal was produced mainly by one large corporation, Rima-murany-Salgotarjan Company, later controlled by German capital, and the state. Nearly all plants were concentrated near Miskolc in Borsod County in northeastern Hungary. Maximum production was reached in 1942 when the raw material bases were temporarily enlarged through territorial acquisitions.

War damage reduced plant capacity, and some of Hungary's best facilities were removed by the Russians, but prewar capacity was approximately restored under the Three-Year Plan. In 1949 production of primary metal exceeded its wartime peak and that of finished metal equaled prewar output. In the first Five-Year Plan, large targets were fixed for primary metallurgy: according to the second version of this plan drawn up in 1951, iron production was to triple by 1954 and that of steel to rise two and a half times. Such levels could not be reached without large new facilities. The construction of a new integrated plant was started at Mohacs on the Danube near the Yugoslav frontier; this plant was expected to process Yugoslav ores. After the Tito-Cominform break in 1948, this project was abandoned in spite of the investment already made, and construction of another plant was begun at Duna-pentele, now Sztalinvaros, south of Budapest. The cost of this ultra-modern and highly advertised project proved to be much higher than originally expected, partly because of its marshy site; it was therefore decided to reduce the size of the plant and to build it in two stages. A large blast furnace and two large open-hearth furnaces were con-structed and placed in operation in 1955, and another large blast furnace and two more large open-hearth furnaces are to be built under the second plan. The Sztalinvaros plant uses Krivoi Rog iron ore, transported via the Danube, and is scheduled to use Hungarian hard coke; in the meantime, all Hungarian plants depend on Polish, Soviet, and East German coke. Until Sztalinvaros reaches full capacity, the old state plant at Diosgyor near Miskolc, which is being modernized, will remain the largest Hungarian primary metal producer. This plant and a few lesser ones nearby, situated close to the Soviet frontier, appear to be the only group of plants in captive Europe that are directly linked with the Soviet wide-gauge railroad system. A large sum of money was invested during the first plan to produce various ferro-alloys and high-grade steel as well as to improve metallurgic technique. Nearly one fourth of all steel is fine steel smelted in electric furnaces.

Under the current plan, iron output is supposed to increase by about 350,000 tons and that of steel by about 600,000 tons; much more rolled and finished steel will be made. If Yugoslav iron ore is now available for Hungary, the prohibitive cost of iron smelting may be greatly reduced. Hitherto, coke made from Hungarian hard coal has been too brittle for use in blast furnaces, and the experimental manu-facture of coke out of brown coal has proved costly and disappointing. It remains to be seen whether locally made hard coke will supply one third of the domestic demand by 1960, as anticipated in the current plan. If the old project of the Oder-Danube Canal were realized, Polish coke could be loaded at Gliwice in Silesia and delivered directly to Sztalinvaros, and Swedish ore brought there by barge from Stettin.

Actual and planned iron and steel production between 1913 and 1960 are shown in Table 4.

Table 4. Iron and Steel Production, Selected Years 1913–1960 (Plan)
(*in thousand metric tons*)

Year	Pig Iron	Crude Steel[a]	Rolled Steel
1913	190	443	...
1938	335	648	470
1942	417	785	...
1949	398	890	470
1953	716	1,543	842
1954 (Plan)	1,280	2,200	890
1954 (Actual)	843	1,491	817
1955	855	1,623	880
1960 (Plan)	1,410	2,240	1,400

Sources: For 1913, League of Nations, *Memorandum on the Iron and Steel Industry* (Geneva, 1927), pp. 40–41; for 1938 and 1942, *Quarterly Bulletin of Steel Statistics for Europe*; for 1949–54, *Statisztikai Szemle* (May 1955), pp. 387–401; for 1954 Plan, *Magyar Kozlony* (Hungarian Gazette), No. 78 (1951), pp. 443–49; for 1955 and 1960 Plan, *Szabad Nep*, April 27, 1956.

[a] Including electrically smelted steel.

Aluminum

Hungary is so rich in bauxite that, were she to process domestically all her annual extraction, she would outproduce all the European states and the Soviet Union and compete with Canada for second place in world output of aluminum. However, this would require much more electric power than Hungarian plants can generate. In addition, the power needed for aluminum smelting must be cheap or cheaply delivered from abroad; othewise it is more profitable to deliver bauxite to sources of cheap power. Hungary has little water power and her coal extraction is expensive; consequently, some of her bauxite and most of her alumina is sold to the Soviet Union, Eastern Germany, Czechoslovakia, and Poland, and less than 10 per cent is processed locally.

The production of alumina (or AL_2O_3) started in Hungary in 1934 and of aluminum in 1935; it made great strides during the war (11,500 tons of aluminum in 1944). Aluminum production for selected years is given in Table 5. However, expansion of the industry began only under the first Five-Year Plan, when the capacity of alumina making was quadrupled. The present capacity of four prewar and two much larger postwar plants seems to exceed present production. The new Inota aluminum plant located at the power plant of the same name is apparently capable of producing more than 20,000 tons of aluminum annually.

Table 5. Bauxite, Alumina, and Aluminum Production,
Selected Years 1938–1960 (Plan)
(*in thousand metric tons*)

Year	Bauxite	Alumina	Aluminum
1938	540	7	1.2
1943	998	...	7.0
1949	560	31	14.5
1954	1,260	132	32.8
1955	1,290	155	37.0
1956 (Plan)	...	...	41.0
1960 (Plan)	1,600	224	47.5

Sources: United Nations Statistical Yearbook 1949/50 (New York, 1950), pp. 159, 265; U.N., *Economic Survey of Europe in 1955* (Geneva, 1956), p. B–39; *Szabad Nep,* April 27, 1956.

Engineering and Machine-Building Industry

Engineering and machine-building on an industrial scale was started in Hungary in the last third of the nineteenth century and developed into an important branch of the national economy prior to 1914. The industry, located mainly in Budapest and vicinity, was heavily hit in 1919 by the violent reduction of the domestic market and the loss of raw material sources. During the inflation years, 1919-24, many plants closed or changed hands. After sound currency was re-established in 1925, most of the engineering and machine-building capacity was concentrated in the hands of three big concerns. One of them, the MAVAG (Hungarian National Iron and Machine Plant), was state owned and linked to the iron and steel plant at Diosgyor. Two others, the Ganz-Danubius and the Manfred Weiss corporations, operated a number of plants in the capital and its vicinity, in which they produced the whole range of metal goods from nails to locomotives, ships, and aircraft; during the war, they also made guns, light tanks and other military vehicles, fighter planes, and aircraft engines. The growth of these corporations was due to the organizational and financial ability of their management and the high level of industrial technique they developed. These companies played such an important role in the Hungarian economy that when they were placed under state control in 1946 as a first step toward nationalization, the government practically controlled the whole metal-processing industry.

Interwar Hungary also had a dozen fairly large machine-building plants not controlled by the big three and generally built around iron and steel foundries and rolling mills. The number of workers and salaried personnel employed in 1938 in the entire metal-processing industry, including primary metallurgy, reached about 100,000; in addition, there were about 40,000 metal-working handicraftsmen. In spite of Hungary's poverty in metallic ores, her 1938 balance of trade in metal and metal goods was favorable. The export of metal goods, machinery, and vehicles more than covered the import of hard fuels, ores, metals and metal goods, industrial equipment, and vehicles.

Between 1938 and 1944, the capacity of the industry was expanded through the installation of new facilities for the manufacture of armaments. A large proportion of this new machinery was lost or looted in 1944-46, but a great effort was made under the Three-Year Plan to rebuild the damaged plants and to increase output. The value of production of the iron, metal, and engineering industries almost doubled between 1938 and 1949 (2,799 million forints at 1947 prices and 5,332 million forints, respectively), a much higher increase than in any other branch of industry. During the Three-Year Plan, nationalization of the engineering industry was completed.

Under the Five-Year Plan (1950-55), an extraordinarily high increase of metal and engineering production was planned, and allegedly generally achieved, in spite of repeated and abrupt changes in investment and production programs. The apparent rise in production of the two industries can be seen from Table 6.

Table 6. Output of Metal and Engineering Industries,
Selected Years 1949–1954
(*in billion Plan forints*)

		Plan for 1954			
Industry[a]	1949 Actual	1949 Version	1951 Version	1953 Version	1954 Actual
Metals[b]	2.42	4.72	6.35	5.80	5.36[c]
Engineering	5.15	11.56	25.23	20.45	18.90
Total	7.57	16.28	31.58	26.25	24.26[c]

Sources: U.N., *Economic Bulletin for Europe, loc. cit.,* p. 96.

[a] All figures quoted before allowance for duplication.

[b] Includes primary metallurgy and production of all metal goods that cannot be qualified as machinery.

[c] Author's estimate.

The duplication in these figures probably reduced 1949 actual output by one third and 1954 actual output by somewhat more than half. Even so, the increase is staggering; it was reached under enormous pressure during the first four years, 1950-53, because in 1954 output shrank by some 10 per cent. These high value indices were not achieved by the few production lines for which absolute figures of output in 1949-54 have been published. The conclusion can hardly be avoided that, if the data quoted in Table 6 are correct, the really great progress in the value of goods produced must have occurred in heavy engineering, for which data were not published and, above all, in the armament industry.

This increase has been achieved through the extension of existing plants and the building of a score of entirely new engineering plants, half of which are in provincial towns with a surplus of population. Moreover, production of heavy industrial equipment was stressed, which required great amounts of iron and steel, of which Hungary is and must remain short. Hungarian planners either believed that they should follow the Soviet program or they were forced to follow it against their judgment.

Output of the metal and engineering industries under the current plan (1956-60) is supposed to continue to increase more rapidly than that of industry in general. The prescribed rate of increase, 70 to 75 per cent, is, however, much slower than under the first Five-Year Plan. Only 3.5 billion forints are to be invested in these industries, of which only one fifth is for the construction of new plants; the rest is to be spent on modernization and expansion of existing facilities. Diesel machinery of all kinds, farm machinery and tractors, most types of rolling stock, machine tools, ball bearings, and power-generating equipment are among the lines expected to develop most rapidly. To counterbalance these, production of some branches is expected to develop slowly, or not at all: freight cars belong to this category. Table 7 gives selected data on the actual and planned output of engineering products.

Shipbuilding and the manufacture of rolling stock and special types of vehicles have long been among the most important Hungarian industries. Their capacity was never fully utilized prior to the last war. High-capacity steam, Diesel, and electric locomotives are manufactured at Budapest, together with passenger coaches and special railroad cars, for which locally smelted aluminum is now available. A comparatively large number of buses and bus bodies are manufactured, some for export. No passenger cars are produced, but trucks are made in prewar assembly plants which have been expanded and modernized. Interwar

Budapest was an important center of rivercraft building, and its shipyards have been expanded.

Table 7. Selected Machinery and Engineering Output,
Selected Years 1949–1960 (Plan)

Item	1949	1954	1955	1960 Plan	1956–60 Plan
	(in megawatts)				
Steam turbines	...	...	240	370	...
	(in million forints)				
Power generators and boilers	...	...	60	194	...
	(in thousand horsepower)				
Diesel motors	...	...	83	567	...
	(in units)				
Steam locomotives	90	230	...	...	...
Electric locomotives	...	...	...	15	...
Deisel locomotives	...	...	...	380	...
Motor trains	...	...	...	...	90
Railroad coaches	...	...	338	805	...
Motorships	...	...	...	...	200
	(in thousands)				
Trucks	3.2	13.5	3.8	6.8	...
Buses and trailers	0.3	1.9	1.4	3.4	...
Tractors	2.6	3.9	...	...	19
Harvester combines	...	1.45[a]	1.5	2.5	10
Metal-working machine tools	...	...	6.1	11.1	...
Motorcycles	9.8	14.6	16.5	54	230
Bicycles	137	174	217	410	1,700
Sewing machines	12.3	28.3	46	68.5	...
Radio sets	71	155[b]	309	455	2,100
Television sets	—	—	—	...	110

Sources: For 1949 and 1954, U.N., *Economic Bulletin for Europe, loc. cit.* p. 96; for 1955 and 1960, "Principles of the Second Five-Year Plan of Hungarian People's Economy," *Szabad Nep,* April 27, 1956.

[a] Figures for 1953.
[b] Figure for 1952.

Tractors were made in interwar Hungary in the Hofherr and Schrantz plant at Budapest, which in the course of the plan is supposed to manufacture about 19,000 caterpillar and universal tractors annually. Farm machinery output is supposed to double by 1960; production will be concentrated on heavy machinery, such as harvester combines, for collective and state farms.

The comparatively small prewar machine tools industry has been greatly enlarged and is supposed to double its output in 1960 to 11,000 pieces. Serial production of small and medium-size machine tools may be regarded as one of the most appropriate aims of Hungarian manufacturing. Mining machinery and hoisting, digging, and other construction and road-making equipment are being produced in Hungary for the first time.

Electric equipment from ordinary bulbs to power generators was made in interwar Hungary by a number of plants; seven large plants were branches of great European concerns and produced also for export to neighboring countries. The Russians carried away the facilities of the large Siemans and Tungsram plants, but the capacity of the remaining plants was gradually rebuilt and expanded, especially those factories making telecommunications equipment. The output of power generators and boilers is supposed to be more than tripled under the current plan. The current plan calls for 2,100,000 radio receivers, mostly for export, and 110,000 television sets are to be made, while production of household electric appliances will be tripled.

Chemical Industry

There is enough coal and oil in Hungary to support the development of an organic chemical industry, but most other basic chemical raw materials are scarce or nonexistent. The modest chemical industry that existed prior to 1914 was greatly expanded during the interwar period, based largely on imported raw materials. Although the industry was not working at full capacity, some products, such as fertilizers and rubber goods, were exported. After some of the best facilities were destroyed or looted in 1944-46, most of the industry was rebuilt in 1947-49. It was supposed to be considerably enlarged under the first plan, but most of the credits budgeted were switched to armaments production. Under the current plan, 5 billion forints will be invested in the chemical industry, which is expected to quadruple production. This new stress is undoubtedly motivated by the regime's desire to develop the production of substitutes for imported metals and textile raw materials, and of fertilizers.

The processing of oil and coal is to be greatly increased. The capacity of a dozen medium-size refineries is sufficient for the processing of locally produced oil, but their production is rather limited. Coke made in gasworks is only good for household uses; the construction of a hard coke plant at Sztalinvaros has been postponed, and the production of hard coke of brown coal at the Kazincbarcika plant (the Borsod chemical combinat) is still in the experimental stage. It is not clear where the estimated 450,000 tons of domestic hard metallurgical coke will be produced by 1960 (one third of total requirements of the iron industry), because distillation of coal was insignificant until 1954. The prospects of developing this branch of industry depend on investment in equipment and are reasonably good. In 1960, 1,550,000 tons of coal are supposed to be chemically processed, compared to less than 400,000 in 1955. Greatly increased output of organic dyes and drugs should follow expansion of the coal-chemical and petrochemical industry.

Very little commercial fertilizer was used in prewar Hungary, largely because of the fertility of its soil, and the careful husbandry of the peasants. However, the more impersonal state and collective farms set up after the war require commercial fertilizer. The building of new fertilizer plants was postponed until the second plan. Imported raw materials are used by superphosphate plants; ammonia and other nitrogenous fertilizers are made in one small prewar plant and at the Borsod combinat; by European standards, the entire fertilizer output was small in 1955. It is supposed to be greatly increased when the Tiszapalkonya chemical combinat, now under construction, and officially the key item of the second plan, is put in operation. This plant, utilizing Romanian natural gas and local coal, is expected to produce in 1960, in addition to nitrogen, plastics based on polyvinyl and polysterene, and synthetic yarn (orlon). This combine, which is being constructed according to a 1952 agreement with Romania, will be modeled on the giant East German and Polish diversified plants.

As can be seen from Table 8, the output of heavy chemicals was small until 1955, when a considerable amount of sulfuric acid was

Table 8. Output of Selected Chemical Goods, Selected Years 1938–1960 (Plan)
(*in thousand metric tons*)

Item	1938	1949	1954	1955	1960 Plan
Sulfuric acid	45	...	...	124	200
Caustic soda	2.7	8.0	11.6	11.7	40.5
Nitrogenous fertilizers	37	79	80	40[a]	150[a]
Phosphorous fertilizers	43	84	160		
Plastics and synthetics	—	—	—	32.1	11.6
Rayon yarn	0.6	0.6	...	...	...
Wood pulp	10	6	...	16.5	46.5
Paper	49.5	72.1	...	106	164

Sources: For 1938, *Hungarian Statistical Yearbook, 1938;* for other years as in Table 7.

[a] Pure content of nitrogen and phosphoric acid.

produced for the first time. This output and that of caustic soda, necessary for aluminum production, are to rise by 1960. Chlorine, oxygen, and other gases, and explosives are produced, as well as some rayon and a considerable amount of rubber goods. Interwar Budapest was noted for its production of hormones and other pharmaceuticals; it now also manufactures a large range of vitamins and antibiotics.

Building Materials Industry

With the one exception of lumber, Hungary possesses all raw materials required for the manufacture of all basic building materials. In 1927-35, approximately 10,000 dwellings were built per year in Hungary in urban areas, half of them in the capital. This was a highly insufficient rate, and Budapest remained one of the most congested major cities in East-Central Europe. Among the principal building materials were cement (396,000 tons in 1938, made in six plants), bricks and tiles (635 million pieces made in 289 brickyards), limestone (925,000 tons), and flat glass (1,678 million square meters).

During the war, the housing fund underwent substantial reduction, particularly in Budapest and vicinity. Building materials plants suffered less from war damage than from nationalization and closing of small enterprises. Under the Three-Year Plan, planned investment in all construction was to equal 2.6 billion forints, of which only 400 million forints, or about 15 per cent, was allotted for housing; but even less was actually spent, and house construction was confined to about 5,200 new apartments built during these three years and about 65,000 apartments reconditioned. In the first version of the first long-range plan, 21.3 billion forints were budgeted for all construction, including 5.1 billion forints for housing. With this amount, 180,000 urban dwellings were to be built, only 65,000 with state money at the cost of 2 billion forints; in the second version of the plan, the number of all dwellings to be constructed was raised to 220,000.

This plan was by no means fulfilled. In 1950, 28,400 dwellings were built, 31,000 in 1951, and only 16,000 each in 1953 and 1954. In 1951, the best year, the building rate equaled about 8 rooms per 1,000 inhabitants, a markedly inferior rate compared with that prevailing in Western Europe. In 1954, the rate fell to one half of that low figure, which was about nine times lower than in Western Germany. Government policy was solely responsible for this housing deficiency, since housing received the lowest priority of all construction.

By 1954, cement production more than doubled, compared with

prewar years (950,000 tons, while 2,100,000 tons was planned) as did flat-glass production; the figure for bricks and tiles is not available, which suggests that production was unsatisfactory. Approximately 200,000 people were employed in 1954 in building and construction, including salaried personnel. An unknown, and undoubtedly very high proportion (perhaps as much as 85-90 per cent) of workers and material were assigned to industrial and other government building.

In 1955, the picture improved somewhat with regard to production of building materials (1,180,000 tons of cement and 1.25 billion bricks), and it was expected to improve further under the second Five-Year Plan. Planned investment in building cannot be separated from other planned investments, but 2 billion forints are to be invested in the building materials industry, and in the building industry itself, 1 billion forints, mainly for new machinery. With regard to housing, 200,000 new apartments, a much smaller figure than originally anticipated, will be constructed. By apartment or dwelling, two or three rooms are usually meant, including kitchen but not a bathroom. If implemented, even this low number will be twice as large as that achieved under the first plan. Half of these dwellings will be state financed; the other half are to be built by prospective tenants from their savings, with the help of state credits, for which 1 billion forints are earmarked. The class character of this project is self-evident since only the élite can save money.

To realize the limited planned volume of new construction and the very high volume of capital building, reconditioning, and maintenance, output of the building industry is expected in 1960 to rise by 54-56 per cent, compared with 1955. Flat-glass production is expected to increase by 56-58 per cent, that of bricks by 56 per cent to 1,950 million pieces, and that of cement by 58 per cent to 1,860,000 tons. Such a rate of increase will necessitate the building of some new plants or at least a considerable expansion of existing facilities. Hungary's production of bauxite concrete has been encouraged, and it will be used more extensively as a building material. Construction will undoubtedly be increased, since Hungary began mass production of building machinery in the early 1950's.

Textile, Clothing, and Footwear Industries

The textile industry is of modern origin, having been established after 1921. Between 1921 and 1935, textile plants came to occupy second place in Hungarian industry, with one fifth of its gross output.

The number of workers employed rose from roughly 16,000 to 65,000, while net output rose fivefold and supplied more than 95 per cent of the country's demand. On the eve of the last war, the textile industry had 335,000 spindles and 14,000 looms; almost all this machinery was imported and highly efficient. Raw cotton was imported (24,400 tons in 1935) as well as most of the wool, silk, and rayon; domestic raw materials included wool (6,700 tons in 1939), flax (4,200 tons), hemp (13,600 tons), and raw silk (40 tons). More than half of the industry was concentrated in and around Budapest. In addition to industrial production, there was a considerable output of homespun linen, woolen, and silk cloth, not included in production statistics.

This industry suffered severe damage in 1944-46, and for years after the war manufactured reparation goods for the Soviet Union. Prewar output of cotton fabrics was equaled in 1949, that of woolens a few years later. Under the first Five-Year Plan, there were plans to erect a score of new textile plants; only two were built, but some factories were enlarged and the number of spindles rose to 440,000 in 1954. Under the current plan, a moderate increase of output is planned in most branches of this industry, with the exception of cotton fabrics.

While official production figures show an increase during the last decade, especially in the cotton industry, it does not follow that there has been a rise in consumption, because of the increase of the population, a marked decline of home spinning and weaving, the high proportion of rejects among the fabrics produced, and the rise of exports. The quality of goods earmarked for domestic consumption deteriorated after the war. The supply of raw materials underwent a change: more domestic rayon yarn is now available, although still more is needed, and there is now some Hungarian-grown cotton; the supply of wool has remained stationary and covers about 30 per cent of requirements, it is expected to increase to 10,000 tons per year at the end of the current plan; flax and hemp production has declined, compared with prewar (2,000 tons of flax and 7,000 tons of hemp in 1952).

The production of cotton fabric increased from 148 square meters in 1938 to 167 million in 1949, 226 million in 1954, and 237 million in 1955; and it is expected to reach 247 million in 1960. For woolens, the respective figures are 20 million square meters in 1938, 13 million in 1949, 12.1 million in 1954, and 25.7 million in 1955. Although there is no official explanation for this sudden jump, planned output for 1960 is 33.7 million square meters. Silk fabrics, i.e. rayon and real silk, were supposed to increase from 20 million square meters in 1955 to 25.5 million in 1960. There are no figures for the postwar processing of flax and hemp. Factory-knitted goods output is expected to increase from 5,038 tons in 1955 to 7,274 tons in 1960. It is interesting to note that, while the entire output of light industry, of which the textile industry represents by far the most important segment, is supposed to increase in the course of the current plan by one quarter, the supply of consumer goods on the domestic market is expected to increase by 40 per cent; this indicates an anticipated reduction in the export of textiles.

The leather industry, of which footwear production was a major part, doubled its output and the number of people employed between 1913 and 1938. It had then at its disposal more good-quality hides than any other country in East-Central Europe. In 1938, it produced about 6.1 million pairs of shoes, including 3.5 million leather ones. In 1955, 12.3 million pairs of leather shoes were allegedly manufactured, and 16.2 million pairs are expected to be made in 1960. An unknown percentage of the present output is exported. The quality of footwear produced is now lower than before the war. As much as 60 to 65 per cent of the hides required by the leather industry are now imported from Latin American and other countries.

Food Industry

Prior to 1918, food-processing plants constituted the largest and most profitable industry. Grain, animal, vegetable, fruit, and other foodstuffs were directed from all over the country to the flour mills, slaughterhouses, and other processing plants of Budapest and vicinity. Many of the products were sold to the industrial areas of the Austrian half of the Dual Monarchy; some, except grain, were also purchased by Germany and other West European countries. Hungarian fat bacon and salami, Tokay and other wines, and paprika were among the internationally known export goods. The turnover of the food industry increased from year to year, and it seemed to be destined to an ever greater development.

After Trianon, this tendency was reversed. There arose a great discrepancy between the capacity of the Hungarian food industry and the limited size of the domestic market. Austrian and Czechoslovakian agrarian policies in the twenties led to the curtailment of Hungarian exports to these countries. During the depression, flour-milling and distilling were most heavily hit. The introduction of new food-processing methods, such as canning and dehydrating, could only partly compensate for the loss of older industries. In spite of these unfavorable circumstances, the food industry remained first among all industrial branches: in 1938, its gross output of 3.7 billion forints (calculated after the war in 1946 prices) exceeded that of the engineering industries (2.8 billion forints).

After the war, the food industry had to produce reparation goods. Practically no money was invested in it under the Three-Year Plan. Under the first Five-Year Plan, 71 new plants were expected to be built and the volume of production nearly tripled in most subdivisions of the food industry. The plan called for a great increase in flour-milling and sugar production, as well as in vegetable and meat canning. Realization of these targets depended, of course, on an anticipated much increased output of basic farm goods, which did not materialize. Only sugar beets and oleaginous plants were produced in greatly increased quantities, and there was some rise, if Hungarian statistical data are to be believed, in production of maize, mutton, and tobacco. Elsewhere, production remained the same or decreased. The weight of animals slaughtered fell from about 575,000 tons in 1938 (when by no means all animals were included in statistics) to 332,000 tons in 1950, and began to rise only a few years later. Only after the introduction of the "new course" did all production indices rise. A great deal of progress was apparently realized under the first plan in refrigeration (cold storage capacity was allegedly doubled), meat processing, butter, and cheese processing; large "bread factories" were built in most big cities; the range of foodstuffs processed was extended, and the preparation of frozen foods on an industrial scale introduced.

Under the second Five-Year Plan, it seems that a slightly higher proportion of various foods may be offered for sale on the domestic market in 1960 than in 1955, provided, of course, that the relatively high farming targets are realized. In 1956-60, 2.3 to 2.4 billion forints are to be invested in the food industry; food output is expected to rise from 45 to 70 per cent. Thus, while the total production of fodder is expected to rise by 25 per cent, the number of cattle by 5 per cent, that of hogs and sheep by 25-30 per cent, and the weight of slaughtered animals by 34 per cent, the output of the meat-processing industry is expected to rise 50-55 per cent.

Production of unprocessed meat is expected to increase from 143,000 tons in 1955 to 219,000 tons in 1960 (about 45 pounds per capita) and that of bacon (the fat Hungarian variety) from 60,000 tons to 79,000 tons. Together with vegetable fats and butter, production of edible fats should increase from 98,900 tons to 132,300 tons in 1960 (disregarding exports). Most Hungarian cooking oil and margarine derives from sunflower seeds.

The separate branches of the food industry can only be briefly dealt with here. Of about 700 large and medium-size flour mills, about 100 of the largest are concentrated in Budapest; their capacity far exceeds actual flour output, which in 1938 and 1951 equaled 1,100,000 tons. The capacity of the 13 sugar refineries also exceeded the widely fluctuating prewar output of sugar (127,400 tons in 1938). From 1948 on, the industry has had to supply large amounts of sugar to the Soviet Union. Sugar beet cultivation is favored, if not actually subsidized by the government, and sugar production has risen. It is expected to increase to 410,000 tons in 1960. Attainment of this target will probably require the erection of new sugar refineries. While sugar output is expected to rise under the current plan by 65 per cent, domestic supply will only rise by 19 per cent. Thus, Hungary intends to export much more sugar than hitherto.

16. TRANSPORTATION
AND COMMUNICATIONS

INTRODUCTION

Until the end of World War I, largely under the influence of the Austro-Hungarian General Staff, transportation policy tended to establish a centralized road and railroad system focused on Budapest. The main railroad lines built before 1918 still represent the backbone of the Hungarian railroad system. Under the Trianon Treaty, Hungary lost about 60 per cent of its railroads and hard-surfaced roads, almost two-thirds of its navigable waterways and its Adriatic port, Fiume.

Efforts to integrate and modernize this truncated network were rather spasmodic. A considerable influence came from the landlords, whose search for markets led them toward Austria and Germany. Consequently, Trianon Hungary developed a communication system with the important veins leading westward. Inter-communication both for railroads and highways lagged. Only in the late 1930's was the construction of better highways begun, with an appropriation of 80 million pengo under a five-year plan for road building. By 1942, Hungary had succeeded in connecting a large number of previously isolated communities to the main road system. However, the railroad lines were comparatively neglected. Lack of capital and the world-wide depression were important factors in this delay.

Prewar Hungary had 815 miles of navigable waterways, including the Danube and its tributaries and the long sliver of Lake Balaton in Transdanubia. After the Danube, the two most important waterways were the Tisza and Koros rivers, which flow through the wheat region of the Great Hungarian Plain. These, however, were navigable only part of the year, being subject to drought in summer and ice in winter. Most river traffic passed up and down the Danube, which before the war had thirteen ports. The most important port, Budapest, drew international traffic with its free facilities at Csepel. In general, the waterway potential had not been exploited.

Budapest was a crossroads for European air traffic. French, Dutch, and German lines stopped there on their way to Bucharest, Athens, Baghdad, and Batavia. The Hungarian Air Transport Corporation (MALERT) made regular flights to Vienna, Prague, Zurich, Arad, Bucharest, and Warsaw, carrying 18,000 passengers in 1936.

Because Hungary had been allied with Germany during the war, the Soviet Union received at Potsdam title to all German-owned property. The Soviet Union exercised these rights in the field of transportation by setting up two "joint companies," in which the control was theoretically shared by Russians and Hungarians. These were MASZOVLET (Hungarian-Soviet Civil Aeronautical Company) and MESZHART (Hungarian-Soviet Navigation Company). In the fall of 1954, they were returned to Hungarian control under the Ministry of Transportation.

POSTWAR RECONSTRUCTION AND COMMUNIST PLANNING

Hungary suffered heavily in World War II, and damage to transportation facilities was particularly costly. Some came from Allied bombing and some from the German retreat in 1944-45. Destruction was severe on the railroads, where nearly half the buildings, a third of the tracks, and almost all the bridges were damaged. Much of the rolling stock was appropriated by the retreating Germans, and then by the "liberating" Russians. War damages to the railroad system amounted to 13.2 per cent of the country's total war damages. Table 1 reveals the impact of war and "liberation" on the rolling stock of the Hungarian railroads.

Table 1. War Losses in Railroad Rolling Stock

	Locomotives	Motor Locomotives	Passenger Coaches	Freight Cars	Total
Stock (1942)	2,875	195	6,205	59,122	68,397
Per cent	100	100	100	100	100
Operating stock (1945)	688	21	1,046	8,767	10,522
Per Cent	24	10.8	16.9	14.9	15.3

Source: Central Statistical Bureau, *Magyar Statisztikai Zsebkonyv* (Hungarian Statistical Pocketbook) (Budapest, 1947), XIV, 229.

Harbor installations sustained heavy damages; and the Germans carried away most of the Danube and Tisza river fleets, although a great part of the floating stock was later returned by the Allies. Road transport, which had not been a significant factor prior to the war, developed during the war as a military transport system. The trucking stock, therefore, shared the fate of other military equipment in being removed by the Germans and Russians.

Economic reconstruction of war-torn Hungary had to begin with transportation. In 1946, a number of bridges were rebuilt over the Danube and the Tisza, and an American loan financed the import of 300 locomotives, but the general performance of the transport services remained far below the prewar level. In 1947, the coalition government began a Three-Year Plan aimed at reconstruction and development. This plan assigned 676 million forints (approximately 58 million dollars at the official rate of exchange), or 25 per cent of the total investment, to transportation and communications. However, as in Czechoslovakia, the spring of 1948 brought further consolidation of Communist power and the speeding up of the plan. The three-year period was cut to 29 months, and the plan ended in December 1949. The actual share of transportation and communications in total investment during the 29 months was approximately 19-20 per cent. Expenditures had been allocated by the original plan in per cent of total transportation expenditures as follows:

	Per Cent
Railroads (total)	50.4
Bridges	8.8
Roads (total)	23.7
Bridges	11.3
Waterways	3.8
Airlines	3.0
Mail, radio, and other	19.1

Source: News from Behind the Iron Curtain, V (March 1956), 16.

By 1949, the traffic on railroads and highways was claimed to be well above the prewar level. Railroad freight volume reached 135 per cent of the 1937 figure, and freight carried in trucks was 245 per cent of the 1937 volume. Waterways, however, had not recovered; the corresponding figure was 98 per cent of 1937. Passenger traffic had risen by 137 per cent on railroads and 30 per cent on long-distance buses.

In January 1950, the regime launched its first Five-Year Plan. This plan followed the pattern of other captive countries in its stress on heavy industry and in its high rate of total investment (21 per cent of the national income).

Transportation and communications were allotted 7.5 billion forints or 15 per cent of the total investment, with a view to increasing transport capacity by 60 per cent over the 1949 level. Industrial output, meanwhile, was to rise by more than 80 per cent, and the output of heavy industry by more than 100 per cent. In May 1951, the plan was revised and generally higher targets were set. Total investments were raised by 67 per cent. While the absolute amount to be spent on transportation and communications was also raised, the share of this sector in total investment fell from 15 to 12 per cent.

In July 1953, after the death of Stalin, Hungary began its "new course." The new Prime Minister, Imre Nagy, admitted that current economic goals were beyond the country's strength and criticized the policy of exaggerated industrialization. The Five-Year Plan was revised again, this time downward. Total investment was reduced by 22 per cent. The share of transportation and communications in this new dispensation was to be 13 per cent of total investment.

The total investment over the five years turned out to be slightly less than the final version of the plan had forecast, or about 67 billion forints. Transportation and communications received 8.7 billion forints. Apparently, this was not enough to enable the transport services to keep pace with increased industrial output. While the total volume of freight transported in 1953 was about double that of 1949, industrial output has risen 254 per cent. An article by Nyilas Andras ("A magyar kozlekedes fejlodese es jelenlegi helyzete" [Development and Present Situation of Hungarian Transportation] in the official statistical quarterly *Statisztikai Tajekoztato* [Statistical Bulletin], No. 4 [1954], 18-27) referred to the "disproportion in the development of industry and transportation" and complained that "not enough care has been devoted to modernization of the transportation system and to building up new transportation means."

The figures below show the decline in the proportion of transportation in planned investment (in per cent of total investment).

Year	Per Cent
1950	19.6
1951	13.7
1952	15.0
1953	10.7
1954	7.2
1955	9.0
1956 (planned)	9.4

Sources: Statisztikai Tajekoztato (Statistical Bulletin), No. 4 (1954); *Szabad Nep* (Free People), November 17, 1955; cited in *News from Behind the Iron Curtain, loc. cit.,* p. 17; *Szabad Nep,* April 20, 22, 1955.

Railroads

Railroads represented the chief means of transport in prewar Hungary, carrying in 1937 about 96 per cent of total freight traffic. At the beginning of 1938, the length of the Royal Hungarian State Railways was 7,646 kilometers (4,751 miles), of which 885 kilometers (550 miles) were double and 6,761 kilometers (4,201 miles) single track. Lines privately owned and operated had a route length of about 527 kilometers (328 miles). From the nineteenth century on, the system was gradually nationalized until about 90 per cent was under the management of the Royal Hungarian State Railways. The total interwar length was 7,823 kilometers (4,860 miles). The total length of the railroads has not changed considerably: the *Oxford Economic Atlas of the World* registered the length of the total network in 1949 as 4,773 miles (about 7,680 kilometers), of which 582 miles (about 940 kilometers) were electrified.

Under the Three-Year Plan, railroads received more than half of the funds allotted to transportation. Most of this went for reconstruction. The blueprint also called for some extension in the length of double-track lines and the electrification of the Budapest-Gyor line. By 1949, six important railroad bridges had been rebuilt, including the southern railroad bridge in Budapest and those over the Tisza and Zagyva rivers in Szolnok. Both electrification of the Budapest-Gyor line and double-tracking of the Budapest-Miskolc line had been completed in 1948.

The system consists essentially of a series of main lines radiating from Budapest. These lines, which are generally well built and can carry axle loads of 16-20 tons, are connected by a large number of light construction lines carrying only 12-13 tons of axle load. The network is comparatively dense, amounting to 15.3 miles for every 100 square miles and 6.1 miles for every 10,000 inhabitants. The European average is about 7 miles per 100 square miles and 5.3 miles per 10,000 inhabitants.

During the Five-Year Plan, railroad capacity was further increased. In the period 1950-53, 404 kilometers of new track were laid, and an additional 110 kilometers were reconstructed. A new line of 45 kilometers was built from Vac to Aszod, and another 23 kilometers from Retszilas to Sztalinvaros, the heavy industrial center. Double-tracking was completed on the Satoraljaujhely-Zahony line and the Budapest-Ujszasz-Szolnok line, both of which are important links with the Soviet Union. The line from Debrecen to Fuzesabony was

also being double-tracked. The marshaling yards of Miskolc and Fer-
encvaros (Budapest) were reconstructed and modernized. The Danube
River bridges at Baja, Taksony, and Ujpest were rebuilt, and new
bridges were completed at Dunafoldvar and Komarom. During the
Five-Year Plan, eight railroad stations were built or reconstructed.

Most of the railroad expansion was in the eastern or border regions
and was directed toward improving connections with the Soviet Union
and other Communist countries (see Table 2). Special attention was
given to the border town of Zahony, where 32 wide-gauge tracks enter
the Soviet Union, and to the important junction at Miskolc, from
which lines run north and east to Kassa (Kosice) in Czechoslovakia,
Przemysl in Poland, and Ungvar (Uzhgorod) in Soviet-occupied
Carpatho-Ukraine. By December 19, 1955, the line from Budapest to
Zahony had been completely rebuilt, the first main line to be rebuilt
in its entirety since the war. Among other improvements, curves were
lengthened and grades reduced. It is claimed that the improvements
will permit an increase of 6 metric tons in average freight car loads,
and it has been stated that replacement of tracks is under way on the
Miskolc line and the Bekescsaba-Lokoshaza line near Romania. (See
Map 3, page 323.)

Rolling stock has shown a rather slow recovery from war damages.
Although substantial additions were made during the Three-Year Plan,
in 1949 there were only 1,500 locomotives, 2,500 passenger cars,
and 35,000 freight cars—still considerably below the 1937/38 level,
while the freight burden had increased by nearly 50 per cent. Rolling
stock increased during the first Five-Year Plan to roughly the prewar
level. New equipment consisted of 33 steam locomotives, 253 passenger coaches, and 3,964 freight cars. Old rolling stock was rebuilt
to the extent of 248 locomotives, 895 coaches, and 7,901 freight cars.
Assuming that the rebuilt equipment represented a net addition to the
operating stock this brought the supply of freight cars to 15 per cent
above the prewar level. Locomotives and passenger coaches, however,
were still about 6 per cent fewer than in 1937/38. (See Table 3.)

The task of the railroads increased faster than their equipment.
According to *Szabad Nep* of May 8, 1955, the volume of freight increased by 30 million tons, nearly doubling the amount transported
in 1949. Passenger traffic grew by 83.6 per cent. Compared with the
prewar year, 1937/38, the railroads in 1954 were carrying two and a
half times the freight load and four times the passenger load. An article
in *Statisztikai Tajekoztato* (No. 4, 1954) admitted that "the immense
results achieved do not conceal the shortcomings in railroad trans-

Table 2. International Railroad Lines

Route	Border Crossing Point	Remarks
Budapest-Banhida-Komarom-Gyor-Hegyeshalom	Hegyeshalom (Hungary) Nickelsdorf (Austria)	Budapest-Vienna main line; route of Arlberg and Orient Express trains; double track; electrified to Hegyeshalom
Budapest-Vac-Szob	Szob (Hungary) Parkan (Czechoslovakia)	Budapest-Prague main line; route of Baltic Orient Express; double track; electrified to Szob
Budapest-Hatvan-Miskolc-Hidasnemeti	Hidasnemeti (Hungary) Cana (Czechoslovakia)	Budapest-Kassa (Kosice) main line; double track and electrified to Miskolc
Budapest-Cegled-Nyiregyhaza-Zahony	Zahony (Hungary) Chop (Soviet Union)	Main east-west line for Soviet traffic to Budapest, Vienna, Bratislava, etc., double track, electrified to Szolnok
Budapest-Szolnok-Bekescsaba-Lokoshaza	Lokoshaza (Hungary) Curtici (Romania)	Budapest-Bucharest main line; route of Arlberg, Orient and Baltic-Orient Express trains; partly double track; electrified to Szolnok
Budapest-Szolnok Puspokladany-Artand	Biharkeresztes (Hungary) Episcopia B. (Romania)	An alternate route for Budapest-Bucharest traffic; partly double track; electrified to Szolnok
Budapest-Kiskunhalas-Kelebia	Kelebia (Hungary) Subotica (Yugoslavia)	Budapest-Belgrade main line; route of the Istambul section of Baltic Orient, Simplon Express; mostly single track
Budapest-Pusztaszabolcs-Siofok-Nagykanizsa-Murakeresztur	Murakeresztur (Hungary) Kotoriba (Yugoslavia)	Budapest-Venice-Rome main line; Budapest-Zagreb traffic; route of Simplon-Orient Express; mostly single track; electrified to Pusztaszabolcs

Sources: Hivatalos Menetrend (Official Timetable), Hungarian State Railways Budapest, 1948, *Kozlekedestudomanyi Szemle* (Transportation Science Review), III, No. 5 (1953).

Table 3. Railroad Rolling Stock, 1937/38, 1949, and 1954

Type	1937/38	1949	1954
Locomotives	1,889	1,500	1,791
Passenger coaches	3,908	2,500	3,648
Freight cars	40,852	35,000	46,865

Sources: Central Statistical Bureau, *Annuaire Statistique Hongrois 1938* (Budapest, 1940) ; *Zycie Gospodarcze* (Economic Life) (Warsaw), No. 9 (1949) ; *Statisztikai Szemle* (Statistical Review) (June 1955) ; cited in *News from Behind the Iron Curtain, loc. cit.,* p. 21.

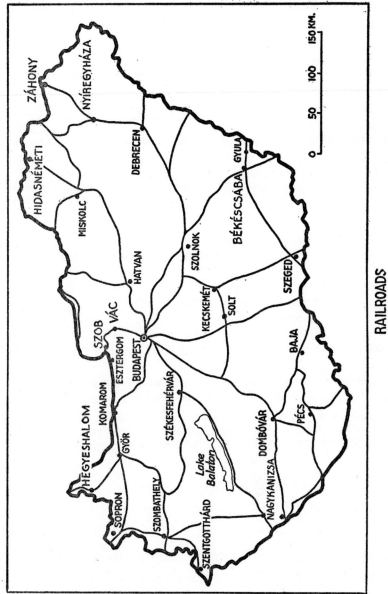

RAILROADS
MAP 3

portation. The greatest difficulty lies in the discrepancy between the actual traffic and the development of the rolling stock." This was echoed in August 1955 by Minister of Transportation Lajos Bebrits, who said that the technical development of the railroads was unequal to its task. If there had been no major breakdown, he added, this was because the railroads had "profited from the experience of the USSR."

In fact, Hungarian railroads have borrowed techniques from the Soviet Union for more intensive use of limited rolling stock. These include the system of norms, workers' competitions, and Stakhanovite movements. For example, the so-called "Two-Thousand-Ton Movement" encourages the formation of 2,000-ton trains (70 cars), and the "Five-Hundred-Kilometer Movement" induces engine crews to run their engines 500 kilometers within 24 hours. Another method has been devised for raising performance to increase the average car load. Thus, for example, the permissible load of a freight car was raised in 1953 in the 15-ton category to 16 metric tons and in the 20-ton category to 21 tons. The most important standard of performance in Communist railroading is the turnaround time of an average freight car, i.e., time between one loading and the next. In Hungary, the average turnaround time was seven days in 1938. By 1949, it had been shortened to 5.6 days; it decreased to 4.7 days in 1950, 3.5 days in 1951, and is approximately the same at present. The performance of the average freight car in 1953 was roughly 173,000 ton-kilometers, compared to 108,000 in France in 1951 and 84,000 in Italy the same year.

Since little has been done to modernize the railroads, technically, the greatly increased tasks called for a considerably larger labor force. The prewar staff, which was well trained and adequate for the level of traffic, totaled 57,891, divided as follows:

	Number of Persons
General and Divisional Headquarters	2,863
Civil engineering	13,074
Locomotive crews	8,383
Station staff	14,228
Train crews	4,844
Running sheds	2,117
Main workshops	6,207
Other grades	6,175
Total	57,891

Source: Great Britain, Ministry of Economic Warfare, *Hungary: Basic Handbook,* Part II, "Economic Survey" (London, 1944), p. 38.

According to the *Magyar Gazdasagkutato Intezet Kozlemenyei* (Publications of the Hungarian Economic Research Institute), of January 30, 1953, the total number of railroad employees was 117,603 at the end of 1952. It is fair to assume that their number has grown since then, more or less proportionately with the growth of freight traffic.

Gyorgy Csanadi, general manager of the railroads, stated in 1955 that most of the loading is still done by hand, a condition that makes any further cut in loading time "almost impossible" *(Szabad Nep,* December 18, 1955). Weeding is also done by hand, although the use of chemicals would save annually 1,300 man-years. The manager noted a general lack of machinery for construction and maintenance. On the other hand, automatic block signals have been installed on the Budapest-Hegyeshalom and the Budapest-Cegled-Szolnok lines. Since March 1955, stagnation in production of electric and Diesel engines has reportedly ended, and more funds have been allotted for mechanization, but the rate of development is still unsatisfactory. Steam engines, Csanadi wrote, "are the largest. . .consumers of the country's coal. They profitably utilize only 4-6 per cent of the consumed energy. The development of coal mining consumes huge sums—if only for this reason, the use of steam engines must be gradually eliminated."

Hungary has a relatively important system of narrow-gauge railroads. They are used in industry to carry freight between plants and to make connections with standard-gauge lines; in the countryside, they are important during harvest time; and they are also used for lumbering operations. During the Five-Year Plan the regime spent about 100 million forints on the narrow-gauge industrial lines and extended the network by 219 kilometers. The estimated volume of freight carried on these lines rose from 580,000 tons in 1950 to 2.2 million tons in 1953. (See Tables 4 and 5.)

Despite the policy shifts and crises which have marked Hungarian planning, the industrial program has advanced far enough to lay a severe strain on the transport system, especially on the railroads, which still carry the major burden.

The situation does not seem likely to change in the near future. According to *Szabad Nep* of November 17, 1955, transportation will receive 9.4 per cent of the total investment budget in 1956. The capacity of the railroads is to be raised "to a greater extent than in former years." Specifically, there are to be 1,150 new freight cars, which is probably an increase of 2-3 per cent of the total stock. Measured against a planned increase of about 10 per cent in the production of heavy industry, and allowing for depreciation of present rolling stock, this implies that the bottleneck will continue.

Table 4. Railroad Freight Traffic, 1937 and 1946–1954

Year	Volume (in thousand metric tons)	Index (1949 = 100)
1937	24,400	74
1946	9,480	29
1947	16,560	50
1948	21,936	66
1949	33,000	100
1950	39,102	118
1951	46,687	141
1952	58,803	178
1953	66,400	201
1954	63,300	192

Sources: Statisztikai Tajekoztato, loc. cit.; Adam Rudzki, *East-Central European Transportation* (Washington, 1955); *Szabad Nep*, May 8, 1955; cited in *News from Behind the Iron Curtain, loc. cit.*, p. 19.

Table 5. Railroad Passenger Traffic, Selected Years 1937/38–1954

Year	Passengers (in thousands)	Index (1949 = 100)
1937/38	78,000	42
1946	65,004	35
1947	96,480	52
1949	185,200	100
1953	338,900	183
1954	340,027	184

Sources: Rudzki, op. cit.; Statistizkai Tajekoztato, loc. cit.; Szabad Nep, May 8, 1955; cited in *News from Behind the Iron Curtain, loc. cit.*, p. 18.

Road Transportation

Hungary's prewar road system consisted of seven main roads converging on Budapest, and numerous interconnecting roads that were hardly suitable for heavy motor traffic. In 1937, there were 30,353 kilometers (18,860 miles) of roads, of which under one fifth were main routes, just over three-fifths were secondary routes, and the remaining fifth consisted of very poor quality rural roads.

Military mobilization and logistic methods as well as the heavy damages sustained by the railroad system gradually increased the importance of road transportation. After the war, in Hungary, as in other captive countries, road transport has developed faster than the rest of transportation. Prior to the war, Hungarian road traffic was negligible. During the Three-Year Plan, nearly a quarter of transport investment went to the road sector, compared with half to the railroads, and during the Five-Year Plan the emphasis increased: road transport received 25 per cent of the investment in the first four years of the plan, while the railroad share declined to 39 per cent.

There is no adequate estimate of the size of the Hungarian road network. The August 15, 1952 *Bulletin* of the Bureau Hongrois de Presse et de Documentation (Paris) stated that the network totaled 25,872 kilometers (16,060 miles), of which one tenth belonged to the over-all state highway system. The Three-Year Plan had called for the completion of repairs to war-damaged roads, which meant the reconstruction of about 20 per cent of the arterial highways and about 40 per cent of the primary and secondary roads, as well as the rebuilding of bridges. Besides this, 1,625 kilometers (1,009 miles) of new roads were to be built. Reconstruction was claimed to have been finished by 1949, though not the building of new roads. The Five-Year Plan, in its original version, provided for 605 kilometers (376 miles) of new arterial highways and 2,250 kilometers (1,397 miles) of new secondary roads, plus a number of bridges. Evidently only part of this program was completed, since the official report on plan fulfillment stated that during five years a total of 1,100 kilometers (683 miles) were added to the highway network. These included three much-publicized roads: one from Miskolc to Satoraljaujhely on the Slovakian border; another in the Transdanubian region from Nagykanizsa on the Yugoslav border along Lake Balaton to Balatonkeresztur; and a third in the same region paralleling the Yugoslav border from Szekszard to Pecs. *Statisztikai Tajekoztato* claimed that at the end of 1953 the total length of asphalt roads was more than twice that of 1937, and the length of concrete roads nearly four times as great.

The number of motor vehicles can likewise only be estimated. At the end of 1938, there were 35,000 vehicles of all types, including 3,800 trucks and 668 buses. In 1947, the total number of vehicles increased to about 48,000, of which 11,000 were trucks and 472 buses. The United Nations *Economic Survey of Europe in 1950* estimated the number of trucks in 1950 at 13,000. During the Five-Year Plan, the number of trucks was to increase by 23,000. However, *Statisztikai Tajekoztato* claimed that in 1953 the number of trucks was "nearly twice as great as in 1950," which suggests a figure somewhere around 25,000.

Hungary has a large auto plant at Csepel, a suburb of Budapest, which produced its ten-thousandth car in March 1952, and since then has made some 15,000. The Ikarusz body and vehicle plant makes long distance buses. Much of the output is exported to other countries of the Soviet bloc, while other motor vehicles are imported.

The official figures for road traffic since the war show enormous development, but it must be remembered that growth started from a very low level. Passengers carried in 1937 amounted to 44 million, including 31 million on city bus lines. In 1949, the total was 99 million, and it increased 192 per cent during the Five-Year Plan to 290 million in 1953. Long distance bus traffic figures are given in Table 6.

Table 6. Long Distance Bus Passenger Traffic, Selected Years
1937–1954

Year	Passengers (in thousands)	Index (1949 = 100)
1937	12,680	77
1949	16,537	100
1953	90,671	548
1954	115,000	695

Sources: Statisztikai Tajekoztato, loc. cit.; Szabad Nep, January 20, 1955; cited in News from Behind the Iron Curtain, loc. cit., p. 18.

Truck transport has grown even more rapidly (see Table 7). Though the regime has not published absolute figures, it claims that the volume of freight carried in 1953 was approximately ten times as great as in 1937, and nearly four times that in 1950.

Table 7. Truck Transportation, 1937, 1938, and 1948–1953

Year	Freight (in thousand metric tons)	Index (1949 = 100)
1937	425	41
1938	460	45
1948	1,006	97
1949	1,033	100
1950	2,514	243
1951	4,764	461
1952	6,808	659
1953	9,606	930

Sources: Rudzki, op. cit.; cited in News from Behind the Iron Curtain, loc. cit., p. 19.

Municipal Transport

The state has taken over public transportation in the larger cities, and perhaps for this reason more information is available than in the case of some other Communist countries, where urban transport is still a municipal concern. Municipal passenger traffic has grown since the war about as much as that of other road transport. Streetcars carried 902 million passengers in 1953, almost two and a half times as many as in 1937. City bus lines carried 199 million passengers in 1953, an increase of more than 500 percent since 1937. (See Table 8.)

Table 8. City Transportation, Selected Years 1937-1954

Year	Million Passengers		Index (1937 = 100)	
	Buses	Streetcars	Buses	Streetcars
1937	31.5	365.9	100	100
1949	82.7	645.2	263	176
1953	199.3	902.1	633	247
1954	227.2	...	721	...

Sources: Statisztikai Tajekoztato, loc. cit.; Szabad Nep, January 20, 1955; cited in News from Behind the Iron Curtain, loc. cit., p. 22.

Budapest has a subway, the oldest in Europe, dating from 1896. One of the most publicized projects of the regime, second only to the steel complex at Szatlinvaros, has been the building of a new express subway. The first line, which was to be completed during the Five-Year Plan, was to run a distance of eight kilometers (five miles) from the People's Stadium to Szell Kalman Square, crossing the Danube at Kossuth Square. The design was very ornate, in the style of the Moscow subway. Construction stopped in 1953 at the beginning of the "new course," and was resumed only late in 1954. It is expected to continue during the next Five-Year Plan.

City rolling stock has not kept pace with the increase in passengers. Although Hungary manufactures streetcars, most are exported, and the number in operation in 1953 was scarcely greater than in 1937 or 1949. The regime has tried to improve the situation by introducing trolley buses, as in the Soviet Union. At first, they were imported from the Soviet Union, but since 1952 Hungary has been making its own. The supply of motor buses, trolley buses, and streetcars is admitted to be inadequate. Szabad Nep stated on January 20, 1955 that passenger traffic in Budapest tripled between 1938 and 1953, but that the number and capacity of vehicles increased only by 15 per cent.

A similar problem exists with taxicabs, which have become increasingly important, because of the almost total lack of private automobiles. In 1937/38, there were 3,150 taxis and cars for rent in the country. Statisztikai Tajekoztato (No. 4, 1954) complains that although taxis in 1953 covered three and a half times as many kilometers as in 1937, the taxi park is smaller than it was in 1937. "The situation is made worse by the fact that a considerable number of taxis are used by the authorities on inspection trips in the country."

Inland Waterways

The Danube is the most important waterway in Hungary and has served as the main international highway from Austria and Germany to the Black Sea and to the Mediterranean Sea. The Hungarian part of the Danube was regulated and canalized in the nineteenth century. At first, it had little importance for Hungary, yet after World War I, the need for a merchant marine, both river and seagoing increased. Prior to World War I, nearly a quarter of Hungary's total foreign trade was carried on her inland waterways, 90 per cent on the Danube.

Hungarian waterways are obstructed by ice and are unnavigable from late December to February. The Danube barges are usually tied up at wintering ports, such as Venek (near Gyor), Budapest, Obuda, Ujpest, Sztalinvaros (formerly Dunapentele), and Baja. Other important harbors are Esztergom, Dunafoldvar, and Mohacs on the Danube, and Szolnok, Csongrad, and Szeged on the Tisza.

The Hungarian part of the Danube is navigable for craft of 900 tons. The Tisza River, which, like the Danube, was internationalized for most of its length by the Treaty of Trianon, provides an outlet for agricultural produce from the rich basin of the Banat. Tisza is generally navigable to Szolnok for craft of 600 tons, and to Tokaj under favorable conditions. The other navigable waterways are of rather local importance and carry mainly agrarian products and timber. The Koros River is navigable to Bekesszentandras for 400- to 600-ton craft. The Drava is navigable to Barcs for vessels of from 400 to 600 tons. The Sio Canal is reportedly navigable for Danube vessels, apparently meaning the standard 900-ton crafts. Table 9 gives the navigability of Hungarian waterways.

The Three-Year Plan allotted only 3.8 per cent of its transportation investment to waterways, showing the relatively minor importance of this form of transport in the first postwar years. In addition to the refloating and reconditioning of river boats, harbor installations were to be improved and the central harbor at Csepel was to be enlarged. The construction of two canals was planned: the Sio Canal, connecting Lake Balaton with the Danube, 110 kilometers south of Budapest (completed in 1948), and a Trans-Tisza Eastern Main Canal which was to cross the Hungarian Plain from the Danube to the Tisza.

The latter project received enormous publicity, but construction on it did not start until 1952. It has since been abandoned.

Table 9. Navigability of Hungarian Waterways

Waterway	Total Length	Navigable Length
	(*in miles*)	
Danube	265	265
Tisza	373	336
Koros	71	71
Drava	69	53
Sio Canal	68	68
Bodrog	35	1
Lake Balaton	77	77
Total	958	871

Sources: *Hungary: Basic Handbook, loc. cit.*, p. 39; L. D. Schweng, *Economic Planning in Hungary Since 1938* (New York, 1951), p. 31.

The Five-Year Plan mentioned the building of five new harbors. The Danube fleet was to be increased by the construction of two passenger steamers, six tugs, fifty-nine barges, and three seagoing vessels. The extent to which all these plans were carried out is not clear. An important new harbor was built at Sztalinvaros to service the big steel plant there. Also, the port of Csepel at Budapest was greatly enlarged, carrying in 1953 three times the traffic it did in 1938. Hungary's floating stock, however, was reported in 1954 to be at the prewar level. Tabulated figures on the increased passenger and freight traffic should, therefore, be viewed against this background. (See Table 10.)

Table 10. Waterways Freight Traffic, Selected Years 1937–1954

Year	Volume (in thousand metric tons)	Index (1949 = 100)
1937	762	102
1938	610	82
1947	280	38
1948	516	69
1949	746	100
1950	1,153	155
1951	1,575	211
1953	1,908	256
1954	1,746	234

Sources: *Statisztikai Tajekoztato, loc. cit.*; Rudzki, *op. cit.*; *Szabad Nep*, May 8, 1955; cited in *News from Behind the Iron Curtain, loc. cit.*, p. 19.

Table 11 shows an interesting trend in Danube shipping between Hungary and the Soviet Union and the other captive countries. Since the new Soviet approach to Yugoslavia, Danube traffic has most likely increased.

Table 11. Transit Trade on the Danube through Yugoslavia,
Selected Years 1937–1953
(*in thousand metric tons*)

	1937	1948	1952	1953
Upstream Traffic				
From Bulgaria to Hungary	3	13	99	106
From Romania to Hungary	291	25	82	83
From Soviet Union to Hungary	—	64	245	118
Downstream Traffic				
From Hungary to Bulgaria	7	24	19	18
From Hungary to Romania	118	18	23	22
From Hungary to Soviet Union	—	120	431	527

Sources: U.N., *Economic Survey of Europe in 1954* (Geneva, 1955), p. 116.

Ships on the Danube carry passengers from Budapest north to Domos and south all the way to Mohacs, near the Yugoslav border. Passenger service also exists on the Tisza and Koros rivers and on Lake Balaton. (See Table 12.)

Table 12. Waterways Passenger Traffic, 1937, 1949, and 1953

Year	Passengers (in thousands)	Index (1949 = 100)
1937	1,863	73
1949	2,552	100
1953	2,801	110

Sources: Statisztikai Tajekoztato, loc. cit.; cited in *News from Behind the Iron Curtain, loc. cit.,* p. 18.

The inadequacy of the floating stock seems to be generally acknowledged by Hungarian transportation experts. The short supply is due not to lack of shipbuilding facilities but to the export of ships to other countries. The Gheorghiu-Dej shipyard at Budapest (formerly Ganz-Danubius) specializes in river and seagoing ships and tankers that can be used on both the Danube and the Mediterranean. Since 1945, it has turned out almost fifty 1,100-ton freighters for the Soviet Union, Egypt, and Communist China, as well as passenger ships for the Soviet

Union. It also produces larger vessels of 1,800 to 3,000 tons. Only one of its freighters has been supplied to Hungary, giving the country a total of six. An article in *Kozlekedestudomanyi Szemle* (Transportation Science Review) in September 1954 suggested that more up-to-date tugs and barges would allow considerable savings in fuel, as well as faster and safer transportation.

Airlines

Hungary now has domestic airline service between Budapest and the major provincial towns. The network is centered on the capital, however, and does not provide regular connections between one provincial town and another. During the Five-Year Plan, the Ferihegy and Nyiregyhaza airports were reconstructed and new airports were built at Nagykanizsa, Kaposvar, Pecs, and Zalaegerszeg. Air transport has been used increasingly for high priority shipments of machine parts and for light materials, such as glass and blood plasma. Some fresh fruits and vegetables are also brought to Budapest by plane. Table 13 shows the increase in airline freight traffic from 1937 to 1953.

Table 13. Airline Freight Traffic, 1937, 1949, and 1953

Year	Volume (in thousand metric tons)	Index (1949 = 100)
1937	.071	18
1949	.392	100
1953	2.723	695

Source: Statisztikai Tajekoztato, loc. cit.; cited in News from Behind the Iron Curtain, loc. cit., p. 18.

Passenger traffic has grown at a somewhat slower rate (see Table 14). In 1952, an "air taxi" service was introduced, providing private charter service between towns having airports.

Table 14. Airline Passenger Traffic, Selected Years 1937-1954

Year	Passengers (in thousands)	Index (1949 = 100)
1937	3.6	11
1949	32.6	100
1953	101.1	310
1954	101.9	313

Sources: Statisztikai Tajekoztato, loc. cit.; Szabad Nep, January 20, 1955; cited in News from Behind the Iron Curtain, loc. cit., p. 18.

17. PUBLIC HEALTH AND SOCIAL SECURITY

DETERMINANTS OF PUBLIC HEALTH

Housing Conditions

Prior to World War II, housing conditions in Hungary were rather backward. Rural housing was inadequate, while rents were high in proportion to incomes. The war of course had a serious effect on the housing situation. Over 80 per cent of the dwellings in Budapest suffered some damage. Of the apartment-room space in Budapest, 23.7 per cent was destroyed, and 1,201 buildings were declared dangerous by the authorities and had to be demolished.

Although reconstruction work started after the war, all efforts were concentrated on repairing war damage, and no new houses had been built until about 1950. *Szabad Nep* (Free People) of May 8, 1955 reported that 100,000 apartments were constructed during the entire Five-Year Plan period. According to the January 22, 1956 issue of *Szabad Nep*, 30,000 apartments were built in 1955. In view of the growth of the population and rapid industrialization, construction fell far below the need of the growing industrial population.

As a result of the Communist housing policy, the availability of dwellings has decreased, and many apartments were taken over for office use. This type of expropriation actually was greatest in the industrial centers. Moreover, apartment houses were not properly maintained, and few improvements have been made since 1943-44. In 1952, apartment houses and larger-size family dwellings were nationalized, and the regime was forced to have these nationalized houses repaired.

Prime Minister Andras Hegedus, in his speech before the National Assembly on November 15, 1955, recognized the impossible housing situation and emphasized that the government was ready to begin improvements. Therefore, the government made more funds available for housing construction. Meanwhile, the number of 2-3 room units now under construction will be reduced, with room-and-kitchen apartments given priority. According to the April 27, 1956 issue of *Szabad*

Nep, the new Five-Year Plan visualizes the construction of 200,000 new apartments in 1956-60, twice the number of units built during the first Five-Year Plan.

Food Consumption and Clothing

Before the last war, the diet of the country as a whole was substantially better than the average for East-Central European countries. Cereals provided fewer calories than in other countries, 60 per cent, compared with over 70 per cent for Romania, Bulgaria, and Yugoslavia. The consumption of maize, a sign of a poor diet, was considerably lower. On the other hand, the consumption of fresh milk, meat, fats, and sugar was much greater in Hungary than in these other countries. Not much butter was consumed, lard being the main source of fats.

Within Hungary, there was a great variation of diet between different parts of the country, and different segments of the population. In western Hungary, well-to-do peasants who had enough pigs and poultry for their own use as well as for sale were well fed. Meat and poultry were consumed three or four times a week, and eggs and vegetables were important in the diet, as were coffee and sugar. In the Great Plain between the Duna and Tisza rivers, the wealthier peasants could afford plentiful supplies of chicken, eggs, and fruit. Throughout this area, large quantities of wheat and lard were consumed but because there were comparatively few cows, there was little milk or butter. In all parts of Hungary, in cities as well as the villages, white bread was used.

Agricultural laborers and their families were undoubtedly the worst fed segment of the population. Their diet lacked adequate supplies of energy and protective foods, and they subsisted mainly on white bread, beans, potatoes, and cabbage, as well as small quantities of fat bacon and pork. Milk, eggs, butter, fruit, and fresh vegetables were consumed only in insignificant quantities. The diet of the lower income industrial workers, like that of the agricultural laborers, was low in quality. During the prewar period, the average daily caloric intake was 2,900. Table 1 gives the annual per capita consumption of the most important foods; the average taken is that of five years prior to World War II.

Following World War II, the democratic Hungarian government was beset by serious financial and economic problems. The war had brought about an enormous shortage of goods and foods, and reparations payments drained the country's resources further. The worker's situation was almost hopeless, for inflation was rapidly increasing, and in most places a month's wages were not enough to purchase a kilo of flour. The most serious inflationary run of the pengo started in July 1945, when the government issued Treasury notes. From then on, most plants and offices paid their employees in food, and barter trading became general. Inflation lasted until August 1, 1946, when the forint was made the new stabilized monetary unit.

Table 1. Average Annual Per Capita Adult Consumption
of Selected Foods, 1936–1940

Item	Kilograms	Pounds
Wheat and rye	160	352
Maize	90	198
Potatoes	100	220
Sugar	11	24
Meat	26	57
Milk (fresh)	80 (liters)	140 (pints)
Butter	1	2
Vegetable oil	1	2
Lard	11	24

Source: Great Britain, Ministry of Economic Warfare, *Hungary: Basic Handbook,* Part II, "Economic Survey" (London, 1944), p. 11.

Stabilization improved the general situation of the working population. Hungarian economic life started anew. The living standard gradually rose and by 1949 approached the prewar level. The living standard of the former middle classes and of peasants with medium-size holdings fell considerably, while that of workers and working peasants increased. When in 1950 the inauguration of the Five-Year Plan signalized a planned economy and collective agriculture on the Soviet model, the situation became even more serious. Low agricultural production, combined with an influx of rural population into the industrial centers, resulted in a disastrous lowering of the living standard. The lowest point was reached in the spring of 1953, when the daily caloric intake fell to between 2,000 and 2,200 per capita. The Communist government realized that this was an untenable situation, and Rakosi made a speech on July 11, 1953 in which he mentioned raising living standards as the "backbone of the Party program." The first government regulation that endeavored to raise the very low living standard was issued on September 5, 1953. As a result, prices dropped on an average of about 17 per cent. Prices on so-called luxury goods were cut the most, while those for essential goods decreased less sharply. Under the terms of the resolution of the Council of Ministers effective March 4, 1954, the prices of certain meats and fats were cut by an average of 10 to 15 per cent.

In spite of these price reductions, however, the average worker was still unable to purchase necessities regularly. His wage at that time was around 900 forints a month. According to official and nonofficial reports, he still had to pay 27 to 28 forints for a kilo of pork and 30 forints for a pound of lard.

According to the boasts of Communist newspapers, the Hungarian workers have never been so well off, and the present standard of living is supposed to be higher than the prewar level. However, this is not true, since even elementary calculations reveal that the average worker can hardly afford to purchase anything but the most essential commodities. The prevailing low wages account for this, and wages are kept low to limit purchasing power.

Table 2 shows the food basket with the prevailing Budapest prices as of December 1955 (11.70 forints equal $1.00 at the official exchange rate).

Table 2. Budapest Weekly Food Basket, 1955
(in forints)

Item			Unit Price		Total Price
	(kilograms)		(per kilogram)		
Bread	2.80		3.00		8.40
Flour	0.50		4.20		2.10
Butter	0.17		66.00		11.24
Veal	0.45		29.00		13.05
Pork	0.20		28.00		5.60
Beef	0.20		21.00		4.20
Lard	0.20		40.00		8.00
Potatoes	1.50		2.40		3.60
Sugar	0.45		10.60		4.77
Cheese	0.10		53.50		5.35
Rice	0.20		20.00		4.00
Noodles	0.20		14.00		2.80
Peas	0.10		11.00		1.10
Beans	0.10		10.00		1.00
Milk	2.4	(liters)	3.30	(per liter)	7.92
Eggs	3.5	(units)	2.40	(per unit)	8.40

The table shows that the price of a weekly basket is 91.53 forints, which means that in a 31-day month the wage earner has to spend 405.33 forints for food.

Table 3 shows how much the wage earners make compared with the food basket price. This table also uses the salary scale of December 1955.

Table 3. Average Salary Relationship to 405.33—Forint Monthly Food Basket, December 1955

Type of Wage Earner	Average Monthly Salary in Forints	Food Basket as Per Cent of Salary
Unskilled industrial worker	750	53.57
Average industrial worker	800	50.66
Semiskilled industrial worker	850	47.68
Semiskilled iron and metal worker	850	47.68
Skilled iron and metal worker	1,250	33.77
Miner	1,250	33.77
Stakhanovite	2,000	20.26
Privileged functionaries	3,000	13.51

In addition to food, the worker's salary must also cover such items as rent, heat, gas and electricity, clothing, and transportation. The price of clothing is particularly high. For example, in December 1955, the price of a man's shirt was 70 forints; a pair of hand-made man's shoes, 460 forints and those of cheapest quality, 200 forints; and a man's ready-made suit 1,350 forints.

On April 29, 1956, a new price reduction was announced. This included a number of consumer goods, mostly clothing. The only food items included were milk and some dairy products, but not butter. Milk sold in bulk was reduced from 3.30 forints per liter to 3 forints. Bottled milk was reduced from 4.20 forints to 3.60 forints. Restaurant meals were reduced by 1 forint, while the average reduction for à la carte items was about 10 per cent.

Hospitals and Medical Facilities

Public health in Hungary made considerable progress between the two wars. On the eve of World War II, Hungary ranked high among the East-Central European countries as far as hospital beds and medical facilities were concerned. The ratio of physicians was even more favorable. There were 11.7 doctors for every ten thousand inhabitants, while the ratio in Austria was 9.9, in Czechoslovakia 7.5, and 3.5 in Yugoslavia. Of course, the mathematical ratio is somewhat misleading, since doctors were unevenly distributed among the population, the vast majority being settled in the cities. In 1938, Budapest alone had 4,668 doctors, or 44 per cent of the total.

Following the war, the situation greatly deteriorated, especially in the capital. After the siege of Budapest, only three thousand hospital beds were in usable condition, compared to seven thousand before the war. Health institutions suffered war damages exceeding 115 million pengo (1938 value). In 1946, reconstruction started and a new upward trend began.

A considerable number of dispensing pharmacies were also destroyed during the war. In 1938, there were 1,355 in the country. In April 1945, only 64 per cent of these were in operation. By July 1946, all except 100 were again in operation, and their number surpassed the prewar figure by March 1, 1948, when there 1,517 pharmacies. This number has not increased. Table 4 shows the prewar and postwar reconstruction and development of health institutions.

Table 4. Number of Hospital Beds and Doctors, Selected Years 1921-1955

Year	Number of Hospital Beds	For Every 10,000 Inhabitants	Number of Doctors	For Every 10,000 Inhabitants
1921	26,451	32.97	4,489	5.60
1930	39,821	46.04	8,196	9.40
1938	48,898	54.00	10,590	11.70
1945	33,163	35.58	...	...
1949	49,500	53.77	9,610	10.44
1950	49,200	52.97	9,660	10.40
1951	52,000	55.45	...	...
1952	53,100	56.14	11,400	12.05
1953	53,800	56.41	12,200	12.79
1954	58,400	60.63	12,700	13.18
1955	61,300	62.87	...	...[a]

Sources: Central Statistical Bureau, *Magyar Statisztikai Zsebkonyv* (Hungarian Statistical Pocketbook) (Budapest, [1948]), XIV (1949) and XV (1948); U.N., *Economic Bulletin for Europe*, VII, No. 2 (August, 1955); *Szabad Nep* (Free People), January 22, 1956 and April 27, 1956.

[a] According to an official announcement, in 1955 there were 13 doctors for every 10,000 inhabitants.

The new Five-Year Plan, published in *Szabad Nep*, April 27, 1956, envisages an increase in the number of doctors by 1960. It is planned to exceed 15 doctors per 10,000 people. During the same period, the number of hospital beds is to be expanded by 7,500.

Although the number of doctors has increased during the last few years, the disproportion between urban and rural areas has become greater than before. It is known that the shortage of doctors is most serious in the area beyond the Tisza River, while relatively fair conditions prevail in Transdanubia.

In some rural areas the village doctor is in charge of as many as seven to ten thousand people. The July 29, 1955 issue of *Szabad Nep* reported that of those who graduated from medical schools in 1954, only 25 per cent were assigned to rural areas. There is an acute shortage of dentists in Hungary. The number of school children is approximately 650,000 and 249 dentists have been assigned to take care of their teeth, which means that each dentist has to take charge of 2,600 children.

While the number of hospital beds has increased, conditions in the hospitals have definitely deteriorated. The January 27, 1954 issue of *Szabad Nep* stated, "Despite expansions made for the sake of greater hygiene, several hospitals and dispensaries are overcrowded, especially children's and maternity wards. . . . Doctors are forced to use the methods of a conveyer belt in a plant . . . . Corridors and waiting halls are jammed with patients."

Medical Training

Prior to the Communist regime, applicants for any of the four medical schools had to be high school or Gymnasium graduates. Under the present regime, admission is granted upon the applicant's passing an entrance examination, which goes beyond general education and scholastic achievements. It examines the candidate's affiliations and family background; in effect, anyone may be barred from admission whose parents do not belong to the class held in favor by the regime.

Ninety per cent of those who are admitted to Hungarian medical schools are supported by state scholarships. A doctor's education and the costs of his medical training cost the state approximately seventy-five thousand forints (about $6,400 at the official exchange rate) over a six-year period. The students are under obligation, as a means of repaying this sum, to serve the state after receiving their degrees. This agreement is really a formality, for new doctors have no choice, since they would not be able to find adequate housing facilities where they could see private patients nor do they have the financial means to purchase medical equipment, which is not for sale on the open market. If a student leaves medical school or the service of the armed forces medical corps, he has to repay the state. The Russian language and the study of Marxism-Leninism are compulsory for medical students. Any student who fails to pass these subjects cannot continue with his other subjects. Attendance records are strictly kept; roll is called often, and a high average grade must be maintained. Contrary to the prewar system, medical students, especially surgeons, are required to practice in hospitals while in medical school. If, upon completion of his medical training, a doctor wishes to specialize in a chosen field, he must first obtain the approval of a committee, consisting of one professor and two medical students.

Recently, a number of excellent, medical textbooks have been published in Hungary. However, there is a paucity of scientific literature on research work, in fact, during the last five years, hardly a single important scientific monograph has been published. The two best-known medical journals currently being published are *Nepegeszsegugy* (Public Health Affairs), a 32-page monthly put out by the Ministry of Health and *Orvosi Hetilap* (Medical Weekly), a century-old weekly, which has become the organ of Soviet medical science.

THE SOCIAL SECURITY SYSTEM

Hungarian social security has a relatively long tradition and a good reputation in Europe. The idea of voluntary associations for mutual aid and benefits developed parallel with the labor movement (see Chapter 13, "Labor").

After World War I, establishment of a vigorous national social insurance system became one of the primary aims of the trade unions. The Workers' Insurance Institute developed into an effective and healthy enterprise jointly controlled by representatives of workers and employees. In the late 1920's, Parliament initiated a series of measures establishing the National Institute of Social Insurance. The state budgeted the yearly deficit of the system, and government representatives supervised the operation of the otherwise autonomous Institute.

The Nazi withdrawals at the end of World War II and the war damages destroyed the financial reserves, assets, and facilities of the Institute. On the other hand, the general deterioration of public health placed unprecedentedly heavy burdens on the newly organized system following the war. The state was able to finance reconstruction of the social insurance institutes during the 1945-47 period.

Organization and Scope

As a result of the postwar legislation, the Hungarian social security system was gradually centralized under the administration of the National Institute of Social Insurance. By 1949, the only exception was the Sickness and Benefit Insurance System of the Hungarian State Railways. Through the process of merger in these years, the National Institute of Social Insurance absorbed the Insurance Institute of Private Employees; the Insurance Institute of Transportation Employees; the Sickness and Benefit Insurance Institute of the State Tobacco Monopoly; the Sickness and Benefit Insurance Institute of Post Office Employees; and the Miners Insurance Fund.

Decree with the Force of Law No. 36 of 1950 proved to be the final step in communizing the Hungarian social security system (September 24, 1950 issue of *Magyar Kozlony* [Hungarian Gazette]). The same regulation closed down such functioning organizations as the National Institute of Social Insurance, and the Sickness and Benefit Insurance System of the Hungarian State Railways. From that time on, the National Council of Trade Unions took over the administration of social security, under the supervision of the Council of Ministers. The Trade Union Council's Social Security Center administers the central office. On the local level, the County Social Security Centers handle the work under the control of national headquarters. In every plant, office, and institution, agricultural cooperatives and in the machine-tractor stations and state-owned agricultural holdings, there is a person or a group in charge of social security matters.

Table 5 gives the number of persons covered by social security insurance, including wage earners and their eligible dependents.

Table 5. Social Insurance Coverage, 1938 and 1947–1955

Date	Number of Insured Persons	Per Cent of Total Population
December 31, 1938	2,800,000	30.9
December 31, 1947	3,000,000	33.0
December 31, 1948	3,300,000	36.0
December 31, 1949	3,800,000	41.1
December 31, 1950	4,400,000	47.3
December 31, 1951	5,200,000	51.0
December 31, 1952	5,300,000	56.0
February 28, 1953	5,500,000	59.2
December 31, 1954	5,800,000	60.0
April 1, 1955	5,850,000	60.0

Sources: Dr. Somogyi and Dr. Ecsedi, "Egeszsegunk helyzete 1950-ben" (State of Health Affairs in 1950), *Statisztikai Szemle* (Statistical Review), III (May 1951), 417–29; *Szabad Nep*, January 20, 1952, April 1, 1955, May 8, 1955; President Kristoff's Report to the Trade Union Congress in *Nepszava* (People's Voice), February 28, 1953.

Although Istvan Kristoff, President of the National Council of Trade Unions, at the Third Congress of the Hungarian Workers' Party stated that 70 per cent of the population, or about 6,700,000 persons, were to be covered by insurance at the end of the first Five-Year Plan (1950-54), the official figure of 5,850,000 persons covered by April 1, 1955 clearly shows that this goal was not reached.

Every worker, agricultural laborer, and university student is covered by social security. With regard to agricultural workers, there are certain specific regulations, since the kolkhozes have signed separate agreements with the social security authorities, and their facilities and benefits are different from those in the other categories.

While for most occupations, social security insurance is compulsory, there are certain occupational groups where it is optional; for example, small businessmen or tradesmen and craftsmen who are self-employed or belong to cooperatives. Members of occupational categories who have formerly participated in the compulsory social security insurance program may continue if they wish.

Sickness Insurance

The present system of sickness insurance is based on a series of decrees issued on December 31, 1955: Decree with the Force of Law No. 39, Cabinet Decree No. 71, and Decree of the National Council of the Trade Unions No. 6.

According to the provisions of these decrees, sickness insurance is extended to workers who are actually employed as well as to those members of their families who are also workers, or are supported by the worker and live in his household. In case of divorce, the divorced member of the family is also covered by the family benefits, provided the person's support has been declared obligatory by the courts.

Sickness insurance does not cover a worker in employment where wages are under 250 forints a month. It does not cover persons who are in a profession which has to be licensed by the authorities. Agricultural workers are excluded, if they farm independently on an agricultural holding (garden, orchard, or vineyard) larger than 5 acres. Domestic employees are not covered if their working hours with one employer are under 30 hours a week. On the other hand, technical administrative and temporary workers of state-owned agricultural enterprises, such as state farms, are covered, as are operators of tractors, harvesting machines, and trucks.

Sickness insurance covers the following categories of unemployed persons: disabled persons receiving state support; pensioners; students in any schools, except higher educational organizations; members of working communities and creative groups; and ministers and church employees.

An agricultural cooperative has the option to sign a sickness insurance agreement with sickness insurance authorities to cover members of the cooperatives. For such insurance, the only option available is that which would cover all members.

The expenses of sickness insurance have to be covered by sickness insurance payments made by the employer, and he is not permitted to make any deductions from his employees' wages for that reason. All expenditures necessary for sickness insurance coverage as well as its general income budget are part of the Hungarian state budget and have to be scheduled as such.

According to law, in case of sickness, a worker or a member of his family is entitled to receive medical care, medicine, and hospital and sanitarium care.

Medical care is free, but the only doctor who can be consulted is the one assigned by the state health organization. Medicines, medical equipment, and sanitarium treatment are also supplied. For these needs, the patient pays 15 per cent of the charges. For dental work, workers as well as eligible members of their families pay between 50 and 75 per cent of the ordinary fee.

Hospitalization is granted only for a year, except in the case of tuberculosis when it may be extended to a maximum of two years. Free hospitalization for family members is limited to 90 calendar days per year.

Disabled workers who cannot earn wages receive a wage compensation. This too is limited to a year, or in the case of tuberculosis to two years as a maximum. If a worker has been employed only one year or less (in the case of tuberculosis two years), prior to his sickness, he can only receive a compensatory salary for the same length of time. A working mother who is unable to continue employment because of the illness of a child younger than a year or who is wet-nursing a child that is being hospitalized receives a special compensation, usually 65 per cent of the wages. For hospitalized workers who support a member of their family, compensation may be increased to 80 per cent of the wages. On the other hand, if they have no family member to support they receive only 50 per cent of their regular wages as compensation. If a worker prior to his disability has been employed by the same employer for two years without interruption and has been a member of a trade union for at least a year, he has the right to claim a 75 per cent wage compensation. For a temporarily disabled person, the wage compensation is 50 per cent of the wages.

Those workers who terminate their employment arbitrarily or who have been discharged as a result of disciplinary action are not eligible to receive any wage compensation in case of sickness and disability. Should a worker who falls into this category re-enter employment with a new employer and subsequently become disabled, his claim for wage compensation constitutes a special case.

In the case of employed working women who become pregnant, medical care as well as the services of a midwife are supplied free. During maternity leave, she receives special wage compensation. If a working woman was employed for three years prior to pregnancy and within that period was covered by sickness insurance for at least a total of 270 days, she receives a 100 per cent wage compensation. If she was covered for at least 180 days, she receives 50 per cent of her wages; while hospitalized or under medical care in connection with childbirth, she receives 80 per cent of her wages. Free medical care as well as free midwife service are also due the wife of a working man.

Working women, in addition to the maternity benefits during pregnancy and at childbirth, receive a special compensation for "motherhood." This motherhood compensation is also due the wife of the working man, if he was covered by sickness insurance for at least 180 days during two years preceding his wife's pregnancy. If the child is born alive and if the mother has been covered by insurance for at least 270 days preceding the birth, the compensation for the first child amounts to 700 forints (about $59 at the official exchange rate); the compensation for additional children is 600 forints each. For stillborn babies, the mother receives 120 forints. A working man's wife receives 460 forints when a child is born, and 120 forints if the baby is stillborn.

Decree No. 7 of 1951 (*Magyar Kozlony* Nos. 17 and 18, January 31, 1951) grants a "special award" for those mothers who have many children. The younger the marriage, the higher the honor and remuneration. According to this decree, mothers of seven or more children, if the youngest child was born after March 8, 1951, receive money awards. The sum is between one thousand and two thousand forints for each child.

While the features of the Communist social security system do not exceed the scope of prewar or democratic postwar security schemes, it is interesting to note the exceptional "generosity" of the Communist regime toward "socialist mothers." A similar trend can be observed in the other East-Central European countries, as well as in the Soviet

Union. The explanation lies in the fact that all Communist regimes pursue a strongly "pro-natal" policy, while large-scale industrialization calls for the mobilization of women. Thus, the regime encourages women to have many children, yet to make them return to the factories and resume work as soon as possible. Therefore, major plants and factories have their own nurseries and kindergartens, where working mothers can leave their children during the day. The system also serves the purpose of Communist pedagogy: the children of working women are left to the state's care and exposed to ideological indoctrination from the earliest age.

In case of death, funeral assistance is provided for the families if the worker has had at least 180 days of insurance during the two years preceding his death. Funeral assistance in the case of a deceased worker is 800 forints. In case of death in a worker's family, the sum varies according to the age of the deceased. If the person is over ten years of age, it is 600 forints; under ten years, 400 forints.

Accident Insurance

A worker receives accident insurance benefits in case of an occupational injury as long as he is unable to resume work or if he is due to retire after the accident. A worker who is covered by accident insurance and his dependents are also entitled to aid in case of certain types of occupational disease. These include: mercury poisoning, silicosis; lead poisoning; anthrax; phosphorus poisoning; arsenic poisoning; benzol poisoning; illness caused by radium and radioactive materials as well as X rays; and cancerous diseases of the skin.

The insured worker who needs medical care for an occupational injury or illness, is entitled to the following: (1) medical treatments, drugs, therapeutic baths, and therapeutic devices; (2) hospitalization; (3) weekly sickness benefits, to the extent and amount prescribed by the law up to the completion of treatment; and (4) allowances for as long as incapacity exists, after treatment and until the worker is able to earn again. This allowance may be either full or partial, depending on the degree of disability. The insured worker is entitled to the full allowance, two-thirds of his last wage, if he is fully disabled. If the worker is not only fully disabled but also must receive permanent medical and nursing treatment, he is entitled to an allowance twice that of the full allowance. The insured is entitled to a partial allowance if he is not totally disabled, but if his earning power is limited as a result of an accident while at work. Should the decrease of earning power be less than 15 per cent, he is not entitled to accident benefits. Should this limitation be over 25 per cent, he can receive it only for two consecutive years.

Should the insured worker die as a result of an occupational accident, the dependents receive death benefits, the amount determined on the basis of the social insurance status of the deceased.

Workers' Family Allowances

The Social Security Center of the Trade Union Council is responsible for the administration of all matters relating to family allowances, which are regulated by a decree issued by the Council of Ministers on February 8, 1953. According to this decree, monthly allowances for families with two children amount to 75 forints; three children, 180 forints; four children, 260 forints; and five children, 350 forints. Single working mothers are entitled to an allowance of 30 forints a month for one child. On the other hand, no family allowance is due for a wife. The family allowance system is financially inadequate to meet the average worker's need; even a family with five children receives less as a monthly allowance that the price of one pair of good shoes. Therefore, the Communists have excluded the great majority of the workers from the family allowance system. The boasted spectacular figures in cases of families with three, four, or five children have only a very limited significance.

Disability and Old-Age Benefits

Only those workers who are over 45 years old and have been insured under social security regulations for a minimum of 520 weeks are entitled to disability benefits. If the worker is under 35 years old, 200 insured weeks are necessary; and between 35 and 45, 300 weeks. The worker is only entitled to disability benefits when a physical illness or a crippled condition limits his earning power to one third of that of his fit colleagues with similar training and occupational background.

Disability benefits were increased under a decree of September 19, 1954. Workers suffering from an occupational injury or disease now receive a basic pension of 80 per cent of their income and a 1 per cent bonus pension for every year worked after January 1945.

Under the Hungarian social security system, pension rights of the workers are regulated by Decree with the Force of Law No. 30 of 1951, which refers to "workers who are covered by Health Insurance and Sickness Benefits, within the framework of the Social Security Insurance . . . as well as the members of the People's Army, on active service" (paragraph 4).

The amount of a pension is determined on the basis of the pensioner's average monthly wage for twelve months prior to his claiming a pension. Those eligible for old-age pensions are men of 60 and women of 50 who have been working for the last ten years and who have been covered by insurance for 520 weeks; members of the People's Army on active service; workers who apply within five years following retirement age (60 for men, 50 for women). Special provisions are made for workers in hazardous occupations: in mines or other subterranean locations, men may retire at 50, after a minimum of 25 years, and women after 20 years; workers who have worked for 15 years under air pressure or abnormal climatic conditions may retire at 50. Parents or grandparents are entitled to a parents' pension if the related worker has supported them for at least a year prior to his death. The pensioner is entitled to a special allowance for his children's education, and in the case of his death the children receive an orphans' allowance. The pensioner is entitled to receive an extra marriage allowance if his spouse is over 60.

The average amount of monthly pensions, based on the average wage, have been increased as follows:

	Forints
October 1, 1947	74.90
March 1, 1948	115.87
January 1, 1952	218.94
March 1, 1954	226.94

Source: *Beke es Szabadsag* (Peace and Freedom), April 21, 1954.

On March 24, 1954, the Council of Ministers increased the old-age pension, effective April 1, 1954. The old-age pension was to be increased for all men over 65 and women over 60, by 8 to 50 per cent; the old-age disability benefits for men under 65 and disability benefits for women under 60, by 4 to 25 per cent; the old-age pensions of miners over the age of 60 by 40 per cent, the old-age pensions of miners' pensioners by 20 per cent; the old-age pension of agricultural workers by 20 per cent; and the pensions of widows of agricultural workers by 25 per cent.

A decree of September 19, 1954 *(Szabad Nep)*, effective October 1, 1954 changed some of the regulations specified by the Decree with the Force of Law No. 30 of 1951, primarily in regard to the amount of pension paid; it also changed the pension age for women from 50 to 55; that for men remains 60.

Although the amount of the pension is still determined from the pensioner's average monthly wage before retiring, the worker now receives 50 per cent of his wages per month rather than 15 per cent, the rate originally set. In addition, he receives 1 per cent (previously 2 per cent) of his wages for every year of work after 1945. At present, the lowest pension is 500 forints a month, except for those workers whose wages are less than 660 forints a month, whose pensions start at 75 per cent of their previous income.

Except for workers in hazardous occupations, men who continue to work after 60 and women after 55 are not eligible for pensions until they retire.

On the surface, the provisions of the new social security decree appear rather generous, compared to earlier benefits. However, a closer examination reveals that the major part of the increased benefits derives from the workers themselves. Prior to this decree, 1 per cent of the workers' nominal wages were withheld as their contribution to the pension fund; as of October 1954, the workers' share was tripled.

This development falls in line with the current political and economic course of the post-Stalinist era. During the last years, the expanding labor force has compelled the regime to comply with some of its demands. In view of the low living standard described in Chapter 13, "Labor," even these increased benefits do not represent a significant improvement, for they cover only the bare necessities.

VI. The Hungarian Revolution

THE HUNGARIAN REVOLUTION

Neal V. Buhler

In the middle of October 1956, Hungary was a secure and absolute Communist police state, ruled by the Party and under the iron control of Soviet occupation troops backing up the Hungarian secret police. Almost ten years of Communist control had changed the whole cultural, political, and social patterns, and every organized non-Communist force had been smashed and broken.

At the end of October, Hungary was an independent state, once again a member of the free family of nations. Virtually every Hungarian secret policeman had been captured, was dead, or was in hiding. The initial Soviet occupation troops had been fought to a standstill by a heroic people who opposed Russian tanks and machine guns with their bare hands and raw courage. Soviet army commanders had promised to evacuate the country. A new government had been formed which for the first time since 1947 represented most of the political desires of the Hungarian people—a government which had announced its independence of Moscow and free elections to come. The trade unions again represented the workers instead of the Communist state, and the peasants were promised a new and better system to replace forced collectivization and compulsory deliveries at low prices. The new government promised to cease persecution of religion and had released Cardinal Mindszenty from his long Communist imprisonment.

Hungary was free. Thousands lay dead in Budapest and in the countryside, but it is no exaggeration to say that the entire nation was delirious with hope and freedom. Human dignity had again been bought by blood and effort.

It was not to last. But the Hungarians didn't know that then. Thousands more were to be sacrificed and killed by Russian troops. Hungary's agony was not over. It was about to begin again. But at the end of October, for the first time in history, a Communist government supported by Russian troops had been overthrown without any outside aid whatever. A whole people had risen, without arms, without foreign aid, and had defeated the troops, and overthrown one of the most vicious and efficient political systems in world history.

352

At the end of October, Hungary was free.

After this section was at the press, on June 20, 1957, the Special Committee on the Problem of Hungary of the United Nations published its *Report*. This 150,000 word document, the result of five months of hearings in Geneva, Rome, Vienna, London and New York, covers almost every aspect of the Hungarian Revolution. It is based on official documents and the expert testimony of over 100 witnesses, none of whom had left Hungary before the Revolution. It may be regarded as definitive, and its objectivity is beyond question. Accordingly, it was felt that the section on the events of the Revolution already written should be replaced by that part of the UN *Report* covering the same area ("A Brief History of the Hungarian Uprising") and that the conclusions of the UN *Report* to that section should also be included.

THE UPRISING

The Twentieth Congress of the Communist Party of the USSR early in 1956 encouraged a movement within the Hungarian Workers' (Communist) Party which aimed at a measure of democratization and national independence and a relaxation of police rule. In March 1956, Rakosi announced that the Supreme Court had established that Rajk and others had been condemned on "fabricated charges". This official admission that crimes had been committed by the regime had profound repercussions in Hungary. It was followed in July by the dismissal of Rakosi and, early in October, by the ceremonial reburial, in the presence of a large crowd, of Laszlo Rajk and other victims of the 1949 trials. Rakosi was succeeded as First Secretary of the Central Committee of the Party by Erno Gero. From the date of Rakosi's fall, the Hungarian people looked for a softening of the regime. Associated in their minds with better days was the former Premier, Imre Nagy, whose period of office from 1953 to 1955 had been marked by a loosening of the controls imposed earlier by Rakosi. Nagy had also been attacked as a deviationist and, while he had escaped trial, had been expelled from the Party and divested of all his offices. His name continued to stand for more liberal policies in the minds of many Hungarian Communists, who wished for his return to public life.

The first protests against the dictatorial regime of the Party were voiced by certain Hungarian writers, as early as the autumn of

1955. Articles published by these writers concerned mainly the doctrine of Party allegiance in literature and interference with creative writers and artists by Party spokesmen and bureaucrats. Although a number of writers were arrested, the scope of these protests gradually widened to take in other grievances of the Hungarian people. In the summer of 1956, the foundation of the Petofi Club provided a new forum for discussions, which were often critical of the regime. This Club was sponsored by DISZ, the official Communist Youth Organization and its debates were mainly attended by young Communist intellectuals.

On 19 October, the Minister of Education, Albert Konya, announced certain changes as a result of requests put forward by Hungarian students. One of these was an undertaking to abolish the compulsory teaching of Russian in schools. This announcement was followed by student manifestations in Szeged and other towns, during which various demands of a more far-reaching character were discussed and adopted. Also on 19 October, news of Poland's move towards greater independence of the USSR was received in Hungary with enthusiasm. Friendship between the two peoples had been traditional for centuries.

News of the Szeged decision [of Szeged University students to set up a non-Communist youth organization, MEFESZ] reached Budapest on Monday morning, 22 October, and various University groups . . . decided to hold meetings during the day. At these meetings events in Poland exercised considerable influence, and solidarity with the Polish workers and youth was widely expressed. Probably the most decisive of all these student meetings was that held at the Building Industry Technological University. . . . In the Great Hall of the University, the Professors, the Party Secretary and Party officials were present with the students. Between 4,000 and 5,000 people attended the meeting, which lasted for about eleven hours, until the early morning of 23 October. A considerable number of workers joined the meeting during the evening. . . .

In the beginning, however, the discussion was restricted to practical demands, for instance, that there should be less teaching of Marxist and Leninist subject and that English, French and German should be taught instead of only Russian. Later during the meeting, voices from all over the Hall called for a discussion of broader problems. . . . Demands were put forward that Imre Nagy should take over the Government, and that the new Government should guarantee human rights to the people of Hungary, as required by the United Nations Charter and the Universal Declaration of Human Rights. . . . One of the Communist youth leaders then went to the microphone and declared that, while Soviet troops were stationed in Hungary, the wished-for political evolution could not take place, as the country was ruled by an imperialist tyranny. Other speakers added that the presence of Soviet troops made impossible free elections, freedom of speech and religion and the enjoyment of human rights. These and other demands were written down as a draft resolution.

Thus, by early evening on 22 October, the aims of the Hungarian uprising had been more or less formulated by University students. The students who improvised this document on a piece of paper torn out of a student's notebook, came largely from working-class or peasant homes; many of them were members of the Communist Party, and the demands were formulated and adopted at a meeting convened by the Communist Youth Organization itself.

About 8:30 P.M., a student delegation went to the radio station, where the censor was willing to pass for the 9:00 P.M. news bulletin five of the ten points but refused permission to broadcast demands for the withdrawal of Soviet troops, free elections, a new economic policy, freedom of the press and new elections within the Communist Party. . . . The student delegation, unwilling that the ten points should be censored for the microphone, returned to the University. The editors of *Szabad Ifjusag* (Free Youth), the organ of DISZ, who had been present at the meeting, affirmed their support of the ten points; but, fearing for their personal safety, they were unwilling to print the demand for the withdrawal of Soviet troops. . . . The *Jovo Mernoke* (The Engineer of the Future), a periodical published by the students of the Building Industry Technological University, published the ten points. To achieve this, five students went to the printing shop and replaced the front page, which had already been set up, by another which contained the ten points. About 2,000 copies of this paper were printed. . . .

The final text of the resolution had been read out to the meeting over the microphone, and students and assistant professors worked throughout the night copying it on all the typewriters available at the University. . . . During the evening, the original ten points became fourteen and later sixteen. The withdrawal of the Soviet troops had become a separate point, and others were inserted which dealt with such matters as the removal of the statue of Stalin and of the Soviet-inspired emblem from the Hungarian national flag. . . .

How the Demonstrations were Initiated and Organized

During the meeting at the Technological University, a representative of the Writers' Union, Zoltan Zelk, announced that the Writers' Union planned to hold a small memorial ceremony next day at the statue of General Jozsef Bem, the national hero of Polish origin who fought with the Hungarians against the Austrians and the Russians in 1848-9. It was therefore decided by the students of the Technological University that they would themselves organize a demonstration, and would invite students of other universities and factory workers to join. . . .

During the evening, the news of the meeting at the Technological University had spread over the city. More and more people had kept coming in, not merely students from other universities and academies, but also workers from Csepel and the Belojanis Factory and miners from Dorog. . . . Early on Tuesday, 23 October, the students' sixteen points appeared all over the city. . . . "Every stenographer and every typist did nothing but copy these things. The Communist Party forbade it in vain. Everyone was talking about it; in conversation, over the telephone, the news spread in a few hours. . . . People pinned the Hungarian national cockade to their clothes, and . . . the whole people became unified . . . the entire system based on lies collapsed in a moment on the morning of 23 October" [participants' description of the atmosphere].

At 10 A.M. on Tuesday, 23 October, Radio Budapest reported that the students had decided to hold "a silent demonstration before the Embassy of the Polish People's Republic, to express the deep sympathy and solidarity of youth in connection with the events in Poland." The Politburo was convened around 12 noon to consider the question of the demonstration. However, at 12:53 the Radio suddenly announced that the Minister of the Interior, Laszlo Piros, had issued a communique to prohibit the "public street assemblies and marches." Several deputations, including one from the Writers' Union, went to see him to point out the risk of serious consequences, since the students would no doubt proceed with their plans in spite of the ban. Mr. Piros stated that, in that case, he would fire on the demonstrators.

The students were already beginning to assemble, when a delegation of five students went to Mr. Piros and declared that the demonstration would go on, whether it was permitted or not. After half an hour's discussion he yielded, and Radio Budapest announced at 2:23 P.M. that the ban had been lifted. Half an hour later the Radio even announced that the Central Committee of DISZ, the communist youth organization, had decided to approve the demonstration and to participate in it.

Demonstrations at the Petofi and Bem Statues

The demonstration was, in fact, already well under way. One group of students assembled around the Petofi Statue in Pest, on the eastern bank of the River Danube, and marched, joined by other groups of students and by more and more workers who came in from the outskirts of the city, to the statue of General Bem in Buda, on the western bank of the river. According to all reports the crowd was unarmed, and orderly and disciplined. Before long, it consisted of some 10,000 people, a number which steadily increased during the afternoon, as students, workers, and many others joined in. It consisted mostly of young people, boys and girls, in high spirits. Many soldiers in uniform were in the crowd including, as Radio Budapest stated at midnight, 800 cadets from the Petofi Military Academy. . . . The demonstrators were carrying Hungarian flags, from which the Communist crest was cut out in the course of the afternoon, some Polish flags, and placards with slogans: "Long live the Youth of Poland" and "For Freedom under the Sign of the Friendship of Bem and Kossuth. . . ."

At the Petofi statue, a well-known actor, Imre Sinkovits, recited Petofi's poem "Up, Hungarians!" At General Bem's statue the President of the Writers' Union, Peter Veres, made a speech and read out the seven points of the Writers' Union. The crowd listened somewhat coolly to this declaration, while the students' sixteen points were received with great enthusiasm.

Demonstration at the Parliament

From General Bem's statue many of the students, as planned, marched in orderly columns back to their Universities. Most of the crowd, however, proceeded across the Danube to the Parliament Building, joined by people from all over the city. The crowd at the Parliament Building and in the adjoining streets about 6 P.M. was estimated to be at least 200,000, perhaps 300,000 strong.

For several hours, the crowd in front of the Parliament persisted in calling for Imre Nagy. Finally, some writer friends of his went to his apartment and persuaded him to come to the Parliament, in spite of the fact that he had no official position. He did so and was received by Ferenc Erdei who asked him to go out on the balcony of the Parliament to appease the crowd. Mr. Erdei first said a few words from the balcony, but the people refused to listen. Mr. Nagy's unprepared address was also very short. There were no microphones. Few in fact, seem to have been able to hear him. . . . It appears that he just asked the crowd to go quietly home. Whether the people could hear him or not, his words had no marked effect—possibly because the crowd had been waiting for so many hours, possibly because they had become exhilarated by a feeling of freedom and had expected some dramatic statement.

These same factors might also in part explain the strong reaction to First Party Secretary Gero's radio speech at 8 o'clock in the evening. Mr. Gero and Prime Minister Hegedus had returned the same morning from a ten-day visit to the Yugoslav Government. The time for the speech had been announced since noon by Radio Budapest. The crowd hoped there would be some new concessions or relaxations in line with developments in Poland. It was expected that Mr. Gero would at least make some reply to the demands of the students, the writers and the demonstrating crowds. It was apparently the truculent tenor of Mr. Gero's address, rather than specific phrases, that infuriated people all over Budapest. The slogans: "Down with Gero", and even "Death to Gero" were heard everywhere. Some of the demonstrators heard the speech from radios placed in open windows, but the majority only heard about it. . . .

Mr. Gero endorsed the resolution of the Central Committee of July 1956 which, he said, had invited the Communist Party to act with unity for Socialist democracy. . . . The achievements of "our People's Democracy" would be jealously guarded against the enemies of the people. The main purpose of these enemies was to shake the people's faith in their Party—the Hungarian Workers' Party—and loosen the ties with the USSR, on which they were heaping slanders and lies. In proclaiming that there was no conflict between "proletarian internationalism" and Hungarian patriotism, Mr. Gero voiced the following appraisal of the events of the day: "We are waging a consistent fight against chauvinism, anti-Semitism and all other reactionary, anti-social and inhuman trends and views. We . . . condemn those who strive to spread the poison of chauvinism among our youth, and who have taken advantage of the democratic freedom ensured by our State to the working people to carry out nationalist demonstrations."

Removal of Stalin's Statue

Already early in the evening of 23 October, crowds had assembled around the huge Stalin statue. Some came from the demonstration at the Bem statue, some from the Parliament Building. A demand for the removal of the statue was one of the students' sixteen points, and some enthusiastic young people climbed the huge monument and set to work on it. At 9:30 the statue fell from its pedestal. . . .

The First Shots

On Tuesday afternoon, 23 October, after the demonstration, a group of students decided once more to demand the broadcasting of their points, and a large crowd proceeded to the Radio Building. The crowd consisted mostly of young people, both men and women, students and workers. No one bore arms. The slogans were the same as earlier in the day and the crowd was still good-natured. However, Gero's speech had an electrifying effect. A delegation had been sent into the Radio Building to negotiate with the Director, Valeria Benke. The demand of the delegation to have all sixteen points broadcast—not just some of them—was refused. The delegation remained in the building, possibly to negotiate further. However, a rumour spread that they were being held captive.

The Radio Building was guarded by the AVH police, and the crowds saw reinforcements, carrying rifles with fixed bayonets, arrive at about 7:30 P.M. and again at about 8:30. . . . Shortly after 9 P.M. tear gas bombs were thrown from the upper floors. One or two minutes later, AVH men rushed from the entrance and began shooting in all directions. . . . The crowd retreated. The bloody clothes of the first dead were carried through the city and people rallied behind them in procession. The news spread speedily through Budapest. Many of the demonstrators in front of the Parliament began to move towards the Radio Building, and the crowd around the Stalin statue hurried there, too, after the statue fell at 9:30 P.M.

Another incident further infuriated the demonstrators. White ambulances with Red Cross licence plates drove through the crowd to the Radio Building—it was assumed to aid the wounded; but the demonstrators discovered, according to eye-witnesses, that they contained AVH police wearing doctors' white coats over their uniforms and that they were transporting arms. . . . Shortly afterwards, three tanks of the Hungarian Army arrived in front of the Radio Station. From the top of their tanks, two Hungarian officers declared that they were not going to shoot at the people. Fire was thereupon opened from the Radio Building, and the officers and several of the demonstrators were killed.

Workers in Csepel and Ujpest and other working class districts learned by telephone that fighting had broken out. They immediately seized what trucks they could find and drove into the centre of Budapest. Many of the workers received arms from soldiers or police they met on their way, while others went to the military barracks where the stores were thrown open, for instance at Angyalfold and Zuglo. About midnight a truck-load of arms from a factory in Soroksar Street arrived at the Radio Building. . . .

Several AVH troop carriers were overturned and burned in the streets around the Radio Building which, from about 11:00 P.M., was under severe attack with light arms. At midnight, the radio announced that "clashes took place at various places in the city between demonstrators and police forces". Some time in the early morning hours, the demonstrators seized the building, or at least part of it, but were driven out again. For the next few days, there was intermittent fighting around the building until it was finally seized by the revolutionaries; the AVH personnel were arrested and taken to barracks for trial.

Late on Tuesday evening, 23 October, part of the crowd went to the offices of the Party paper, *Szabad Nep*, and demanded publication of the sixteen points. The AVH fired on the crowd and some were killed, but later in the night, after they had obtained arms, the demonstrators succeeded in occupying the whole building.

Further Developments

During the night, several book shops selling Russian books were broken into. Russian books were thrown out into the streets in piles and burnt. No looting took place, however, either this night or in the days that followed. . . . During Wednesday, 24 October, the revolutionaries began to occupy district police stations, usually without opposition, and district Communist Party Headquarters. In the latter they found arms. Thus, more arms came into the hands of the people. The witnesses maintained that, without the intervention of the Soviet troops, there would have been order in the city in a day or two, since only the AVH were firing on the crowds, and many members of the army and the police supported the uprising. There seems, in fact, not to be a single report of any member of the Hungarian military forces or of the ordinary police opening fire on the people.

The first Soviet tank patrol was seen in the city at 2:00 A.M. on Wednesday, 24 October. On the same day, fierce fighting developed between the Soviet troops and the revolutionaries, supported by part of the regular Hungarian Army, particularly at the Kilian Barracks and at the Corvin Block. The population became increasingly embittered against the Russians, particularly because several incidents were reported of Russian tanks opening fire without provocation on unarmed crowds. . . .

Parliament Building on 25 October

There were many people at the Parliament Building waiting for Prime Minister Nagy to appear, probably 20-25,000, perhaps more, half of them women and children, some even with babies in arms. Between 11 A.M. and 12, when the demonstrators arrived at the square with the Soviet tanks, AVH police, and possibly Soviet soldiers, stationed on the roof-tops of the surrounding buildings, opened fire on the crowd with machine-guns. Other Soviet tanks approached from the side streets, and, according to witnesses, fire was exchanged between them and the Soviet tanks which had arrived at the square with the demonstrators. . . . Many of the casualties were women and children. Estimates of the number killed vary from 300 to 800. A member of the staff of the British Legation counted twelve truckloads of corpses being removed from the square later in the afternoon.

Meanwhile, during these same days, events in Budapest had produced repercussions all over Hungary. Revolutionary Councils and Workers' Councils in factories were being enthusiastically set up throughout the country and were discussing their programmes for action.

Revolutionary Political Developments

The political developments of October 23 to 25 are difficult if not impossible to reconstruct precisely. Certainly Gero was still in control of the Party, and thus of the government on October 23, when, on his return from Yugoslavia, he made his radio speech. This was after the demonstrations had begun, and Imre Nagy certainly had no official position when he was brought by friends to address the crowd from the balcony of Parliament on the evening of October 23. Sometime after this, Imre Nagy went, or was taken, to Communist Party headquarters, where an emergency session of the Politburo had begun at 10:22 P.M. The first Soviet tanks had appeared at about 2 A.M. on the morning of October 24, and were soon in action, although no official announcement was made of the Soviet intervention until 9 A.M.

What real changes had taken place in the government were unclear to the population. Imre Nagy had been referred to on the radio as Premier, but who had declared martial law and who had called in the Soviet troops was unknown. It appeared from the radio announcements that these were measures of the new Nagy leadership. Most of those who had supported Nagy turned against him on October 24 and 25, as it appeared that he was actually supporting the suppression of the people. In point of fact, however, Nagy was kept incommunicado in Communist Party Headquarters during "Wednesday, Thursday and most of Friday, 24, 25, and 26 October," according to the UN *Report*, which continues:

> The first shots at the Radio Building marked the beginning of a hard-fought, five-day battle, in which the people of Budapest found themselves in combat with Soviet armour and with the AVH. The ordinary police sympathized with the insurgents, giving them weapons or fighting at their side. Certain units of the Hungarian Army fought as such on the side of the insurgents, but the Army as a whole

disintegrated from the start of the uprising. Wherever they could succeed in doing so, Hungarian soldiers handed over weapons and ammunition to their fighting compatriots and, in very many cases, deserted, individually or in groups, to their ranks. However, in general, the senior officers were pro-Soviet and the insurgents mistrusted them. There was no single instance recorded of Hungarian troops fighting on the Soviet side against their fellow countrymen.

The freedom fighters, most of whom were workers, with a proportion of students, usually fought in small groups. . . . A frequent weapon used against Russian tanks was the "Molotov cocktail". . . . Such improvised methods proved highly effective against the power of Soviet armour, which found it difficult to manoeuvre, especially in narrow streets. . . .

Revolutionary and Workers' Councils

Most of the available Soviet forces had been dispatched to Budapest and, meanwhile, there was comparatively little fighting in the provinces. Here, the first days of the uprising saw a transfer of power from the Communist bureaucracy to the new Revolutionary and Workers' Councils. These Councils represented a spontaneous reaction against the dictatorial methods of the regime. The Revolutionary Councils took over the various responsibilities of local government. There were also Revolutionary Councils or Committees in the Army, in Government departments and in professional groups and centres of activity such as the radio and the Hungarian Telegraph Agency. Members of the Councils were usually chosen at a meeting of those concerned. They were intended to prepare for the setting up of a genuinely democratic system of government. The Councils also put forward various political and economic demands, calling for the withdrawal of Soviet troops, free and secret elections, complete freedom of expression and the abolition of the one-party system. The most influential of these bodies was probably the Transdanubian National Council, which represented the people of Western Hungary. Using the Free Radio Station at Gyor, this Council demanded that Hungary should renounce the Warsaw Treaty and proclaim her neutrality. Should its demands not be accepted, it proposed to set up an independent Government.

The Workers' Councils were set up in a variety of centres of work, such as factories, mines, industrial undertakings and so on. They also put forward political demands and wielded considerable influence. However, their principal purpose was to secure for the workers a real share in the management of enterprises and to arrange for the setting up of machinery to protect their interests. Unpopular measures such as that of establishing "norms" of production for each worker, were abolished. The emergence of Revolutionary and Workers' Councils throughout Hungary was one of the most characteristic features of the uprising. It represented the first practical step to restore order and to reorganize the Hungarian economy on a socialist basis, but without rigid Party control or the apparatus of terror.

Political Developments

This massacre [before the Parliament building on October 25] in which many people lost their lives, shocked the nation. The Hungarian people did not know at this time that Mr. Nagy was detained at the Communist Party Headquarters when the Russian tanks were firing on the unarmed crowd. On the same day, the insurgents derived some encouragement from the news that Erno Gero had been replaced as First Secretary of the Central Committee of the Party by Janos Kadar. The following day Mr. Gero sought the security of Soviet tanks—and later Soviet territory. The former Premier, Andras Hegedus, Vice-Chairman of the Council of Ministers, also fled from the Communist Headquarters.

Mr. Nagy was now free to move to the Parliament Building. On 27 October, he formed a Government into which he invited both Communist and non-Communist Ministers. These included Zoltan Tildy, former Head of State, Bela Kovacs, former Secretary-General of the Independent Smallholders, and Ferenc Erdei of the National Peasants. The non-Communists, however, were serving in a personal, non-party capacity and several "Stalinists" were retained.

With the departure of Messrs. Gero and Hegedus, the Central Committee of the Hungarian Workers' (Communist) Party announced that the Government would start negotiations with the USSR for the immediate withdrawal of Soviet forces. On 28 October, Mr. Nagy's Government ordered a cease-fire. Fighting stopped largely on the insurgents' terms. Apart from the successful adoption of guerilla tactics by the fighters, larger groups of the insurgents had withstood Soviet tanks in strongholds such as the Corvin Block. At the Kilian Barracks, Hungarian Army units had fought successfully against repeated attacks under their leader, Colonel Pal Maleter, who had gone over to the insurgents after being sent with instructions to fight against them.

Mr. Nagy clarifies his position

On the same day when Mr. Nagy's Government ordered a cease-fire, the Prime Minister announced that he would abolish the AVH, after the restoration of order. Popular resentment against the AVH was so universal and so deep that Mr. Nagy was obliged to take this decisive step on the following day, 29 October. As a result, he was himself freed for the first time from the control of the AVH. The fall of a regime for which, in all Hungary, only the AVH was prepared to fight, followed as an inevitable consequence. On 30 October, Mr. Nagy announced that the Cabinet had abolished the "one-party system." Speaking in the name of the Communist Party, Mr. Kadar, still First Secretary of its Central Committee, agreed with this step to avoid, as he said, "further bloodshed." Zoltan Tildy, former leader of the Smallholders Party, announced that free elections would be held throughout Hungary. Representatives of both the Smallholders and National Peasants entered the Inner Cabinet in which they had, between them, as many posts as the Communists. A post was set aside for a Social-Democratic nominee.

Once the AVH had been disbanded, Mr. Nagy felt free to explain his actions on and immediately after 24 October. A series of statements was made by himself, or on his behalf, in the press and on the radio. The most important of these declared that Mr. Nagy had not signed any decrees asking for Soviet military intervention or proclaiming summary jurisdiction. It was also stated that he had not subsequently approved of the invitation to the Soviet forces. These clarifications and the political steps taken by Mr. Nagy served to dispel popular doubts regarding his attitude towards the uprising, and his popularity rapidly returned.

Although a cease-fire had been ordered on 28 October, a few isolated skirmishes took place after that date, but the cease-fire became fully effective by the time the new Cabinet took office on 30 October. That same day saw the beginning of a withdrawal of Soviet armed forces from Budapest. The general expectation was that negotiations for their complete withdrawal from Hungarian territory would soon attain their objective. A number of revolutionary organs, the new political parties and newspapers beginning to appear on the streets all joined the Government in its efforts to stop the last manifestations of lawlessness which had occurred. . . . Hundreds of buildings in Budapest had become ruins as a result of the gunfire, and thousands more were severely damaged, although some areas of the city had suffered little.

The days that followed the cease-fire, up to 4 November, saw the people of Budapest take the first steps to clear away rubble and broken glass, to restore order and to bring life back to normal conditions. It was generally agreed that everyone would resume work on Monday, 5 November. The disbanding of the AVH and the renewed confidence in Mr. Nagy, together with the victory of those who had fought in the uprising, combined to create a general feeling of well-being and hopefulness, which impressed all observers. Meanwhile, political prisoners whom the AHV had detained and tortured were released by the people. The most celebrated political prisoner to regain his freedom was Cardinal Mindszenty, who returned to Budapest and broadcast to the nation. . . . On 1 November, the freedom fighters, while maintaining their identity, agreed to be amalgamated into a National Guard whose members would be the only Hungarians apart from the Army and police, authorized to bear arms.

On 3 November, the Government was again reconstituted. Several Communists were dismissed, some of them having been ousted from their offices by the staff of their respective Ministries. Three Ministries each were allotted to the Communists, the Social Democrats, the Independent Smallholders, and two to the Petofi Party. . . . Reassuring statements were issued by various leaders regarding the policy to be followed. A Minister of State, Ferenc Farkas, himself a member of the National Peasant Party, announced that the four parties were unanimously agreed to retain from the socialist achievements everything which could be used in a free, democratic and socialist country, in accordance with the will of the people. The peasant parties did not agree on all issues with the Social Democrats, but they also were solidly opposed to the restoration of large estates, as they were to the forced collectivization and obligatory deliveries of produce imposed by the Communist regime.

The Communist Party itself realized that a drastic overhaul of its methods would be necessary to regain the confidence of its disillusioned supporters. . . . On 1 November, Mr. Kadar read over Budapest Radio a message from the Preparatory Committee of what was to be a reformed party under the name of the Hungarian Socialist Workers' Party. The new party would defend the cause of socialism and democracy, "not by slavishly imitating foreign examples, but by taking a road suitable to the economic and historic characteristics of our country. . . . "We do not want to be dependent any longer; we do not want our country to become a battlefield". . . .

Declaration of Neutrality

On the morning of 1 November, Mr. Nagy . . . told the Soviet Ambassador that he had received authoritative information on the entry of new Soviet military units into Hungary. This, he informed the Ambassador, was a violation of the Warsaw Treaty and the Hungarian Government would denounce the Treaty if the reinforcements were not withdrawn. . . . At 2:00 P.M., Mr. Nagy telephoned the Ambassador and informed him that new Soviet troops had crossed the frontier within the last three hours. For this reason,

effective immediately, Hungary was withdrawing from the Warsaw
Treaty. At 4:00 P.M., the Council of Ministers, which included
Mr. Kadar, approved this action without dissent and, at the same
meeting, adopted a Declaration of Neutrality for Hungary. At 5:00
P.M., the Council of Ministers invited the Soviet Ambassador to a
meeting and informed him of these decisions. The same news was
conveyed by the Hungarian Government to various heads of diplo-
matic missions in Budapest, who were also told of a request by
Mr. Nagy to the United Nations, asking for the aid of the four
Great Powers in defense of Hungary's neutrality.

Soviet Forces Intervene Again

While news came in of the massing of Soviet armoured forces,
negotiations continued for the withdrawal of Soviet troops from
Hungary. By the afternoon of 3 November, agreement appeared to
be near and only certain technical details of the withdrawal remained to be settled. A Hungarian delegation consisting of the
Minister of Defense, now General Maleter, the Minister of State
Ferenc Erdei, the Chief of Staff General Kovacs, and Colonel Szucs
was invited to settle these details at the Soviet Military Command
at Tokol near Budapest, at 10 P.M. The Hungarian negotiators attended a banquet given in their honour by the Soviet military representatives at Tokol. It was nearly midnight when the party was
interrupted by the arrival of General Serov, Chief of the Soviet
Security Police, who entered the room accompanied by NKVD officers
and ordered the arrest of the Hungarian delegation.

Communication having been interrupted between Mr. Nagy's
Government and General Maleter, considerable anxiety was felt at
the Parliament Building regarding developments. During the night
. . . numerous telephone calls came from industrial districts surrounding Budapest and from various Revolutionary Councils in the
provinces. They all reported that Soviet forces, in battle formation,
were steadily advancing, and the Revolutionary organs asked
urgently for permission to oppose them by force of arms. It has
been estimated that some 2,500 Soviet tanks and 1,000 Soviet supporting vehicles were in Hungary by 3 November. All strategic
centres, airfields, railroads and highways had been brought under
Soviet control. Mr. Nagy, however, gave specific instructions not to
open fire on the Russian troops, since he understood that a successful outcome of the negotiations for withdrawal of the Soviet troops
was still expected. These instructions were not changed until news
was received that Mr. Kadar had set up another Government, whereupon Mr. Nagy summoned a Cabinet meeting at which it was decided to resist the Soviet troops by force of arms. At 5:20 A.M.

Mr. Nagy announced over Budapest Radio that Soviet troops had attacked the capital "with the obvious intention of overthrowing the legal Hungarian democratic Government." He declared that the Government was at its post and that the Hungarian troops were in combat. Battles were, in fact, being fought on the arterial roads at the approaches to Budapest. Notwithstanding the overwhelming power of the Soviet forces, barricades hastily erected by the Hungarian fighters presented a first obstacle to the Russian advance. The Hungarian Army, the National Guard, and groups of freedom fighters, mostly equipped only with light weapons fought side by side against the advancing tanks. Shortly after 8 A.M. Budapest Radio broadcast its last message before going off the air. This was an appeal to the writers and scientists of the world to help the people of Hungary.

Mr. Kadar Forms a Government

At 5:05 A.M., only a quarter of an hour before Mr. Nagy broadcast news of the second Soviet intervention, another radio station had announced the formation of a Hungarian Revolutionary Worker-Peasant Government by Mr. Kadar. . . . At 6 A.M. Mr. Kadar's voice was heard over the same wavelength announcing the composition of his Government. He declared that reactionary elements were seeking to overthrow socialism in Hungary and to restore the capitalists and landowners to power. The new Government, he said, had requested the help of the Soviet troops to defeat these "reactionary forces."

Mr. Kadar gave no explanation of his change of attitude since his broadcast supporting Mr. Nagy on the night of 1 November. There is no evidence that he had taken any steps to disassociate himself from Mr. Nagy's policies or to resign from his Government. It is known that he visited the Soviet Embassy after his broadcast on the night of 1 November, but he was present at negotiations with representatives of Revolutionary Councils the following day. If the circumstances in which he constituted his Cabinet are obscure, so also are his movements and those of his fellow Ministers at the time. According to witnesses, Mr. Kadar was in Moscow early in November and he and his Ministers made no public appearance in Budapest until they took the oath of office on 7 November. The controlling authority in Hungary was the Soviet Military Command, which issued orders to the Hungarian people regarding the surrender of arms, falling within the province of civil administration. There is no evidence to suggest that any Hungarian group opposed the actions of Mr. Nagy which, in most cases, merely reflected what the Revolutionary and Workers' Councils had insisted upon from the outbreak of the uprising.

After the Soviet forces had occupied Budapest, local resistance continued in various centres. Bitter fighting went on until Tuesday evening, 6 November, when most of the Hungarian fighters ran out of ammunition. Some centres within the city continued, however, to resist until the 8th and in the outlying industrial districts fighting went on until the 11th. Heavy destruction and considerable loss of life were caused by the Soviet armed forces, which often directed gunfire into buildings lining the streets. During this second armed intervention by Soviet forces, the fiercest fighting took place in working class suburbs of Budapest, such as Ujpest and Csepel Island. The workers at Csepel refused several Soviet calls to surrender and held out until the evening of 9 November, despite the use of artillery against them from various directions, supplemented by aerial bombardments. At the important industrial centre of Dunapentele, formerly Sztalinvaros, the workers showed an equal determination to resist the Soviet troops. On 7 November, during an all day battle, they repelled a Soviet attack from three directions using a large armoured force, self-propelled guns and tactical airforce. . . .

The Abduction of Mr. Nagy

Mr. Nagy left the Parliament Building at about 6 A.M. on 4 November and sought asylum at the Yugoslav Embassy. Later in the day, other leading Hungarians, including the widow of Laszlo Rajk, with fifteen women and seventeen children, sought asylum in the same building. During negotiations between the Yugoslav Government and Mr. Kadar that took place in November, the Yugoslav Government proposed that Mr. Kadar should provide a written guarantee that Mr. Nagy and his party would be allowed to return freely to their homes or, if this were not possible, to go to Yugoslavia. A suggestion by Mr. Kadar that the Nagy party should seek refuge in Romania was rejected by Mr. Nagy. Other demands by Mr. Kadar's Government considered unacceptable by Mr. Nagy were that he should resign from his position in the Government, should offer a self-criticism of his activities and should declare himself in sympathy with Mr. Kadar's Government. Eventually, the Yugoslav Government wrote to Mr. Kadar that it would agree to the departure of Mr. Nagy and his friends only if Mr. Kadar, as President of the Hungarian Government, guaranteed in writing that the party would be granted safe conduct to proceed freely to their respective homes. In his reply, Mr. Kadar confirmed in writing that the Hungarian Government did not desire to apply sanctions against Imre Nagy and the members of his group for their past activities.

The next day, 22 November, at 6:30 P.M. a bus arrived at the Yugoslav Embassy to take the party to their homes. Soviet military personnel arrived and insisted on entering the bus, whereupon the Yugoslav Ambassador asked that two Embassy officials should accompany the bus, to make certain that Mr. Nagy and his party reached their homes as agreed. The bus was driven to the Headquarters of the Soviet Military Command, where a Russian Lieutenant-Colonel ordered the two Yugoslav officials to leave. The bus then drove away to an unknown destination escorted by Soviet armoured cars.

In a *note verbale*, the Yugoslav Government condemned the Hungarian action as "a flagrant breach of the agreement reached." The note declared that Mr. Nagy and his party had refused to go to Romania and it condemned the Hungarian action as completely contrary to the generally accepted practices of international law. Notwithstanding this reaction, Mr. Kadar's Government announced publicly that Mr. Nagy and some of the colleagues who had sought refuge in the Yugoslav Embassy had gone to Romania in accordance with a request they had submitted previously. . . .

Soviet Military Occupation

The action of the Soviet Military Command in intervening in an arrangement between Mr. Kadar's Government and the Yugoslav Embassy illustrates the degree of his subordination to the Soviet forces. Having taken over Hungary by armed intervention, the Soviet authorities were compelled by reason of the administrative vacuum to administer a country whose popularly supported Government they had overthrown. The Soviet-installed Government of Mr. Kadar commanded no following in the country, with the exception of individual members of the former AVH, a few senior officers of the Hungarian Army and a small segment of former Communist Party officials, who had been dismissed during the uprising. Having broken the armed resistance of the Hungarian people in a massive attack, the Soviet authorities found themselves facing the passive resistance of the Hungarian population. This was particularly marked in the case of the workers who had borne the brunt of most of the fighting. In the industrial and mining districts, they steadily maintained their demands.

Finding themselves confronted by this nation-wide resistance, the Soviet Military Command began by resorting to mass arrests. Many of the people thus apprehended had not been directly involved in the fighting. In numerous cases, the captives were not transferred to the Hungarian authorities, but were crowded on trains or in trucks and deported, under Russian escort, to the USSR. In some instances, because of action by the Hungarian resistance and the railway workers, it was found necessary to run the trains entirely with Russian personnel. No accurate figures exist regarding the numbers of Hungarian citizens deported, but these certainly run into thousands. By January 1957, some of these had been returned to Hungary, but it would appear that a considerable number still remain in the USSR.

In an effort to win popular support, Mr. Kadar announced that the policy of his Government would include the implementation of various demands put forward during the uprising. These included raising the workers' standard of living, factory management by Workers' Councils and the abolition of compulsory deliveries of agricultural produce by the peasants. These promises, however, failed to satisfy the Hungarian people, who continued to press for the withdrawal of Soviet troops, free elections and the return of Mr. Nagy. Since 23 October, industrial production had been completely disrupted in Hungary and the position continued to deteriorate after 4 November, since the workers refused to resume work until the Government gave evidence that it would meet their demands.

As in the time of Mr. Nagy's premiership, the Workers' Councils were still the principal channels through which such demands were conveyed to Mr. Kadar's Government. The outcome of the negotiations was wholly unsatisfactory to the Councils. On 14 November, the factory Councils established the greater Budapest Workers' Council in order to present a united front. Until its abolition on 9 December, this Council strove to reach an agreement with Mr. Kadar and his Government. It became clear from the Government's attitude that it was in no position to satisfy the workers' demands. Meanwhile, in order to secure control of the country, new security forces were organized, including many former members of the AVH. Through arrests of members of Workers' Councils and through the infiltration of trusted Party members into key posts, the power of the Councils was steadily undermined. When the Greater Budapest Workers' Council declared a forty-eight-hour protest strike to take place on 11 and 12 December, the Government issued a decree to abolish all Workers' Councils above factory level. Decrees were also issued instituting the death penalty for a large category of offenses, including participation in strikes.

Hungarian factories had remained practically idle for nearly two months. Electric power plants had produced only a minimum amount of electricity due to the slow-down strike of the Hungarian coal miners. However, the weapon of passive resistance by the Hungarian workers could not be employed indefinitely. Dire necessity had enforced a resumption of work by mid-December, when the Hungarian workers found themselves in factories and coal mines which contained a novel element—the presence of Russian soldiers.

Recent Developments

Other steps taken by Mr. Kadar's Government to establish control over the Hungarian people include the opening on 20 December of a State Information Office to control the press. The Revolutionary Council of Intellectuals was dissolved on 9 December and the Writers' Union, which had branded the Soviet intervention in Hungary as a "historic mistake," was disbanded on 21 April. The Petofi Club also ceased to function and Hungarians were without any forum where they could exchange ideas. All hope of a coalition Government vanished although, in negotiations between Mr. Kadar and the major democratic parties, the latter made it clear that they accepted public ownership of the means of production and were willing to "defend the socialist achievements." By the beginning of 1957, non-Communist organizations had, in effect, been excluded from any role in public life. It was officially stated that the Social Democratic Party will not be allowed to function, while leaders of the Smallholders Party have retired from public life and the Petofi Party has virtually dissolved itself. The mandate of the present Party has virtually dissolved itself. The mandate of the present Hungarian Assembly was due to expire on 17 May 1957. However, this mandate has been extended for two years by amendment to the Constitution, thereby depriving the Hungarian people of the exercise of their fundamental political right to participate in the function of Government through elected representatives of their own choice.

Summary of Conclusions

The Committee has summarized its conclusions as to the essential facts about the Hungarian uprising under thirteen points. The essence of these conclusions is as follows:

(i) What took place in Hungary was a spontaneous national uprising, caused by long-standing grievances. One of these was the inferior status of Hungary with regard to the USSR;

(ii) The uprising was led by students, workers, soldiers and intellectuals, many of them Communists or former Communists. Those who took part in it insisted that democratic socialism should be the basis of the Hungarian political structure, and that the land reform and other social achievements should be safeguarded. It is untrue that the uprising was fomented by reactionary circles in Hungary or that it drew its strength from "Imperialist" circles in the West;

(iii) The uprising was not planned in advance, but actually took participants by surprise. Its timing was connected with Poland's successful move for greater independence from the USSR and with the disappointment caused by the speech of Mr. Erno Gero on his return from Yugoslavia on 23 October, when it was hoped that he would adopt a sympathetic attitude towards the popular demands voiced on 22 October by the Hungarian students;

(iv) It would appear that the Soviet authorities had taken steps as early as 20 October to make armed intervention possible. Evidence exists of troop movements, or projected troop movements, from that date on, and Soviet troops from outside Hungary were used even in the first intervention. In Hungary, signs of opposition were evident before 23 October;

(v) The demonstrations on 23 October were at first entirely peaceable and no evidence has been discovered that any demonstrations intended to resort to force. The change was due to the action of the AVH in opening fire on the people outside the Radio Building and to the appearance of Russian soldiers in Budapest as enemies in combat;

(vi) Mr. Nagy has established that he did not issue any invitation to the Soviet authorities to intervene and the Committee has no evidence as to the circumstances in which an invitation was issued or as to whether such an invitation was issued at all. Similar considerations apply to the alleged invitation by Mr. Kadar's Government for the Soviet troops to intervene on the second occasion. There is abundant evidence that Soviet preparations for this intervention had been under way since the last days of October;

(vii) Mr. Nagy was not at first free to exercise the full powers of the Premiership. By the time the grip of the AVH had been loosened, the real power lay with the Revolutionary and Workers' Councils. Mr. Nagy, seeing that his countrymen were united in their desire for other forms of Government and for the departure of the Soviet troops, threw in his lot with the insurgents;

(viii) During the few days of freedom, the popular nature of the uprising was proved by the appearance of a free press and radio and by general rejoicing among the people;

(ix) A number of lynchings and beatings by the crowds concerned, in almost all cases, members of the AVH or those who were believed to have co-operated with them;

(x) Steps taken by the Workers' Councils during this period were aimed at giving the workers real control of nationalized undertakings and at abolishing unpopular institutions, such as the production norms. Meanwhile, negotiations were proceeding for the complete withdrawal of Soviet troops and life in Budapest was beginning to return to normal;

(xi) In contrast to demands put forward at this time for the re-establishment of political rights, basic human rights of the Hungarian people were violated by the Hungarian Governments before 23 October, especially up to the autumn of 1955, and such violations have been resumed since 4 November. The numerous accounts of inhuman treatment and tortures by the AVH must be accepted as true. In an attempt to break the revolution, numbers of Hungarians, including some women, were deported to the Soviet Union and some may not have been returned to their homes;

(xii) Since the second Soviet intervention on 4 November there has been no evidence of popular support for Mr. Kadar's Government. Mr. Kadar has proceeded step by step to destroy the power of the workers. Strong repressive measures have been introduced and general elections have been postponed for two years. He refuses in present circumstances to discuss withdrawal of the Soviet troops. Only a small fraction of the 190,000 Hungarians who fled the country have accepted the invitation to return;

(xiii) Consideration of the Hungarian question by the United Nations was legally proper and paragraph 7 of Article 2 of the Charter does not justify objections to such consideration. A massive armed intervention by one Power on the territory of another with the avowed intention of interfering in its internal affairs must, by the Soviet Union's own definition of aggression, be a matter of international concern.

Post-Revolution Hungary

The UN *Report* speaks for itself. The following short section, based on fragmentary information and incomplete statistical data, is an attempt to evaluate the impact of the Revolution.

Demographic Factors

Dead and Wounded. Official figures on dead and wounded released by the Kadar regime are patently false. As of January 15, 1957, these were given as 2,500 to 3,000 dead (of which 1,800 to 2,000 in Budapest) and about 13,000 wounded (of which 11,500 in Budapest). An estimate by the Indian Ambassador was that of 25,000 Hungarians dead in Budapest alone, and 7,000 Russians, as of December 13, 1956. It is probable that at least another 10,000 freedom fighters were killed in the countryside, mostly by Soviet troops, after November 4. The sex ratio of dead as given by the Kadar regime (84 per cent men, 16 per cent women) may very well be accurate, as may the 20 per cent of dead given as below 20 years of age. It is probable that 85 per cent of the dead lie in the 16-35 year range.

There were probably over 100,000 wounded in the Revolution. Considering the chaotic conditions and the lack of adequate medical care and supplies during the fighting, the ratio of dead to wounded was probably appreciably higher than would be the case in regular warfare. As the heaviest fighting took place in Budapest, it is probably that the majority of dead were city-dwellers.

Emigration. The major demographic loss was due to emigration during and immediately after the Soviet reoccupation, when thousands of Hungarians escaped to Austria and to a lesser extent to Yugoslavia. The 193,216 refugees who had fled Hungary for Austria and Yugoslavia up to the end of April 1957, mostly consisted of young people, approximately 70 per cent below 30 years of age.

The effect of the demographic loss by emigration, great as it is numerically, is even greater qualitatively. Overwhelmingly in the reproductive age brackets, proportionately better educated, and possessing a greater degree of technical skills than the national average, Revolutionary demographic losses will inevitably show a cumulative effect on Hungary's demographic structure and economic potential.

The majority of escapees have indicated a desire to settle in the United States, Canada, Western Europe, and South America. As of January 1, 1957, of the 169,627 who had arrived in Austria, 64,904 were still there, 23,963 had gone to the United States, 16,072 to the United Kingdom, 11,555 to West Germany, 10,317 to Switzerland, 9,968 to Canada, 8,846 to France, 4,021 to Sweden, 3,970 to the Netherlands, 3,545 to Italy, 3,170 to Australia, 3,100 to Belgium, 1,437 to Israel, 1,015 to Denmark, and 3,744 to other countries. Since that time a majority of the escapees to Austria have been resettled (bringing the total to over 30,000 in the United States) in 27 countries. Of the total of 13,186 Hungarian escapees still in Yugoslavia as of June 2, 1957, 8,600 had been promised havens in other countries.

It is notable that despite a full-fledged campaign by the Kadar regime (including a firm promise that no reprisals would be taken against them) and the difficulties and hardships of life in temporary resettlement camps in Austria and Yugoslavia, only a very small minority (well under 5 per cent) of escapees have elected to return to Hungary.

Deportations. To quote the UN *Report,* the deportations "run into thousands." It would seem that somewhere between 20,000 and 35,000 are still being held in camps in the USSR.

The Revolution, has thus cost Hungary a total demographic loss of at least 250,000. The loss (to a country of only ten million people) of such a large percentage of her most vigorous and capable citizens, cannot speedily, if ever, be repaired, whatever the political future may hold.

The Constitutional System and Government

The first Kadar government, formed at Szolnok under Soviet aegis and control, consisted of Kadar as Premier, Ferenc Munnich, Minister of Interior, Gyorgy Marosan, Minister of State, Imre Horvath, Minister of Foreign Affairs, Istvan Kossa, Minister of Finance, Antal Apro, Minister of Industry, Imre Dogei, Minister of Agriculture, and Sandor Ronai, Minister of Commerce. Some reshuffling and addition occurred later, when new members were added on March 1 and May 9. The first meeting of the Hungarian National Assembly since the Revolution was held on May 9, 1957. During the three-day meeting the number of Cabinet posts was increased from 12 to 21 by a unanimous show of hands after simply being presented by Speaker Sandor Ronai as a proposal of the Presidium, the twenty-one-man government executive body. Almost all the new Cabinet members had served under previous Communist regimes. It was announced that 28 of the 298 members of Parliament had "resigned" since the last session in August, including Rakosi and Gero. The general elections, set for May 1957, were simply "posptoned," and the current Parliament extended its own mandate for an additional two years. The new Cabinet, as approved on May 9, was as follows:

Minister	Cabinet Post	Date of Appointment
Janos Kadar	Chairman of the Council of Ministers (Premier)	11/12/56
Ferenc Munnich	First Deputy Chairman of the Council of Ministers	3/1/57
Antal Apro	Deputy Chairman of the Council of Ministers	5/9/57
Gyorgy Marosan	Minister of State	11/12/56
Imre Horvath	Minister of Foreign Affairs	
Imre Dogei	Minister of Agriculture	
Bela Biszku	Minister of Interior	3/1/57
Frigyes Doleschall	Minister of Public Health	3/1/57
Gyula Kallai	Minister of Culture	3/1/57
Geza Revesz	Minister of Defense	3/1/57
Istvan Antos	Minister of Finance	5/9/57
Ferenc Nezval	Minister of Justice	5/9/57
Janos Csergo	Minister of Smelting and Machine Industry	5/9/57
Sandor Czottner	Minister of Heavy Industry	5/9/57
Mme. Jozsef Nagy	Minister of Light Industry	5/9/57
Istvan Kossa	Minister of Transportation and Postal Affairs	5/9/57 5/9/57
Jeno Incze	Minister of Foreign Trade	5/9/57
Janos Tausz	Minister of Domestic Trade	5/9/57
Imre Kovacs	Minister of Food Supplies	5/9/57
Rezso Trautmann	Minister of Building Construction	5/9/57
Odon Kishazi	Minister of Labor	5/9/57

Arpad Kiss was simultaneously confirmed as President of the National Planning Office, and Geza Szenassy was appointed Prosecutor General. As the Communist "Rakosi" Constitution of 1949 is still in force, there has been no need to make any changes. It is flexible and ambiguous enough to provide legal cover for whatever measures the regime wishes to enforce. The only constitutional amendments by the Kadar regime have been to include the Kossuth emblem in the coat of arms of the Hungarian People's Republic and to delete the Communist emblem from the national flag.

Politics and Political Organizations

The reconstituted Hungarian Socialist [Communist] Workers' Party has faced grave difficulties in recruiting members.   More than six months after the Soviet establishment of the Kadar regime, it had less than 300,000 members in Hungary, compared to some 900,000 before the Revolution. Virtually all the leading Stalinists except Rakosi and Gero have come out of hiding in Hungary or returned from their temporary hiding places in Prague or the Soviet Union, and have again assumed leading roles in the government and in Party organizations.

The re-established "mass organizations" are completely Party-controlled. The following are the surviving and reconstituted mass organizations as of May 1957:

MSZSZOSZ—Magyar Szabad Szakszervezetek Orszagos Szovetsege (National Association of Free Hungarian Trade Unions): KISZ—Kommunista Ifjusagi Szovetseg (Communist Youth Association); MATISZ—Magyar Forradalmi Ifjumunkas Szovetseg (Hungarian Revolutionary Young Workers' Association); EPOSZ—Egyesult Paraszt Ifjusag Orszagos Szovetsege (National Association of Unified Peasant Youth); OSZSZ—Orszagos Szabadsagharcos Szovetseg (National Association of Freedom Fighters); SZOVOSZ—Szovetkezetek Orszagos Szovetsege (National Association of Cooperatives); and MNDSZ—Magyar Nok Demokratikus Szovetsege (Democratic Association of Hungarian Women). No former paramilitary organizations have been re-established by the Kadar regime.

National Security

Army. That the Hungarian Army supported the Revolution or maintained a benevolent neutrality was perhaps the greatest shock sustained by world communism and the leadership of the USSR. After years of indoctrination and an enormous investment in equipment and training it became clearly evident that the Hungarian Army was Hungarian and not Communist. Only at the higher command levels was there any support for the Communist Party, and even here there was no unanimity.

The Kadar regime has been significantly quiet about plans for a new army. It is doubtful if a reactivated army anywhere near the pre-Revolutionary 170,000 man force is planned. For the moment the Soviet troops are not being replaced by Hungarian units except for frontier guard duty.

It is indicative that the Kadar regime had to go down to the level of colonel to find a new Chief of Staff, Colonel Ferenc Ugrai, appointed in February 1957, and it is significant that General Pal Maleter and

his aide, both to be tried for their lives by the Kadar regime for participation in the Revolution, were ranking officers in the Communist army.
The pre-Revolutionary military budget was cut by more than 50 per
cent for 1957, and it is likely that the money officially allocated to
national defense is in reality mostly slated for the new political police.

Internal Security. The detested AVH was officially abolished by
a law of December 30, which transferred its duties to the regular
police. Security was at first the province of the Soviet troops, but the
regime formed the so-called "R" groups on November 9, and gradually
integrated them into the *Karhatalom,* or armed militia, which comprised all the armed forces of the Kadar government. A new political
police was set up to replace the notorious AVH on December 18,
around a core of remaining AVH men. Colonel Gyula Horvath, who
took an active part in the trial of Laszlo Rajk, is the current head of
the police, appointed in the spring of 1957. The Workers' Militia was
created February 18, 1957. This is a Communist armed force to ensure
"order and protection of factories and work places." The new police
organization is weaker and not as well organized as the old one. Many
of the regular police, as opposed to the AVH, went over to the freedom
fighters, and all pre-Revolutionary army and police forces, with the
single exception of former AVH members, appear somewhat suspect
by the regime.

Security Measures. A continuing check has been made of those
involved in the uprising. Physicians and hospitals have been required
to give the re-established secret police the names of persons attended
during the Revolution, and all Budapest residents are required to
report their movements during the suspect period. New identity cards
are being issued. The exact number of executions is unknown. It
would appear from well-authenticated reports that over 2,000 death
sentences have been passed and at least 300 have been executed since
the suppression of military resistance.

There appear to be between 20,000 and 22,000 persons held in
Hungarian prisons, and an unknown number in reactivated and new
concentration camps. The notorious Recsk and Kistarcsa camps have
been reopened, and a special camp at Obuda has reportedly been set
up for "trouble-making" children under 14.

Religion

The Revolution proved that ten years of anti-religious propaganda
and all the devious anti-church machinations, overt and covert, of an

anti-religious state, had failed absolutely to destroy the basic religious beliefs of the Hungarian people. The Kadar regime's religious policy, effected through the Department of Church Affairs in the Ministry of Education, is essentially that of Rakosi, and in general it may be said that the religious clock has been turned back to 1953, although the government has been circumspect in not attacking religion openly, in an apparently vain effort to placate the population.

It is noteworthy that one of the first measures of the Kadar regime, in an attempt to gain support, was a decree permitting children to get religious instruction in the schools, although this right was shortly so curtailed as to make it meaningless. The major campaign to infiltrate and split if not capture the churches, through rump organizations of fellow-traveling "peace priests" and Protestant clergymen, has been revived and intensified. Bishop Laszlo Dezsery of the Evangelical Church, who replaced Bishop Ordass when he was jailed by the Communists in the early days of the Rakosi regime, is again one of the leading religious regime spokesmen. Former Bishop Janos Peter of the Reformed Calvinist has become chairman of the regime's Hungarian Institute for Cultural Relations. Continuing efforts have been made to infiltrate the Hungarian Reformed Church, a campaign which was not greatly hindered prior to the Revolution when Bishop Bereczky was President of its Synod. The Reverend Richard Horvath, the Secretary of the Hungarian Movement of Priests for Peace before the Revolution, suspended by Cardinal Mindszenty during the Revolution, would continue his activities with greater zeal had he not been excommunicated by Pope Pius XII in February 1957.

Although the government has arrested the Reverend Egon Turcsanyi, Cardinal Mindszenty's secretary, and some other priests and pastors, it has generally not carried out any mass arrests of the clergy, nor has it closed any churches. A recent decree contains detailed instructions on the church appointments which require the consent of the government, retroactive to October 1. This decree sets up the legal machinery for the government to remove church officials elected during the Revolution or abolish church reorganizations effected at that time.

Education

University, high school, and elementary education came to a halt as the schools closed during the Revolution. Lower schools began to reopen after November 4, but the universities did not begin to reopen until January 14, and the Budapest universities did not reopen until February 1, 1957.

Marxism-Leninism was again made compulsory in high schools and universities, as was Russian language instruction. The question of religious education in the schools was declared closed when it "reverted to the status of September." Thus officially all the educational demands and gains achieved during the Revolution were wiped out.

The government has threatened "Draconic measures" against those "who do not want to study or teach" according to strict government regulations, and a threat was made in the early spring of 1957 to close the universities "if students do not heed government warnings."

Press, Propaganda, and Culture

The new cultural line, while paying lip-service to liberalization, has been steadily increasing control over all cultural and artistic freedom and its expression, and increasing power of old-line Stalinist bureaucrats in control of the Ministries and departments dealing with cultural affairs and the press. A forecast of things to come was the Parliament speech of Bela Karcsony on June 5, 1957, calling for a sweeping purge of all Hungarian intellectual life to eliminate "the rear guard action of the cultural counter-revolution."

Virtually all the writers who sparked the cultural revolt are silenced, in jail, or dead, with the exception of the few who escaped to the West. Gyula Hay, Zoltan Zelk, Tibor Tardos, Sandor Novobacky and Pal Loecsei, all Communists, were among the first to be arrested. Of the Hungarian writers supporting the new regime, few were important before the Revolution, and fewer were talented. They include Bela Illes, Gyorgy Boloni, Zoltan Hera, Imre Dobozi, Erno Urban, Jozsef Fodor, Sandor Gergely, and Lajos Barta.

The press is reverting to the dullness and conformity of the Rakosi period. Nothing has changed but the names of the major periodicals. Of major organs, the Party *Szabad Nep* has become *Nepszabadsag*, the trade union *Nepszava* has become *Nepakarat*, the daily Budapest *Esti Budapest* is now *Esti Hirlap*, the literary weekly *Irodalmi Ujsag* is now called *Elet es Irodalom*, the daily youth paper *Szabad Ifjusag* has become the weekly *Magyar Ifjusag*, and *Magyar Nemzet*, the former organ of the People's Patriotic Front, has been suppressed.

Health, Welfare, and Social Security

The Revolution, discounting those wounded, does not appear to have had a major impact on national health, largely due to emergency and Red Cross aid.

While approximately 25,000 apartments and housing units were destroyed in Budapest, the housing situation is not appreciably worse than before, when it was described as "bad" to "desperate." The enormous emigration of escapees has probably resulted in a net gain in housing, even taking housing damage into consideration.

In the welfare and social security fields many new measures have been adopted. Some unemployment "bonuses" have been paid, and pensions and family allowances are in the process of being raised, but not enough to cover increased living costs due to a recognizable post-Revolutionary inflation. The Tax on Childlessness has been abolished, and eligibility for old-age pensions has been extended to men at the age of 59 and women at the age of 54. The government has also declared it would remedy past "wrongs caused by the illegal stopping of pension benefits." Income taxes have been changed to fall more heavily on the upper brackets, ranging up to 56 per cent on gross incomes over 50,000 forints ($4,282 at the official rate of exchange).

The Economy

There are no accurate economic statistics available, and prediction, dangerous in any circumstances, is absolutely foolhardy in post-Revolutionary Hungary. Nevertheless, some trends are evident by mid-1957, and some extremely hazardous guesses may be attempted. Under no circumstances should any figures given in the following section be accepted as more than indicative.

Hungary's economy came to a standstill October 23, and her industrial plant was gravely injured in the subsequent fighting and Soviet military occupation. Over-all damage to the economy has been variously placed at 16, 14, 12, and 20 billion forints by different regime spokesmen from Kadar to Parragi. The last figure is probably the most accurate. The economy has made only a very slow recovery since the beginning of 1957. The over-all production index had probably risen to some 70-80 per cent of what it was before the Revolution by the late spring of 1957, and the figure would not even be that high if it were not for the fact that 1957 agricultural production is reckoned at 90-95 per cent of 1956.

Agriculture and Food Supply. The post-Revolutionary agricultural production picture is no clearer than the political situation on the agricultural front. All that is certain is that the peasants were firmly opposed to the pre-Revolutionary regime, that they supported the freedom fighters as best they could, and that they remain opposed to the Kadar regime.

Early in 1957 it was announced that 8 per cent of the food supplies had been destroyed during the uprising, and in its first few months most food stocks were released by the regime to prevent a shortage. During recent years Hungarian grain imports have varied between 400 and 500 thousand tons, and about the same amount will be needed this year.

Government agricultural policy is roughly the same as before October with one notable exception: forced deliveries of agricultural produce were abolished during the Revolution and have not been fully reimposed. This has resulted in increased farm prices in the free market, and it is hoped this incentive will be reflected in greater 1957 production. Collectivization remains a regime objective, although the peasantry has been assured it will be completely voluntary. There were slightly over 5,000 state and collective farms at the beginning of the Revolution, during which most dissolved themselves. It was announced that at the beginning of 1957 the number of collectives had fallen to 1,599. The regime had been able to raise this figure to something between 2,000 and 2,500 by the late spring of 1957. Much of the equipment, livestock, and supplies of the collectives and state farms disappeared during the Revolution, as did some equipment from the MTS; with the exception of heavier equipment, which may be damaged, it will be difficult or impossible for the state authorities to get it back.

Industry and Planning.   Industrial production for 1957 will probably reach 60-70 per cent of that planned for 1956, providing there is no further major upheaval, and providing domestic coal production and additional coal imports together reach the pre-Revolution 1956 figures. For light industry, not quite so heavily dependent on coal, the figure may reach 70-80 per cent.

The 1957 budget and state plan contain figures little more than indicative of the true situation, as the value of the forint is considerably less than pre-Revolution due to inflation, and statistical juggling for propaganda effect is clearly evident. It was admitted that national income would fall some 9 billion forints below that planned for 1957 before the Revolution, but 2 billion more than actual national income for 1956 (during which national income plummeted to almost nothing for the months of November and December). The value of industrial output was slated to be 2.4 per cent higher than that of 1956, but 7 per cent less than that for 1955.

The proportion of the budget allotted heavy industry was cut from 56 per cent in 1956 to 53 per cent for 1957, the proportion allotted light industry raised proportionately. The major features of the budget were the halving of defense expenditures and the slashing of investment in heavy industry. Unlike all previous plans, new investment was negligible by Communist standards. Capital investment was cut almost in half, and most of the new allocations were slated for "reconstruction." It had previously been announced that during 1957, "large-scale construction will be stopped temporarily."

The 1957 plan may be regarded as an "emergency" plan to replace the projected second Five-Year Plan (1957-61) which had to be scrapped before it could go into effect. A new Three-Year Plan is to follow.

Mining. Not counting the general political and industrial unrest, the major regime economic problem is the lack of coal, which is at the root of the low level of over-all industrial output, and controls the output of iron, steel, and electric energy.

The regime recognizes coal production as the key to its economic survival, and has concentrated all its energies on the problem, but it is not likely to be solved. The labor force in the coal mines had dropped from 90 thousand before the Revolution to 50 thousand at the beginning of 1957, and daily output, which had averaged about 78,000 tons had only recovered to about 50,000 in the early spring. Massive imports (at least 4,000,000 tons in 1957) will not end the shortage. The government has announced that "25 per cent of foreign trade will be represented by coal imports." The situation is bad in the whole mining sector, but not so desperate as in coal.

The Revolution confirmed rumors of the existence of major uranium deposits in the Mecsek Mountains, but despite reports that huge shipments had been made to the Soviet Union, only about 65 tons of ore (not including samples) seem to have been exported before the Revolution, although uranium mining was controlled in its entirety by Soviet personnel. Samples reportedly contained from .7 to 3 per cent uranium, a high, but not spectacular content. That the deposits were considered important by Soviet experts is indicated by reported pre-Revolution plans to erect a refinery, and barracks for 25,000 workers near Pecs.

Under the Kadar regime the mines (at Kovagoszollos, near Pecs) are again under Soviet supervision, and mining is reportedly being stepped up under a team of 100 Soviet experts who arrived in Hungary early in 1957. The only information released by the Kadar regime has been that Hungary is selling uranium ore to the Soviet Union "at world market prices."

Labor and Productivity. The replacement of the norm system by that of hourly and task wages in most factories during the Revolution lowered productivity. To lure striking workers back to their jobs the regime granted wage increases from 8 to 15 per cent which went into effect at the beginning of 1957, but these increases were largely canceled out by a later decree ruling that past "illegal or additional" wage payments were to be deducted from workers' wages in installments.

A Manpower Rationalization decree, which states those who cannot be employed "for any reason" must be dismissed, was the excuse to purge all labor elements in production considered anti-regime (4,000 of the 32,000 workers in the Csepel Works have been dismissed).

Worker productivity may be estimated at somewhere between 75-85 per cent of the pre-Revolutionary figures, although it naturally varies from industry to industry and from factory to factory. The shortages and irregular supply of raw materials further cut productivity, as work must often be slowed down or suspended.

Labor competitions have been reintroduced, as has a modified norm system. Infiltration and suppression of Workers' Councils and trade unions, increased Party interference and control in factories and work places, and the introduction of repressive measures, up to the death penalty, are part of the new labor policy.

Due to lack of coal, many plants consuming power were forced to close down and an official government estimate on the eve of 1957 was that from 100 to 200 thousand workers would lose their jobs as a result of these measures. Post-Revolutionary purges in the swollen bureaucracy and Party organizations threw additional thousands of unemployed on the labor market, as did the virtual disbandment of the army. The regime went so far as to comment that the escape of thousands of workers would be beneficial in easing the unemployment crisis. Although many of the workers unemployed at the beginning of 1957 will be absorbed by the end of the year, unemployment and underemployment will haunt Hungary for months and probably years to come.

Transportation and Communications. The Revolution resulted in serious losses of motor vehicles, and some railroad stock, as well as busses and streetcars in Budapest. Other communications were not seriously affected, wrecked radio stations and telephone exchanges being comparatively easily repaired. One serious aftermath of the Revolution is the appalling state of the road system, badly battered and cut up by the tread of heavy Soviet tanks.

Exports, Imports, and Foreign Aid.   Exports will probably be cut by at least 50 per cent over-all for 1957; foodstuffs exports will practically cease. Hungary's needs, which can only be satisfied by imports, have increased enormously since the Revolution. It is unofficially estimated that Hungary owed about $200,000,000 to Western countries even before the Revolution for past imports of grain, fats, machinery, and materials. The West will hardly grant the Kadar regime any loans, and Hungary is in no economic position to accumulate foreign exchange by exports.

After ten days of negotiations in Moscow, an economic agreement was signed March 28, 1957 by Hungary and the Soviet Union under which Hungary was said to have won "very great" economic assistance in money and raw materials, including iron ore and coke for steel production. Under this agreement the Soviet Union promised to supply Hungary with 110 million rubles' (27.5 million dollars at the official rate of exchange) worth of goods "this year," and a long-term loan, of which 750 million rubles (including 200 million rubles in free currency) can be used this year. Hungary was also released from payments on her previous one billion forint "debt" to the Soviet Union. Communist China has agreed to grant Hungary an additional 100 million ruble credit.

Hungary's battered economy will thus be even more closely tied to the Soviet bloc than before, but she will be a heavy drain on the Soviet and captive economies, already under stress. The Soviet Union has supplied some grain and livestock feed, and it is probable that the minimum necessary additional amounts until the fall harvest will be provided by the Soviet bloc and purchases in the West.

International Developments

The impact of the Revolution on international affairs was enormous, both in the Communist and Free worlds.

United Nations.   A special meeting of the Security Council was called by the United Nations on October 28, 1956 to consider "The situation in Hungary," and when the efforts of the Security Council were blocked by the Soviet membership and veto power in that body, an emergency special session of the General Assembly on November 4 passed a resolution calling upon the USSR to cease intervention in the internal affairs of Hungary and requesting the Secretary-General to "observe directly" the Hungarian situation and report to the Assembly "at the earliest possible moment."

The Kadar government and the USSR refused to cooperate with the United Nations, and rejected all requested United Nations action, refusing to allow the entrance of the Secretary-General himself or United Nations observers. Short of military action, there was little possibilty of enforcing the United Nations' resolutions.

The timing of the Israeli invasion of Egypt, and the Suez military action undertaken by the United Kingdom and France during the Hungarian Revolution was unfortunate, to put it very mildly. It allowed the Soviet Union to muddy the international waters in and outside the United Nations, and to make the false claim that Soviet intervention was completely "legal," because "invited," while the Israeli invasion was "clear-cut aggression as part of a British-French imperialist plan." Under the circumstances, United Nations action has been limited to moral condemnation of the Kadar regime and of the Soviet action which established it.

A Special Committee on the Problem of Hungary, composed of the representatives of Australia, Ceylon, Denmark, Tunisia, and Uruguay, was established by the General Assembly on January 10, 1957. After five months of hearings and study, the *Report of the Special Committee on Hungary*, was released June 20, 1957. This 150,000 word report, on which much of this section is based, is a scathing indictment of the role of the Soviet Union during and after the Revolution, and of the repressive measures of the Rakosi regime and their readoption and implementation by the current government. It has created world-wide indignation, but further United Nations action was still undetermined at the time of publication.

Hungarian-Soviet Agreement on Soviet Military Forces. Finally, on May 27, 1957, a Soviet-Hungarian agreement was signed in Budapest, under which Russian military forces would appear likely to remain in Hungary as long as "necessary." The number of Soviet troops and their location were to be determined on the basis of special agreements "to be negotiated." The Soviet accord with Hungary is similar to agreements previously signed with Poland, East Germany, and Romania. On paper, at least, the stationing of Soviet troops in Hungary "does not affect the sovereignty of the Hungarian state" and such troops will "not interfere in the internal affairs of Hungary." Crimes committed by Soviet troops or members of their families are henceforth to be dealt with "by Hungarian courts." Movement of Soviet troops "outside their normal posts" will be carried out only "with the approval of the Hungarian authorities." Hungary is, of course, to remain a member of the Warsaw Pact.

The Communist World. It may be said that the official reaction in Communist countries varied according to the distance they had traveled from Stalinism. Czechoslovakia, Romania, Bulgaria, and Albania have supported the Soviet position and the Kadar regime more vehemently than Moscow itself.

Poland's anti-Stalinist Gomulka regime, the installation of which in the face of Soviet threats triggered the Revolution, supported it wholeheartedly up to the second Soviet intervention, and the entire Polish people, even including the rank and file of the Party, were united in support of the Revolution. Unlike the other captive states, Poland has never echoed the Soviet explanation that the Revolution was an uprising "fomented and organized by Western imperialists" and carried out by "Horthyites, reactionaries, and Fascist agents." Nevertheless, Poland's difficult international position has been responsible for official, if half-hearted, support of the Kadar regime and Soviet policy on the "tragic" Hungarian Revolution.

Yugoslavia has consistently maintained the position that the Revolution began as a genuinely democratic movement. This and the Nagy abduction from the Yugoslav Embassy, gave rise to a serious rift between the Soviet Union and Yugoslavia, and it appeared at first that the virulent Soviet and captive state anti-Tito campaign was to be resumed. By June, however, an uneasy truce appeared to have again descended on the always stormy Soviet-Yugoslav relationship. While both Poland and Yugoslavia have failed to pretend there was no democratic Revolution, both countries have announced that the best thing for Hungary under the circumstances is to support the Kadar regime.

Communist China, although supporting the Soviet position as the leader of the "socialist peace camp" has been somewhat less than enthusiastic in supporting the Soviet description of the Revolution as "counter-revolutionary." Chou En-lai, leading a Chinese delegation to Moscow and the captive capitals, visited Budapest early in 1957 and evidenced Chinese support for the Kadar regime, but speeches and statements by Mao Tse-tung have made it clear that his government considered Revolutionary demands were justified by past Communist mistakes and "contradictions" in Hungary.

The Revolution had an enormous impact on the Communist parties in the Free World, whose members could follow the true course of events through the press. Thousands of prominent long-time members withdrew from the large Party organizations in Italy, France, and other Western countries, and even the miniscule British and American parties were split. Not since the Hitler-Stalin pact had such large scale defections and losses been suffered by these Communist parties. The defection of such major Communist writers as Howard Fast, and telegrams of protest at the arrest of Hungarian writers signed by such cultural figures as Pablo Picasso and Jean Paul Sartre have further weakened the Communist movement in destroying what little prestige it had been able to maintain among intellectuals up to the Revolution.

There is evidence that even in the Soviet Union the people and the Party have been far from unanimous in support of Soviet military action in Hungary. The Soviet intelligentsia, and particularly the writers, would appear to be the most heavily disaffected by Soviet military action. Communist ideological and intellectual apologists abroad have been hard pressed to find a valid defense for the brutal suppression of a workers' Revolution by the tanks of the "workers' state," and the imprisonment and execution of convinced Hungarian Communist intellectuals whose major crime was an attempt to put true Marxist theory into practice.

POST-REVOLUTIONARY OUTLOOK

The Kadar regime, or any forseeable Communist Hungarian government, must find itself in a difficult if not impossible situation. Given the political atmosphere, in which the vast majority of the Hungarian people is united in hatred of its government and contempt for its ideology, there are but two choices. The first would be a genuine broadening of the government to include non-Communist elements. As the Revolution so quickly showed, this could result in the overthrow of the Communists and the establishment of a non-Communist and anti-Soviet democracy, which could not be allowed to develop by the Kadar regime or the Soviet Union. The only alternative is force and terror; but force and terror, as the Revolution also showed, are self-defeating in the long run.

As a result of the Revolution, Russia can never again feel easy in her relations with her satellites, she can no longer count on them as military assets, and Hungary at least will be an economic liability to the entire bloc for some time to come. But coupled with the Yugoslav defection, the Gomulka Declaration of Independence, and the emergence of an Asian rival for world Communist leadership, it is imperative, if only for prestige purposes, that Hungary be maintained a Soviet satrapy.

A return to Stalinist methods can best ensure continued Communist control in Hungary, even though Stalinism is historically outmoded. It would appear that the future Communist policy indicated for Hungary, based on the first six months following the Revolution, is to consist of a judicious mixture of force and concessions, with the emphasis on force. But as the Revolution finally showed, concessions made to a people united against an imposed and hated regime lead to more demands, while ruthless terror eventually leads to a rebellion of desperation. China, a country which has recently provided some new slogans for Communist ideologues, has an ancient proverb applicable to the Communist dilemma in Hungary. "Who rides the tiger cannot dismount."

Appendix

BIOGRAPHICAL SKETCHES
of Leading Figures of the Communist Regime
as of August 1956

ACS, LAJOS: Member of the Party Secretariat, member of the Central Committee of the Party, member of the Politburo, member of Parliament.

Born: About 1915, Hungary.

Career: Nothing is known of his prewar activities. After the war, he was associated with the personal secretariat of Rakosi. He then went to Moscow to train at the Upper Party School of the Soviet Communist Party. In 1950, he returned to Hungary and in February 1951 the Party Congress appointed him alternate member of the Central Committee of the Hungarian Workers' (Communist) Party. On May 17, 1953, he became a member of Parliament, and on June 27, 1953, in the course of the reorganization of the Party, he became a member of the Secretariat and of the Politburo. At the same time, he was appointed member of the Central Committee.

APRO, ANTAL: Deputy Prime Minister, member of the Central Committee of the Party, member of the Politburo, member of Parliament.

Born: 1910, Hungary; the son of a worker.

Career: Prior to World War II, he was a member of the Building Workers' Union and of the underground Communist Party. He was sent to the Soviet Union in 1942 in a penal battalion, from which he escaped. In 1943-44, he was active in the Moscow cadre school. He was sent back to Hungary in the spring of 1944 to maintain liaison with organized labor on behalf of the Communist Party.

In 1945 he became a member of the Politburo and the Central Committee, and in 1948 of the Organization Committee of the Communist Party. From August 1948 to January 1952, he was Chairman of the National Council of Trade Unions, from January 6, 1952 to July 1953, Minister of Building Industry, and from November 25, 1953, Deputy Prime Minister without Portfolio.

An organizer rather than a theoretician, Apro has a dynamic personality and is a good speaker. After Rakosi and Gero, he is the oldest member of the Politburo. He has always been a faithful follower of the Moscow line.

BATA, ISTVAN: Minister of Defense, member of the Central Committee of the Party, alternate member of the Politburo, member of Parliament.

Born: 1910, Hungary; of a working-class family.

Career: A streetcar conductor in Budapest, Bata joined the outlawed Communist Party in 1930. After World War II, he became Party Secretary in the Budapest third district. He went to Moscow for special military training and returned to Hungary in 1949 and became a member of Parliament and a member of the General Staff. He was appointed as Chief of the General Staff in October 1950 and held this position until July 4, 1953, when he was appointed Minister of Defense.

He was an alternate member of the Central Committee of the Party from March 1951 to June 27, 1953, when he was elected a full member and an alternate member of the Politburo.

BEBRITS, LAJOS: Minister of Transportation and Postal Affairs.

Born: 1891, Hungary; of a middle-class family.

Career: After his graduation from high school, Bebrits joined the Hungarian State Railway service, being employed as a clerk at the Temesvar (Timisoara) station. He became a member of the Social Democratic Party and participated in the 1919 Commune, although he did not become a Communist. Temesvar became part of Romania under the Trianon Peace Treaty. Bebrits organized a strike of the railroad employees, was found guilty by the Romanian authorities and was forced to emigrate. He visited practically every Western European country and was banished from each in quick succession because of his revolutionary activities. He came to the United States, met with the same fate, and was finally offered political asylum by the Soviet Union. He settled in Moscow where he spent a long time, attending first the Upper Party School, then a course for railroad engineers and contributed to *Dolgozok Lapja* (The Workers' Paper), a periodical published in Moscow and smuggled into Hungary. Sent back to Hungary after the war, he became president of the Hungarian State Railways. He was later, on November 15, 1945, appointed Deputy Minister of Transportation under Erno Gero and finally on February 18, 1949, Minister of Transportation and Postal Service.

DOBI, ISTVAN: Chairman of the Presidium.

Born: 1892, Per, Hungary; of a peasant family.

Career: Dobi who was obliged to work on the farm from early child-hood never had an opportunity to receive formal education. His aspira-tions for social equality were fostered by members of the local branch of the Social Democratic Party in neighboring Komarom (Komarno). He soon became a member of that party, partaking in various oppositional activities of the organization. However, in the 1930's he was alienated from the Social Democrats by what he considered their exclusive devo-tion to the cause of the workers as opposed to that of the peasantry and joined the then recently reorganized Independent Smallholders' Party. He campaigned for the Smallholders in the general elections of 1935. During the war, he served in the Army as a guard in a labor brigade for anti-Nazi elements where he was known for his humaneness. In 1945, he was nominated by the Smallholders' Party as candidate for deputy to the Parliament and was elected on November 4, 1945. On March 1, 1946, he became Minister of Agriculture in Ferenc Nagy's Cabinet. He served as Minister until November 20, 1946, then again from April 17, 1948 to December 8, 1948. Twice he was Minister without Portfolio: from November 15, 1945 to March 1, 1946 and from May 30, 1947 to Septem-ber 24, 1947. At the end of 1947, he was made president of the Small-holders' Party and editor in chief of its official organ, *Kis Ujsag* (Little Gazette). On December 9, 1948, he was appointed Prime Minister and finally on August 14, 1952, Chairman of the Presidium.

Dobi's Communist sympathies reinforced by his visits to the Soviet Union, enabled him to remain in the good graces of the regime. His excessive alcoholism makes him a conveniently pliable instrument in the hands of Communist leaders.

FARKAS, MIHALY: Former member of the Central Committee of the Party, former member of Parliament.

Born: 1904, Hungary; of proletarian parents.

Career: Farkas has a grammar school education. He joined the under-ground Communist Party in the mid-twenties. He left for Czechoslovakia in 1930 where he became an organizer of the Communist youth movement. In 1932, he was Secretary of the Kassa (Kosice) branch of the Party. He fled Czechoslovakia in 1940, went to Moscow, and finally returned to Hungary in the wake of the Soviet troops in December 1944.

Between 1945 and 1951, he was Assistant Secretary-General of the Com-munist Party, renamed Hungarian Workers' Party in 1948. From 1945 to June 27, 1953, he was a member of the Politburo and member of the Central Committee, and Minister of Defense from September 9, 1948 to July 4, 1953.

During the reshuffle of the top offices of the Party on June 27, 1953, he lost all his Party and government positions, but temporarily rose to prominence again. He became in August 1953 the fourth member in the Secretariat and a member of the Politburo. On April 14, 1955, he again lost his positions and on July 21, 1956 he was expelled from the Party.

GASPAR, SANDOR: Secretary-General of the National Council of Trade Unions, alternate member of the Politburo, member of the Central Committee of the Party, member of Parliament.

Born: 1917, Hungary.

Career: Before World War II, he worked as an auto mechanic in a Budapest factory, and joined the illegal Communist Party during the war. He became an executive member of the Iron Workers' Trade Union in 1947. From 1949 to 1951, he was Deputy Secretary-General of the Iron Workers' Trade Union and from 1951 to April 30, 1955 President of the Hungarian Railroad Workers' and Boatmen's Trade Union. From March 1953 to April 30, 1955, he was secretary and an executive member of the National Council of Trade Unions, and on April 30, 1955, he became President of the National Council of Trade Unions. He has been a member of Parliament from May 1949 and a full member of the Party's Central Committee from October 1946. He became an alternate member of the Politburo on July 18, 1956.

GERO, ERNO: First Secretary of the Party, top-ranking member of the Central Committee and Politburo, member of Parliament.

Born: 1898, Tergebec, Hont County, Czechoslovakia; of a middle-class family.

Career: Gero wanted to enter the medical profession but interrupted his studies in March 1919 during the time of the proletarian dictatorship in Hungary and joined the Communist Party. After the Commune collapsed, he carried out secret missions for the Party and, in 1921 to avoid imprisonment, fled to Czechoslovakia and from there to Russia. In Moscow, he became an official of the Comintern and was assigned to its foreign policy section. In 1930, he was sent to Paris. In 1936, he was named adviser to Negrin, President of the revolutionary Spanish Republic. After the end of the Civil War in Spain, he returned to Moscow where he was given confidential assignments in the Ministry of Foreign Affairs. The termination of World War II found him working for the Soviet Ministry of Internal Affairs, and in December 1944 he returned to Hungary as an MVD colonel.

From December 1944 he has been a member of the Politburo, Secretariat, and Central Committee. From May 11, 1945 to November 15, 1945, he was Minister of Commerce; from then until February 18, 1949, Minister of Transportation. From December 9, 1948 to June 8, 1949, he was also Minister of Finance; from June 8, 1949 to November 16, 1952, Minister of State; from June 11, 1949 to November 24, 1952, President of the People's Economic Council; and from November 16, 1952 to July 4, 1953, Deputy Prime Minister. On July 4, 1953, he was appointed first Deputy Prime Minister and Minister of the Interior. In the course of the 1953 government reshuffle, he became third member of the Politburo. On July 7, 1954, he was relieved as Minister of the Interior. After the fall of Imre Nagy in April 1955, he again became the second-ranking Communist in the country after Rakosi. When Rakosi resigned on July 18, 1956, Gero succeeded him as Party First Secretary.

Gero belongs to the left-wing faction of the Party, to those following the orthodox line. He speaks Russian, English, German, Spanish, and French. He is one of the most prominent economic experts in the regime and is a good organizer. Lacking a sense of humor, Gero is an extremely severe and demanding person. Ascetic in his habits, he works from 16 to 18 hours a day.

HAZI, ARPAD: Minister of State Control, member of the Central Committee of the Party, member of Parliament.

Born: 1908, Bihar County, then Hungary.

Career: Hazi was a skilled worker and joined the outlawed Communist Party in the thirties. Although he never left Hungary, he was unknown in that country until 1945 when he abruptly came into the public spotlight on being elected a member of the Central Committee of the Party. In the same year, he became one of Rakosi's lieutenants and deputy commissioner of Pest County as well as member of Parliament. In 1949, Hazi was selected to head the State Control Center and in 1951 became a member of the Politburo. He was appointed Minister of the Interior on April 21, 1951 and reputedly organized the mass deportations of undesirable elements from the capital. On November 16, 1952, he became Deputy Prime Minister and in March 1953 he was among the delegation of four Hungarians attending Stalin's funeral.

His career suffered a severe setback in the Government and Party shake-up of June 1953. He was stripped of his post in the Politburo on June 27 and of his Deputy Prime Ministership on July 4; however, on July 25 he was again permitted to function as head of the State Control Center and after the establishment of the Ministry of State Control he became its Minister on August 27, 1955.

HEGEDUS, ANDRAS: Prime Minister, member of the Central Committee of the Party, member of the Politburo, member of Parliament.

Born: 1919, Sopronfelsoszentmiklos, Sopron County, Hungary; of a peasant family.

Career: Hegedus joined the Communist Party only in 1945. He attended Gyorffy College and after 1945 took an active part in preparing the land reform. He toured the country and urged the peasants to form land reform committees. The Party soon discovered his abilities as an organizer and a speaker and he was invited to Party headquarters. In 1948, he was sent to Moscow to study at the Upper Party School (attached to the Central Committee of the Soviet Communist Party). On returning to Hungary, he rose rapidly, on March 1, 1951 becoming a member of the Party's Central Committee and thirteenth member of the Politburo. On June 27, 1953, he was elected fifth member of the Politburo.

Late in 1949 he was appointed Deputy Minister of Agriculture. From January 6, 1952 to July 4, 1953, he was Minister of State Farms, from then First Deputy Prime Minister, and on April 18, 1955 he was appointed as Prime Minister.

Hegedus belongs to Rakosi's closest circle; he is a so-called "center" figure for Rakosi. A well-educated Communist, he speaks Russian and German, and is one of the most intelligent, though not dynamic, members of the young Communist generation. He has a good sense of humor, likes to eat and drink well.

HIDAS, ISTVAN: First Deputy Prime Minister, member of the Central Committee of the Party, member of the Politburo, member of Parliament.

Born: 1918, Budapest; son of a metallurgical worker.

Career: Hidas learned the metallurgical trade, and from his youth was active in trade union work; in 1939, he joined the Social Democratic Party. He gained influence in the underground Communist movement and in 1943 joined the Communist Party.

In 1945, he was Party Secretary in Budafok, and in 1946 was transferred to the cadre department of the Party headquarters. From the fall of 1946 to 1950, he was managing director of MAVAG (Hungarian National Iron and Machine Plant). In 1949, he became a member of Parliament, and from July 1950 to November 16, 1952 he was Party Secretary for Budapest. From then on his career soared to great heights, and he became one of the most trusted associates of Rakosi. Hidas made several trips to Moscow and was also a member of the Hungarian Delegation to the Nineteenth Soviet Party Congress. In 1951, he became member of the Organizing Committee and alternate member of the Politburo. On November 16, 1952, he was appointed Deputy Prime Minister and on June 27, 1953 a member of the Politburo. On July 4, 1953, he was appointed Minister of Heavy Industry. On November 1, 1954, he was again appointed Deputy Prime Minister without Portfolio, and became First Deputy Prime Minister on July 30, 1956.

Hidas belongs to the new Communist generation. He is a talented organizer, a good speaker, an intelligent person. His theoretical knowledge does not measure up to that of those belonging to the front line. Although Hidas likes to drink, he is a reticent person.

KADAR, JANOS: Member of the Party Secretariat, member of the Central Committee of the Party, member of the Politburo.

Born: 1912, Kapoly, Hungary; of proletarian background.

Career: A construction worker in his early youth, Kadar received very little education. In 1928, he joined the Construction Workers' Union. He became secretary-general of the illegal Communist youth movement in 1932. Subsequently, he was arrested three times, the last of these detentions occurring in 1937 when he was already a member of the underground Party's Politburo. Kadar became one of the organizers of the Hungarian resistance movement after 1941. He organized the illegal Party press and directed the distribution of Communist publications, such as *Szabad Nep* (Free People), the official Party organ, founded in 1943. After the occupation of Budapest by the Red Army in January 1945, he was named Deputy Chief of Police for Budapest. He was elected in the same year to the Politburo, to the Central Committee of the Party, and as Deputy Secretary-General of the Party. From the fall of 1945, he has been head of the Department of Organization of the Party. He became Minister of the Interior on August 3, 1948 and held this post until June 24, 1950.

In May 1951, he was purged, but his case has never been tried; he lost all his positions. In spring 1954 he was released from prison and became Party Secretary of the thirteenth district of Budapest. On July 18, 1956, he was re-elected to the Politburo.

KISS, KAROLY: Chairman of the Control Commission, member of the Central Committee of the Party, member of the Politburo, member of Parliament.

Born: 1903, Hungary.

Career: He attended only four years of grammar school and at the age of nineteen joined the illegal Communist Party. In 1932, he used the Social Democratic Party as a cover for his activities. He worked in the Leather Workers' Union but was expelled in 1936 as a Communist agitator. Sent to the Russian front in 1942 with a battalion composed of undesirable elements, he deserted and was dispatched by the Red Army to Moscow.

In the spring of 1944, he returned to his native land, which was under German occupation, and assumed leadership of the Communist Party and forwarded secret reports to Moscow until the end of hostilities. He has been a member of Parliament since 1945, and also head of the Party Cadre Division. He was elected in 1951 to the Organization Committee, to the Politburo, and to the Central Committee. In the same year, he became Chairman of the Control Commission.

He served as Foreign Minister from May 13, 1951 to November 16, 1952, when he was named Deputy Prime Minister. On June 27, 1953, he was relieved of his posts as Deputy Prime Minister and as member of the Politburo.

On July 18, 1956, he was re-elected to the Politburo.

KOSSA, ISTVAN: First Deputy Chairman of the National Planning Bureau, alternate member of the Central Committee of the Party, member of Parliament.

Born: 1904, Balatonlelle, Hungary.

Career: He finished grammar school and arrived in Budapest at eighteen where he joined the Social Democratic Party. In 1933, he became secretary of the Streetcar Employees' Union and later a member of the Trade Union Council. In 1940, he joined the underground Communist Party. In 1941, the right-wing Hungarian government sent him with a forced labor battalion to the Ukraine where he deserted. In 1943, he emerged in Moscow as head of the Hungarian section in the Provincial Political Academy of the Communist Party. In the fall of 1944, he was parachuted into Hungary where he helped organize the Communist Party until the German forces surrendered.

He was a member of the Central Committee from May 1945 to March 1951 and then alternate member. He was also a member of the Politburo from October 1946 to March 1951.

At the end of World War II, he became Secretary-General of the National Council of Trade Unions. He has been a deputy in Parliament since November 4, 1945 and served as Vice Chairman of the House from November 15, 1945 to August 1947.

Kossa lost his position as Secretary-General of the National Council of Trade Unions on August 3, 1948 and became Minister of Industry but resigned on June 8, 1949. Between that date and February 25, 1950, he served as Minister of Finance. From February 25, 1950 to May 1951, he was President of the National Wage Committee, from that time to January 6, 1952 he was President of the State Office for Church Affairs. From January 6, 1952 to December 23, 1952, he was Minister of Smelting and Machine Industry. During the functioning of the Ministry of General Machine Industry from December 23, 1952 to July 4, 1953, Kossa headed this Ministry. On July 4, 1953, he lost his Cabinet rank and became First Deputy Minister of Smelting and Machine Industry. In spring 1954, he was appointed President of the Office of Labor Reserves, and in the summer of 1955 he became First Deputy Chairman of the National Planning Bureau.

KOVACS, ISTVAN: Member of the Party Secretariat, member of the Central Committee, member of the Politburo, Party Secretary for Budapest, member of Parliament.

Born: 1911, Budapest; of a middle-class family.

Career: Kovacs was very young when he joined, as an employee, the underground Communist Party. In 1931, he was arrested for illegal Communist activities and sentenced by the Budapest Military Court to 11 years of imprisonment. He completed his term in 1942 but due to the war, instead of being released, was sent to a concentration camp from which he was freed in 1945.

In 1945, he became a leading member of the Communist Party, working in the organization section, and from 1947 to 1950 Party Secretary for Budapest. In 1948 he was elected member of the Central Committee and the Organizing Committee of the Party. In 1949 he became secretary of the Central Committee. On May 13, 1951, he was appointed Deputy Chairman of the Presidium. In 1952, he was appointed Party Secretary for Borsod County and in June 1953 again as Budapest Party Secretary. Since April 18, 1955, Kovacs has been a member of the Politburo and since November 12, 1955 a member of the Party Secretariat. He has no government position.

Kovacs is an extremely cultured Communist with a theoretical background, of Rakosi's circle; a very good organizer, talented speaker and writer, he is useful in every post. He has a good sense of humor, likes to eat and drink well, and has a tremendous capacity for work.

KRISTOFF, ISTVAN: President of the Revision Committee of the Party, Secretary of the Presidium of the People's Republic, member of Parliament.

Born: 1910, Hungary; of proletarian stock.

Career: Kristoff joined the youth organization of the trade union movement before World War II. During the war, he drifted toward the Communists whose youth organization he joined, but his name was not connected with any significant activity. After the war, he worked for Istvan Kossa, Secretary-General of the National Council of Trade Unions. He was subsequently sent to Russia and graduated from the Upper Party School in Moscow. In 1949, he was selected as head of the Organizational Department of the Party Headquarters, and at the same time was a member of the Party Organizational Committee. In 1951, he was elected to the Politburo and to the Central Committee of the Party. In January 1952, he was named Secretary-General and in February 1952, chairman, of the National Council of Trade Unions. In May 1953, he was elected a member of Parliament.

He was relieved of his membership in the Politburo and Central Committee by the Third Congress of the Party on May 30, 1954. He was elected at the same time President of the Revision Committee of the Party. He was relieved of his post as Chairman of the National Council of Trade Unions on June 26, 1954. He became Secretary of the Presidium of the People's Republic on February 8, 1956.

MAROSAN, GYORGY: Deputy Prime Minister, member of the Central Committee of the Party, member of the Politburo.

Born: 1908, Hungary.

Career: As a young man he joined the Social Democratic Party. Before World War II, he was President of the Bakers' Trade Union. After the war, he became Deputy First Secretary of the Social Democratic Party. He was a member of Parliament from 1945 to 1950. Among the first to betray the Social Democratic Party he was instrumental in its forced merger with the Communist Party in 1948. As a reward he was made Deputy First Secretary of the "united" Party and served as Minister of Light Industry from June 8, 1949 to August 5, 1950. In 1950, he was arrested and released in the spring of 1956. The Party rehabilitated Marosan on July 18, 1956 by appointing him a member of the Politburo and the Central Committee. He became Deputy Prime Minister on July 30, 1956.

MEKIS, JOZSEF: Deputy Prime Minister, member of the Central Committee of the Party, member of the Politburo, member of Parliament.

Career: He joined the outlawed Communist Party during World War II. After the war, he became Director of the Salgotarjan Steel Plant, from 1947 to 1948. In October 1948, he became Secretary-General of the Iron Workers' Trade Union and he served until June 1954. He was Vice Chairman of the National Council of Trade Unions from 1949 to June 25, 1954 and then President of that organization from June 26, 1954 to April 30, 1955.

Mekis has been a member of Parliament from May 1949. He was Vice Chairman of Parliament from July 4, 1953 to April 18, 1955, when he was elected Deputy Prime Minister.

He was an alternate member of the Control Commission of the Party from October 1946 to June 1948. He became a member of the Central Committee in June 1948 and alternate member of the Politburo on May 30, 1954, and a full member on April 18, 1955.

MOLNAR, ERIK: Minister of Justice, member of the Central Committee of the Party, member of Parliament.

Born: 1894, Hungary.

Career: Molnar studied at universities in Vienna, Rome, and Budapest. Reportedly taken prisoner by the Russians during World War I, when he returned to Hungary he joined the Social Democratic Party. He was arrested several times during World War II by the Hungarian police, and joined the outlawed Communist Party in 1944.

After the war, he became Minister of Public Health from December 23, 1944 to September 24, 1947. From September 24, 1947 to June 30, 1948, he was Minister of Foreign Affairs, and from October 1948 to September 1949, ambassador to Moscow. On June 14, 1950, Molnar was appointed Minister of Justice, serving until November 16, 1952, when he again was Minister of Foreign Affairs, until July 4, 1953. In July 1953, he was appointed President of the Supreme Court, and on November 1, 1954, Molnar was again shifted to the position of Minister of Justice. He has been a member of the Central Committee from June 1948.

NAGY, IMRE: Former Prime Minister and second-ranking member of the Politburo.

Born: 1896, Hungary.

Career: Born of a family of devout Calvinists, he graduated from high school, was drafted into the Austro-Hungarian Army and sent to the Russian front in World War I. Taken prisoner, he joined the Revolution and became a member of the Bolshevik Party. Nagy returned to Hungary a few years after the termination of hostilities but had to flee in 1929 to avoid arrest. Back in Moscow, he was employed by the Agrarian Institute for which he worked throughout World War II. In December 1944, he reappeared in Hungary to become one of the pillars of the Hungarian Communist Party. In the renamed (Hungarian Workers') Party, he retained his previous membership in the Politburo and Central Committee and in 1951, was named a member of the Secretariat of the Party.

He has held the following Cabinet posts since 1944: Minister of Agriculture from December 23, 1944 to November 15, 1945; Minister of the Interior from November 15, 1945 to March 23, 1946; Minister of Crop Collection from May 8, 1950 to November 16, 1952; Deputy Prime Minister from November 16, 1952 to July 4, 1953; Prime Minister from July 4, 1953 to April 18, 1955 in the so-called "new course."

Nagy was a member of Parliament from 1945 to 1955, having served as Chairman of Parliament from September 15, 1947 to August 23, 1949. In the Party shake-up of June 27, 1953, he became the second-ranking member of the Politburo. On April 14, 1955, he lost all his positions in the Party, from which he was expelled, on April 18, in the Government.

PETER, GABOR: Former head of the Hungarian State Defense Authority, former member of the Central Committee of the Party.

Born: 1906, Hungary.

Career: A tailor's assistant, he rallied to the Communist cause in the early thirties and later functioned as secret courier, traveling between Budapest and Moscow. In the meantime, he was repeatedly convicted as a Communist. In Moscow, he came into personal contact with Stalin. From 1943, he was among the organizers of the resistance movement of the Party, especially in Budapest, closely cooperating with Laszlo Rajk. In January 1945, since part of the capital was already under Soviet control, Peter founded the Political Police in Budapest. Starting in late 1945, he shared in the leadership of the Hungarian Communist Party and in the following years, as head of the State Defense Authority, he handled the practical aspects of eliminating the oppositional elements and the "right-wing" Communists. In 1948, he was named member of the Central Committee.

Peter was arrested by the State Defense Authority in January 1953 along with a group of police officers, and convicted of machinations aimed at the overthrow of the government and harming the public good; he was sentenced to life imprisonment on March 13, 1954.

PIROS, LASZLO: Minister of the Interior, member of the Central Committee of the Party, alternate member of the Politburo, member of Parliament.

Born: 1917, Hungary.

Career: A cobbler by trade, Piros joined the outlawed Communist Party while still a teenager. He was first imprisoned as a Communist and then, in 1942, sent to Russia with a labor brigade. He later deserted to the Soviet forces, worked with Istvan Kossa in Moscow and fought as a partisan behind the German lines in 1944. In the fall of 1944, he was parachuted into Hungary where he helped organize the resistance movement and participated in it until the occupation of the country by the Red Army. He was named Assistant Secretary-General of the National Council of Trade Unions in 1945 in which capacity he again closely cooperated with Kossa. In September 1948, Piros gave up his office with the National Council of Trade Unions to head the Frontier Guards. In 1950, he was appointed Deputy Chief of the State Defense Authority which he was designated to head after the purge of Gabor Peter in January 1953. On July 4, 1953, he was appointed Deputy Minister of the Interior, and on July 7, Minister, technically giving up his position as Chief of the State Defense Authority but in fact retaining it, since that organization was simultaneously brought under the jurisdiction of the Ministry of the Interior.

Piros was an alternate member of the Central Committee from June 1948 to March 1951, then member. After being an alternate member of the Politburo from June 1950, he was named a regular member in March 1953 but again lost his membership on June 27 of the same year. He became an alternate member again on April 18, 1955.

RAJK, LASZLO: Former Minister of the Interior, former member of Politburo.

Born: 1909, Udvarhely, Hungary; son of an artisan.

Career: Rajk joined the Communist youth movement and was arrested for organizing a Communist student group in 1930. After his release, he worked as a bricklayer, organizing the construction workers' strike of 1935. He fought in the Spanish Civil War in 1937 as Party Secretary of the Matyas Rakosi Battalion. Escaping from Spain after the defeat of the Republican forces, he was interned in France. Returning to Hungary in 1941, he was again interned and later convicted and imprisoned. Released in summer 1944, he became Secretary of the Central Committee of the illegal Communist Party. Arrested as the Hungarian Nazi regime came to power, he was taken to Sopronkohida and later to a concentration camp in Germany. In May 1945, Rajk returned to Hungary, becoming a member of the Politburo and the Central Committee; he was also elected member of Parliament. He was appointed Minister of the Interior on March 23, 1946 but had to resign on August 3, 1948, becoming Foreign Minister. On June 8, 1949, he was arrested, convicted of treason—especially for his Titoist activities—by the Budapest People's Court, and executed in October 1949. In March 1956, following the Twentieth Soviet Party Congress he was publicly "rehabilitated" by the Party.

Laszlo Rajk, the second-ranking Communist as Minister of the Interior acted with the vilest brutality in crushing efforts to achieve democracy, in jailing democratically minded politicians, in trampling upon the Hungarian Constitution and the right to free elections.

RAKOSI, MATYAS: Former First Secretary of the Party, former member of the Central Committee and Politburo, member of Parliament (resigned July 18, 1956).

Born: March 9, 1892, Ada, Bacs-Bodrog County, Hungary; of a middle-class family.

Career: After graduating from high school in 1910, Rakosi enrolled in the Commercial Academy in Budapest. In 1910, he became member of the Social Democratic Party, and in 1911-12 acted as secretary of the Galilei Circle, a society of radical youth. Sent to Hamburg and London on a scholarship, he became closely acquainted with Marxism. At the beginning of World War I, he was drafted into the Austro-Hungarian Army, sent to the Eastern front, and was soon captured by the Russians. Brought to Chita and then to Petrograd as a prisoner, he made the acquaintance of Lenin, who sent him to Moscow to the Central Office of the Communist Party, and there Rakosi became a specialist in organizing underground cells. When he returned to Hungary after the war, he was not only a confidant of Lenin but a well-trained agent of the Party.

On November 20, 1918, he was, together with Bela Kun, one of the founders of the Hungarian Communist Party. On March 21, 1919, at the outbreak of the first Communist revolution in Hungary, Rakosi was Deputy People's Commissar for Commerce and Transportation and from April 3, 1919 he became People's Commissar for Production. After the fall of the Commune on August 1, 1919, he fled to Austria with Bela Kun and was arrested by the Austrian police. In 1920, he was banished from that country by the Austrian authorities. Traveling to Russia, he participated in the Second Congress of the Comintern as a delegate from Hungary. Between 1920 and 1924, he functioned as Secretary of the Comintern and in this capacity toured European countries. In December 1924, Rakosi was ordered to return to Hungary to reorganize the outlawed Party there. Hungarian police arrested him and his clique on September 22, 1925. First he was tried by a Summary Court on November 14-16, 1925, then from July 12 to August 5, 1926 by a civil court and was sentenced to eight and a half years' imprisonment. Close to the completion of this term, he was again tried from January 14 to February 8, 1935 by a civil court and in second instance by a Supreme Court from June 27 to July 1, 1935 and sentenced to life imprisonment, for crimes committed during the 1919 Communist revolution.

Several times the Soviet Union intervened unsuccessfully in his behalf. Finally on October 30, 1940, at the time of the short-lived Russo-Hungarian *rapprochement*, Matyas Rakosi and Zoltan Vas were surrendered to the Soviet Union in exchange for Hungarian flags captured by the Russian Army during the 1848 War of Independence and which were still held in Moscow. From November 6, 1940, Rakosi lived in Moscow, where he took out Soviet citizenship papers, married a Russian woman, and worked for the People's Commissariat for Foreign Affairs. He became Stalin's confidant, reporting directly on the activities of the illegal Hungarian Communist Party to the Soviet dictator. He worked in the Hungarian Section of the Commissariat for Foreign Affairs.

In December 1944, he returned to Hungary in the wake of the Russian troops, and he was chosen Secretary-General of the Hungarian Communist Party. From November 15, 1945 to August 14, 1952, he was Deputy Prime Minister and from then until July 4, 1953, Prime Minister. As a result of the new policy of "collective leadership" on June 27, 1953, the Communists abolished the position of Secretary-General of the Party. Rakosi then became First Secretary of the Party. After the July 4, 1953 government reshuffle, Rakosi was not given a position in the Government. However, he remained top-ranking Communist in Hungary until July 18, 1956 when he was replaced by Erno Gero.

Rakosi is an excellent organizer, an outstanding orator, and a skilled writer. He is one of the most prominent theoreticians and speaks German, English, French, Italian, Turkish, and Russian. Although vain he has a keen sense of humor and is a pleasant conversationalist.

REVAI, JOZSEF: Deputy Chairman of the Presidium, member of the Central Committee of the Party, member of the Politburo, member of Parliament.

Born: 1898, Hungary; of a middle-class family.

Career: A high school graduate, Revai early became a leading columnist of the Communist press, Bela Kun's personal secretary, and an editor of *Voros Ujsag* (Red Paper) during the 1919 revolution. After the fall of the Commune, he fled to Vienna. During the following years, he worked in Austria, Germany, and Czechoslovakia and periodically even visited Hungary clandestinely. In 1930, while on one of these trips, he was arrested by the Hungarian police and convicted of illegal Communist activities. Released in the thirties, he escaped to Russia, went to Moscow and became an official in the Hungarian section of the People's Commissariat for Foreign Affairs. In this capacity, he supervised the Hungarian-language broadcasts of Radio Moscow.

He returned to Hungary in December 1944 in the wake of the Soviet armed forces. He was immediately appointed a member of the Politburo and Central Committee. From February 1945 to 1951, he was editor in chief of *Szabad Nep* (Free People), official Communist daily newspaper. From June 8, 1949 to July 4, 1953, he functioned as Minister of People's Culture. Until late in 1952, he was the third-ranking member of the Politburo, and from then the sixth. In June 27, 1953, he was stripped of his membership in the Politburo and became Deputy Chairman of the Presidium. One of the chief Communist ideologists, a member of the board of editors of *Tarsadalmi Szemle* (Social Review), on July 18, 1956 he was re-elected to the Politburo.

RONAI, SANDOR: Chairman of Parliament, member of the Central Committee of the Party, alternate member of the Politburo.

Born: 1892, Hungary.

Career: Ronai finished grammar school. He joined the Social Democratic Party in 1918, and became a member of the Workers' Council during the first Commune. He served as Social Democratic Party secretary in Miskolc between the two world wars. Frequently arrested and interned during World War II, he became a prominent Social Democrat after the war, winning a seat in Parliament. He became a member of the Executive Committee of the Social Democratic Party. He helped to throw his party into the hands of the Communists and was rewarded by being elected a member of the Politburo and Central Committee of the newly created Hungarian Workers' Party in June 1948, technically a result of the merger of the Social Democratic and Communist parties. In March 1951, he was also elected a member of the Committee of Organization of the Party. On June 27, 1953, Ronai lost his position in the Politburo,

Committee of Organization, but he is still a member of the Central Committee. He became an alternate member of the Politburo on July 18, 1956.

From July 25, 1945 to November 15, 1945, he served as Minister of Food; from November 15, 1945 to June 8, 1949, as Minister of Commerce; from June 8, 1949 to May 8, 1950, as Minister of Foreign Trade; from May 8, 1950 to August 14, 1952, as Chairman of the Presidium. Since August 14, 1952, he has been Chairman of Parliament.

SZAKASITS, ARPAD: Former President of the Hungarian People's Republic, former President of the Party.

Born: 1888, Hungary; of an artisan class.

Career: Szakasits started as a stonecutter, joined the trade union movement of which he became a prominent member. In 1918, he became a staff member and in 1939, editor in chief of *Nepszava* (People's Voice), Social Democratic daily. He emerged as one of the leaders of the Social Democratic Party before World War II. In 1944, when the party was forced to go underground, he became its head. In October of that year, he signed a pact with the Communists, establishing cooperation between the two parties. He headed the Social Democratic Party from 1945 to 1948 as Secretary-General, was President of the Budapest City Council and of the Provisional National Council in 1945. He also served as Deputy Prime Minister from November 15, 1945 to July 30, 1948. In June 1948, he was elected President of the Hungarian Workers' (Communist) Party, the result of the merger of the Social Democratic and Communist parties. He rose to the Presidency of the Republic on August 23, 1948, then to the President of the People's Republic from August 20, 1949 to April 26, 1950, when he was arrested. Reportedly released and rehabilitated in the summer of 1956.

SZALAI, BELA: Member of the Secretariat, member of the Central Committee of the Party, member of the Politburo, member of Parliament.

Born: 1922, Hungary.

Career: Szalai joined the outlawed Communist Party during World War II, organizing student resistance. After the war, he became President of the Hungarian High School and University Students' Association (MEFESZ). From 1948 to 1949, he was President of the National Association of People's Colleges (NEKOSZ) and at the same time Vice President of the People's Federation of Hungarian Youth (MINSZ). Between 1951 and June 1953, he was Director of the Teachers College.

His career rose rapidly after June 27, 1953 when he became an alternate member of the Politburo and a full member of Central Committee of the Party. On May 30, 1954, he became a full member of the Politburo and on September 4, 1955 a member of the Party Secretariat. He has been a member of Parliament since May 1948. He was President of the National Planning Office from July 4, 1953 to November 1, 1954 and from then to September 5, 1955, Minister of Light Industry. Now he has no government position.

VAS, ZOLTAN: President of Farmers' Cooperative Association, member of the Central Committee of the Party, member of Parliament.

Born: 1900, Budapest; of a lower middle-class family.

Career: Vas joined the Communist Party while still a youth and actively participated in the 1919 Commune and was briefly arrested in 1919. Forced to flee to Austria, he took part in Communist activities in Czechoslovakia, Germany, and Austria between 1919 and 1921, and in 1921 he went to Moscow. Commissioned to build up the outlawed Communist Party in Hungary, he was sent back to Budapest with Matyas Rakosi in December 1924, and was arrested by the police on September 22, 1925. Sentenced to life imprisonment Vas along with Rakosi was handed over to the Soviet authorities on October 30, 1940 in exchange for national relics of the 1848 Hungarian War of Independence. He was subsequently given the rank of colonel in the Red Army. It was his job to select among Hungarian prisoners of war those to be sent to Communist seminars. In the fall of 1944, Vas returned to Hungary, where he helped to organize the National Front of Independence in Szeged.

Appointed Commissioner of Public Supplies for Budapest early in 1945, he was instrumental in alleviating the agonizing food shortage in the capital. He was mayor of Budapest from spring to November 1945. From then to June 1949, he became Secretary-General of the Supreme Economic Council. On June 11, 1949, he was appointed Chairman of the National Planning Bureau. He served there until January 1953 when he became Director of the Komlo coal mines. In the summer of 1953, he became Secretary of the Council of Ministers. On January 24, 1954, he lost his post and became President of the Farmers' Cooperative Association.

Vas has been a member of the Central Committee from 1945. He was elected an alternate member of the Politburo in June 1948 and a full member in March 1951, which membership he lost on June 27, 1953.

VEG, BELA: Member of the Secretariat, member of the Central Committee of the Party, member of Parliament.

Born: Approximately 39 years old, Hungary.

Career: Before and during World War II, Veg was an iron worker in Budapest. He did not participate in public life. After the war, he joined the Communist Party and was shortly given an assignment at Party headquarters. First, he worked in the cadre division, then was sent to Moscow where he graduated at the Upper Party School of the Soviet

Communist Party. After his return to Hungary, Veg was again assigned to the cadre division of the Party. On May 17, 1953, he became a member of Parliament. After the reorganization of the Party on June 27, 1953, he was elected member of the Secretariat and also became a member of the Central Committee.

His career rose under Imre Nagy, but he never reached the Politburo. Although not a member of Politburo, judging from the attention paid to him in the press he appears to be in the "top leadership."

ZSOFINYECZ, MIHALY: Director of the Rakosi Works, member of the Central Committee of the Party, member of Parliament.

Born: 1906, Hungary; of a proletarian family.

Career: Zsofinyecz worked in the Hofherr and Schrantz Machine Works between the two world wars. Becoming a member of the Social Democratic Party in 1923, he was elected spokesman for his co-workers. He joined the outlawed Communist Party in 1944 and became chairman of the Hofherr and Schrantz workers' committee following the Soviet occupation. In 1947, he was appointed director of the nationalized Hofherr and Schrantz Works. His career rose to greater heights on June 8, 1949 when he became Minister of Heavy Industry. From December 16, 1950 to January 6, 1952, he was Minister of Smelting Machine Industry and again from July 4, 1953 to October 10, 1954. From January 6, 1952 to July 4, 1953, he was Minister of Semi-Heavy Industry and also Minister of Smelting Industry from December 23, 1952 to July 4, 1953. On October 10, 1954, Zsofinyecz became Director of the Rakosi Works and lost all his ministerial positions.

He became a member of Parliament in May 1949. In June 1950, he became an alternate member of the Politburo and member of the Central Committee and in March 1951, a member of Politburo. He lost his Politburo membership on May 30, 1954.

PARTY AND GOVERNMENT LEADERS
AS OF AUGUST 1956

I. PARTY LEADERS

Political Committee (Politburo)

Full Members:

Erno Gero	Istvan Kovacs
Lajos Acs	Jozsef Mekis
Istvan Hidas	Gyorgy Marosan
Antal Apro	Janos Kadar
Andras Hegedus	Jozsef Revai
Bela Szalai	Karoly Kiss

Alternate Members: Istvan Bata
Laszlo Piros
Sandor Ronai
Sandor Gaspar

Secretariat

First Secretary: Erno Gero

Secretaries:

Lajos Acs	Istvan Kovacs
Bela Veg	Gyula Egri
Bela Szalai	Janos Kadar

Central Party Control Commission

Chairman: Karoly Kiss

Central Revision Committee

Chairman: Istvan Kristoff

Principal County Party Committee First Secretaries

County	Official
1. Bacs-Kiskun	Jozsef Nemeti
2. Baranya	Mihaly Gabri
3. Bekes	Jozsef Biro
4. Borsod-Abauj-Zemplen	Rudolf Foldvari
5. Csongrad	Karoly Nemeth
6. Fejer	Imre Sebes
7. Gyor-Sopron	Janos Hortobagyi
8. Hajdu-Bihar	Gyula Barczi
9. Heves	Mihaly Komocsi
10. Komarom	Kalman Nagy
11. Nograd	Jozsef Hajdu
12. Pest	Janos Kukucska
13. Somogy	Istvan Toth
14. Szabolcs-Szatmar	Sandor Varga
15. Szolnok	Ferenc David
16. Tolna	Laszlo Kiraly
17. Vas	Rudolf Kovacs
18. Veszprem	Imre Pardi
19. Zala	Istvan Denes

Members of the Central Committee

Erno Acs, Lajos Acs, Erzsebet Andics, Janos Antal, Antal Apro, Laszlo Badari, Istvan Bata, Valeria Benke, Andor Berei, Zoltan Biro, Janos Boldoczky, Gergely Boros, Janos Csergo, Sandor Czottner, Ferenc David, Imre Dogei, Tibor Erdey-Gruz, Gyula Egri, Laszlo Farkas, Laszlo Foldes, Rudolf Foldvari, Istvan Friss, Erno Gallo, Sandor Gaspar, Erno Gero, Jozsef Harustyak, Jeno Hazai, Arpad Hazi, Ede Hebelt, Andras Hegedus, Ferenc Herczeg, Istvan Hidas, Imre Horvath, Marton Horvath, Mrs. Imre Juhasz, Janos Kadar, Gyula Kallai, Arpad Kiss, Karoly Kiss, Istvan Kovacs, Jozsef Kobol, Gyorgy Marosan, Janos Matolcsi, Tivadar Matusek, Jozsef Mekis, Imre Mezo, Erik Molnar, Erno Molnar, Imre Molnar, Mrs. Jozsef

Nagy, Kalman Nagy, Maria Nagy, Sandor Nogradi,
Gyorgy Non, Rezso Nyers, Karoly Olt, Laszlo
Piros, Kalman Pongracz, Matyas Rakosi, Anna
Ratko, Jozsef Revai, Sandor Ronai, Jozsef Suhajda,
Istvan Schumeth, Ferenc Szabo, Istvan Szabo,
Janos Szabo, Jozsef Szakali, Bela Szalai, Zoltan
Szanto, Andras Szobek, Janos Tausz, Zoltan Vas,
Mrs. Istvan Vass, Tibor Vagvolgyi, Bela Vegh,
Gyula Vida, Mihaly Zsofinyecz.

II. LEADERS OF THE PARTY MASS ORGANIZATIONS

Federation of Working Youth

First Secretary: Jozsef Szakali

Trade Union

Chairman of the National Council: Sandor Gaspar

III. GOVERNMENT LEADERS

Presidium (Presidential Council) of the People's Republic

Chairman
(President):   Istvan Dobi, appointed on August 14, 1952.

His predecessors: from August 20, 1949 to April
26, 1950: Arpad Szakasits; from May 8, 1950 to
August 14, 1952: Sandor Ronai. Presidents of the
Republic from February 1, 1946 to July 30, 1948:
Zoltan Tildy; from July 30, 1948 to August 20,
1949: Arpad Szakasits.

Deputy Chairmen: Jozsef Revai
Daniel Nagy

Secretary: Istvan Kristoff

Members: Erzsebet Andics, Lajos Acs, Sandor Barcs, Sandor
Gaspar, Erno Gero, Istvan Kovacs, Janos Gosz-
tonyi, Jozsef Harustyak, Arpad Hazi, Erno Mihalyfi,
Laszlo Nanasi, Gyorgy Parragi, Matyas Rakosi,
Sandor Ronai, Istvan Rusznyak, Jozsef Seregely,
Pal Szabo.

National Assembly

Chairman
(President) of
the National
Assembly: Sandor Ronai, appointed on August 14, 1952.

His predecessors: from December 23, 1944 to November 29, 1945: Bela Zsedenyi; from November 29, 1945 to February 5, 1946: Ferenc Nagy; from February 7, 1946 to June 4, 1947: Bela Varga; from June 4, 1947 to September 15, 1947: Arpad Szabo; from September 15, 1947 to August 23, 1949: Imre Nagy; from August 23, 1949 to May 19, 1951: Lajos Drahos: from May 19, 1951 to August 14, 1952: Imre Dogei.

Deputy

Chairmen: Jozsef Nagyistok
Mrs. Istvan Vass

Council of Ministers

Chairman
(Prime
Minister): Andras Hegedus, appointed on April 18, 1955.

His predecessors: from December 23, 1944 to November 15, 1945: Bela Dalnoki-Miklos; from November 15, 1945 to February 1, 1946: Zoltan Tildy; from February 4, 1946 to May 30, 1947: Ferenc Nagy; from June 4, 1947 to December 8, 1948: Lajos Dinnyes; from December 9, 1948 to August 14, 1952: Istvan Dobi; from August 14, 1952 to July 4, 1953: Matyas Rakosi; from July 4, 1953 to April 18, 1955: Imre Nagy.

First Deputy
Chairman
(First Deputy
Prime Minister): Istvan Hidas, appointed on July 30, 1956.

His predecessors: from July 4, 1953 to July 30, 1956: Erno Gero; from July 4, 1955 to April 18, 1956: Andras Hegedus. Erno Gero acted as Minister of State from June 8, 1949 to November 16, 1952. This post, equivalent to the first deputy chairmanship, was abolished in 1952.

Deputy
Chairmen
(Deputy Prime
Ministers):   Antal Apro, appointed on November 25, 1953.
Ferenc Erdei, appointed on November 15, 1955.
Jozsef Mekis, appointed on April 18, 1955.
Gyorgy Marosan, appointed on July 30, 1956.

Their predecessors: from November 15, 1945 to
August 14, 1952: Matyas Rakosi; from November
15, 1945 to July 30, 1948: Arpad Szakasits; from
November 15, 1945 to March 1, 1946, then from
May 30, 1947 to September 24, 1947: Istvan Dobi;
from March 1, 1946 to May 30, 1947: Istvan
Szabo; from November 16, 1952 to July 4, 1953:
Erno Gero, Arpad Hazi, Karoly Kiss, and Imre
Nagy. Istvan Hidas from November 16, 1952 to
July 4, 1953 and from November 1, 1954 to July
30, 1956.

Minister of
Foreign Affairs: Imre Horvath, appointed on July 30, 1956.

His predecessors: from December 23, 1944 to May
30, 1947: Janos Gyongyosi; from May 30, 1947
to September 24, 1947: Erno Mihalyfi; from September 27, 1947 to June 30, 1948: Erik Molnar;
from August 3, 1948 to June 8, 1949: Laszlo Rajk;
from June 8, 1949 to May 13, 1951: Gyula Kallai;
from May 13, 1951 to November 16, 1952: Karoly
Kiss; from November 16, 1952 to July 4, 1953:
Erik Molnar; from July 4, 1953 to July 30, 1956:
Janos Boldoczky.

Minister of
the Interior: Laszlo Piros, appointed on July 7, 1954.

His predecessors: from December 23, 1944 to No-
vember 15, 1945: Ferenc Erdei; from November
15, 1945 to March 23, 1946: Imre Nagy; from
March 23, 1946 to August 3, 1948: Laszlo Rajk;
from August 3, 1948 to June 24, 1950: Janos
Kadar; from June 24, 1950 to April 21, 1951:
Sandor Zold; from April 21, 1951 to November 16,
1952: Arpad Hazi; from November 16, 1952 to
July 4, 1953: Jozsef Gyore; from July 4, 1953 to
July 7, 1954: Erno Gero.

Minister of
Defense:

Istvan Bata, appointed on July 4, 1953.

His predecessors: from December 23, 1944 to November 15, 1945: Janos Voros; from November 15, 1945 to August 20, 1946: Jeno Tombor; from August 20, 1946 to March 14, 1947: Albert Bartha; from March 14, 1947 to September 24, 1947: Lajos Dinnyes; from September 24, 1947 to September 9, 1948: Peter Veres; from September 9, 1948 to July 4, 1953: Mihaly Farkas.

Minister of
Justice:

Erik Molnar, appointed on November 1, 1954.

His predecessors: from December 23, 1944 to July 25, 1945: Agoston Valentiny; from July 25, 1945 to June 14, 1950: Istvan Riesz; from June 14, 1950 to November 16, 1952: Erik Molnar; from November 16, 1952 to February 8, 1953: Gyula Decsi; from February 8, 1953 to July 4, 1953: Bela Kovacs; from July 4, 1953 to November 1, 1954: Ferenc Erdei.

Minister of
Agriculture:

Janos Matolcsi, appointed on November 15, 1955.

His predecessors: from December 23, 1944 to November 15, 1945: Imre Nagy; from November 15, 1945 to March 1, 1946: Bela Kovacs; from March 1, 1946 to November 20, 1946: Istvan Dobi; from November 20, 1946 to September 24, 1947: Karoly Baranyos; from September 24, 1947 to April 17, 1948: Arpad Szabo; from April 17, 1948 to December 8, 1948: Istvan Dobi; from December 9, 1948 to June 8, 1949: Istvan Csala; from June 8, 1949 to July 4, 1953: Ferenc Erdei; from July 4, 1953 to November 1, 1954: Andras Hegedus; from November 1, 1954 to November 15, 1955: Ferenc Erdei.

Minister of
Finance:

Karoly Olt, appointed on February 25, 1950.

His predecessors: from December 23, 1944 to July 25, 1945: Istvan Vasary; from July 25, 1945 to November 15, 1945: Imre Oltvanyi; from November 15, 1945 to August 30, 1946: Ferenc Gordon; from August 30, 1946 to March 14, 1947; Jeno

Racz; from March 14, 1947 to December 9, 1948:
Miklos Nyaradi; from December 9, 1948 to June
8, 1949: Erno Gero; from June 8, 1949 to February
25, 1950: Istvan Kossa.

Minister of
Education: Albert Konya, appointed on July 30, 1956.

His predecessors as Minister of Religion and Public
Education: from December 23, 1944 to November
15, 1945: Geza Teleki; from November 15, 1945
to November 8, 1946: Dezso Keresztury; from
November 9, 1946 to March 14, 1947 this post was
vacant. From March 14, 1947 to February 25, 1950:
Gyula Ortutay. On February 25, 1950, the name
of the Ministry was changed to Ministry of Education and Jozsef Darvas was appointed Minister.
The Ministry of Higher Education was established
on December 23, 1952; Tibor Erdey-Gruz was
appointed simultaneously with the setting up of
this Ministry. The Ministry was abolished on July
4, 1953, and Tibor Erdey-Gruz remained Minister
of Education until July 30, 1956.

Minister of
People's Culture: Jozsef Darvas, appointed on July 4, 1953.

His predecessors: from June 8, 1949 to July 4,
1953: Jozsef Revai. The Ministry of People's Culture is a change from the Ministry of Propaganda.
Ministers of Propaganda after the war: from November 15, 1945 to November 20, 1946: Antal
Balla; from November 20, 1946 to March 14, 1947:
Jozsef Bognar; from March 14, 1947 to September
24, 1947; Erno Mihalyfi. This Ministry was closed
on September 24, 1947, and revived under the
name of Ministry of People's Culture on June 8,
1949.

Minister of
Public Health: Jozsef Roman, appointed on February 20, 1955.

This Ministry was formerly called the Ministry of
Public Welfare until May 8, 1950. Ministers: from
December 23, 1944 to September 24, 1947: Erik
Molnar; from September 24, 1947 to June 8, 1949:
Karoly Olt; from June 8, 1949 to April 19, 1953:
Anna Ratko; from April 19, 1953 to February 20,
1955: Sandor Zsoldos.

Minister of Trans-
portation and
Postal Service: Lajos Bebrits, appointed on February 18, 1949.

His predecessors: from November 15, 1945 to February 18, 1949: Erno Gero. The Ministry of Transportation and Postal Affairs was divided from January 6, 1952 and July 4, 1953. Minister of Postal Affairs in this period: Antal Katona.

Minister for Crop
Collections: Andras Szobek, appointed on July 7, 1954.

This Ministry was set up on May 8, 1950. Ministers: from May 8, 1950 to November 16, 1952: Imre Nagy; from November 16, 1952 to July 7, 1954: Jozsef Tisza.

Minister of Food: Rezso Nyers, appointed on July 30, 1956.

His predecessors: from December 23, 1944 to July 25, 1945: Gabor Farago; from July 25, 1945 to November 15, 1945: Sandor Ronai; from November 15, 1945 to November 20, 1946: Karoly Baranyos; from November 20, 1946 to September 24, 1947: Janos Eross. At that time this Ministry was discontinued until January 6, 1952, when Ivan Altomare was appointed Minister until July 30, 1956.

Minister of
State Farms: Gyorgy Pogacsas, appointed on November 1, 1954.

This Ministry was established on the same day. From January 6, 1952 to July 4, 1953 a Ministry of State Agriculture and Forestry functioned headed by Andras Hegedus.

Minister of
Domestic
Commerce: Jozsef Bognar, appointed on June 8, 1949.

This Ministry was set up on June 8, 1949, when the Ministry of Commerce was divided in two parts —the Ministry of Domestic Commerce and the Ministry of Foreign Trade. After the war, the Ministers of Commerce were: from December 23, 1944 to May 11, 1945: Jozsef Gabor; from May 11, 1945 to November 15, 1945: Erno Gero; from

November 15, 1945 to June 8, 1949, date when the Ministry was divided, Sandor Ronai. On July 4, 1953, the two ministries were merged again, under the name Ministry of Domestic and Foreign Trade, and headed by Jozsef Bognar. On July 7, 1954, the Ministry of Foreign Trade was once again separated from this department.

Minister of
Foreign Trade: Laszlo Hay, appointed on July 7, 1954.

The Ministry was formed on June 8, 1949. Ministers: from June 8, 1949 to May 8, 1950: Sandor Ronai; from May 8, 1950 to July 4, 1953: Andras Szobek. During the period from July 4, 1953 to July 7, 1954, the Ministry was integrated into the Ministry of Domestic and Foreign Trade.

Minister of
Construction: Lajos Szijjarto, appointed on October 9, 1951.

His predecessors: from May 11, 1945 to November 15, 1945: Ferenc Nagy; from November 15, 1945 to July 22, 1946: Jozsef Antal; from July 22, 1946 to March 14, 1947: Endre Misteth; from March 14, 1947 to September 24, 1947: Peter Veres; from September 24, 1947 to February 25, 1950: Jozsef Darvas; from February 25, 1950 to October 9, 1951: Laszlo Sandor. The Ministry of Building Industry was established on January 6, 1952 and until its abolishment on July 4, 1953, was headed by Antal Apro.

Minister of
Light Industry: Mrs. Jozsef Nagy, appointed on September 5, 1955.

This Ministry was formed on June 8, 1949 after the abolishment of the Ministry of Industry. From the day of its formation to August 5, 1950 Gyorgy Marosan was Minister, from August 5, 1950 to November 1, 1954: Arpad Kiss; from November 1, 1954 to September 5, 1955: Bela Szalai.
Ministers of Industry after the war: from December 23, 1944 to June 8, 1945: Ferenc Takacs; from June 8, 1945 to February 21, 1948: Antal Ban; from February 21, 1948 to August 3, 1948 with a temporary assignment: Arpad Szakasits; from August 3, 1948 to June 8, 1949—to the end—Istvan Kossa.

The Ministry of Heavy Industry was also set up on June 8, 1949, after the abolishment of the Ministry of Industry. Minister of Heavy Industry: from June 8, 1949 to December 16, 1950: Mihaly Zsofinyecz. By that time, the Ministry was abolished, re-established on July 4, 1953, under Minister Istvan Hidas. On October 10, 1954, the Ministry was once again abolished.

Minister of Smelting and Machine Industry:

Janos Csergo, appointed on October 10, 1954.

His predecessors: from December 16, 1950 when the Ministry was established to January 6, 1952: Mihaly Zsofinyecz; from January 6, 1952 to December 23, 1952: Istvan Kossa. From December 23, 1952 to July 4, 1953, the administration of the Machine Industry was taken away from the Ministry which during this period was called "Ministry of Smelting Industry" under Mihaly Zsofinyecz. On July 4, 1953, machine industry was re-assigned to the Ministry, headed by Mihaly Zsofinyecz until October 10, 1954. Ministry of General Machine Industry was established on December 23, 1952 and abolished on July 4, 1953, under Minister Istvan Kossa. Ministry of Semi-Heavy Industry was established on January 6, 1952, and abolished on July 4, 1953, under Mihaly Zsofinyecz.

Minister of Chemical Industry:

Gergely Szabo, appointed July 30, 1956.

Prior to this date it was called Ministry of Chemical and Power Industry; under Istvan Hidas from October 10 to November 1, 1954, and Arpad Kiss from November 1, 1954 to July 30, 1956. Established on December 23, 1952, the Ministry of Chemical Industry functioned under Minister Gergely Szabolcs until July 4, 1953.

Minister of Mining and Power:

Sandor Czottner, appointed October 10, 1954. The Ministry was established on December 16, 1950 and until its temporary abolishment on July 4, 1953 was headed by Sandor Czottner. From October 10, 1954 to July 30, 1956, it was called Ministry of Coal Mining Industry; power supplies were administered by the Ministry of Chemical and Power Industry (see above).

Minister of
City and Town
Administration: Janos Szabo, appointed on February 2, 1954.

The Ministry was established on January 23, 1954. Ministry of Local Industry was set up on January 6, 1952 and until its abolishment on July 4, 1953 was headed by the same, Janos Szabo.

Minister of
State Control: Arpad Hazi, appointed on August 27, 1955.

The Ministry was established on August 20, 1955. Prior to this date, it functioned as an independent agency without Cabinet rank, called State Control Center, under the chairmanship of Arpad Hazi.

IV. EXECUTIVE OFFICERS OF
MAJOR GOVERNMENT AGENCIES

President of the
Supreme Court: Jozsef Domonkos

Prosecutor
General: Gyorgy Non

Chairman of the
National Plan-
ning Bureau: Andor Berei, appointed on November 1, 1954.

His predecessors: from June 11, 1949 when it was established to January 1953: Zoltan Vas; from January 1953 to July 4, 1953: Ferenc Herczeg; from July 4, 1953 to November 1, 1954: Bela Szalai. People's Economic Council existed during the period from June 11, 1949 to November 24, 1952, under the chairmanship of Erno Gero. Its functions were transferred to the Council of Ministers as of December 1, 1952.

Chairman of the
Labor Reserve
Bureau: Janos Pecsi

Chairman of the
Central Bureau
of Statistics: Gyorgy Peter

Chairman of the
State Office for
Church Affairs: Janos Horvath

Chairman of the
Hungarian
Academy of
Science: Istvan Rusznyak

BIBLIOGRAPHY

BIBLIOGRAPHICAL WORKS

Bobula, Ida. "The Hungarian Material of the Library of Congress." Microfilmed MS of the Mid-European Studies Center, No. 131, 1951, Library of Congress, Washington.

Borzsak, Istvan. *A magyar klasszikus-filologiai irodalom bibliografiaja 1926-1950* (Bibliography of the Hungarian Literature on Classic Philology). Budapest, 1952.

Kozocsa, Sandor. *A magyar irodalom bibliografiaja, 1945-49* (Bibliography of Hungarian Literature, 1945-49). Budapest, 1950.

Petrik, Geza. *Bibliographia Hungarica 1712-1910.* 10 vols. Budapest. 1885-1928.

Trocsanyi, Gyorgy. *Magyar nemzeti bibliografia* (Hungarian National Bibliography). Karcag, 1938.

Stolz, George (comp.). *Forced Labor in the Soviet Orbit: A Selective Bibliography.* Mid-European Studies Center, Mimeographed Series, No. 20. New York, March 15, 1954.

Sztachova, Jirina. *Mid-Europe—A Selected Bibliography.* New York, 1953.

STATISTICS

Annuaire Statistique Hongrois 1938. Budapest, 1940.

Az 1949 Evi Nepszamlalas (Population Census of 1949). Budapest, 1952.

Blazek, Miroslav. *Hospodarska geografie Ceskoslovenska* (Economic Geography of Czechoslovakia). Prague, 1952.

"Family Statistical Returns of the 1949 Census," *Statisztikai Szemle* (Statistical Review). (Budapest), III (April 1951).

Free Europe Press Research Staff. *Miscellaneous Statistical Data on Hungary 1950-52.* New York, 1952.

Hungary. Central Statistical Bureau. *Magyar Statisztikai Zsebkonyv* (Hungarian Statistical Pocketbook). Vol. XIII (1946). Budapest, [1947].

———. Central Statistical Bureau. *Magyar Statisztikai Zsebkonyv* (Hungarian Statistical Pocketbook). Vol. XIV (1947). Budapest, [1948].

————. Central Statistical Bureau. *Magyar Statisztikai Zsebkonyv* (Hungarian Statistical Pocketbook). Vol. XV (1948). Budapest, [1949].

————. Central Statistical Bureau. *Potfuzet Magyarorszag helysegnevtara 1952 evi kiadasahoz* (Supplement to the 1952 Gazetteer on Hungary). Budapest, 1953.

International Labour Office. *Yearbook of Labour Statistics 1943/44.* Geneva, 1945.

————. *Yearbook of Labour Statistics 1947/48.* Geneva, 1949.

Plan Fulfillment Reports of the Central Statistical Bureau, *Statisztikai Szemle,* (Statistical Review), January and April 1951, January and April 1952, January and April 1953 and *Hungarian Bulletin,* February 1953.

Populatia Republicii Populare Romane la 25 Ianuaria 1948 (Population of the Romanian People's Republic on January 25, 1948). Bucharest, March 1948.

"Provisional Results of the Population Census [of Yugoslavia]," *Statisticki buletin* (Statistical Bulletin) (Belgrade), No. 1 (July 1950).

Report of the Central Bureau of Statistics on Economic Progress and Trends of Material and Cultural Standards of the Population During the First Five-Year Plan 1950-1954, *Hungarian Review,* No. 6 (June 1955).

Statistical Year-Book of the League of Nations 1930-31. Geneva, 1931.

Statistical Yearbook of the League of Nations 1942-44. Geneva, 1945.

United Nations. *Demographic Yearbook 1953.* New York, 1953.

————. *Economic Survey of Europe Since the War.* Geneva, 1953.

————. *National and Per Capita Incomes, Seventy Countries, 1949.* Statistical Papers, Series E, No. 1. New York, 1951.

————. *National Income and Its Distribution in Under-developed Countries.* Statistical Papers, Series E, No. 3. New York, 1951.

————. *National Income Statistics 1938-1948.* Lake Success, 1950.

————. *Population and Vital Statistics Reports.* Series A, Vols. VI and VII. New York, 1954, 1955.

————. *Statistics of National Income and Expenditure.* Statistical Papers, Series H, Nos. 1-5. New York, 1952-1954.

————. *Statistical Yearbook 1954.* New York, 1954.

————. *Statistical Yearbook 1955.* New York, 1955.

United States. Bureau of the Census. *International Population Reports.* Series P-91. Washington, 1955.

LAND AND PEOPLE

Blanchard, Raoul. *A Geography of Europe.* New York, 1935.

Boldizsar, Ivan. *Magyarorszag. Utikonyv* (Hungary. Travelogue). Budapest, 1955.

Bulla, Bela, and Mendol, Tibor. *A Karpat-medence foldrajza* (Geography of the Danube Basin). Budapest, 1947.

Czako, Elemer, and Viski, Karoly. *A magyarsag neprajza* (Hungarian Ethnography). 4 vols. Budapest, n.d.

"The Change in the Class Structure of Our Society Reflected by Figures," *Szabad Nep* (Free People), March 31, 1955.

Elekes, Dezso. *Hazank, nepunk, szomszedaink* (Our Homeland, People and Neighbors). Budapest, 1941.

Frumkin, Gregory. *Population Changes in Europe Since 1939*. New York, 1951.

Kenez, Bela. *Nep es fold* (People and Land). Budapest, 1917.

Kirk, Dudley. *Population in the Interwar Years*. Geneva, 1946.

Kovacs, Aloysius. "Commentary on the Development of Population in Hungary." MS of the International Institute of Intellectual Co-operation, League of Nations, Paris, 1939.

Kuczynski, Robert R. *The Balance of Births and Deaths*. Washington, 1931.

Kulisher, Eugene M. *Europe on the Move—War and Population Changes, 1917-47*. New York, 1948.

Loczy, Louis de, and Papp, Charles. *Geological Map of Hungary*. Budapest, 1922.

Moore, Wilbert E. *Economic Demography of Eastern and Southeastern Europe*. Geneva, 1945.

Notestein, Frank W., and Others. *The Future Population of Europe and the Soviet Union*. Geneva, 1944.

Petri, Edith. *Geographie de la Hongrie*. Budapest, 1950.

Poniatowski, Jozef. "The Population of Intermarium," *Eastern Quarterly* (London), III (October 1950), 18-28, and IV (July 1951), 24-37.

Princz, Gyula. *Magyarorszag foldrajza* (Geography of Hungary). Budapest, 1942.

Prinz, Gyula, and Others. *Magyar fold, magyar faj* (Hungarian Land, Hungarian People). 4 vols. Budapest, 1936-38.

"Satellite Demography—Hungary," *News from Behind the Iron Curtain*, IV (February 1955).

Szabo, Laszlo. *Magyarorszag foldrajza* (A Geography of Hungary). Budapest, 1954.

Szabo, Zoltan. *Cifra nyomorusag—A Cserhat, Matra, Bukk foldje es nepe* (Disguised Poverty—Land and People of the Cserhat, Matra and Bukk [Mountains]). Budapest, n.d.

Szel, Tivadar. *L'effet d'industrialisation au point de vue du mouvement de la population*. Budapest, 1937.

Thompson, Warren S. *Population Problems*. New York, 1953.

Vernant, Jacques. *The Refugee in the Postwar World*. New Haven, 1953.

Woytinsky, W. S., and Woytinsky, E. S. *World Population and Production*. New York, 1953.

GENERAL

Baldwin, Roger N. (ed.). *A New Slavery—Forced Labor*. New York, 1953.

Baranski, Leon. *East and Central Europe*. New York, 1943.

Basch, Antonin. *The Danube Basin and the German Economic Sphere*. New York, 1943.

Beamish, Tufton. *Must Night Fall?* London, 1950.

Betts, R. R. (ed.). *Central and South East Europe 1945-1948*. London, 1950.

Black, C. E., *Communist Europe*. New York, 1953.

———. "Constitutional Trends in Eastern Europe 1945-48," *Review of Politics*, XI (April 1949), 196-207.

———. *Readings on Contemporary Eastern Europe*. New York, 1953.

———. "Soviet Policy in Eastern Europe," *Annals of the American Academy of Political and Social Science*, 263 (May 1949), 152-64.

Black, C. E. (ed.). *Challenge in Eastern Europe*. New Brunswick, N. J., 1954.

Bodrin, V V. *Vengerskaya Narodnaya Respublika* (The Hungarian People's Republic). Moscow, 1952.

Campbell, John C. "Diplomacy on the Danube," *Foreign Affairs*, XXVII (January 1949), 315-27.

———. "The European Territorial Settlement," *Foreign Affairs*, XXVI (1947), 796-818.

Carlton, Richard K. *The Economic Role of Forced Labor in Eastern Europe*. Mid-European Studies Center, Mimeographed Series, No. 35. New York, June 28, 1954.

Carlton, Richard K., and Others. *Forced Labor in the "People's Democracies."* New York, 1955.

Central and Eastern European Conference. *Human Freedom is Being Crushed—The Story of Deportations Behind the Iron Curtain*. Washington, 1951.

Chardonnet, Jean. *Géographie économique de l'Europe Danubienne et de la Pologne*. Paris, 1949.

Civil Affairs Handbook, Hungary. Army Service Forces Manual M 369-7, October 28, 1944.

Clarion, Nicolas. *Le Glacis Soviétique: Théorie et Practique de la Démocratie Nouvelle*. Paris, 1948.

Creed, Virginia. *Hungary*. New York, 1941.

Daniel, Clifton. "East Bloc Says Joint Army Will Counter Bonn in NATO," *The New York Times*, December 3, 1954.

——. "The Soviet Bloc Plans Joint Army Staff," *The New York Times*, December 1, 1954.

De Sola Pool, Ithiel, and Others. *Satellite Generals, A Study of Military Elites in the Soviet Sphere*. Stanford, Calif., 1955.

Elekes, Dezso. *A mai Magyarorszag* (Hungary Today). Budapest, 1947.

Eppstein, John. *Hungary*. Cambridge, England, 1945.

Farberov, N. P. *Gosudarstvennoe pravo stran narodnoi demokratii* (State Law of the People's Democratic Countries). Moscow, 1949.

Free Europe Press Research Staff. *Analytic Survey of Major Trends in the Soviet Sphere* (July 1953-July 1954). New York, 1954.

——. *Critical Bibliography of Communist Purges and Trials in the Soviet Union and in the 'People's Democracies'*. New York, 1953.

——. *New Policies in the Soviet Sphere*. New York, 1953.

——. *Satellite Agriculture in Crisis*. New York, 1954.

George, Pierre. *L'économie de l'Europe Central slave et Danubienne*. Paris, 1949.

Georgescu, Teohari. "Political Foundations of the People's Democratic System," *For a Lasting Peace, for a People's Democracy*, June 11, 1949, 4-5.

Gluckstein, Ygael. *Stalin's Satellites in Europe*. London, 1952.

Gmanaberov, G. A. "Problems of State and Law in the Countries of People's Democracy," *Current Digest of the Soviet Press*, I (September 13, 1949), 10-16.

Graham, Malbone W., Jr., and Binkley, Robert. *New Governments of Central Europe*. New York, 1924.

Great Britain. Ministry of Economic Warfare. *Hungary: Basic Handbook*. Pt. I, "Historical, Political and Social"; Pt. II, "Economic Survey"; Pt. III, "Map Section." London, 1944.

Gross, Feliks (ed.). *European Ideologies*. New York, 1948.

Grunwald, Constantin de. *Portrait de la Hongrie*. Paris, 1939.

Gsovski, Vladimir (ed.). *Economic Treaties and Agreements of the Soviet Bloc in Eastern Europe, 1945-1951*. 2nd ed. New York, 1952.

Gurian, W. (ed.). *The Soviet Union: Background, Ideology, Reality*. Notre Dame, Ind., 1951.

Gyorgy, Andrew. *Governments of Danubian Europe*. New York, 1949.

Halecki, Oscar. *Borderlands of Western Civilization: A History of East-Central Europe*. New York, 1952.

Hertz, F. O. *The Economic Problem of the Danubian States, A Study in Economic Nationalism*. London, 1947.

Hoptner, J. B. *The Soviet Orbit*. Mid-European Studies Center, Mimeographed Series, No. 3. New York, November 16, 1953.

Howard, Harry N. "New Links in the Soviet Alliance System," *Documents and State Papers*, I (March-April 1949), 12-13.

Isbert, Otto Albrecht. *Ungarn*. Berlin, 1941.

Ivan, Colonel. "The Development of the Armed Forces of Cominform Countries," *Review of International Affairs* (Belgrade), January 16, 1953, pp. 7-9.

———. "An Opinion That Pressure of USSR and Its Satellites on Yugoslavia Has Abated," *Review of International Affairs* (Belgrade), June 1, 1952, pp. 13-14.

Jackson, E. F. *Social Accounting in Eastern Europe in Income and Wealth*. Series IV, International Association for Research in Income and Wealth. London, 1955.

Joint Committee on the Economic Report. *Trends in Economic Growth —A Comparison of the Western Powers and the Soviet Bloc*. Washington, 1955.

Kertesz, Stephen D. "Human Rights in the Peace Treaties" in *Law and Contemporary Problems*. Durham, N. C., 1949.

———. "The Plight of Satellite Diplomacy," *Review of Politics*, XI (April 1949), 26-62.

Kulski, W. W. "The Soviet System of Collective Security Compared with the Western System," *American Journal of International Law*, 44 (July 1950), 453-76.

Macartney, Carlile Aylmer. *Hungary*. London, 1934.

———. *National States and National Minorities*. London, 1934.

———. *Problems of the Danube Basin*. Cambridge, England, 1942.

Mankovsky, B. S. "The New Stage in Development of the People's Democracies as States of the Socialist Type," *Current Digest of the Soviet Press*, 2 (October 14, 1950), 3-8.

Martin, Ebon. *World Communism Today*. New York, 1948.

Mende, Tibor. *Hungary*. London, 1944.

Mitrany, David. *The Effects of the War in Southeastern Europe*. New Haven, 1936.

Neumann, Robert G. "U.S. Foreign Policy and the Satellite States," *Review of Politics*, XI (April 1949), 220-36.

Nicolson, Harold. "Peacemaking in Paris: Success, Failure or Farce," *Foreign Affairs*, XXV (1947), 190-203.

Oberländer, Theodor. "Übervölkerung in Ostmitteleuropa," *Baltische Monatshefte*, July-August 1933.

Opie, Redvers, and Associates. *The Search for Peace Settlements*. Washington, 1951.

Pasvolsky, Leo. *Economic Nationalism of the Danubian States.* London, 1928.

Peselj, Branko M. *The Industrialization of Peasant Europe.* New York, 1953.

———. "Legal Trends in the People's Democracies," *George Washington Law Review,* XXII, 513 (1954).

Radisich, Elemer. *Dunataj* (Danube Region). Budapest, 1946.

Revai Nagy Lexikona (Revai's Great Encyclopaedia). Budapest, n.d.

Roucek, Joseph S. (ed.). *Central-Eastern Europe: Crucible of World Wars.* New York, 1946.

———. "Moscow's European Satellites," *Annals of the American Academy of Political and Social Science,* 271 (September 1951).

Royal Institute of International Affairrs. *Agrarian Problems from the Baltic to the Aegean.* London, 1944.

Rudzinski, Alexander W. *The Myth of Satellite Sovereignty.* Mid-European Studies Center, Mimeographed Series, No. 26. New York, April 26, 1954.

Rudzki, Adam. *East-Central European Transportation.* Washington, 1955.

———. *Organization of Transportation in Captive Europe.* Mid-European Studies Center, Mimeographed Series, No. 10. New York, January 4, 1954.

———. *Railroad Systems in Captive Europe.* Mid-European Studies Center, Mimeographed Series, No. 13. New York, January 25, 1954.

———. *Roads, Waterways and Seaports of Captive Europe.* Mid-European Studies Center, Mimeographed Series, No. 15. New York, February 8, 1954.

Salvini, Luigi (ed.). *Ungheria d'oggi.* Rome, 1939.

Sanders, Irwin T. "Changing Status of the Peasant in Eastern Europe," *Annals of the American Academy of Political and Social Science,* 271 (September 1951), 78-93.

Schacher, Gerhard. *Die Nachfolgestaaten Osterreich, Ungarn, Tschechoslowakei und ihre Wirtschaftliche Kräfte.* Stuttgart, 1932.

Schweng, Lorand D. "Recent Agricultural Developments in Eastern Europe," *Journal of Farm Economics* (London), XXXIII (February 1951), 15 ff.

Seton-Watson, Hugh. *Eastern Europe Between the Wars 1918-1941.* Cambridge, England, 1946.

———. *East European Revolution.* London, 1950.

Sharp, Samuel L. *Nationalization of Key Industries in Eastern Europe.* Washington, 1946.

———. *New Constitutions in the Soviet Sphere.* Washington, 1950.

Shepherd, G. *Russia's Danubian Empire.* New York, 1954.

Spulber, Nicolas. *The Economics of Communist Eastern Europe.* Cambridge, Mass., 1954.

Stadtmüller Georg. *Geschichte Südosteuropas.* Munich, 1950.

Steanu, P. B. "Constitutionalism in the Satellite States," *Journal of Central European Affairs,* XII (April 1952), 56-69.

Stowe, Leland. "Satellites in Arms," *Life,* December 17, 1951.

Sulzberger, C. L. "Russia Rearms Germany—Plus Its Former Axis-Allies," *The New York Times,* January 12, 1955.

Tensions Within the Soviet Captive Countries. Part 7, "Hungary." Washington, 1954.

Ulam, Adam B. "The Cominform and the People's Democracies," *World Politics,* III (January 1951), 200-17.

United States. Department of State. *Paris Peace Conference 1946—Selected Documents.* Conference Series 103. Washington.

Wanklyn, Harriet. *The Eastern Marchlands of Europe.* New York, 1941.

Warriner, Doreen. *Revolution in Eastern Europe.* London, 1950.

Wszelaki, Jan H. "Petroleum for Power in Red Europe," *World Oil,* CXXXIV (May 1952), 252-56.

———. "The Rise of Industrial Middle Europe," *Foreign Affairs,* XXX (October 1951), 123-34.

Yakobson, Sergius. "The Soviet Concept of Satellite States," *Review of Politics,* XI (April 1949), 184-95.

Zagoroff, S. D. "Rise and Decline of Peasant Freedom in the Danubian Countries," *Zeitschrift des Instituts für Weltwirtschaft an der Universität Kiel.* Band 69, 1952, Heft 2. Hamburg, 1952.

HISTORY AND POLITICS

Andics, Erzsebet. *A magyar munkasmozgalom az 1914-18as vilaghaboru alatt* (Hungarian Labor Movement During the 1914-18 World War). Budapest, 1950.

Apponyi, Albert, Count. *Lectures on the Peace Problem and on the Constitutional Growth of Hungary.* Budapest, 1911.

Bandholts, Harry Hill. *An Undiplomatic Diary.* New York, 1933.

Beer, Janos (ed.). *Magyar alkotmanyjog* (Hungarian Constitutional Law). (Includes text of 1949 Constitution.) Budapest, 1951.

Bethlen, Stephen, Count. *The Treaty of Trianon and European Peace.* New York, 1934.

Bohm, Vilmos. *Ket forradalom tuzeben* (In the Fire of Two Revolutions). Budapest, 1947.

Cabinet Decree No. 45 of 1950 (II.4) M. T. on Military Draft Regulations, *Magyar Kozlony* (Hungarian Gazette), February 4, 1950.

Cabinet Decree No. 4,353 of 1949 (268) M. T. on the Organization of the State Security Authority, *Magyar Kozlony* (Hungarian Gazette), December 28, 1949.

Deak, F. *Hungary at the Paris Peace Conference.* New York, 1942.

Decree No. 274,000 of 1949 (II.19) B. M. Concerning the Change in the Organization of the Police, in *Minisztertanacsi es Miniszteri Rendeletek 1949* (Cabinet and Ministerial Decrees). Vol. I, pp. 605-14. Budapest, 1950.

Eckhart, Ferenc. *Magyarorszag tortenete* (History of Hungary). Budapest, 1940.

————. *A Short History of the Hungarian People.* London, 1931.

Eisenmann, Louis. *Le compromis Austro-Hongrois de 1867.* Paris, 1904.

Farberov, N. P. (ed.). *Konstitutsiia i osnovnye zakonodatelnye akty vengerskoi narodni respubliki* (Constitution and Basic Acts of the Hungarian People's Republic). Moscow, 1951.

Farkas, Mihaly. *A beke arcvonalan* (On the Peace Front). Budapest, 1949.

Feher Konyv—a magyar koztarsasag es demokracia elleni osszeeskuves okmanyai (White Book—Documents on the Conspiracy Against the Hungarian Republic and Democracy). Official record. Budapest, 1947.

Free Europe Press Research Staff. *Chronology of Events in Hungary, 1952.* New York, 1953.

————. *Chronology of Events in Hungary, 1953.* New York, 1954.

————. *Hungary in the Year 1951.* New York, 1952.

————. *Hungarian Party Congress, May 24-30, 1954.* Research Report. New York, 1954.

Gabor, Robert. *Organization and Strategy of the Hungarian Workers' (Communist) Party.* 2nd ed. revised. New York, 1952.

Garami, Erno. *Forrongo Magyarorszag* (Hungary in Ferment). Leipzig, 1922.

Hantos, Elemer. *The Magna Carta of the English and of the Hungarian Constitution.* London, 1904.

Hogye, Michael. *The Paris Peace Conference of 1946: Role of the Hungarian Communists and of the Soviet Union.* New York, 1954.

Homan, Balint. *Geschichte des Ungarischen Mittelalters.* 2 vols. Berlin, 1940-43.

Homan, Balint, and Szekfu, Gyula. *Magyar Tortenet* (Hungarian History). 8 vols. Budapest, n.d.

Horthy, Nikolaus von. *Ein Leben für Ungarn.* Bonn, 1953.

Horvath, Barna. *A Magyar kozjog kis tukre* (A Short Outline of Hungarian Public Law). New York, 1953.

Hungary. Minister of the Interior. *A kozsegi tanacselnokok tanfolyamanak eloadasai* (Lecture Courses for the Village Council Presidents). Budapest, 1951.

———. Ministry of Foreign Affairs. *Liberated Hungary 1945-1950*. Budapest, 1950.

Illes, Bela. "Hungarian Troops in the Second World War," *Tarsadalmi Szemle* (Social Review) (Budapest), XI (June 1951), 443-50.

Ivan, Colonel. "The Treaty on Austria and Aggressive Soviet Strategy in the Balkans," *Review of International Affairs* (Belgrade), March 16, 1953, pp. 7-9.

Jaszi, Oscar. *Revolution and Counterrevolution in Hungary*. London, 1924.

———. *The Dissolution of the Habsburg Monarchy*. Chicago, 1929.

Kallai, Gyula. *A magyar fuggetlensegi mozgalom* (The Hungarian Movement for Independence). Budapest, 1949.

Kallay, Nicholas. *Hungarian Premier: A Personal Account of a Nation's Struggle in the Second World War*. New York, 1954.

Kann, R. A. *The Multinational Empire. Nationalism and National Reform in the Habsburg Monarchy 1848-1918*. New York, 1950.

Kaszonyi, N. *Die Rassenverwandtschaft der Donauvölker*. Zürich, 1931.

Kertesz, Stephen D. *Diplomacy in a Whirlpool: Hungary Between Nazi Germany and Soviet Russia*. Notre Dame, Ind., 1953.

———. "The Methods of Communist Conquest: Hungary 1944-47," *World Politics*, III (October 1950), 20-54.

Knatchbull-Hugessen, C. M. *The Political Evolution of the Hungarian Nation*. London, 1908.

Kosary, Dominic G. *A History of Hungary*. New York, 1941.

Kovacs, Imre. *The Hungarian People's Republic*. 2nd ed. revised. New York, 1951.

———. *Im Shatten der Sowjets*. Zürich, 1948.

Laszlo Rajk and His Accomplices Before the People's Court. Official Record. Budapest, 1949.

Law No. 62 of 1948 Concerning the Military Penal Code, in *1948 Ev Hatalyos Jogszabalyai* (Statutory Provisions of 1948), pp. 114-30. Budapest, 1949.

Lukinich, Imre. *History of Hungary*. London, 1937.

Magyar Dolgozok Partja Kozponti Vezetosege (The Central Committee of the Hungarian Workers' Party). *A Magyar Dolgozok Partja Szervezeti Szabalyzata* (Organizational Statutes of the Hungarian Workers' Party). Budapest, 1954.

Magyar Munkasmozgalmi Intezet (Hungarian Institute of Labor Movements). *A Magyar Tanacskoztarsasag, 1919* (The Hungarian Soviet-Republic 1919). Budapest, 1950.

Bibliography 433

————. *A Rakosi Per* (The Rakosi Trial). Budapest, 1950.

A Magyar Nepkoztarsasag alkotmanytervezete (Draft Constitution of the Hungarian People's Republic). Budapest, 1949.

A Magyar Nepkoztarsasag fontosabb torvenyei es kormanyhatarozatai (The Most Important Laws and Governmental Resolutions of the Hungarian People's Republic). Budapest, 1952, 1953.

May, Arthur J. *The Hapsburg Monarchy, 1867-1914.* Cambridge, Mass., 1951.

Macartney, C. A. *Hungary and Her Successors. The Treaty of Trianon and Its Consequences 1919-1937.* New York, 1937.

Mod, Aladar. *400 ev kuzdelem az onallo Magyarorszagert* (400-Year Struggle for an Independent Hungary). Budapest, 1950.

Montgomery, J. F. *Hungary: The Unwilling Satellite.* New York, 1947.

Nagy, Ferenc. *The Struggle Behind the Iron Curtain.* New York, 1948.

Nyaradi, Nicholas. *My Ringside Seat in Moscow.* New York, 1952.

Paloczy-Horvath, G. *In Darkest Hungary.* London, 1945.

Pisky, Frederick S. "The Case of Forced Labor in Hungary (1953)." Microfilmed MS of the Mid-European Studies Center, No. 351, 1956, Library of Congress, Washington.

Rakosi, Matyas. *A dolgozo nep alkotmanya, Rakosi Matyas beszede az orszaggyules 1949 augusztus 17-en tartott ulesen* (The Constitution of the Working People, Matyas Rakosi's Speech at the Session of the National Assembly Held August 17, 1949). Budapest, 1949.

————. *Nepi demokraciank utja* (The Path of Our People's Democracy). Budapest, 1952.

————. *Valogatott beszedek es cikkek* (Selected Speeches and Articles). Budapest, 1950.

Redlich, Joseph. *Emperor Francis Joseph of Austria: A Biography.* New York, 1929.

Revai, Jozsef. "The Character of a People's Democracy," *Foreign Affairs,* XXVIII (October 1949), 143-52.

————. *Elni tudtunk a szabadsaggal* (We Did Make Use of Freedom). Budapest, 1949.

Revesz, Mihaly (ed.). *A reakcio ellen—a Szocialdemokrata Part harca* (The Social Democratic Party's Fight Against Reaction). Budapest, 1945.

Schoenfeld, Arthur H. F. "Soviet Imperialism in Hungary," *Foreign Affairs,* XXVI (April 1948), 554-66.

Sebestyen, Endre. *Kossuth.* Pittsburgh, Pa., 1950.

Seton-Watson, R. W. *Racial Problems in Hungary.* London, 1908.

————. *Treaty Revision and the Hungarian Frontiers.* London, 1934.

Sulyok, Dezsö. *Zwei Naechte Ohne Tag.* Zurich, 1948.

Szabo, Istvan. *A magyar parasztsag tortenete* (History of the Hungarian Peasantry). Budapest, 1940.

Szabo, Jozsef. *A Magyar Nepkoztarsasag alkotmanyjoganak vazlata* (An Outline of the Constitutional Law of the Hungarian People's Republic). Szeged, 1949.

Szanto, Bela. *A magyarorszagi proletariatus osztalyharca es diktaturaja* (The Class Struggle and Dictatorship of the Hungarian Proletariat). Vienna, 1920.

Szekfu, Gyula. *Harom nemzedek es ami utana kovetkezik* (Three Generations and What Comes Next). Budapest, 1938.

———. *Magyarorszag Tortenete* (History of Hungary). Budapest, 1933.

Szemere, Bertalan. *Hungary from 1848-1860.* London, 1880.

Szerenyi, Simon. *Leleplezesek a kommunizmus napjaibol* (Unveiling the Days of Communism). Budapest, 1919.

Taubinger, Laszlo M. V. "Militärstaat Sowjetungarn," *Ost Probleme* (Bonn), VII (October 28, 1955), 1662-68.

Taylor, A. J. P. *The Hapsburg Monarchy, 1815-1918.* London, 1949.

Teleki, Paul, Count. *The Evolution of Hungary and Its Place in European History.* New York, 1923.

Tezner, Friedrich. *Die Wandlungen der Österreichisch-Ungarischen Reichsidee.* Vienna, 1905.

"The Third Congress of the Hungarian Working People's Party," *New Hungary,* Supplement, IV (June-July 1954).

United States. Department of State. *America's Interests in Hungarian Struggle for Independence.* Documents and State Papers, Vol. I., No. 5. Washington, 1948.

———. House of Representatives. Select Committee on Communist Agression. *Communist Takeover and Occupation of Hungary.* Special Report No. 10. 83rd Cong. Washington, 1954.

Varga, Laszlo. *The Legal Aspects of Forced Labor in Hungary.* New York, n.d.

Weltner, Jakab. *Forradalom, Bolsevizmus, Emigracio* (Revolution, Bolshevism, Exile). Budapest, 1929.

———. *A szocialdemokrata part es a beke* (The Social Democratic Party and the Peace). Budapest, 1919.

Zlatapolskii, D. L. *Gosudarstvenny stroi vengerskoi narodnoi respubliki* (The Structure of Government of the Hungarian People's Republic). Moscow, 1951.

ECONOMY

"The Agricultural Labour Situation in Hungary," *International Labour Review,* XXV (May 1932), 673-78.

Alcser, Jeno. "On Making Our Irrigation System More Economical," *Agrartudomany* (Agricultural Science), III (July 1951), 384-88.

Andresen, Karsten. *Die Deutsch-Ungarischen Wirtschaftbeziehungen und das Problem ihrer engeren Gestaltung.* Rostock, 1935.

Az 5 eves terv masodik evenek feladatai (The Tasks of the Second Year of the Five-Year Plan). Budapest, 1951.

Bebrits, Lajos, Minister of Transportation. Monitored speech to Hungarian Railroad Workers. Radio Budapest, August 14, 1955.

Bernatsky, Kornel. *Production Systems in Hungarian Agriculture.* Mid-European Studies Center, Mimeographed Series, No. 34. New York, June 21, 1954.

Brunauer, Sandor. "The History of the Hungarian Labor Movement." Microfilmed MS of the Mid-European Studies Center, No. 269, 1953, Library of Congress, Washington.

————. "Social Legislation in Hungary." Microfilmed MS of the Mid-European Studies Center, No. 132, 1950, Library of Congress, Washington.

Buday, Kalman. *The International Position of Hungary and the Succession States.* Budapest, 1931.

Buletin de la Bureau Hongrois de Presse et de Documentation. (Paris), August 15, 1952.

"Concerning the New Model Statutes for Producers' Cooperatives," *Jogtudomanyi Kozlony* (Legal Science Review), IX (January-February 1954), 20-25.

Csikos, Hantos, and Rezler. *Magyar Gazdasagi Elet* (Hungarian Economic Life). Budapest, 1944.

Csorba-Mikita, Istvan. *Gondolatok a Szabad Magyarsag Agrarpolitikajahoz* (Reflections on the Agricultural Policy of a Free Hungary). Zurich, 1950.

"The Development of the Labor Class Reflected by Figures," *Szabad Nep* (Free People), March 27, 1955.

Donat, Ferenc. "Producers' Cooperatives in Hungary," *For a Lasting Peace, for a People's Democracy,* No. 13 (40), July 1, 1949.

Eckstein, Alexander. "National Income and Capital Formation in Hungary, 1900-1950." (Forthcoming in *Income and Wealth,* Series V, International Association for Research in Income and Wealth.) Cambridge, England, 1956.

————. "Land Reform and the Transformation of Agriculture in Hungary," *Journal of Farm Economics,* XXXI, No. 3 (August 1949).

"The Economy of Hungary 1950-1954," United Nations *Economic Bulletin for Europe,* VII, No. 2 (August 1955).

Erdei, Ferenc. Speech to National Conference of Outstanding Cooperatives and Machine Tractor Stations, in *Szabad Nep* (Free People),
December 28, 1951.

Farkasfalvy, Sandor. "Industry," *Magyar Statisztikai Szemle* (Hungarian
Statistical Review), XIV, No. 4 (1936), 455.

──────. "The State of Manufacturing Industry in 1939," *Magyar Statisztikai Szemle* (Hungarian Statistical Review), XVIII, No. 11
(1940), 953.

Feher, Lajos. "The Central Problem of Hungary's New Peasant Policy:
Alliance with the Middle Peasants," *Tarsadalmi Szemle* (Social
Review), IX (March 1954), 33-56.

──────. "Export and Agriculture," *Szabad Nep* (Free People), November 5, 1954.

Fellner, F. "Le Revenue National de la Hongrie Actuelle," *Buletin de
l'Institut International de Statistique*, XXV, No. 3.

──────. "Die Verteilung des Volksvermögens und Volkseinkommens der
Länder der Ungarischen heiligen Krone zwischen dem heutigen
Ungarn und den Succession Staaten," *Metron*, III, No. 2 (Novem-
ber 1923).

──────. "Das Volkseinkommen Österreichs and Ungarns," *Statistische
Monatschrift*, Vol. XXI (1916).

──────. "Das Volkseinkommen, seine statistische Erfassung und sein
heutiger Stand in verschiedenen Ländern," in *Der Internationale
Kapitalismus und die Krise* (Festschrift f. Julius Wolf), ed. by
S. V. Kardorff and others. Stuttgart, 1932.

Franklyn, Harriet. "The Birth of Peasant Hungary in Europe," *The
Geographical Journal* (January 1941), 18.

Free Europe Press. *Communist Land Policy in Hungary.* New York,
January 1954.

──────. *Satellite Agriculture in Crisis.* New York, 1954.

Free Europe Press Research Staff. *The New Hungarian Economic Policy
—Three Speeches by Imre Nagy and Matyas Rakosi.* New York,
1953.

Gabor, Robert. *The Bolshevization of the Hungarian Trade Unions (1945-
1951)* New York, 1952.

Geller, K. *Die Strukturänderungen der ungarischen Volkswirtschaft nach
dem Kriege und die Stellung Ungarns im mittel-europäischen Wirtschaftsraum.* Münster, 1938.

General Assembly of the National Bank of Hungary. *Reports of the Board
of Directors of the National Bank of Hungary on the Business Years
1947 and 1948, to the 22nd and 23rd Ordinary Annual Meeting,
March 1948 and March 1949.* Budapest, 1948, 1949.

Gero, Erno. "With the Five Year Plan Toward Socialism," *Szabad Nep*
(Free People), December 10, 1949.

————. *Harcban a Szocialista Nepgazdasagert* (Fighting for the Socialist People's Economy). Budapest, 1950.

————. "The Policy of the Hungarian Workers' Party in the Countryside," *For a Lasting Peace, for a People's Democracy*, No. 23 (26), December 1, 1948.

Hajpal, G. "Magyarorszag Nemzeti Jovedelme" (National Income of Hungary), *A Magyar Gasdasagkutato Intezet Kozlemenyei* (Bulletin of the Hungarian Institute of Economic Research), March 31, 1947.

Hegedus, Andras. "On the Development of Agricultural Production," *Szabad Nep*, (Free People), December 30, 1953.

Hilton, Howard J., Jr. "Hungary: A Case Story of Soviet Economic Imperialism," *United States Department of State Bulletin*, No. 25 (August 27, 1951), 323-27.

Hivatalos Menetrend (Official Timetable of the Hungarian State Railways, Bus Lines, Air Lines and Waterways). Budapest, 1948.

Horst-Eberhard, Otto. *Die Industrialisierung Ungarns*. Berlin, 1941.

Hungary's Three-Year Plan. Published by the *Hungarian Bulletin*. Budapest, 1957.

Ihrig, Karl. "Agrarian Reform in Hungary," *International Review of Agriculture*, November-December 1931.

International Labour Office. *The Law on the Contract of Employment of Agricultural Workers in Austria, Germany and Hungary*. Studies and Reports, Series K. No. 10. Geneva, 1930.

Jaszai, Samu. *A Magyar Szakszervezetek Tortenete* (History of the Hungarian Trade Unions). Budapest, 1925.

Jelentes a haromeves terv elso everol (Report of the First Year of the Three-Year Plan). Budapest, 1948.

Judik, Jozsef. "The Three-Year Economic Plan," *Magyar Kozgazdasagi Szemle* (Hungarian Economic Review), LXX, No. 1-2 (1947).

Kemeny, George. *Economic Planning in Hungary 1947-49*. London, 1951.

Kerek, Mihaly. "Agricultural Land Reform in Hungary," *Hungarian Quarterly* (Budapest), Autumn 1940.

Kovacs, Imre. *Agrarian Problems in Hungary*. New York, 1950.

Kovacs, Peter. "On the Problems of the Worker-Peasant Alliance," *Tarsadalmi Szemle* (Social Review), VI (February 1951), 105-16.

Kovrig, Bela. *Magyar Tarsadalompolitika (1920-1945)* (Hungarian Social Policy [1920-1945]). New York, 1954.

Kuthy, Olga. *Geographical Aspects of Land Utilization in Hungary*. New York, 1942.

Ladik, George. *Water Supply in Hungary*. New York, 1954.

Law No. 25 of 1949 on the First Economic Five-Year Plan of the Hungarian People's Republic, in *Torvenyek es torvenyereju rendeletek*

1949 (Laws and Decrees with the Force of Law 1949). Budapest, 1950.

League of Nations. *European Conference on Rural Life: Hungary.* Geneva, 1939.

Magyar Gazdasagkutato Intezet Kozlemenyei (Publications of the Hungarian Economic Research Institute). Budapest, January 30, 1953, November 15, 1954.

Magyar Ipari Munkatudomanyi Intezet (Hungarian Industrial Labor Research Institute). *Az eletszinvonal alakulasa Magyarorszagon* (Development of Standard of Living in Hungary). Budapest, 1944.

Magyar Munkasmozgalmi Intezet (Hungarian Institute of Labor Movements). *A magyar munkasmozgalom kialakulasa (1848-1890)* (Development of the Hungarian Labor Movement). Budapest, 1951.

Magyarorszag gazdasaga es a 3-eves terv (Hungary's Economy and the Three-Year Plan). Budapest, 1948.

Major, Robert. *Ket vilaghaboru kozott* (Between Two World Wars). Budapest, 1942.

Matolcsy, M., and Varga, S. *The National Income of Hungary 1924/25-1936/37.* London, 1938.

Michael, L. G. *Agricultural Survey of Europe—Hungary.* Technical Bulletin No. 160, United States Department of Agriculture, January 1930.

Mid-European Studies Center Staff. *The Hungarian Oil Industry.* New York, 1954.

Mod, Aladar. "Our Agricultural Production," *Tarsadalmi Szemle,* (Social Review), VIII (April-May 1953), 416-41.

Moricz, Miklos. "Landless Agricultural Workers in Hungary," *International Labour Review,* XXVII (October 1933), 518-30.

Nagy, I. "On Measures of Hungarian Working People's Party and Government Aimed at Raising the Standard of Living," *For a Lasting Peace, for a People's Democracy,* July 17, 1953.

——. "For Steady Rise in Standard of Living," *For a Lasting Peace, for a People's Democracy,* February 5, 1954.

Nagy, Ivan E. "Agriculture and the Agricultural Economic Policy of Hungary," in *Agricultural Systems of Middle Europe, a Symposium,* ed. by O. S. Morgan. New York, 1933.

Nagy, Tamas. "Hungarian National Income and Its Distribution, Past and Present," *Tarsadalmi Szemle* (Social Review), V, No. 12 (1950), 982-98.

Neubauer, J. "Le Montant du Revenu National Hongrois," *Journal de la Société Hongroise de Statistique,* Vol. XVII (1939).

Nyilas, Andras. "Development and Present Situation of the Hungarian

Transportation," *Statisztikai Tajekoztato* (Statistical Bulletin), No. 4 (1954), 18-27.

Oteves Tervunk: Beketerv (Our Five-Year Plan: a Peace Plan). Budapest, 1951.

Oxford Economic Atlas of the World. Oxford, 1954.

Pisky, Frederick S. "Employment of Women in Hungary (1953)." Microfilmed MS of the Mid-European Studies Center, No. 354, 1956, Library of Congress, Washington.

———. "History of Labor in Hungary—Chronological Tables 1848-1954." MS of the Mid-European Studies Center, New York, 1954.

———. *Labor Discipline in Hungary*. Mid-European Studies Center, Mimeographed Series, No. 11. New York, January 11, 1954.

———. "The New Trade Unions in Hungary (1953)." Microfilmed MS of the Mid-European Studies Center, No. 353, 1956, Library of Congress, Washington.

———. "Standard of Living in Hungary (1953)." Microfilmed MS of the Mid-European Studies Center, No. 352, 1956, Library of Congress, Washington.

"La Planification de l'Economie Hongroise," *Etudes et Conjencture*, II, No. 14-15 (July-August 1947).

Pogacsas, Gyorgy. "Resolutions of the Council of Ministers on Improving Animal Husbandry in Hungary," *Magyar-Szovjet Kozgazdasagi Szemle* (Hungarian-Soviet Economic Review), IV, No. 11-12 (1950).

Prigrada, Anthony. *Danube Waterways*. Mid-European Studies Center, Mimeographed Series, No. 5. New York, November 30, 1953.

———. *International Agreements Concerning the Danube*. Mid-European Studies Center, Mimeographed Series, No. 6. New York, December 7, 1953.

"Principles of the Second Five-Year Plan of the Hungarian People's Economy," *Szabad Nep* (Free People), April 27, 1956.

Rakosi, Matyas. "Address to the Second Congress of the Hungarian Workers' Party, February 1951," *For a Lasting Peace, for a People's Democracy*, No. 9 (121), March 2, 1951.

———. "Report at the Central Committee of the Hungarian Working People's Party, Plenum of October 31, 1953," *For a Lasting Peace, for a People's Democracy*, November 20, 1953.

Rath, Steven. "Electric Power in Hungary." MS of the Mid-European Studies Center, New York, 1955.

———. "The Hungarian Coal Industry." Microfilmed MS of the Mid-European Studies Center, No. 289, 1954, Library of Congress, Washington.

———. "Manufactured Gas Production in Hungary." Microfilmed MS of the Mid-European Studies Center, No. 290, 1954, Library of Congress, Washington.

Reports Delivered at the Hungarian National Assembly November 15-16, 1955. Supplement to the *Hungarian Review,* No. 12 (1955).

"Resolution of the Central Committee of the Hungarian Workers' Party and the Council of Ministers of the Hungarian People's Republic on the Development of Agricultural Production [December 1954]," *Hungarian Bulletin,* 1954.

Rezler, Julius S. "Local Administration in Hungary, with Emphasis on Price Control and Trade Union Controls in Communist Hungary (1952)." Microfilmed MS of Mid-European Studies Center, No. 291, 1956, Library of Congress, Washington.

————. *A magyar nagyipari munkassag kialakulasa (1867-1914)* (Development of Hungarian Labor in Manufacturing Industry). Budapest, 1945.

————. "A magyar szakszervezeti mozgalom 1945 elott" (Hungarian Trade Union Movement Before 1945). Microfilmed MS of the Mid-European Studies Center, No. 148, 1952, Library of Congress, Washington.

Rezler, Julius S. (ed.). *Magyar gyari munkassag* (Hungarian Industrial Workers). Budapest, 1940.

Schweng, L. D. *Economic Planning in Hungary Since 1938.* New York, 1951.

————. *Political, Social and Economic Developments in Post-War Hungary.* Washington, 1950.

Standard Oil Company (New Jersey) and Oil Production in Hungary by MAORT 1931-1948. New York, 1949.

Stowe, Leland, "Hungary's Agrarian Revolution," *Foreign Affairs,* XXV (1947), 490-502.

Szabo, Ervin. *Gazdasagi szervezet es huberiseg* (Economic Structure and Feudalism). Budapest, 1915.

Szabo, K. "The Role of the Free Market in the New Period," *Tarsadalmi Szemle* (Social Review), August-September 1954. Translated by the Mid-European Studies Center, New York, 1955.

Teleki, Paul, Count. "Die Weltpolitische und Wirtschaftliche Lage Ungarns in Vergangenheit und Gegenwart," *Zeitschrift für Geopolitik,* III, No. 6, pp. 408 ff.

Toma, Adam. "Naturalized Plants to Diminish Hungarian Imports," *Magyar-Szovjet Kozgazdasagi Szemle,* IV, No. 11-12 (1950).

"Transportation and Tourism in Bolshevized Hungary," Pt. I and II, *Magyarorszagi Esemenyek* (Report on Hungary), VII, Nos. 9-10, 11-12 (1955).

"Transportation in Hungary," *News from Behind the Iron Curtain,* V (March 1955), 15-22.

United Nations. Economic Commission for Europe. *Economic Survey of Europe.* Annual 1948-1954. Geneva.

———. Economic Commission for Europe. *European Agriculture: A Statement of Problems.* Geneva, 1954.

United Nations Food and Agriculture Organization. *Commodity Series,* especially the following: No. 4. *Dairy Products.* February 1948; No. 6. *Vegetables and Fruits.* No. 1, May 1948; No. 10. *Grain Bulletin.* January 1949; No. 12. *Meat and Livestock.* May 1949; No. 14. *Fibers.* August 1949.

———. *Farm Mechanization.* Washington, September 1950.

———. *Forestry and Forest Products, World Situation.* Washington, August 15, 1946.

Varga, Laszlo. *The Position of the Hungarian Worker Between January 1, 1950 and November 1952.* New York, 1953.

Vas, Zoltan. "The Completion of the Three Year Plan: a Victory for our People," *Tarsadalmi Szemle* (Social Review), V, No. 3. (1950), 131-51.

———. "Five-Year Plan in Hungary," *For a Lasting Peace, for a People's Democracy,* March 17, 1950.

———. "Nemzeti jovedelmunk kerdesei" (Questions of our National Income), *Gyozelemre visszuk a beke tervet* (We Shall Carry out Victoriously the Plan of Peace). Budapest, 1951.

———. *Az Oteves Terv masodik evi feladatai* (Tasks of the Second Year of the Five-Year Plan). Budapest, 1951.

———. "Zavershenie Trekhletnego Plana—Pobeda Nashego Naroda" (The Completion of the Three-Year Plan—a Victory of our People), *Planirovanie Narodnogo Khoziaisva Vengrii, Sbornik Materialov* (Planning of Hungarian People's Economy, Collection of Materials). Moscow, 1950.

Veres, Peter. "Address on the Socialization of Agriculture," *Szabad Szo* (Free Word), December 5, 1948.

Weltner, Jakab. *A gazdasagi harc* (The Economic Struggle). Budapest, 1919.

CULTURE AND SOCIETY

Altalanos konyvjegyzek (General Catalogue of Books). Vol. I (1946) and II (1947). Budapest, 1947, 1948.

Authorized White Book: Cardinal Mindszenty Speaks. New York, 1949.

Balics, Lajos. *A Romai Katholikus Egyhaz tortenete Magyarorszagon* (History of the Roman Catholic Church in Hungary). 3 vols. Budapest, 1885-1890.

Baranyai, Lipot. *A klasszikus kultura es a mai ember* (Classical Culture and Contemporary Man). Budapest, 1942.

Bauhofer, Janos Gyorgy. *History of the Protestant Church in Hungary.* London, 1854.

Benedek, Marcel, and Others. *Irodalmi lexicon* (Encyclopaedia of Literature). Budapest, 1927.

Beothy, Zsolt. *A magyar irodalom tortenete* (History of Hungarian Literature). 2 vols. Budapest, 1899-1900.

Bucsay, Mihaly. *Bibliothek des Protestantism im Mitleren Donauraum.* Halle, 1940.

Csicsery-Ronay, Istvan. *Russian Cultural Penetration in Hungary.* 3rd ed. New York, 1952.

Demokracia (Democracy). Budapest, 1945.

Fabian, Bela. *Cardinal Mindszenty.* New York, 1949.

Farkas, Gyula. *Kultur der Ungarn.* Potsdam, 1939.

Five Years of Hungarian Protestantism 1945-50. Budapest, n.d.

Fogarasi, Belane. *A kolhoz szinhaz* (The Kolkhoz Theater). Budapest, 1949.

"For Strong Discipline in Our Schools," *Szocialista Neveles Kiskonyvtara* (Series on Socialist Education), No. 20 (1951).

Free Europe Research and Publication Service. *The Red and the Black —The Church in the Communist State.* New York, 1953.

Geleji, Dezso. *Magyarorszag 1944-ben* (Hungary in 1944). Budapest, 1945.

Hankiss, Jean. *Lumiere de Hongrie aspects de la civilisation Hongroise.* Budapest, 1935.

Hegedus, Geza. *A polgari irodalom stilusiranyai* (Trends in Style of the Bourgeois Literature). Budapest, 1947.

Hungarian Newspapers and Periodicals, Catalogue 1956. Budapest, 1956.

Hungarian People's Republic. Washington Legation. *The Relationship Between Church and State in the Hungarian People's Republic.* Washington, n.d.

Hungary. Ministry of Foreign Affairs. *The Reform of Public Education.* Budapest, 1947 (?).

Inkeles, Alex. *Public Opinion in Soviet Russia.* Cambridge, Mass., 1950.

Irodalmi tajekoztato (Literary Catalogue). Budapest, 1941.

Juhasz, William. *Blueprint for a Red Generation.* New York, 1952.
———. *Persecution of Churches Behind the Iron Curtain.* New York, 1952.

Kiraly, Deme, and Szabolcsi. *Magyar Konyv* (Hungarian Book). Budapest, n.d.

Klebelsberg, Kuno, Count. *Beszedei, cikkei es torvenyjavaslatai* (Speeches, Articles and Legislative Acts). Budapest, 1927.

Kornis, Gyula. *Hungary and European Civilization.* Budapest, 1938.

Levai, Eugene. *"Black Book" on the Martyrdom of Hungarian Jewry.* Zurich, 1947.

Lukacs, Gyorgy. *A polgari filozofia valsaga* (The Crisis of Bourgeois Philosophy). Budapest, n.d.

Markham, R. H. (ed.). *Communists Crush Churches in Eastern Europe.* Boston, 1950.

Mayer, Claudius F. "Contemporary Medical Affairs in Captive Hungary," *The Military Surgeon,* III (July-December 1952), 114-27.

Morris, Max. *Hungary Builds a New Education.* London, 1950.

Ortutay, Gyula. *A muvelodes es politika* (Culture and Politics). Budapest, 1949.

Nagy, Tibor. "Problems of Housing Policy and Administration," *Allam es Kozigazgatas* (State and State Administration), December 1955.

"Questions on the Moral Education of Youth," *Szocialista Neveles Kiskonyvtara* (Series on Socialist Education), No. 10 (1950).

Racz, Endre. *Az ujabbkori magyar muvelodes szelleme* (The Spirit of Recent Hungarian Civilization). Budapest, 1946.

"Resolutions of the Council of Ministers on Price Reductions," *Szabad Nep* (Free People), September 5, 1953, March 14, 1954, and April 29, 1956.

Revai, Jozsef. *Marxizmus, nepiesseg, magyarsag* (Marxism, Volksism, Magyarism). Budapest, 1948.

Ronay, Gyorgy. *A regeny es az elet* (Life and Fiction). Budapest, 1947.

Rudas, Laszlo. *Materialista vilagnezet* (Materialistic Ideology). Budapest, 1950.

Somogyi and Ecsedy. *Az egeszsegugy helyzete 1950-ben* (Public Health Affairs in 1950). Budapest, 1950.

"Soviet Cultural Collaboration," *The World Today,* X (May 1954), 197-209.

Szabolcsi, Bence. *A muvesz es kozonsege* (The Artist and His Public). Budapest, 1952.

Szerb, Antal. *Magyar irodalomtortenet* (History of Hungarian Literature). Budapest, 1947.

United Nations. *Yearbook on Human Rights for 1951.* New York, 1953.

Vincze, Laszlo. *Politika es iskola* (Politics and Schools). Budapest, 1948.

PERIODICALS[1]

A Kereszt (The Cross). Fortnightly, published by the National Peace Committee of Hungarian Catholic Priests. Budapest. 1956: VII.

Allami Gazdasagok (State Farms). Official monthly for the workers of state farms. Budapest. 1956: VIII.

American Political Science Review. Quarterly, published by the American Political Science Association. Menasha, Wis. 1956: L.

The Annals of the American Academy of Political Science. Bimonthly. Philadelphia. July 1956: CCCVI.

Aussenpolitik. Monthly. Stuttgart. 1956: VII.

Az Ut (The Way). Weekly of the Hungarian Reformed (Calvinist) Church. Budapest. 1956: IX.

Banyaszati Lapok (Mining News). Monthly, published by the National Association for Mining and Metallurgy. Budapest. 1956: LXXXIX.

Beke es Szabadsag (Peace and Freedom). Weekly, published by the National Peace Council. Budapest. 1956: VIII.

Bulletin Analytique de Documentation Politique, Economique et Sociale Contemporaine. Bimonthly, published by the Presses Universitaires de France. Paris. 1956: XI.

Bulletin Catholique Hongrois. Monthly, published by the National Peace Committee of Hungarian Catholic Priests. Budapest. 1956: II.

Bulletin of the Institute for the Study of the History and Culture of the USSR. Monthly. Munich. 1956: III.

Bulletins on Soviet Economic Development. Series 1-2, Nos. 1-8 (May 1949—May 1953). University of Birmingham.

Corvina. A Hungarian digest. Vols. 1945-48. Budapest.

The Current Digest of the Soviet Press. Weekly, published by the Joint Committee on Slavic Studies. New York. 1956: VIII.

Csalad es Iskola (School and Family). Monthly, published by the Ministry of Education. Budapest. 1956: VI.

Csillag (Star). Literary journal of the Association of Hungarian Writers. Budapest. 1956: X.

Eastern Review. Quarterly (in English, French and German). Vienna. Vols. 1948-1949.

The Eastern Quarterly. Published by the Institute for Eastern Affairs. London. Vols. 1948-1953.

---

[1] Roman numerals indicate volume number of year given.

East European Accessions List. Monthly publication of the Library of Congress. Washington. 1956:VI.

Elelmezesi Ipar (Food Industry). Monthly, published by the Scientific Association for Agriculture and Food Industry. Budapest. 1956: X.

Elet es Tudomany (Life and Science). Weekly, published by the Society for the Popularization of Social and Natural Sciences. Budapest. 1956: XI.

Epuletgepeszet (Building Installations). Bimonthly, of the Scientific Association for Building Construction. Budapest. 1956: V.

Esti Budapest (Budapest Evening News). Daily, published by the Budapest Committee of the Hungarian Workers' (Communist) Party and the Budapest City Council. Budapest. 1956: V.

Ethnographia (Ethnography). Quarterly, published by the Hungarian Ethnographical Society. Budapest. 1956: LXVII.

Europa-Archiv. Fortnightly, published by the Institut für Europäische Politik und Wirtschaft. Frankfurt a. Main. 1956: XI.

Der Europäische Osten. Monthly. Munich. 1956: II.

Evangelikus Elet (Evangelical Life). Weekly, published by the Press Department of the Evangelical (Lutheran) Church. Budapest. 1956: XXI.

Faipar (Lumber Industry). Monthly, published by the Scientific Association for Wood Industry. Budapest. 1956: VII.

Foldrajzi Ertesito (Geographical Gazette). Quarterly, published by the Geographical Research Institute of the Hungarian Academy of Science. Budapest. 1956: VI.

Foldrajzi Kozlemenyek (Geographical News). Quarterly, published by the Hungarian Geographical Society. Budapest. 1956: LXXX.

For a Lasting Peace, for a People's Democracy. Weekly organ of the Cominform. Bucharest. 1956: X.

Foreign Affairs. Quarterly, published by Council on Foreign Relations. New York. 1956: XXXIV.

Foreign Policy Bulletin and Headline Series. Bimonthly, published by the Foreign Policy Association. New York. July 20, 1956: No. 118.

Forum. Literary, critical, and sociological review published by the Forum Club, an independent, but later Communist front organization. Budapest. Vols. I-III, 1946-48.

Freies Leben. Weekly of the "German Working Men in Hungary." Budapest. 1956: III.

Gazdasagstatisztikai Tajekoztato (Economic Statistical Bulletin). Quarterly, published by the Supreme Economic Council and the Central Bureau of Statistics. Budapest. Vols. I-III, 1947-49.

Gep (Machinery). Monthly, published by the Scientific Association for the Machine Industry. Budapest. 1956: IV.

Highlights of Current Legislation and Activities in Mid-Europe. Monthly publication of the Mid-European Law Project, Library of Congress. Washington. 1956: IV.

Journal of International Affairs. Published twice a year, Columbia University. New York. 1956: X.

Hungarian Agricultural Review. English digest of Hungarian books and periodicals on agriculture, published by the National Agricultural Library. Budapest. 1956: V.

Hungarian Heavy Industries. English quarterly of the Hungarian Chamber of Commerce. Budapest. (Reportedly beginning in 1956.)

Hungarian Review. Official propaganda monthly of the Hungarian government. Budapest. 1956: II.

Hungarian Technical Abstracts. Selected abstracts of articles published in Hungarian technical journals. Budapest. 1956: VIII.

Hungary. Official propaganda magazine of the Hungarian government. Budapest. 1956: V.

International Affairs. Quarterly, published by the Royal Institute of International Affairs. London. 1956: XXXII.

Irodalmi Ujsag (Literary Journal). Weekly of the Hungarian Writers' Association. Budapest. 1956: VII.

Jarmuvek, Mezogazdasagi Gepek (Vehicles and Agricultural Machines). Monthly, published by the Scientific Association for Machine Industry. Budapest. 1956: III.

Jogtudomanyi Kozlony (Legal Science Review). Monthly, published by the Institute for Political Science and Jurisprudence. Budapest. 1956: XII.

Journal of Central European Affairs. Quarterly, published by the University of Colorado. Boulder, Colo. 1956: XVI.

Kohaszati Lapok (Metallurgical Review). Monthly, published by the National Association for Mining and Metallurgy. Budapest. 1956: LXXXIX.

Kozgazdasagi Szemle (Economic Review). Monthly, published by the Hungarian Academy of Sciences. Budapest. 1956: III.

Kozlekedestudomanyi Szemle (Transportation Science Review). Monthly, published by the Scientific Association for Transport and Transport Construction. Budapest. 1956: VI.

Kozneveles (Public Education). Biweekly, published by the Ministry of Education. Budapest. 1956: XII.

Libertatea Noastra (Our Freedom). Fortnightly, published by the Cultural Association of Romanians in Hungary. Budapest. 1956: VI.

Ludas Matyi (Matyi the Gooseboy). Satirical weekly, unofficial Party organ. Budapest. 1956: XII.

Magyar Energiagazdalkodas (Hungarian Power Economy). Monthly, published by the Scientific Association for Power Economy. Budapest. 1956: IX.

Magyar Epitoipar (Hungarian Building Industry). Monthly, published by the Scientific Association for Building Industry. Budapest. 1956: V.

Magyar Epitomuveszet (Hungarian Architecture). Monthly, published by the Association of Hungarian Architects. Budapest. 1956: V.

Magyar Kozlony (Hungarian Gazette). Official organ for government publications. Budapest. 1945——.

Magyar Nemzet (Hungarian Nation). Daily, published by the Patriotic People's Front. Budapest. 1956: XII.

Magyar Nemzeti Bibliografia (Hungarian National Bibliography). Monthly, published by the National Szechenyi Library. Budapest. 1956: I.

Magyar Radio (Hungarian Radio). Weekly program guide, published by the Hungarian Radio Office. Budapest. 1956: XII.

Meres es Automatika (Measuring and Automation). Monthly, published by the Scientific Association for Measuring Technique and Automation. Budapest. 1956: IV.

Monthly List of Books Catalogued in the Library of the United Nations. Geneva. 1956: XXIX.

Monthly List of Selected Articles. Published by United Nations Library. Geneva. 1956: XXVII.

Muszaki Elet (Technical Life). Fortnightly, published by the Association of Societies for Technics and Natural Sciences. Budapest. 1956: XI.

Muvelt Nep (Cultured People). Weekly, semi-official organ of the Ministry of Popular Culture. Budapest. 1956: VII.

Nasa Sloboda (Our Freedom). Weekly of the Democratic Association of Slovaks in Hungary. Budapest. 1956: VII.

Nase Novine (Our Newspaper). Weekly of the Association of Yugoslavs in Hungary. Budapest. 1956: IX.

Nepegeszsegugy (Public Health Affairs). Budapest. No. 7, 1951.

Nepszava (People's Voice). Daily, published by the National Council of Trade Unions. Budapest. 1956: LXXXIV.

News from Behind the Iron Curtain. Monthly, published by the Free Europe Committee. New York. 1956: V.

Nok Lapja (Women's Gazette). Weekly of the Democratic Association of Hungarian Women. Budapest. 1956: VII.

Novaya Vengriya (New Hungary). Russian weekly digest of the Hungarian press, published by the Hungarian Telegraphic Agency. Budapest. 1956: V.

Orvosi Hetilap (Medical Weekly). Budapest. Vol. 1950-54.

Ost-Europa. Bimonthly, published by the Deutsche Gesellschaft für Ost-europakunde. Stuttgart. 1956; VI.

Osteuropa-Recht. Published twice a year by the Deutsche Gesellschaft für Osteuropakunde. Stuttgart. 1956: II.

Pedagogiai Szemle (Pedagogical Review). Bimonthly, published by the Ministry of Education. Budapest. 1956: VI.

Penzugyi Szemle (Financial Review). Monthly of the Ministry of Finance. Budapest. 1956: V.

Political Science Quarterly. Published by Columbia University. New York. 1956: LXXI.

Problems of Communism. Bimonthly publication of the United States Information Agency. Washington. 1956: V.

The Review of Politics. Quarterly, published by the University of Notre Dame, Ind. 1956: XVIII.

Revue Historique. Quarterly, published by French University Press. Paris. 1956: LXXX.

Slavonic and East European Review. Published twice a year by the University of London. 1956: XXXIV.

Soviet Studies. Quarterly, published by the University of Glasgow. 1956: VIII.

Sowjetwissenschaft. Bimonthly, published by the Gesellschaft für Deutsch-Sowjetische Freundschaft. Berlin. 1956: III.

Statistische Praxis. Monthly, published by the (East German) Central Statistical Office. Berlin. 1956: XI.

Statisztikai Szemle (Statistical Review). Monthly, published by the Central Bureau of Statistics. Budapest. 1956: XXXIV.

Statisztikai Tajekoztato (Statistical Bulletin). Quarterly, published by the Central Bureau of Statistics. Budapest. 1955: V.

Szabad Fold (Free Land). Weekly of the Hungarian "working peasantry," semi-official Party organ. Budapest. 1956: V.

Szabad Ifjusag (Free Youth). Daily, published by the Central Committee of the Union of Working Youth. Budapest. 1956: VII.

Szabad Muveszet (Free Art). Monthly, published by the Association of Hungarian Painters, Sculptors, and Craftsmen of Fine Worksmanship. Budapest. 1956: XI.

Szabad Nep (Free People). Daily, central organ of the Hungarian Workers' Party. Budapest. 1956: XIV.

Szazadok (Centuries). Bimonthly, published by the Society of Hungarian Historians. Budapest. 1956: LXL.

Szinhaz es Filmmuveszet (Theater and Film Art). Monthly, published by the Hungarian Dramatic and Film Art Society. Budapest. 1956: VII.

Szinhaz es Mozi (Theater and Cinema). Weekly program guide. Budapest. 1956: IX.

Szovjet Kultura (Soviet Culture). Monthly of the Ministry of Popular Culture. Budapest. 1956: VIII.

Tarsadalmi Szemle (Social Review). Monthly, published by the Central Committee of the Hungarian Workers' Party. Budapest. 1956: XI.

Tarsadalombiztositas es Munkavedelem (Social Insurance and Protection of Labor). Monthly of the National Council of Trade Unions. Budapest. Vols. 1950-54.

Termeszet es Tarsadalom (Nature and Society). Monthly magazine of the Society for the Popularization of Social and Natural Sciences. Budapest. 1956: CXV.

Uj Elet (New Life). Monthly, published by the National Office of Hungarian Jews. Budapest. 1956: XII.

Uj Ember (New Man). Weekly, published by the National Presidium of Actio Catholica. Budapest. 1956: XII.

Uj Hang (New Voice). Literary journal of the Association of Hungarian Writers. Budapest. 1956: V.

Uj Ido (New Time). Hungarian edition of the Soviet weekly *Novoye Vremja* (New Times). Budapest. 1956: II.

Uj Vilag (New World). Weekly of the Hungarian-Soviet Friendship Society. Budapest. 1956: IV.

Uj Zenei Szemle (New Musical Review). Monthly, published by the Association of Hungarian Musicians. Budapest. 1956: VII.

United Nations Economic Bulletin for Europe. Published three times a year. Geneva. 1956: VIII.

———. *Monthly Bulletin of Statistics.* New York. 1956: X.

Valasz (Reply). Independent monthly. Budapest. Vols. VII-IX, 1947-49.

Valosag (Reality). Monthly, published by the Hungarian Democratic Youth Association (MADISZ). Budapest. Vols. I-III, 1945-47.

Vigilia. Religious, social, cultural, and literary monthly of the Roman Catholic Church. Budapest. 1956: XXI.

Vierteljahrshefte für Zeitgeschichte. Quarterly, published by the Institut für Zeitgeschichte. Munich. 1956: IV.

Wissenscaftlicher Dienst Südosteuropa. Monthly, published by the Südost-Institut München (Munich). 1956: V.

Zeitschrift für Geschichtswissenschaft. Bimonthly. Berlin. 1956: IV.

Zeitschrift für Ostforschung. Quarterly, published by the Johann Gottfried Herder-Forschungsrates E. V. Marburg a. d. Lahn. 1956: V.

Index

Note: Numbers in italics refer to maps and tables.